Home Management

Ruth E. Deacon
Iowa State University

Francille M. Firebaugh
Ohio State University

Houghton Mifflin Company • Boston

Atlanta • Dallas • Geneva, Illinois • Hopewell, New Jersey

Palo Alto • London

Home

Management

Context

and

Concepts

Contents

Preface

The primary purpose of this book is to provide undergraduate students and teachers with a meaningful framework for studying the managerial activity of individuals and families. The authors hope that the usefulness of the book will extend beyond the formal classroom, however. Persons who work directly with families—extension agents and social workers, for example—can use this book as a reference on management. The book is particularly oriented to the professional's need for an approach which promotes objective interpretation of the full range of managerial variations. But it is equally possible for those who want to read the book from their own perspective to gain insight into their own managerial style.

We came individually, and under different circumstances, to an interest in trying to clarify managerial processes. Interest grew, and one of us, after a frustrating period in working directly with families on their managerial problems, wrote to the department head: "We can teach the management process, but we have difficulty helping others, much less ourselves, understand what to observe when we see it in action . . . . Is it possible to find any technique or techniques by which we can help both professionals and families to . . . evaluate what is needed in a given situation?"

Eventually, similar concerns led us to research as an avenue for continuing the search. This was possible at the same institution, and it led to an exciting period of mutually stimulating work. During the developmental period, the guidance of Dr. Elizabeth Maccia, a researchers' researcher, was invaluable. Since she believed in the development of theory as a justifiable objective of research, she promoted adaptation of applied areas of appropriate conceptualizations from the basic fields. And she introduced us to the possibilities of the systems approach at a time when advances in interpretation of the open and adaptive social-system model were only beginning. Findings from the research that followed are presented in the text where applicable, but this book has been the medium for further development and elaboration of the original conceptual framework published in 1966.

Thus, while the book is a byproduct of research, it is in turn a natural outcome from the original motivation to undertake research—to find a means whereby the substance and creativity of management may be more meaningful and functional in our lives. The systems model has served our purpose in a number of ways. A social system exists in an environment, and the interacting relation to that context has mutual effects. Management, therefore, is subject to the environmental conditions of the household or family, and also has its effects. The household or family unit is, in turn, one which acts on and is acted upon by other systems of the larger society.

The systems format encompasses the more traditional aspects of process, content, and function, and places them in an appropriate relation to each other. A continuing thread through the book is the recognition of the mutually interdependent contributions of process and content to effective management. A systems approach does not permit bias in favor of one or the other—both are necessary and neither is sufficient alone. Even so, the weight of the discussion is on the structuring of major managerial components and their functional relationships. The intent of such structuring is to promote consistency in interpretation of the functional roles of the various parts of the managerial system and of the managerial system within the family system. We believe such clarification is a step in identifying the way in which the various other content areas within and outside home economics relate and contribute to effective management, and vice versa.

We recognize the individuality of each person's and each family's managerial state and approach. Applications are seen as unique; the managerial components are universal, organizing concepts interrelated through dynamic processes leading to varied responses to the diverse contexts and contents of situations. An analytical approach is necessary, and we have tried to provide a framework to promote it.

Such an undertaking comes about with the support and assistance of many friends, co-workers, family members, and institutions. The Ohio Agricultural Research and Development Center supported the original research; the administration and faculty of the School of Home Economics, The Ohio State University, gave encouragement. Members of the School's Division of Management, Housing and Equipment all deserve particular recognition for their many contributions—consideration of conceptual ideas during developmental stages, evaluations from introductions into teaching, constructive criticism of drafts. We appreciate each of them, especially Jean S. Bowers, Kristan R. Crosby, and Geraldine Olson for their substantive suggestions. Graduate students who served on the original project and who were in our classes and seminars in home management and family economics stimulated ideas in all stages of the research and the book.

Carole A. Vickers' continuing contributions are particularly noteworthy—she used the text in her home management class at Marshall University, helped us use the students' candid evaluations, and then developed the Instructor's Manual. We are deeply grateful to her. The constructive suggestions and reactions of the formal reviewers were helpful. These reviewers were Doris Beard, of Sacramento State College; Karen Craig, of Southern Illinois University; Carol Engebretson, of Louisiana State University; Martha Plonk, of Oregon State University; Rose Steidl, of Cornell University; and Florence Walker, of the University of Nebraska, Lincoln. The informal reviewers, Eva D. Wilson and Linda Glenn, were equally helpful.

We are indebted to Margaret V. Richter for her personal interest in typing and retyping drafts, her care and accuracy in form and citations, her development of the bibliography, and many other kinds of assistance. Editing, duplicating, proofreading, drafting of charts and other help, both personal and operational, were contributed by John D. Firebaugh, for which we both express appreciation.

Ruth E. Deacon
Francille M. Firebaugh

Home Management

Introduction

As individuals and as families, we manage our personal affairs within a constantly changing world. Compared to earlier generations, we live in a world that has grown smaller through rapid transportation and instant communication. Not only do new opportunities present themselves, but also new forces invade our personal sphere. The observation that change is inevitable may be trite, but it is also true.

Every student has observed how roommates come and go, how sudden illness within a family can alter plans, how the decisions of large companies to move their plants to new locations can upset workers and their families. Brothers and sisters marry and leave the parental home. Grandparents retire, and their retirement affects not only their lives but also the lives of others.

How we respond to change depends on the situation in which we find ourselves at the moment of change. Our response further depends on the depth of our insight into the problems and challenges resulting from change and on our individual resourcefulness in discovering ways to cope with the new circumstances.

To manage well we do not necessarily have to know management concepts and processes on a formalized level, but knowing about management makes it possible for us to:

1. be able and willing to analyze our own management;
2. recognize and understand the ways in which others manage; and
3. help others with their management problems.

To understand the managerial complexities of today's living we need a framework within which to examine our activities and responsibilities in relation to the family and the larger segments of society. An adequate framework not only reflects the dynamic changes within a household —those easily identified because they affect us personally—but also the less obvious interchanges between the household and the larger environment. The total managerial effect is greater than the sum of the individual components.

The study of home management should reflect this wholeness, or total-ity; therefore, the organizing concept best suited to the overall view is the systems approach to management. As background for later concentration on the managerial system and its components, we shall first explore the nature of open family systems.

Part One

Context of Home Management

A Systems Approach to the Family

1.

All of us have our own concepts of the family: the word evokes pictorial and emotional memories that are distinctly ours and no one else's. But if we are to enrich our knowledge with an overview of the family in relation to its environment and to extend our perspective to include the larger society, we must first set aside our highly personal concepts and try to understand the concept of the family as a social system.

THE FAMILY AS A SYSTEM

What Is a System?

One writer defines systems as "interrelated elements or parts having a boundary and functional unity within a larger system."[1] Another writer describes a *system* as a coordinated set of parts for accomplishing goals.[2] A system is *closed* when factors outside the system do not affect it; it is *open* when it both affects and is affected by the environment.

---

1. Charles R. Dechert, "The Development of Cybernetics," *The American Behavioral Scientist* 8 (June 1965): 17.
2. C. West Churchman, *The Systems Approach* (New York: Delacorte Press, 1968), p. 29.

5

In what way does the family (or other unit that functions as a family) meet these criteria? Primarily, the individuals who comprise a family unit work together to reach goals. The lifestyles of the members may vary widely: one may be an avid reader who surrounds himself with books; another may be an enthusiastic sportsman who lives largely outdoors; and still another may be involved in civic and social events. Yet within the household, they all function to maintain the home. The majority of families in any community represent the traditional type, in which the members are related by blood, by marriage, or by adoption. However, the proportion of households composed of unrelated individuals has increased gradually in the past years and is now one in four (see Table 10-2). We must recognize, therefore, that there are many households other than traditional ones, which range from single individuals to communes. Since families are dynamic units, they may change during a few years from several members to just one individual because members grow up or because of separation, divorce, illness, or death.

A *boundary*—which is another criterion used to define systems —separates the family system from other systems. Within each unit, concerns for personal relationships, responsibilities for personal maintenance and development, and the management of family resources differentiate the family system from outside systems.

The boundaries of social systems, however, are not always easy to identify. For example, a divorced mother living in a mobile home on her parents' property remains separate from her parents in some ways, although she may eat with them frequently and even share laundry facilities. On weekends when the children visit their father, she may reassume the role of a single woman with no immediate obligation to participate in activities with her family.

Major Family Functions

However fuzzy the boundaries, the family system exists as long as the members work together to meet goals that either the group desires or society demands. The major functions that society expects of families include the following, although not all are possible or even accepted to the same degree by individual units:

1. the provision of food, clothing, and shelter for the physical maintenance of each individual,

2. an increase in family size through reproduction or the adoption of children and the release of children when they have matured,
3. socialization of children for adult roles in the family and in other social groups,
4. maintenance of order within the family and between the family members and outsiders,
5. maintenance of family morale and motivation to carry out tasks in the family and in other groups,
6. production of goods and services necessary to maintain the family unit.[3]

To fulfill the indicated expectations of society, the family must be adaptive and growth supporting.

Subsystems

All systems may have subsystems that fill the same conditions as the system and play a functional role in the larger system.[4] When we see a system in the overall perspective, we recognize that a system may also be a subsystem. Families, for example, are subsystems of a community system, and the community is a subsystem of a county system, and so on. The family system contains a personal and a managerial subsystem; the function of the managerial subsystem is to plan and implement the use of family resources to meet family demands.[5]

Interaction with Other Systems

Families continually interact with their physical environments and with other systems, including the economic, political, and social-cultural systems. One writer describes the *environment* as a set of conditions and properties that are not a part of the system but are still able to influence it.[6] In systems language, the common boundary between two systems is known as the *interface* and is a barrier to be overcome in systems exchange. We shall consider interfaces and their importance in Chapter 5.

---

3. Reuben Hill, "Modern Systems Theory and the Family: A Confrontation," *Social Science Information* 10 (October 1971): 16.
4. Dechert, p. 19.
5. Ruth E. Deacon, "Toward a Philosophy of Home Management," speech, January 24, 1966, Oregon State University, Corvallis, Oregon.
6. Russel L. Ackoff, "Toward a System of Systems Concepts," *Management Science* 17 (July 1971): 662–63.

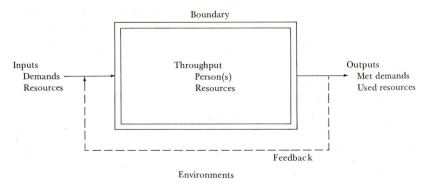

FIGURE 1.1 *The family system.*

Input, Throughput, Output

Figure 1.1 illustrates ways in which the family system interacts with its environment. No family can exist for long without resources. No family remains free from outside demands, as we have already noted. When these resources and demands enter into the family sphere, we call them *inputs.* Input is basically matter, energy, and information, but resources and demands are identified as terms more specific to the family system. As the family uses the resources and meets the demands, both the used resources and the met demands leave the family system and go out again into the environment as *outputs.* The process of passing them through the family sphere is known as *throughput,* or transformation.

To illustrate: the head of the household brings home a weekly paycheck, which becomes a part of the family resources. At the same time, the mailman delivers a notice that indicates certain property taxes are due. Both the check and the taxes represent inputs. A check is sent to pay the tax, thereby using up a part of the family resources and simultaneously meeting a demand. Both the used resources and the met demand constitute outputs. Planning for ways to make the funds available, considering other demands, and writing the check become the throughput, or the transforming process. If the family has anticipated the need for funds to pay the tax, it may have a sense of satisfaction that will promote readiness for the next installment. If funding the payment is difficult and if a late payment involves a penalty, the family may resolve to make a plan to have the money ready when the next payment is due. In this case, it has limited satisfaction from the way it met the demand. In either case, the degree of satisfaction has an effect on the way it anticipates the next payment. This process of output returning in part to the family as input is known as *feedback*.

"Information concerning the outputs or the process of the system is fed back as an input into the system, perhaps leading to changes in the transformation process and /or future outputs."[7]

The Nature of Feedback

Feedback can be either negative or positive. For example, consider the family who owns property which a realtor wants to buy and turn into a parking lot. Sale of the property would require the family to move away from friends and relatives, and, although the price offered would enrich the family resources, the family declines to sell. This refusal illustrates *negative feedback* in that it reinforces earlier goals of the family related to housing and has a stabilizing effect on the family. Had the family accepted the realtor's offer to buy, the acceptance would have constituted a *positive feedback* that would, in turn, have encouraged the family to move, to adjust, and to expand to meet a new situation. In this sense, positive feedback fosters change.

Negative feedback has been defined as a stabilizing influence that triggers measures to maintain the system in a desired state. Positive feedback reflects deviations from anticipated effects and promotes change.[8]

The Family as an Adaptive Unit

The open family system adapts to social change more frequently than do other systems. Several points are critical in the family's adaptation to other systems.[9] First, other social systems adapt according to their goals. The goals of the welfare department, for instance, may sometimes be incompatible with the goals of certain families, but the welfare department does not change its goals. Second, the family system tends to relinquish its

---

7. Fremont E. Kast and James E. Rosenzweig, "General Systems Theory: Applications for Organization and Management," *Academy of Management Journal* 15 (December 1972): 450.
8. Walter Buckley, *Sociology and Modern Systems Theory* (Englewood Cliffs, N. J.: Prentice-Hall, Inc., 1967), p. 58.
9. Clark E. Vincent, "Family Spongia: The Adaptive Function," *Journal of Marriage and the Family* 28 (February 1966): 33–34.

goals when they conflict with those of other social systems. For example, if the school system requires its teachers to attend a conference on a school day and the working parents require their children to be in school, then the family, and not the school, adapts to the conflict in goals and finds a way to keep the children at home or with a relative or neighbor for the day. Finally, the family system often adapts for lack of alternatives. The single parent of a sick child may have to wait long hours in a hospital emergency room for the child to receive attention because limited resources allow few alternatives. Some families "buck the system" rather than adapt; they may organize into groups to try to change the system.

Families show remarkable resilience in response to changes in the environment. They respond in several ways:

1. by adjusting temporarily to external forces such as when a flood or other natural disaster strikes and compels the family to move elsewhere until it has time to plan for the future;
2. by moving to more congenial surroundings as, for example, when a child's difficulty in dealing with social pressures in a school prompts the family to relocate; and
3. by reorganizing the family system to cope with an unexpected change in the environment.[10]

For instance, a husband must accept a lower-paying job because of automation within the plant where he works. To meet this new crisis, the family may shift household tasks in order to release the wife for outside employment.

Although we characterize the family as adaptive, in some families the static tendencies may equal or exceed the dynamic qualities. In a dynamic system, one component acts on another; in a static system, components are relatively fixed in relation to each other.[11] When a family struggles to survive in extreme poverty, circumstances may be so complex and demanding and motivations so low that no response seems worthwhile. A relatively static system then occurs.

Naturally, since families differ, the responses of open family systems vary. With very different initial circumstances or conditions, two families

---

10. Buckley, p. 58.
11. Ronald G. Havelock, *Planning for Innovation Through Dissemination and Utilization of Knowledge* (Ann Arbor, Mich.: Center for Research on Utilization of Scientific Knowledge, 1971), pp. 2–3.

may arrive at similar conclusions or find themselves in similar situations.[12] In systems terminology, this phenomenon is called *equifinality*. And yet relatively similar opportunities and beginning orientations can lead to different outcomes—a phenomenon that is called *multifinality*. Families may differ considerably in their adaptive and growth-supporting qualities. Two couples that start married life with widely different resources may later attain resources that show approximately the same net worth when they retire. On the other hand, families who purchase similar houses in the same neighborhood may sell them at considerably different prices because of differences in the maintenance of or improvements to the property, assuming that the same market conditions prevail at the time of both sales.

The concepts of equifinality and multifinality are important from the managerial perspective because they emphasize the need to consider factors that contribute to differences in families at a given point in time. Differences among families in their present situations may be due to differences in their adaptive responses to other systems and to their decisions as growth-supporting units.

Interrelated Subsystems

The family system functions to meet the needs of its members through the personal and managerial subsystems. The personal subsystem sets the tone for the family—evolves the basic values of individuals, develops personalities, and socializes the young family members.

Within the personal subsystem, dynamic interactions of social relations have impact on the personality. If the system is composed of one individual, major social influences may take place in external environments; but all personal and social experiences have an impact on the personality, adapting it to change or reinforcing current behavior. This process evolves faster or slower at various times or with different persons and has commensurate effects on the managerial system.

Society assigns the primary responsibility for assisting in the personality development of children to the family, but this responsibility is shared in many ways—through the educational system, religious institutions, and so on.

The field of social psychology treats personality development, and the

---

12. Buckley, p. 79.

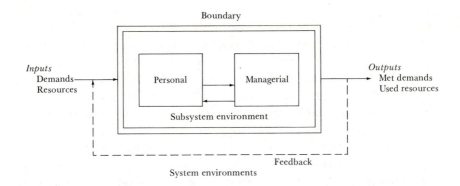

FIGURE 1.2 *The family system with personal and managerial subsystems.*

term "psycho-social" might aptly name the subsystem in that field. How-ever, social and psychological factors also influence managerial capabilities such as in cognitive processes of decision making.

The personal subsystem has resource inputs such as information and energy, and value laden demands which are translated into goals consist-ent with the needs and desires of the person's personality. We shall not, however, pursue the structure and processes of the personal subsystem in this book. Our concern focuses on the managerial subsystem and its gen-eral relation to the personal subsystem.

As we consider subsystems, remember that they, too, have input, throughput, feedback, and environment (Figure 1-2). The major outputs of the personal subsystem to the managerial system—which are the family's goals and value based objectives—become inputs into the mana-gerial system. As we talk of these subsystems, we must also recognize that each member of the household is a part of both the personal and the managerial subsystems. Each has his own goals and values, and each, to some degree, manages his own affairs. When a small child hides a treas-ured toy from the rough handling of an older brother, that child is managing his resources. When an adult with a lively interest in social trends acquires the tuition for a night class, he has called on the manager-ial subsystem to support the value he places on knowledge. In this way, management helps one to attain goals by making realistic plans from nebulous desires. When either the individual budget or the family budget is tight, feedback from the managerial subsystem to the personal subsys-tem may cause a change in goals. Management instrumentally supports the personal subsystem by clarifying goals, developing programs to pursue these goals, and overseeing efforts to accomplish the goals. Management functions to meet demands, whether these demands are individual or family goals, or unexpected events that require action and use resources to meet the demands. As we have noted, resources are also a part of input to the family system. They are of specific importance in the managerial system since any addition to resources, depletion from the resources, or change in the form of resources affects the managerial subsystem's input.

The purchase of a new car can perhaps illustrate the close interrelations between the personal and managerial subsystems of the family. Concern about energy conservation and air pollution may indicate the wisdom of buying a small car. At the same time, the family may desire a large, powerful automobile. And so concern and desire come in conflict. Goal outputs from the personal subsystem affect the family's satisfaction with output from the managerial subsystem by giving direction to goals against which managerial output is measured. Through preliminary planning, management can contribute insights that help to resolve the value conflict and clarify the goal through a feedback relation with the personal system. This integral relation is important because satisfaction with output from the management system is measured against the personal system's goal expectation.

SUMMARY

The family is an open, adaptive, and growth-supporting system which is an identifiable entity. The family system has two interrelated subsystems—personal and managerial—which function to meet family needs. Resources and demands are the input of the system which are transformed into met demands and used resources. These resources may remain within the family system or enter the environment.

Several systems concepts are particularly important in the family system: feedback as part of output, which affects succeeding input; equifinality—reaching the same situation with different initial conditions; and multifinality—having similar initial conditions with dissimilar end conditions. These concepts help to develop awareness of differences in families with similar backgrounds who vary in the way they adapt and respond to other systems. A basic aim of this book is to recognize differences in the management of families and the factors contributing to the differences.

DEFINITIONS

Definitions of systems concepts relating to open, adaptive and growth-supporting families are given throughout this chapter and appear here for reference.

System is a set of parts coordinated to accomplish a set of goals.[13]

Boundary is a region separating one system from another.[14]

Interface is a boundary common to two systems.

Input and output are matter, energy, or information exchanged between systems.

Throughput is matter, energy, or information transformed by the system from input to output.

Feedback is the portion of output reentering the system as input to affect succeeding output.[15]

Negative feedback is output information promoting corrective measures to restore the system to the desired or expected outcome.[16]

Positive feedback is output information reflecting deviations from anticipated effects and promoting change.[17]

Environment is a set of elements, conditions, and properties outside a system that can produce changes in the system.[18]

Open systems interchange with the environment.[19]

Equifinality is similar end results following from different initial conditions.[20]

Multifinality is different end results following from similar initial conditions.[21]

---

13. Churchman, p. 29.
14. F. Kenneth Berrien, *General and Social Systems* (New Brunswick, N. J.: Rutgers University Press, 1968), p. 21.
15. A. D. Hall and R.E. Fagen, "Definition of Systems," *General Systems* 1 (1956): 23.
16. Buckley, p. 59.
17. Buckley, p. 58.
18. Ackoff, pp. 662–63.
19. Kast and Rosenzweig, p. 450.
20. Buckley, p. 79.
21. Buckley, p. 79.

The Family, Other Social Systems, and Environments

2.

Individual and family systems are part of a network of social, biological, and physical systems, each interacting with and affecting the other. The complex of interactions in a developed democratic country form the basis of our discussion. In this chapter we shall first consider the physical environments as the setting for interactions of the family with other social systems. Next, we examine the political, economic, and social-cultural systems in relation to the family system, especially the managerial subsystem.

PHYSICAL ENVIRONMENTS

"The most critical problem facing humanity today is an ecological one of relating human societies harmoniously to their environments," according to Ripley and Buechner.[1] Even minor environmental changes can have far-reaching effects. We can think of the world as a system with numerous open and closed systems which act and interact.[2] A growing awareness of environmental problems can increase recognition of systems interrelationships. Figure 2.1 shows the interactions between the family and other systems, with two-way arrows indicating back and forth actions between systems.

---

1. S. Dillon Ripley and Helmut K. Buechner, "Ecosystem Science as a Point of Synthesis," *Daedalus* 96 (Fall 1967): p. 1192.
2. Kenneth E. Boulding, "The Economics of the Coming Spaceship Earth," in *Environmental Quality in a Growing Economy,* ed. H. Jarrett (Baltimore: The Johns Hopkins University Press, 1966), pp. 3–20.

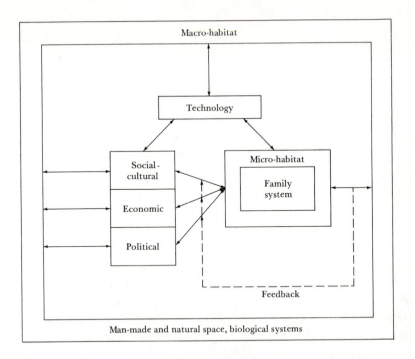

FIGURE 2.1 *Interactions among family and other systems.*

Social systems interact in a *macro-habitat*, which includes man-made and natural space and the biological contents of the physical environment. Space structured as buildings and highways, natural space such as parks and undeveloped areas, and the accompanying biological systems such as marine, plant, and animal life are within the macro-habitat. We may think of the macro-habitat as the reservoir of available natural resources. The *micro-habitat* is the setting of individuals and families—the shared environment of the personal and managerial subsystems. Over time, parts of the macro-habitat shift to the micro-habitat and back. We bring fuel into the home for heating and cooling; we use wood as material in building houses on land that was formerly a part of open space. The shift from the macro-habitat to the micro-habitat takes place through systems interchanges which are primarily economic. Changes in the macro-habitat from micro-units may be in the form of residues or, more positively, through conservation and other improvement practices.

Inevitably, the micro-habitat changes as the family grows, as resources make purchases possible, and as the interests and values of family members change. In both the micro- and the macro-habitats many of the changes are the result of technology.

Technology

Mesthene defines *technology* as knowledge organized for useful purposes.[3] Diverse technological developments, ranging from freeze-dried coffee to transistorized radios have changed our lifestyles. They change the environments and the forms of available goods and services, thus influencing the family and other social systems.

Technology provides such benefits as expanded experiences, longer life, and greater mobility. But its unwanted effects are extensive: smog, noisy air conditioners and airplanes, and water pollution. Our society is newly awakened to the effects of technology because of the recent awareness of environmental quality and relatively sensitive ecological balances. In the past, the costs to correct such abuses as the emission of factory effluents or automobile exhausts ("external effects" or "externalities") have not been charged to either the producer or the user. We need adequate ways to account for such costs.[4]

Some observers feel we are on a technological treadmill with far-reaching changes affecting more than just our environment. Rising material levels of living decrease our free time, thereby reducing the net benefits of the improved living level.[5] It takes time to earn money to purchase these additional goods, and it takes time to use, care for, and maintain them. A greater affluence, therefore, results in a sacrifice of time. The technology that brings us independence from others via the automobile, self-service stores, and movies at home may also increase our feelings of loneliness.[6] These changing conditions continually affect the managerial and personal subsystem relations within the family systems.

The benefits from these goods and services can distract us from recognizing the problems these same goods and services create and can delay or

---

3. E. G. Mesthene, *Technological Change* (Cambridge, Mass.: Harvard University Press, 1970), p. 25.
4. Robert M. Solow, "The Economist's Approach to Pollution and Its Control," *Science* 173 (August 6, 1971): 498–503.
5. Staffan Burenstam Linder, *The Harried Leisure Class* (New York: Columbia University Press, 1970), p. 144.
6. Philip E. Slater, *The Pursuit of Loneliness* (Boston: Beacon Press, 1970), p. 26.

actually hinder us from taking actions on the problems. Even acknowledged problems may seem too difficult to correct. For years, auto deaths and injuries increased while consumers demanded little change. But recently, consumer advocate groups have pressed for and achieved some improved safety measures through engineering technology.

It is important that we clarify our values and sharpen our goals for desired goods and services.[7] We may or may not buy products with the latest technological advances, depending on what is genuinely significant to us. Planning takes on added importance in a technologically advanced society. When technological advances reduce the physical requirements of work in the home, as has been the case in the United States, the mental aspects of work increase.[8] Recognition of such shifts in emphasis is significant to an effective managerial system.

Interaction with the Family System

The family system interacts with the "land, water, air, space, the solar system, plants and animals, sources of food and energy."[9] Many family resources originate in the environments, and the family changes the matter and energy into forms they need. An example is the laundering of clothes. Resources needed for the system are energy for operating the machine and heating the water; water for the entire process; and products such as detergent, fabric softener, and bleach. Water containing dirt, detergent, and other laundry products, is an output which is returned to surface water, while the remainder goes to the atmosphere. The inputs and outputs of this process are given in Table 2-1.

Actions to improve the environmental quality are generally corrective or preventive, and families are primarily involved with corrective actions. A single family can improve its micro-habitat and contribute to improvement of the larger environment by their considered choices and practices. When many families are involved, they can have a major corrective impact on the environment. As possible corrective actions—in the example of clothes washing—families might alter the frequency of laundering, reduce the temperature of the water used, reduce the amount of laundry

---

7. Leland W. Howe, "Group Dynamics and Value Clarification," *Penneys Forum* (Spring/Summer 1972): p. 12.
8. Rose E. Steidl and Esther Crew Bratton, *Work in the Home* (New York: John Wiley & Sons, 1968), p. 59.
9. Nancy C. Hook and Beatrice Paolucci, "The Family as an Ecosystem," *Journal of Home Economics* 62 (May 1970): 317.

products used, and substitute products with maximum degradability. The goals of clean clothes and a clean environment are met in different degrees by these actions.

Preventive actions from outside sources could be a modified design in washing machines to require less water, less energy, and so on. Future

TABLE 2-1.
The interaction of the family system and physical environments in clothes washing as an example.

Inputs to family system
  Resources (for one load of clothes)
    Material
      Automatic washer
      Supplies
        Detergent (1½ cups)
        Fabric softener (1 oz.)
        Bleach (1 cup)
      Energy
        Washer (0.2 KWH)
        Hot water heater (4.0 KWH)
      Water (45 gals.)
        Hot (20 gals.)
        Cold (variable amounts)
      Soiled clothes
    Human
      Time
      Physical capacity
  Demand
    Goal—Clean clothes

Throughput—planning and implementing necessary processes

Outputs to physical environments
  Used resources
    Waste water (containing dirt, detergent, and other laundry products)
        (approximately 45 gals.)
    Waste energy (electrical energy converted to mechanical energy, degraded to heat
        energy)
    Waste containers for products
      Detergent (1 container every 14 loads with 49-oz. box)
      Fabric softener (1 container every 33 loads with 33-oz. container)
      Bleach (1 container every 16 loads with 1-gal. container)

Outputs to family system
  Used resources
    Time used
    Human effort used
  Met demands
    Met goal—clean clothes

preventive actions may lead to developments in the use of sonic energy for washing clothes and dishes. The aim of preventive actions is to avoid or minimize the creation of residuals rather than to treat them afterwards.[10]

Families create residuals from goods "consumed" by the household, and they contribute to the need for corrective and preventive actions. Automobile exhausts, gases from space heating and incineration, sewage, and solid wastes such as garbage, junk autos, and appliances are some of the residuals to be dealt with.[11] As individuals and as families we can help minimize waste-disposal problems by choosing durable and reusable products with maximum degradable or recycling qualities. But our interactions with external systems must also be effective if our individual commitments to pollution control are to have a positive net effect. Is it environmentally advantageous to drive a polluting automobile to deliver a bundle of waste items for recycling? What are the alternative uses of the time spent in preparing the materials for recycling as well as for delivering them? To minimize such related costs, we need good transfer points. For broad-scale involvement of households, separation of waste must be easy, and collection must be both convenient and dependable.

The problem of solid wastes produced by the family system is evident in the short life span of household equipment for any individual (Figure 2-2). A single owner uses the washing machine for less than ten years. The longest-lasting household appliance is the sewing machine, with a life expectancy for one owner of almost twenty-five years. Automobiles and mobile homes are important solid-waste disposal problems. Car life varies with the condition and origin of the car and with the driver's age and sex. New cars have 6.2 years of expected use by one owner, while used cars have 4.1 years of expected use. American cars exceed the expected years of use of foreign cars by over two years (6.3 years compared to 3.9 years). A car driven by a woman has longer expected years of use (4.9 years) than does a car driven by a man (3.9 years); the driver's age is directly related to expected years of use. Younger persons expect to use a car fewer years than do older persons.[12]

---

10. Report of the National Goals Research Staff, "Toward Balanced Growth: Quantity with Quality," (Washington, D. C.: U.S. Government Printing Office, 1970), p. 72.

11. Allen V. Kneese, R. U. Ayres, and Ralph C. D'Arge, *Economics and the Environment* (Baltimore: The Johns Hopkins Press, 1970), pp. 51–65.

12. Jean L. Pennock and Carol M. Jaeger, "Household Service Life of Durable Goods," *Journal of Home Economics* 56 (January 1964): 24–25.

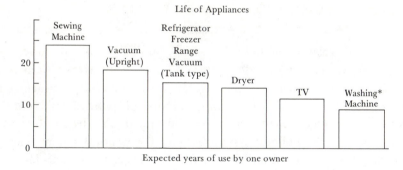

FIGURE 2.2 *Expected years of use by one owner of household appliances.*

Source: Jean L. Pennock and Carol Jaegar, "Household Service Life of Durable Goods," *Journal of Home Economics* 56 (January 1964): 23.

The packaging of less-durable products with products that have long-lasting residuals also creates special disposal problems. Metal and plastic caps and crowns accumulate at the rate of 338 per person per year, tin cans at the rate of 250 per person per year, and bottles and jars at the rate of 135 per person per year.[13] In urban areas, family systems contribute solid wastes such as paper, grass, brush cuttings, garbage, ashes, and metal, amounting to 1600 pounds per person per year.[14]

There are potentially compounding problems that evolve from the interaction of the family with the physical environments: population growth and pollution; expansion of consumer goods and pollution; increased power demands, interlocking systems and vulnerability to failures; continued demand for single-family dwellings and urban sprawl. Much remains to be understood about factors affecting environmental quality, but family choices are an important part in the ecological balance between the physical and biological systems of our micro- and macro-habitats. These problems interrelate with the interactions of the family with other social systems.

---

13. President's Science Advisory Committee, "Restoring the Quality of Our Environment," Report of the Environmental Pollution Panel (Washington, D. C.: The White House, November 1965), p. 11.

14. President's Science Advisory Committee, p. 11.

POLITICAL AND ECONOMIC SYSTEMS

The relation of individuals and families to the political and economic systems seems close whenever a paycheck arrives with income taxes and social security payments withheld. We hold the political system responsible for achieving society's goals through policies, laws, regulations, and the means to implement and enforce them. The family system interacts with the political system because the political system reaches directly into the lives of individuals and families as the various levels of political influence impinge on their activities. Regular expenditures by families have a major relationship with the economic system and depend largely on family earnings—another important aspect.

Interaction with the Family System

Figure 2-3 illustrates the three-way relationship of the family system with the political and economic systems. The diagram shows, perhaps more clearly than previous diagrams, that the output of one system is the input of another system. Inputs are labeled as "demands" and "supports," consistent with the terminology for inputs identified earlier as demands and resources for the family system.[15]

The political system demands (D^1) that the family consider the system's laws to be binding, and it enforces this demand. The political system encourages the family to develop politically responsible citizens. The family receives support (S^1) in various forms of protection—physical, both personal and property, and civil. In addition, the political system provides various goods and services such as education and recreational parks which can be made available more advantageously through public sharing of resources than through private means. The political system also provides other services to families who are not able to maintain their members at a level the society considers basic.

From the perspective of the family system, demands (D^2) placed on the political system seem somewhat diffuse. As individuals, we have the op-

---

15. David Easton, *A Framework for Political Analysis* (Englewood Cliffs, N. J.: Prentice Hall, Inc., 1965), p. 50. Support is used by Easton with the same connotation as resources or means for meeting demands. In the political context, the means are more often expressed as evidence of support—e.g., vote in "support" of a law to raise taxes in "support" of a given program. Such support is necessary in providing a consensus to make authoritative or binding allocation of values.

portunity to vote on certain issues, but few such issues have a direct bearing on our daily decisions. Our representatives at all levels of government decide most issues. Letters concerning particular issues may help sway legislative decisions, but we often feel that their influence on consumer problems or other matters relating to family welfare is limited. Involvement with an organized group is more likely to have an effect in expressing needs and making demands for desired reforms than our individual effort.

However, opportunities for the family to support the political system (S^2) are more apparent. These include tax payments, responsible voting, adherence to laws, and the fulfillment of other civic obligations such as jury duty.

The family expects (D^5) that the economic system will provide opportunities for family members to participate in productive processes through labor and through investments. The family also expects the economic system to make goods and services available that the family may purchase at acceptable prices with reasonable protection of market values. The actual purchases of the family and the provision of productive resources are supportive (S^5) to the economic system on terms of exchange that are reasonable and/or agreeable.

The economy, on the other hand, expects (D^6) that families will purchase goods and services and will provide the economy with productive resources at a price. As families respond to these and other demands, their aggregate choices of goods and services make up market demand —that is, the total amount of a good or service that consumers will buy at a given time and a given price. The family receives (S^6) dependable goods and services and a fair return for its participation in production processes only to the extent that the economic system supports the family system's demands.

The relation of the political system to the family and economic systems is to set the ground rules and protect the interests of members of each system (S^1, S^4) in response to expressed needs and in keeping with societal values (D^2, D^3). The political system expects adherence to established policies and regulations (D^1, D^4); family systems demonstrate their support (S^2, S^3) through actual adherence and performance of civic responsibilities.

The interactions among family-economic-political systems have grown in scope and in complexity. Although each input-output relation in Figure 2.3 has important implications for family management, we shall expand

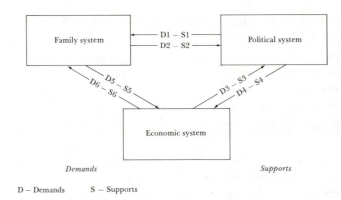

FIGURE 2.3 *Interrelationships of the family system with political and economic systems.*

Output of political system; input to family system

D1 Anticipated adherence to laws and other regulations; politically socialized members.

S1 Protection; provision of services, programs and policies to meet needs

Output of family system; input to political system

D2 Expressed values, needs—formal (in support of issues) or informal (letters, meetings).

S2 Tax payments; obeying laws and other regulations; military service; court duty; voting.

Output of economic system; input to political system

D3 Specifications for protective and facilitating mechanisms.

S3 Adherence to regulations; tax payments.

Output of political system; input to economic system

D4 Response to policies and regulations protecting producers and consumers—safety, equity, security.

S4 Protection and facilitating mechanisms consistent with societal and other system values.

Output of family system; input to economic system

D5 Expectation of goods and services available at an acceptable price; opportunities to participate in productive processes; reasonable protection at the market.

S5 Actual expenditures for consumer goods and services; provision of labor and other productive resources at reasonable and agreeable terms.

Output of economic system; input to family system

D6 Expectation that a quantity of goods and services will be purchased and that labor and other productive resources will be provided at a price.

S6 Reasonable return for labor and other productive outputs; dependable goods and services at acceptable prices.

only two for illustrative purposes: direct support of individuals and families with special economic needs, and public goods and services.

Direct Support for Special Economic Needs. Families, local governments, and private agencies have historically provided minimal support for individuals and families faced with inadequate resources and the adverse effects of economic risks. By economic risks we mean conditions such as unemployment or underemployment, aging, disability or illness, and death or absence of wage earners[16]—conditions that make it difficult or impossible for a family or individual to cope with economic responsibilities.

Both labor and management increasingly respond to these needs through benefits provided in union agreements and through other actions. Group health plans and community social agencies also provide expanded services. While these sources of support continue to meet special and local needs, a number of factors have brought a broader approach to meeting these needs through federal programs.

Technological advances initiated many of the conditions that have led to a more organized approach to security oriented programs: increased life expectancy brought anxieties about extended periods of no income; industrial expansion, which was made possible in part by geographic mobility, also weakened family and employer ties. Different parts of the country have various levels of vulnerability to economic fluctuations and to natural disasters. Differences also exist in the resources available in various regions for dealing with these vulnerabilities.

The passage of the Social Security Act of 1935 (S^1) recognized demands for programs on a national scale (D^2). The act is a comprehensive bill, which includes programs related to the broad range of economic risks of families. It provides for unemployment insurance programs, and all states currently participate. Benefits to unemployed workers vary from state to state, but tend to be about fifty per cent of most recent earnings up to a maximum amount over a payment period of about six months. The program of unemployment insurance has received general support as an important mechanism for bringing relative economic stability to families in times of stress.

The most comprehensive government program of economic support to individuals and families is Old-Age, Survivors, Disability, and Health In

---

16. Charles I. Schottland, "Government Economic Programs and Family Life," *Journal of Marriage and the Family* 19 (February 1967): 71–123.

surance (OASDHI) of the Social Security Administration. "This basic contributory program covers about nine out of ten persons working for a living."[17] Provisions are family related because benefits accrue to survivors and dependents of workers covered by the program. The system is a social effort to help families spread earnings over their lifetimes, to provide minimum support for retirement, and to share the risk of disability or premature death of the wage earner.

Employers and employees each contribute to the social security tax, and the tax rates are set in relation to overall program needs, on an insurance basis, rather than to individual prepayment of potential benefits.[18] When the program began, many individuals became eligible for maximum benefits with minimum contributions. As we approach the time when those who receive benefits will have contributed throughout their working lives, and with increasing taxes, the prepayment concept may become more realistic; inputs to the system may more nearly equal anticipated returns. In earlier stages, the program was apparently supplementary to, and not in competition with, private efforts. Certain questions arise which we cannot answer at the moment. For example, will the program continue to be supplementary as benefits are expanded to meet inflationary pressures and to provide for additional economic risks? As the program matures and rates of taxation are higher, how will social security returns and costs compare to private programs?

Public assistance provides for persons who do not have adequate means to meet the basic necessities for living. Such assistance is not based on prepayment by the recipients, but is related to specific causes from which the need arises. Old-Age Assistance, Aid to Families with Dependent Children (AFDC), Aid to the Blind, Aid to the Permanently and Totally Disabled, and Medical Assistance are programs of the Social Security Act administered by the states. Although the Aid to Dependent Children program has grown considerably and is now the largest of these forms of assistance,[19] per capita payments to recipients is lower than for the other public assistance programs.

---

17. U.S. Dept. of Health, Education, and Welfare, Social Security Administration, *Social Security Programs in the United States* (Washington, D. C.: U.S. Government Printing Office, 1973), p. 1.
18. U.S. Dept. of Health, Education, and Welfare, *Social Security Programs in the United States*, pp. 20–47.
19. *Social Security Bulletin* 36 (February 1973): 58–59.

Needs not covered by the OASDHI aspects of the Social Security Act may qualify for the General Assistance Programs of states and localities. The varied circumstances of persons needing assistance and the varied philosophies of local governing groups make eligibility criteria difficult to develop and administer. A basic level of support, which families or individuals must have for decent living, is a changing one. Changing general levels of living bring changing values. For this reason, a fair poverty line is often considered a relative rather than an absolute question.[20] (See Chapter 10.)

The complexities and inequities in administering current public welfare programs have led to income maintenance proposals that would assure all individuals and families a basic level of income. The major criticism of the proposals is that with a "guaranteed" income base, individuals or families might have less incentive to work. Some of the proposals include definite advantages for working. The usual proposal is a tax payment to families reporting incomes under a defined poverty level, hence the negative income tax concept. The tax payment would be reduced on a graduated basis to promote incentives for work. Available studies indicate that incentives for the husband to earn at given levels are not lessened, although he may have the alternative to seek a better-paying job and work fewer hours. Income earnings of other family members may be reduced.[21]

Public Goods and Services. We have noted that the availability of community goods and services such as parks, playgrounds, libraries, and so on are important resources for families in their management.[22] The economic value of public goods and services is often difficult to assess.[23] The importance of these resources to families may go unrecognized because of the same difficulties of evaluation. Apparently higher-income families make relatively more use of public goods and services than do lower-income families. Opportunity to use the resources, awareness of

---

20. S. M. Miller and Pamela A. Roby, *The Future of Inequality* (New York: Basic Books, Inc., 1970), chap. 2.

21. Irwin Garfinkel, "The New Jersey Income Maintenance Experiment," *Journal of Consumer Affairs* 6 (Summer 1972): 9.

22. Paulena Nickell and Jean Muir Dorsey, *Management in Family Living*, 4th ed. (New York: John Wiley & Sons, Inc., 1967), p. 84.

23. Richard A. Musgrave, "Cost-Benefit Analysis and the Theory of Public Finance," *Journal of Economic Literature* 7 (September 1969): pp. 799–800.

their potential value, or other convenience and social factors may affect such decisions.[24]

Education is probably one of the most far-reaching and influential governmental services relative to family managerial behavior. Traditionally, government-supported education in the United States has been considered necessary to promote responsible decision making by the citizens. As the scope of education grows, state and federal involvement and support are increasing. The programs range from complete or partial support of formal education to less formal vocational and rehabilitation programs for helping people adapt to changing economic and social conditions. All the programs have direct and indirect influence on personal management decisions as to earning ability or the effective use of earnings.

A public good is equally available to all, and one person's use does not alter another person's enjoyment or basis for access to its use, except temporarily. A private market is not likely to exist for these public goods because they are ordinarily difficult to divide into small units for private use. An example of a good shared frequently by a group or by the public is water recreation facilities.

In the future, our interest in public goods will probably increase. Concern for the quality of life or relief from the maintenance of private goods, such as boats or second cars, may generate support for more cultural centers, public recreational facilities, or efficient city transit systems. If these changes occur, more creative participation of private interests with government at all levels will be needed.

The concept of social balance in the distribution of resources is basic to decisions about the division between private and public goods and services.[25] People decide on the amount of private income they are willing to exchange for public goods and services. Alternative uses of public funds must also be evaluated carefully to insure the highest social returns. The problems and questions raised in the previous discussion suggest

---

24. Glen Morris, Richard Pasewark, and John Schultz, "Occupational Level and Participation in Public Recreation in a Rural Community," *Journal of Leisure Research* 4 (Winter 1972): 25-32.
    John J. Lindsay and Richard A. Ogle, "Socioeconomic Patterns of Outdoor Recreation Use Near Urban Areas," *Journal of Leisure Research* 4 (Winter 1972): 19–24.
25. John Kenneth Galbraith, *The Affluent Society* (Boston: Houghton Mifflin Co., 1958), p. 260.

areas in which the family-political-economic systems interchange needs more study from the family perspective.

The Family as a Micro-Economic System

The economic processes and roles of individuals and families have changed as the interdependence with the general economic system has grown. For many families, exchanging time and services for wages or salaries has increased their levels of living—a point we shall consider later in this chapter.

From a systems perspective, the interaction of time and service for wages and salaries is part of the family exchange with the general economy. Table 2-2 shows these interactions as inputs and outputs between the micro-unit and the economic, government or political system, and community organization systems.

The family exchanges labor and other productive activities with the general economy for income including profits and rents. Part of the income becomes the family's output (expenditures) for goods and services.

TABLE 2.2

Family micro-economic system inputs and outputs.

Family micro-economic system inputs	Family micro-economic system outputs
From the economic system	*To the economic system*
Wages and salaries, profits from self-employment, rent	Labor entrepreneurship, and other productive activities
Interest and dividends	Savings and investments (temporary)
Goods and services	Consumption expenditures
From the political system	*To the political system*
Services, benefits, subsidy payments, tax incentives	Taxes
Transfer payments such as social security	Services
From community organizations	*To community organizations*
Services and monetary assistance	Money, goods, and services

Another part of the income may be set aside temporarily as savings and investments available for future use. Until they are used, these resources are available to the general economy through financial institutions and capital stock companies. Returns to the family in interest and dividends may be used or reinvested according to family preference or need.

Input-output relationships other than family market exchanges with the general economy occur with other societal systems. Tax payments are family output, which may return as inputs to the very same families in the form of general community benefits or services, such as police or fire protection and education. Taxes may also support public resources—libraries and recreational facilities. Or, taxes may be transferred to other families through grants, subsidies, assistance or other program payments, which may be translated into goods and services through exchange with the general economy.

Families contribute to other families, to community agencies, to churches, or to social organizations in many ways. Transfers may be in the form of expertise such as that provided by volunteer firemen or workers in a community drive to reduce costs, or in goods which are also in lieu of costs, or in money to cover costs. But, regardless of the form these transfers may take, the output of resources from the family has tangible value as inputs to the general community.

Outputs may be separated from inputs in time and form. Social security taxes are partly a current output and partly a claim for future input. Economic activity may occur entirely within the family system with no apparent interchange with the general economy, but many activities have a partial external involvement. For example, a gardening family may buy seeds as the only direct exchange with the general economic system. Planting, cultivating, harvesting, and consuming (except utilities) may be economic activities without external exchange; the gardening tools used in these activities may have been a previous external purchase.

Interaction of the General Economic and Family Systems

The choices of families as producers and consumers influence the general economy and affect the available family resources. Spending decisions affect family lifestyle and are the source of market demand. The family's capabilities and circumstances influence choices among available alternatives within the opportunities and constraints of the general economy. The interaction of the family with the general economic system is mutually responsive when consumers use information to make choices that reflect their needs. The mutual nature of the interaction breaks down when monopolistic elements cause resources to flow in directions and in quantities that do not reflect the consumer's desires.

Employment. A major transaction between family and economic systems is the family's participation in the labor force. The family's income depends on its inputs into the economy and the economy's response in terms of output. Self-employment offers one source of income, but the major source of family income is from wages and salaries. The percentage of the personal income of individuals and families derived from wage and salary disbursements was 67 per cent in 1971.[26]

Families are probably more aware of trends in the labor force when they are personally affected. The increasing number of young adult workers who are 25–34 years old[27] is an important trend to a person over 40 who is looking for a job. The continual shift toward service-producing industries (government, transportation, public utilities, trade, finance, services, and real estate) is significant to a worker in a goods-producing industry who is replaced by a computerized operation. The increase in part-time employment is important to the person looking for a second job and to the man or woman who only wants part-time employment because of other commitments, such as school or household responsibilities. If present trends hold, by 1980, one out of every seven persons will be employed on a part-time basis.[28]

In American families the husband is generally the main wage earner, although a growing number of wives and mothers are employed. The percentage of wives who are in the labor force has increased from just over 20 in 1948 to over 40 in 1971 (see Figure 2.4). If we translate these overall trends on women's employment into work histories, we find that the histories take the form of an "M." Employment reaches the first peak before and shortly after a woman marries, then drops while her children are young, and returns again to the early marriage level as her children become less dependent.

---

26. U.S. Dept. of Commerce, Bureau of the Census, *Statistical Abstract of the United States: 1972* (Washington, D. C.,: U.S. Government Printing Office, 1972), p. 317.

27. U.S. Dept. of Labor, Office of the Assistant Secretary for Policy, Evaluation, and Research, "U.S. Manpower in the 1970's," (Washington, D. C.: U.S. Government Printing Office, 1970), p. A-37.

28. U.S. Dept. of Labor, "U.S. Manpower in the 1970's."

FIGURE 2.4 *Participation of married women in the labor force, 1960-1972.*

Source: Howard Hayghe, "Labor Force Activity of Married Women," *Monthly Labor Review* 96 (April, 1973): 34.

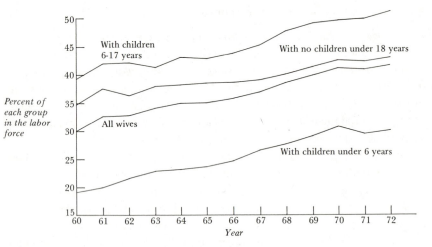

Participation of married women in the labor force, by age.

Source: Howard Hayghe, "Labor Force Activity of Married Women," *Monthly Labor Review* 96 (April, 1973): 33.

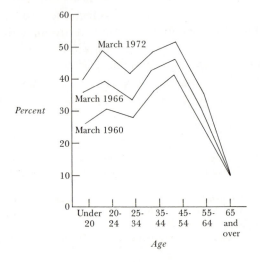

The rate of participation in the labor force is highest for wives in the lower-middle income levels. As the husband's income reaches higher levels, the rate of the wife's participation declines. A working wife adds an average of more than 25 per cent to the family income.[29] This contribution can be critical at lower-income levels.

The effects of employment and occupational choices on management in homes are discussed in Chapter 4.

Standards and Levels of Living. A *standard of living* is the quantity and quality of goods and services that an individual or group desires, while the *level of living or consumption* refers to the goods and services currently consumed. The standard of living, in the economic context, is a social or individual goal or aspiration, and the level of living or consumption is the actual situation. Whenever the gap between the standard and the level of living is narrow, individuals and families feel secure about their economic welfare.[30] The difference between the standard of living and the level of consumption is considered to be a strong motivating force toward closing the gap.[31] Once we reach our preferred lifestyle or our desired level of living—whether as individuals or as families—we try to maintain it, especially whenever a reduction in the standard is threatened.[32]

To some extent, families take on the standard of living of their peers or the larger society. Achieving the standard becomes the family system's goal, and the managerial system responds to the goal. Social standards influence the choices families make about their individual standard and level of consumption. The process of choosing includes at least four levels of decisions:

1. considering societal living standards,
2. accepting or rejecting the majority's consumption standards as bases for judging quality and performance of goods and services,

---

29. Howard Hayghe, "Labor Force Activity of Married Women," *Monthly Labor Review* 96 (April 1973): 33.

30. Richard S. Weckstein, "Welfare Criteria and Changing Tastes," *American Economic Review* 52 (March 1962): 133–53.

31. "Report of the Family Economics Concepts Committee," pp. 266–293 in *Issues in Family Economics,* Proceedings of a National Conference (Washington, D. C.: American Home Economics Association, 1967).

32. Hazel Kyrk, *The Family in the American Economy* (Chicago: The University of Chicago Press, 1953), pp. 12–13.

3. choosing the individual lifestyle and living level,
4. selecting specific goods and services within the lifestyle and level.[33]

In the United States we have what may be called a standard package of household items, which are nominally the same for broad ranges of population groups. Variations come in special features or models for certain groups. Moving from one group to another is easier when a family can adapt the standard package than when the family has a completely new set of expectations.[34] The change from associating with a group of married college students to a group of young professional couples often involves a transitional period of apartment living before the young couple purchases a suburban home. During the transitional period, the couple adapts the standard package of goods to the interim situation; then adjusts later to the increased expectations in the new package of goods.

Some groups, particularly youth, seek unique expressions of their lifestyle. Individuals who want freedom from conformity to a standard package of goods by seeking the unique are actually participating in the evolution of another standard package. Changes in fashion and in conformity are accepted elements of choice making in an open society.

Changes made in expenditures appear to be related to our opportunities for expanded consumption (Table 2.2). Once we have satisfied hunger, our food intake is limited, due to the inelasticity of the human stomach. Although we can increase the quality and quantity of our clothing, we can wear only a limited number of items at one time. Housing has greater opportunities for expansion, and so do the other items—even medical care, which can be expanded in scope to include more preventive measures and more complex long-run treatments. Changes in spending within each category respond somewhat in relation to the capacity of consumers for either quantitative or qualitative expansion of consumption.

SOCIAL-CULTURAL SYSTEM

Culture defines the meaning and content of a society; changes in culture occur through social processes. Because of this interrelation, the social and cultural aspects are considered together in this section.

33. Howard Roseborough, "Some Sociological Dimensions of Consumer Spending," *Canadian Journal of Economics and Political Economy* 26 (August 1960): 454–64.
34. David Riesman and Howard Roseborough, "Careers and Consumer Behavior," in *Consumer Behavior*, ed. Lincoln H. Clark (New York University Press, 1955). 2: 1–18.

TABLE 2.3

Relative importance of Consumer Price Index components, United States city average for urban wage earners and clerical workers, by commodity, for selected years.

Components	1935–39 a	December 1952 b	December 1963 c	December 1972 d
All items	100.0	100.0	119.1	119.5
Food	35.4	29.6	22.4	22.5
Housing	33.7	32.5	33.2	33.9
Apparel and upkeep	11.0	9.2	10.6	10.4
Transportation	8.2	11.3	13.9	13.1
Health and recreation			19.5	19.8
Medical care	4.0	5.1	5.7	6.4
Personal care	2.4	2.0	2.8	2.6
Reading and recreation	2.9	5.3	5.9	5.7
Other goods and services	2.4	5.0	5.1	5.1

Gloria P. Green, "Relative Importance of CPI Items," *Monthly Labor Review* 88 (November 1965): 1347. U.S. Dept. of Labor, Bureau of Labor Statistics, "The Consumer Price Index for July 1973," Washington, D. C.: U. S. Government Printing Office, October 1973, p. 8.

a Value weights based on expenditure survey 1934–36.

b Value weights based on estimates of average family expenditures in 1952, derived from consumer expenditure survey 1950, revised after 1963 revision of index.

c Value weights based on expenditure survey 1960–61, adjusted for price changes between the survey dates and December 1963.

d Value weights based on expenditure survey 1960–61, adjusted for price changes between the survey dates and December 1972.

Culture

Culture reflects the customs of a society and provides guidelines for future behavior.[35] *Culture* is the composite of observed and expected behavioral patterns, beliefs and values, and their accompanying symbols and objects.

Cultural values and patterns are learned, primarily through the family system. Children are instilled with the important values and behavior patterns of the culture. More than one-third of an anthropologist's 73-item list of traits common to all cultures are part of the personal and family

35. Mary Ellen Goodman, *The Individual and Culture* (Homewood, Ill.: The Dorsey Press, 1967), p. 39.

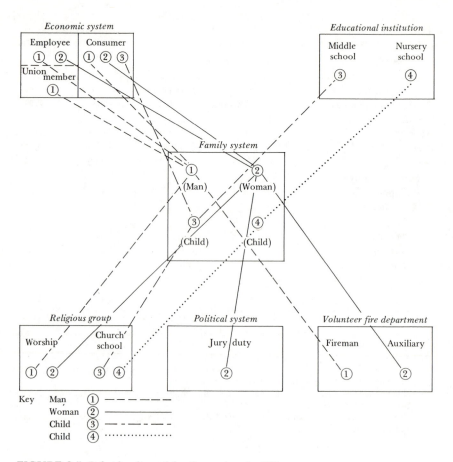

Economic system

Employee | Consumer
① ② | ① ② ③
Union member
①

Educational institution

Middle school ③ | Nursery school ④

Family system
① (Man) | ② (Woman)
③ (Child) | ④ (Child)

Religious group
Worship | Church school
① ② | ③ ④

Political system
Jury duty
②

Volunteer fire department
Fireman | Auxiliary
① | ②

Key | Man | ① | — — — — —
| Woman | ② | —————
| Child | ③ | — · — · —
| Child | ④ | ············

FIGURE 2.5 *Role pluralism of family members in different systems.*

systems.[36] Examples of family and personal items are food taboos, marriage, hair styles, meal times, housing, and cleanliness training.

Frequently, cultural values and patterns are subject to stress, such as in the United States since the early 1960's. Families are responsible for the socialization of children, but the parental role during rapid change is difficult. In simple societies, members can learn the total heritage; in large, complex societies, members are likely to learn only a small portion of the

36. Bernard Berelson and Gary A. Steiner, *Human Behavior* (New York: Harcourt, Brace & World, Inc., 1964), p. 649.

total culture. An orientation to individual expression may be part of the cultural heritage and may also be a result of an inability to comprehend the total. Rapid change can be a source of stress.

Cultural values carry a sense of commitment and moral obligation, and behavior is often prescribed in relation to values. Cultural expectations thus limit the scope of managerial involvement. An example of this is the family structure in the state of Kerala in India. The strong matriarchal society identifies the woman as the decision maker and manager of the household.

However, in complex societies cultural values and patterns are more general, and a wide range of behavior is acceptable.[37]

Social Interaction

In our discussion of social interaction, we shall focus on the interrelation of the family system with other social systems and we shall stress social status and interaction through multiple roles of family members. Family members penetrate other systems, and the extent and kind of roles outside the family system affects their social status. Social relations within the family are also influential, although they are outside the scope of this discussion.

Social status is "the perceived relationship of a person, a social group, or a category of person to others."[38] In the household, the social position is based on the male head, if there is one. Acker and others are urging considered study of the female contribution to status, because of increased numbers of unattached individuals, increased women's participation in the labor force, the women's movement, and women's place in the social structure.[39]

In relatively open social systems, such as in the United States, mobility between social positions is part of the way of life. However, regulations, hostility, and inability to meet the financial requirements can form barriers to penetrating other systems. Formidable barriers exist when the family attempts to make a drastic change in social positions. "A class as-

37. Talcott Parsons, *The System of Modern Societies* (Englewood Cliffs, N. J.: Prentice-Hall, Inc., 1971,) pp. 14–15.
38. Thomas E. Lasswell, *Class and Stratum* (Boston: Houghton Mifflin Co., 1965), p. 43.
39. Joan Acker, "Women and Social Stratification: A Case of Intellectual Sexism," *American Journal of Sociology* 78 (January 1973): 182.

pires to and struggles for mobility only to the next higher rank(s), the more distant ones being considered too far away for realistic approach."[40]

Similar systems are, however, more open than dissimilar ones. "The more distinguishable the class or caste in physical appearance, the slower its group mobility (for example, Negroes as compared with white immigrants in this country)."[41] Further, "The longer a minority group has been in a society, the more it is assimilated into the values of the larger community, and the less visibly ethnic it is, then the better are its chances at upward mobility."[42] It may also be the case that the longer a group is viewed as a minority, the more difficult it is to move upward.

Larger systems, such as cities, are more open to changes in social status than are small communities. "Working-class youths raised in a big city are more likely to move upward than those raised in a small town; there are more stimuli for mobility in the city, fewer restrictions, more anonymity and more opportunities."[43]

The effect of the family system on geographic and occupational mobility is not clear. A person's occupational mobility seems to be more related to his social status and residential migration than to family ties.[44] Social status is characterized and complicated by many individual and family involvements in different systems. This involvement is *role pluralism.*[45]

Role is the aggregate of the rights, privileges, duties, and obligations of a person in one social position in relation to those of persons in other positions.[46] In their various roles, family members may face conflicts in their loyalties to different systems, such as loyalty to the economic system in the role of wage earner and loyalty to the family system in the role of parent. The conflict described here is between systems and not within the family system, as when mother and wife roles or mother and daughter-in-law roles conflict, except as these conflicts relate to roles in other systems.

Role pluralism for individuals may be overly demanding. A person must allocate his time and resources among different roles and accompanying

---

40. Berelson and Steiner, p. 465.
41. Berelson and Steiner, p. 465.
42. Berelson and Steiner, p. 470.
43. Berelson and Steiner, p. 470.
44. Bert N. Adams, "Isolation, Function, and Beyond: American Kinship in the 1960's," *Journal of Marriage and the Family* 32: (November 1970), 589.
45. Parsons, p.12.
46. Theodore R. Sarbin and Vernon L. Allen, "Role Theory," in *The Handbook of Social Psychology* eds. Garder Lindzey and Elliot Aronson, (Reading, Mass.: Addison-Wesley Publishing Co., Inc., 1968), I, 497.

obligations.[47] In the example in Figure 2-5, family members are assuming fifteen separate roles in other systems. Conflict occurs when a person simultaneously holds roles with incompatible expectations. A woman on jury duty, whose regular work is piling up for her return and who finds that the school has scheduled a "parent" meeting while the jury is in session, is likely to experience role conflict.

Incompatible expectations may frustrate a college student who lives at home with the family, who holds membership in a social organization, and who regularly dates one person. Each group may expect primary loyalty to a particular role, and strain occurs when there is no agreement on role priority. In general, loyalty conflicts arising from role pluralism can be partially resolved by easing role expectations.[48] The frustrated college student, for example, could change membership in the social organization from an active to an inactive status and thereby ease the expectations of one group. Coping with role conflict begins with influencing one's roles rather than being controlled by them.[49]

Cultural guidelines are less distinct as social interactions become more complex. The openness, size, and similarity of systems influence opportunities for social interchange. Social mobility and multiple roles are evidences of continuing change. Individual decisions and increased complexity of choices are progressing at accelerating rates.[50]

SUMMARY

Interaction between systems is a central theme in this overview of the family's relation to its environments and to other social systems.

Individual and family interactions with physical environments have had positive and negative effects. Positive interchanges are esthetically and functionally creative uses of space and productive use and control of material resources to serve our needs and goals. Negative effects are reduced environmental quality, requiring both preventive and corrective measures to improve the situation. Households can contribute to corrective actions.

---

47. Sarbin and Allen, p. 539.
48. Parsons, p. 15.
49. Douglas T. Hall, "A Model of Coping with Role Conflict: The Role Behavior of College Educated Women," *Administrative Science Quarterly* 17: (December 1972), 486.
50. Alvin Toffler, *Future Shock* (New York: Random House, Inc., 1970), chap. 2.

The effects of technology permeate the physical environments and the household as well. Technology, as knowledge and processes applied to practical problems, is closely related to the functional aspects of home management.

The political system is becoming more widely involved in the family system through formal and informal means. Through policies, rules, and regulations the political system affects the programs, the products purchased by the family, and the services that the political system renders.

Ideally, the interactions of the family as a micro-economic system with the general economy are mutually beneficial exchanges. Families are experiencing benefits such as generally higher levels of living, shorter work weeks, opportunities to specialize in their productive activities, and increasing amounts of discretionary income. At the same time, we sense the limits of the impact of an individual consumer choice and action.

As individuals and as families we get the basis for most of the value content and role identification from interactions with the social-cultural system. Our participation in activities and our roles affect our individual status. The openness, size, and similarity of systems affects the potential interactions and the ease of penetrating barriers.

Interactions between the family, and the political, economic, and social-cultural systems and the physical environments are far from the ideal of mutual benefit. Improvements can be made within each system, and change is imperative in the interrelation with the physical environments.

DEFINITIONS

Macro-habitat is the man-made and the natural space and biological contents of the physical environment of the family system.

Micro-habitat is the man-made and the natural space and biological contents of the physical environment of the personal and managerial subsystem within the family system. It is the shared environment of the family.

Technology is knowledge organized for useful purposes.[51]

Micro-economic system contains the economic actions of the family or any well-defined group of individuals.[52]

---

51. Mesthene, p. 25.
52. James Mitchell Henderson and Richard E. Quandt, *Micro-economic Theory* (New York: McGraw-Hill Book Company, 1971), p. 6.

Standard of living is the quantity and quality of goods and services desired for consumption by an individual or group.

Level of consumption is the goods and services currently utilized.

Culture is the composite of observed and expected behavioral patterns, beliefs and values, and their accompanying symbols and objects.

Social status is the perceived relationship of a person, a social group, or a category of person to others.[53]

Role is the aggregate of the rights, privileges, duties, and obligations of a person in one social position in relation to those of persons in other positions.[54]

Role pluralism is the involvement of an individual in many different systems.[55]

---

53. Lasswell, p. 43.
54. Sarbin and Allen, p. 497.
55. Parsons, p. 12.

Part Two

Concepts of Home Management

Management as a System

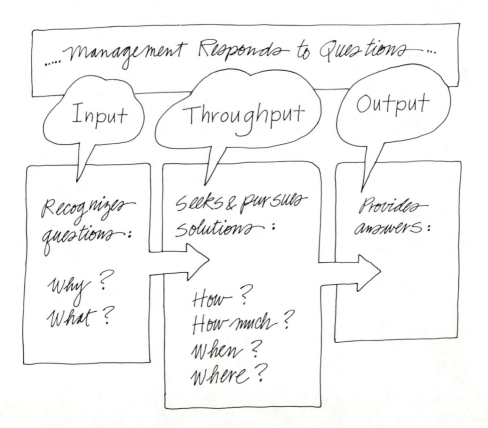

..... Management Responds to Questions ...

Input

Recognizes questions:

Why?
What?

Throughput

Seeks & pursues solutions:

How?
How much?
When?
Where?

Output

Provides answers:

3.

From time to time, we have all noticed that some of our friends consistently accomplish what is important to them, while others never quite meet their goals. The ways in which people manage their resources is a part of the difference. A systems approach helps us understand the total management situation of individuals and families by considering their many interrelationships with other systems. This chapter focuses on the managerial system as a subsystem of the family.

COMPONENTS OF THE MANAGERIAL SYSTEM

The managerial systems of individuals and families relate to other subsystems of the family as well as to the political, social-cultural, and economic systems and the physical environments. The wholeness, or totality, of the situation is important to our understanding of management. In part, it is the system's input and output that demonstrates the managerial activity. Management is not a general, rigid set of rules and actions, but is a set of flexible responses to a particular situation. Its actions are goal directed and are related to available or obtainable resources; a single action is not isolated in time, but is related to the past and the future. Input, output, and feedback cross the boundaries of open systems such as the family system. Feedback promotes management flexibility by alerting the system to growth possibilities. A general definition of management encompasses its interrelationships: *management* is planning the use of resources and then implementing the plans to meet demands. In the following sections on input, throughput, output, and feedback we shall briefly examine planning, implementing, resources, and demands and then study each component in some detail as the subject of a separate chapter. "Management," "home management," "family management," and "personal management" refer to this total management view.

Inputs

As we have said in earlier chapters, demands and resources are the inputs to family systems and their subsystems. *Demands* are goals and/or events that require action. *Goals* are value-based objectives, and *events* are unexpected occurrences that require action. Demands may originate from either inside or outside the family system.

Sources of External Demands. Families and individuals are bombarded with requests, requirements, and expectations from outside the family. The personal and managerial systems deal with these demands. The most binding demands are regulations from the political systems such as school attendance for a given number of years, obedience to laws, and zoning restrictions.

Events may originate with the macro-habitat. Natural disasters —tornadoes, floods, earthquakes—are the most dramatic examples of events requiring the action of the affected individuals and families. Effective management of resources is very important at such times.

The macro-habitat also provides the setting for many individual or family activities. Public buildings, open spaces, parks, and highways are all part of the macro-habitat in addition to rivers, lakes, animals, and, of course, the weather. Regulations in the use of the macro-habitat place demands on the family; laws for anti-pollution devices on cars, sewage treatment, highway and airway regulations must be responded to by the family. Where the regulations are binding, it is the political system that enforces them, even though they emanate from the macro-habitat.

Technology is another source of external demands. Technological developments constantly change the products that reach consumers through economic processes. Families and individuals must respond to these technological developments. Sometimes the family has too much information about a product, and at other times, not enough. An overload of information can be confusing. Where there is insufficient basic information, the effects of the product on the family or its environment may be neglected.

External demands also come from the social-cultural system, which expects children to be socialized and which develops behavioral norms. Although behavioral norms may vary from region to region, they frequently dictate the types of occupations that are acceptable to the culture as well as certain attitudes toward sex. These norms are strong enough to be demands. The expectations may range from the amount of formal education deemed desirable and the age when youth should become independent to the social and religious affiliations considered congenial to the particular culture. A family, however, may still choose whether or not to accept the behavioral norms. When the circumstances are complex, they may lead to accelerated change.

Sources of Internal Demands.   The micro-habitat of the family system is its structured and natural space and biological systems. Demands may come from this shared environment which includes (1) the living unit and surroundings, (2) all the objects available to enhance the environment or promote the purposes of each member, and (3) the biological systems, including plants, animals, and individual family members.

Family members have biological needs, such as food and water, but they also have many other requirements which the managerial system must accommodate. The teenager's plea to use the car for a date or for new clothes before a party is probably processed by the personal subsystem, but the family's decisions about the requests are made through the managerial system.

Goals.   Goals give direction to management; they originate primarily in the personal subsystem of the family or the individual. Management can help clarify and order goals.

If a family holds many goals, its management is probably more complicated.[1] Assessing goal priorities can be difficult; management can help by assisting in the realistic appraisal of the goals. If goal priorities are unclear because value priorities are unclear, management becomes more complex. For a clearer reading on values, feedback from the managerial subsystem to the personal subsystem may be needed. Figure 3.1 indicates this feedback.

---

1. Francille Maloch and Ruth E. Deacon, "Proposed Framework for Home Management," *Journal of Home Economics* 58 (January 1966): 31. Francille Maloch and Ruth E. Deacon, "Components of Home Management in Relation to Selected Variables," Research Bulletin 1042 (Wooster, Ohio: Ohio Agricultural Research and Development Center, 1970).

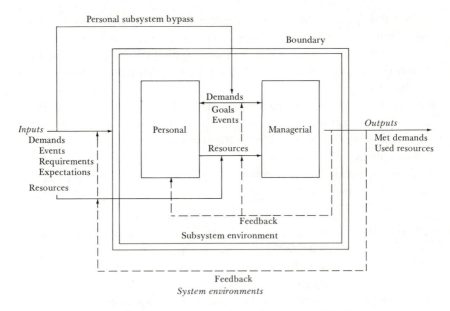

FIGURE 3.1 *Sources of demands and resources of the managerial subsystem.*

Some expectations from external systems may bypass the personal system and go directly to the managerial subsystem. This process is also shown in Figure 3.1. For the family or individual who has decided to support certain community fund drives annually, when the request arrives, the decision is how much to give, not whether to give. The personal subsystem goal is a continuing one and permits the managerial subsystem to function predominantly in allocating money to this particular cause.

When the city notifies the family that sidewalks must be repaired within thirty days or the city will make the repairs and bill the family, this demand probably bypasses the personal subsystem and goes directly to the managerial subsystem to be processed. In either example—to aid the fund drive or to adhere to an ordinance—establishing the original goal involves the personal system.

Events. Events as inputs are pertinent, unexpected, or low-probability occurrences that require action. An external event that reaches the family system is the result of a series of circumstances and is the output of some system. A raging hurricane is an external event and so, too, is a school fair, in the common meaning of events. Although the hurricane and the annual school fair are outputs of physical and social systems, respectively, the hurricane is more likely to be a pertinent and unexpected occurrence that requires action by the family. The family may participate in the school fair as part of its planned interaction with the school, in which case the fair could not be considered an unexpected occurrence. However, if the family does not participate in the fair but is caught in a traffic jam because of an unanticipated parade in connection with the fair, then that becomes a minor event to be coped with.

Internal events, ranging from a home accident to a forgotten birthday, may also occur. Both are the result of a series of circumstances. Events which the family interprets as pertinent and requiring action, such as remembering the birthday belatedly, will vary according to the family's values. To some events, such as those that relate to health, the family has a standing commitment. When such events arise, the managerial subsystem responds directly.

Resources. The critical criterion of a resource is that it be the means for achieving goals or for meeting the demands placed upon the family by certain events. Resources may become available from activities internal to the family system or through interactions with other systems. In either case, the available resources are those which individuals or families own or have control over. Resources may be classified as human and material.

Human resources inside the family system are the skills, abilities, and knowledge of the persons who are members of the system. If the family sometimes prefers the knowledge, skills, or abilities of others outside the family, these may be obtained by exchanging money or time or by receiving assistance in the form of gifts. *Material resources* are the goods already available for consumption or that will be used to produce other goods, and the savings and investments which represent potential claims on goods or services. Resource characteristics and resource allocation are discussed more fully in Chapter 6.

Throughputs

The components within the boundary of a system help explain its dynamics. Throughput is the activity inside the system boundary. We can measure a system's overall effectiveness by comparing the output (the results achieved) with input (what was wanted and available). But such an analysis would not, for example, reveal why some families (with similar resources) more nearly achieve goals than do others.

The effects of throughput are reflected in the differences in input and output. The term "black box" describes the unknown throughput. Boulding observes that "a pure 'black box' behavioral science, which studies only inputs and outputs and makes no attempt to pry off the lid of the behavior unit to see what is inside, suffers from almost fatal limitations."[2]

For the management of home and personal affairs we analyze the throughput in terms of planning and implementing—two of the components in the definition given earlier. *Planning* is a series of decisions concerning standards and/or sequences of action. *Implementing* is putting plans and procedures (standards and sequences) into effect by controlling and facilitating actions.

Figure 3.2 illustrates planning and implementing as major subsystems within the boundary of the managerial subsystem. The inputs to planning are the demands and resources. Since planning decisions involve standards and sequences of action needed to meet demands, the two planning subsystems are called standard setting and action sequencing. Plans are shown as the output of planning, with standards and sequences identified as their major parts. The feedback arrows shown from planning to the personal subsystem and from plans to planning indicate the openness of the subsystem components.

The repeated use of plans is a common and practical way to simplify everyday living. A repeat-use arrow—indicated in Figure 3.2 by a solid line—shows the bypass from the demand and resource inputs, before they reach the planning subsystem, to the output marked "plans." This indicates that output from previous planning is useable for the current purpose. More attention is given to single-use and repeat-use plans in Chapter 7.

Although planning is always future oriented, plans vary in specificity from situation to situation. During the planning process, *standards* evolve. These are measures of quality and/or quantity resulting from the families' attempts to reconcile resources with demands. Standard setting brings the two inputs of demands and resources into a realistic relationship.

Decision making, as the term implies, is the making of choices or the resolving of alternatives. Decision making is important in personal management, yet it is not unique to it, nor is the concept of planning.

In setting standards, the family or the individual assesses resources, searches for further information, develops alternatives, considers these al-

---

2. Kenneth E. Boulding, *Economics as a Science* (New York: McGraw-Hill Book Company, 1970), p. 54.

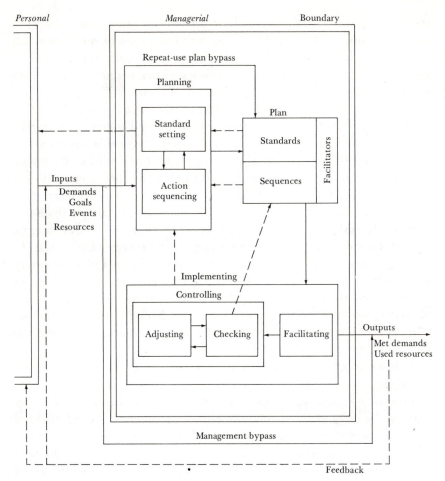

FIGURE 3.2 *The managerial system.*

ternatives in relation to goals and available resources, and arrives at a decision. The subject of these deliberations varies from problem to problem,
but the end product, the plan, defines some achievable qualitative and/or
quantitative aspect(s) of something. When we buy a radio, for instance, we
complete the processes of searching, developing alternatives, and weighing the alternatives. The total process defines quality and quantity factors
(content) such as tone, size, reception, and style. This is standard setting.
When we have decided on the relative importance of these features in

relation to purpose and cost, we have a plan with criteria (standards) to guide our buying. The final purchase will have a set of qualitative and quantitative characteristics. However, we may not consciously choose a radio on the basis of all the characteristics, either because some do not matter or because we have little awareness of them.

A *sequence of action* is an order among or within tasks. In the illustration of shopping for a radio, the plan development and execution may take place in one or several shopping trips. The major sequencing activity may be to schedule the shopping so that we can make the best choice within the available time. A sequence (the order for doing the shopping in this example) must be consistent with the established standards. If the store farthest away is more likely to have the widest choice, starting at that store may be the best sequence. Standards and sequences, ordinarily integral parts of a total plan, need not be developed at the same time.

After standard(s) and sequence(s) are developed into a plan consistent with resources and demands, implementing the action is the other task of management. If the implementation completes the action without complications, the plan's effectiveness can be evaluated. Standards and sequences more specifically represent the original goal and become the goals to be met through implementation.

In the example of shopping for a radio, suppose we did not base the sequence on the scope of selection, but instead sequenced stores from the nearest to the farthest. Suppose also that our time ran out before we reached the most likely store at the end of the line and we still had not found an acceptable product. We would then have to choose between either an alternate sequencing plan or a change in preferred standards for the radio. In either case, we would probably have to change the use of time or the money resources.

The problem lies with the original plan, but can corrections be made in the implementing phase of management? To answer the question, we need definitions of two components of implementing: *controlling* is checking actions for conformity to plans and, if necessary, adjusting standards and/or sequences. *Facilitating* is assisting the progress or flow of actions by capitalizing on individual and/or environmental factors. According to these definitions, the radio situation is a controlling problem (if the standards of the original plan were adequately checked). When it is possible to change either standards or sequence (but not both) in order to continue implementing the plan, the basic plan can be adjusted without altering the goal. If new information and limited time necessitate a change in both the standards and the sequence, then we need a new plan.

As implied above, *checking* is examining actions for conformity to the planned standards and sequences. The nature of checking varies with the specific task or situation. A task such as vacuuming a rug may involve almost continuous checking against a standard. A task of getting all members of the family to a meeting on time is more complex. There may have to be spot checking to see that one person is not far behind the others in getting ready. The type of checking in industrial quality control also varies. In manufacturing space-ship parts, each item may be carefully inspected and tested; for mass-produced, small household appliances, parts are often randomly checked for quality.

Adjusting is altering the planned standard or sequence of action. After our checking determines that the planned standard or sequence will not bring the desired outcome, we may have to change the plan. An intervening event may alter the situation or the original planning may prove inadequate: the electricity goes off for an hour and causes delays or, as in the radio illustration, the sequencing is poor. Inadequate or incorrect information may lead to unanticipated variations that require adjustments. The newly painted walls, for instance, may appear darker than we anticipated and may not be in harmony with the draperies we had planned to buy. Or an improperly balanced checkbook may show more money than is actually in the bank account. If changes in either standards or sequence can keep the plan intact, an adjustment will allow the plan to be implemented. Otherwise, a new plan with new standards and sequences is needed.

We have noted earlier that implementing has two components. The role of the controlling component is to increase the likelihood that the expected outcomes (toward which planning was directed) will actually occur. The role of the facilitating component is to assist the progress or flow of actions by capitalizing on individual and/or environmental factors. Facilitating factors may have a positive or negative effect, depending on the situation.

An environment that promotes the flow of work helps sequencing. A highly skilled typist cannot achieve high standards from a poor typewriter. The typist's skill may even make it harder to adjust to the machine's idiosyncracies.

Facilitating actions may be built into the plan, as are standards and a schedule, or the environmental setting may be used or modified to facilitate actions. For instance, in applying a sealer to a blacktop driveway, we may take advantage of the right weather and temperature to facilitate easy spreading and quick drying. Facilitation affects only the plan's ease of execution and not its sequence or standards. For a young mother who plans to shop for groceries, facilitating might be writing a grocery list consistent with the store layout and then leaving the children home with their father. By this plan, she promotes easier shopping in two ways.

Sometimes our habits and skills support facilitating actions, but at other times a reluctance to change or an insistence upon demonstrating our skills may slow the action. Nevertheless, new products and changing situations call for new attitudes, new skills, and new facilitating actions. For example, a sewing machine with numerous attachments offers many ways to facilitate sewing, but correct use of the attachments calls for new skills. And yet an experienced seamstress may derive greater satisfaction from her habitual way of sewing.

Output and Feedback

As noted before, outputs of the managerial system are called met demands and used resources, which result from transformations inside the boundaries of the managerial system in response to demands and resource inputs. The *met demands* component of output is the satisfaction or meaning we derive from demands. Output to the personal system is the satisfaction and meaning we derive from accomplishing goal and event demands. Output to external environments reflects supported or unsupported demands placed on the family system.

The *used resources* component of output represents a shift in the stock of available means. The shift may reduce resources, such as when management involves consumption or sharing. If resources are exchanged, the outcome reflects a shift in the makeup of the resource stock of an individual and/or family unit. Producing, saving, or investing are reallocations intended to increase the stock of available means.

When a young couple purchases a term life insurance policy on the husband's life, the family system resources are exchanged with an insurance company outside the system for protection for a time period. The new policy may bring a young family a sense of security, which is a met demand of the personal system. The purchase may represent a choice among alternative consumption desires—additional savings or protection against the economic risk of untimely death.

Feedback is the portion of output that reenters a system as input to affect succeeding output. Feedback is a positive or negative response to action that reflects to the managerial and personal subsystems the effects of any changes in plans in interpreting subsequent steps. Perhaps the couple decides that insuring the wife's life will increase their protection, thereby stimulating a new goal of the managerial system. Or, an awareness of changing needs for protection may evolve during this managerial experience, and the couple may resolve to review their insurance program periodically, thus developing a new goal.

Feedback within a system is the internal mechanism that operates when standards are checked during implementing. It provides an immediate opportunity either to make actions more consistent with the plans or to change the goals.

Nonmanaged Actions

The management bypass line of Figure 3.2 needs a brief explanation. It is drawn directly from demands and resources to the output line of met demands and used resources and lies outside the management boundary. It is an unconsidered response to a desire that meets the demand and uses resources, but is not part of managerial components and processes. It may be a student's response to an impulse either to see a movie and forget a paper due tomorrow or to buy an item solely on the basis of the seller's charisma. A common explanation is that "I wanted to do it no matter what." Such actions, albeit impulsive, have managerial implications because they are likely to affect later management. The feedback line from output to resources, demands, and the personal system reflects nonmanaged as well as managed actions.

The situations in the illustrations of nonmanagement just given might also have been managed. Even if the student had weighed the desire to go to a movie against the cost of staying up late or of being late with the paper, he or she might still have decided on the same action. The item that the persuasive salesperson promoted could have been one that the student needed and considered to be a good choice. The actions could have been managed through basic management processes.

When actions are not managed, resources already planned for one purpose may be used for the nonmanaged action. The effects of the resource use feedback to affect succeeding resource inputs; the effects of demands that are met through nonmanagement also feed back. The seriousness of the imbalance in resources and demands due to nonmanagement depends partly on the extent of resource use and their availability as well as on demands.

An Example of a Managerial System

An example from an undergraduate class in home management illustrates the components of management just discussed. The home economics student is married to a man in military service overseas and she is employed part time. She has found that two teeth need capping as soon as possible. The example is not exhaustive in goals or alternatives.

External Resource: University-subsidized dental clinic

Personal Subsystem

Input
    Event: Dentist says two teeth need to be capped as soon as possible.
Output
    Goals: To keep husband free from worry
           To maintain and improve present appearance
           To maintain current level of savings
           To be prepared for emergencies
           To avoid indebtedness
           To maintain current academic standing

Managerial Subsystem

Input
    Resources: Monthly allotment check (already committed)
               Wife's part-time job (present earnings already committed)
               Savings account
               Time before husband returns
    Goals: From personal subsystem

Throughput
  Planning:
    Standard setting
    Get information on cost of capping teeth (both in lost work time and money) and possibility of working extra hours

  Consider alternatives:
    1. Cap teeth.
       Use savings and risk another emergency. Restore savings by extra work. Cut back current expenditures wherever possible.

Plan: (Output of planning)
    Standards
    Cap (quality) two teeth (quantity).

    Lower amount in savings account to less than desired for a short period (quantity).

    Restore savings to present level (quantity) by time husband returns.

    Set more specific standards for closer expenditure control for current living (quality and quantity).

2. Postpone capping teeth.
    Maintain savings for more important emergency. Risk effect on appearance. Work extra hours to increase savings before capping. Risk additional decay or dental problems.

3. Do not cap teeth.
    Risk long-run effect on teeth and appearance. Maintain savings for more important emergency. Avoid extra time pressures.

Sequencing
Get information on timing of payment and employers' preferences for work hours consistent with study and class time.
Alternatives:
    1. Payment may be postponed until final appointment.
    2. Extra work hours may be on Saturday mornings (4 hours weekly for a shorter time or two hours for longer period).

Sequence
Decision: Work two extra hours for longer period of time (permitting regular study time).

See supervisor for permission to change work hours. Call for appointment to begin work on capping as soon as possible. Make more detailed schedule when extra work and dental hours are set. Take work-hour change notice to payroll clerk.

Implementing:
Controlling
Checking. Check amount of money set aside with the amount decided on for each week. See that amount spent for groceries and entertainment is the same or less than in the past. Have a specific list of things needed from the grocery store to check against when buying.
Adjusting. Extend length of time two extra hours per week if not able to save at rate planned.
Facilitating
Go out with friends who want to save on entertainment. Work the extra two hours during the first of the week because it is easier to maintain schedule.

Output
To personal system
    Met goals: Satisfaction of having teeth capped for personal appearance.
              Satisfaction of not involving husband.
              Satisfaction of having restored savings to pre-event level.
              Satisfaction of not having indebtedness.
              Satisfaction of maintaining academic standing.
To economic system
    Longer hours employed; increased earnings.
    Payments to dentist.
    Savings account used temporarily and restored to previous status.

QUESTIONS ABOUT MANAGEMENT

Several questions may arise from this introduction to home management, from the example, and from widely held ideas about the content of management. Answers to most of the questions should be found in later chapters; below are preliminary responses to questions that are often asked.

1. What is the relation of the system to decision making?

Decisions are an integral part of all of management, and the components provide a way to classify decisions—planning decisions, goal-setting decisions.[3] Goal setting is a form of decision making, whether initiated in the personal subsystem or reformulated in the planning aspect of management. In the managerial subsystem, planning develops standards and/or sequences. Decisions also take place during implementing, for example, such as when we are checking on how well actions conform to plans and when we are guiding adjustments.

The decision-making process involves recognizing that a decision is needed, identifying, weighing, and choosing among or resolving alternatives. The process is used throughout the system.

2. What is the relation of home management as a system to the home management process?

A systems approach includes environmental effects on the system and the potential of the system for affecting the environments. Both approaches stress the importance of planning and implementing, but the relationship of planning and implementing to input and output is more visible through a systems approach. The process is only part of the system.

3. What is the role of evaluation in the managerial subsystem?

Over the years, the managerial process has included planning, controlling, and evaluating. In the management subsystem the decisions are based on criteria and are thus evaluated decisions, or value judgments. The criteria or standards for decisions in implementing are set during planning; and the criteria for decisions in planning are goals or value-based objectives, which are inputs to management from the personal subsystem. Therefore, evaluating is not just a final process of judging out-

---

3. Elizabeth W. Crandall, "Conceptual Framework I: The Three-Step Managerial Process," in *Conceptual Frameworks: Process of Home Management,* Proceedings of a Home Management Conference (Washington, D. C.: American Home Economics Association, 1964), pp. 17–34.

comes (although that occurs as part of feedback): it takes place thoughout the system to foster consistency of the output with the value based objectives.

4. What are the qualities of a good manager?

Good managers are generally effective in reaching goals, but it is unlikely that all effective managers have equal facility with all managerial components. Some people enjoy some phases of management more than other phases. This may, but need not, relate to the competence they feel. For some, the creative part of planning may be interesting while the actual implementation is a chore; for others, the activity and its sense of accomplishment may be more enjoyable. Good managers may choose to develop their strengths while remaining acceptably effective in other areas, or they may strive to develop each part equally well and find all phases interesting and important.

If one aspect is emphasized, the others should be well understood because the component given more attention needs to compensate for less attention to the others. If a manager finds some activity uninteresting, it may mean that someone else should be hired to do the activity, or a coworker or family member who enjoys that activity should do it. The balance of expertise to seek is the one that most nearly accomplishes the desired end and brings the most satisfaction in the process. Managerial style varies with individuals and circumstances, and that is one reason why managers who start with different resources or skills may arrive at the same place (equifinality) or vice versa (multifinality).

5. What is the relation of the management system to household work?

Work is part of the goal-directed output of management. The management system is focused on goals and resources rather than centered on work. If work is managed, it will more likely be in keeping with the desired lifestyle.

Certain day-to-day activities must be done, and management is concerned with these because they have an important part in reaching family-system goals. For example, household tasks, such as dishwashing or packing for a vacation trip, meet specific needs.

SUMMARY

Management is an open, dynamic subsystem of the family, and part of its output of met demands and resource use become input to affect succeeding output. Management is important to the system's adaptive quality, being oriented to each situation rather than prescribing a generalized set of actions; it directs the individual's or family's resource use to meet the system's goals in the best way.

The macro-habitat and the social-cultural, economic, and political systems influence goals of individuals and families, and unexpected occurrences called events can elicit managerial behavior. Actions that use resources but are not considered responses to the total situation are called nonmanaged.

DEFINITIONS

Management is planning and implementing the use of resources to meet demands.

Demands are goals and/or events requiring action.

Goals are value-based objectives.

Events are unexpected or low-probability occurrences that require action.

Resources are means for meeting demands.

Planning is a series of decisions concerning standards and/or sequences of action.

Implementing is putting plans and procedures (standards and sequences) into effect by controlling and facilitating actions.

Standard is a measure of quantity and/or quality, which reflects the reconciliation of resources with demands.

Decision making is choosing or resolving alternatives.

Sequences of action are the order among tasks or parts of a task.

Controlling is the checking of actions against plans and adjusting standards or sequences.

Facilitating is assisting the progress or flow of actions by capitalizing on individual and/or environmental factors.

Checking is the examination of actions in relation to planned standards and sequences.

Adjusting is a change in the planned standard or sequence of action.

Met demands component of output is the relation of the outcome to the demands in terms of anticipated meaning or satisfaction.

Used resources component of output is a shift in the stock of available means.

Feedback is the portion of output which reenters as input to affect succeeding output.

Selected Factors That Influence Home Management

4.

In this chapter, we shall consider the nature of selected situations that are common in some way to all families. These are by no means all the factors that influence home management but they are important in a situation at a point in time. Yet their influences vary from family to family and for the same family over the years.

Families and individuals with similar beginnings may end up quite differently in later life because of their decisions about education, employment changes, and child spacing–(multifinality). Other families or individuals may be different at the start and yet reach similar goals through different opportunities–(equifinality).

The factors considered here are family composition, health, personality, race, education, occupation, social position, and the micro-habitat, especially housing. Precise evidence about the effects of these factors is not yet available in some cases; in other cases, the factors are interrelated so that the separate presentation of factors oversimplifies the situation.

FAMILY COMPOSITION

Family Life and Role Stages

The composition of the family varies widely from family to family, and the variations become even greater when the term "family system" is used synonymously, as it is here, with "household system." One system might be made up of a brother and sister and the brother's children, or of several couples living together with or without children, or of husband, wife, and children traditionally known as the nuclear family group.

Usually we describe the traditional nuclear family in terms of family life stages, which span the family from its beginning to the death of either spouse. Categories indicate the stage of a family at a given point in time. The stages may be in terms of:

1. position of the family, such as birth of the first child,
2. age composition of the family,
3. father's employment status,
4. years of marriage, and
5. combinations of criteria, such as the age of the oldest child and the ages or school relationship of the other children in the family.[1]

Family life stages predict the economic behavior of families better than does the age of household head alone.[2] A recent study of financial goals (input to the managerial system), decisions, and crises identified four categories in the economic family life span: the foundation stage (0–4 years of marriage), the developmental (5–19 years of marriage), the assessment, achievement, and readjustment (20–39 years of marriage), and the retirement stage (40 and more years of marriage).[3] These will be discussed more fully in Chapter 10.

The traditionally accepted social role of homemakers or housewives closely parallels family life stages. Lopata, in a treatise on "Occupation: Housewife," describes the stages as: becoming a housewife, the expanding circle, the full-house plateau, and the shrinking circle.[4]

Stages from three different emphases are given in Table 4.1. Similarities exist in the stages for family life, economic behavior, and social role of housewife. The discussion here is primarily directed toward the social role of housewife.

In the first stage of the social role, "becoming a housewife," the consumer responsibilities change as the wife makes purchases for the house-

1. Reuben Hill, "Decision Making and the Family Life Cycle," in *Social Structure and the Family: Generational Relations*, eds. Ethel Shanas and Gordon F. Streib (Englewood Cliffs, N. J.: Prentice-Hall, Inc., 1963), p. 116.
2. Roy H. Rodgers, *Improvements in the Construction and Analysis of Family Life Cycle Categories* (Kalamazoo, Mich.: Western Michigan University, 1962), p. 57.
3. Cleo Fitzsimmons, Dorothy A. Larery, and Edward J. Metzen, "Major Financial Decisions and Crises in the Family Life Span," North Central Regional Research Publication No. 208 (Lafayette, Ind.: Purdue University Agricultural Experiment Station, 1971).
4. Helena Z. Lopata, *Occupation: Housewife* (New York: Oxford University Press, 1971), pp. 32–44.

TABLE 4.1
Family life cycle stages.

Family life cycle[1]	Family life span (economic)[2]	Social role cycle[3]
Married couples Married couple without children	*Foundation years* 0–4 years of marriage	*Becoming a housewife*
Childbearing families Oldest child birth to 30 months		*The expanding circle* Birth of children
Families with preschool children Oldest child 2½–6 years	*Developmental years* 5–19 years of marriage	

Families with school children
Oldest child 6–13 years
		*The full-house
		plateau*
		Youngest child enters
		  school, until he
		  leaves home: no more
		  children likely

Families with teenagers Oldest child 13–20 years		
Families as launching centers First child gone to last child's leaving home	*Assessment, achievement, and readjustment years* 20–39 years of marriage	
Middle-aged parents Empty nest to retirement		*The shrinking circle* Children gone from home; later, widowhood
Aging family members Retirement to death of one or both spouses	*Retirement years* 40+ years of marriage	

[1] Evelyn M. Duvall, *Family Development* (Philadelphia: J. B. Lippincott Company, 1971), pp. 116–117.
[2] Cleo Fitzsimmons, Dorothy A. Larery, and Edward J. Metzen, "Major Financial Decisions and Crises in the Family Life Span," North Central Regional Research Publication No. 208 (Lafayette, Ind.: Purdue University Agricultural Experiment Station, 1971).
[3] Helena Z. Lopata, *Occupation: Housewife* (New York: Oxford University Press, 1971), pp. 29–43.

hold instead of primarily for herself. Task allocations change. In the time before there are children, tasks may be shared more evenly and in less specialized fashion, especially if the wife is employed outside the home.[5]

---

5. William Silverman and Reuben Hill, "Task Allocation in Marriage in the United States and Belgium," *Journal of Marriage and the Family* 29 (May 1967): 357–58.

In the expanding-circle stage, changes brought about by the birth of the first child may affect home management. Families today may make fewer changes than in the past, with the wife continuing to work outside the home. Schedules and organization of household work must usually change; if the wife is no longer employed, the costs of having and maintaining children on a reduced income must be faced.[6] Many husbands may be more involved in their employment and less available to help with household tasks.[7] For the wife not currently employed outside the home who was previously employed outside the home, the absence of work rhythm, the freedom from supervision, and the reduced need to integrate her work with others may give an openness to home responsibilities never before experienced.[8] This openness can be either a problem or an advantage, but many homemakers experience difficulties in focusing or organizing their activities.

The full-house plateau is marked by the presence of children at home and the likelihood that no more children will be born. Women respond to the stage primarily in three different ways—by emphasizing the family and remaining in the home; by being employed outside the home full time; and by keeping in touch with outside roles through part-time employment or heavy commitments to volunteer work.[9] Income from the husband's earnings are relatively high during the later part of this stage, but expenditures are also often high, especially for families who are providing education beyond high school for their children.

The shrinking circle begins when the first child marries or leaves home. The husband may resume responsibility for household tasks he did not perform during the child-rearing period.[10] In the later part of this stage, changes occur in many areas of responsibility. Fewer decision-making situations are present in employment, and widowhood often occurs.

Critics of these typical stages of family life and social role point to the fact that these stages obviously pertain to an idealized family. Progression from marriage, birth of a child, marriage of the child, and death of one

6. Daniel F. Hobbs, "Parenthood as a Crisis: A Third Study," *Journal of Marriage and the Family* 24 (August 1965): 370.
7. Silverman and Hill, pp. 357–58.
8. Lopata, pp. 34–35.
9. Helena Z. Lopata, "The Life Cycle of the Social Role of Housewife," *Sociology and Social Research* 51 (October 1966): 12.
10. Silverman and Hill, pp. 357–58.

spouse may characterize the majority of families, but there are many families where these events do not follow such a defined pattern. Families are broken by divorce, separation, desertion; some families do not have children;[11] other families omit some stages; families may have one set of children and then another, or remarry and have another set, so that stages overlap. The economic-behavior stages give a time dimension in number of years of marriage and only indirectly reflect the role-age composition of family members.

For our complex family and social situation we need a more inclusive concept. One enlarged family life stage concept is situational sequence. Such a sequence could conceivably include the age and school attainment of the oldest child, the number and sex of siblings, education of the parents, occupation, and the like.[12]

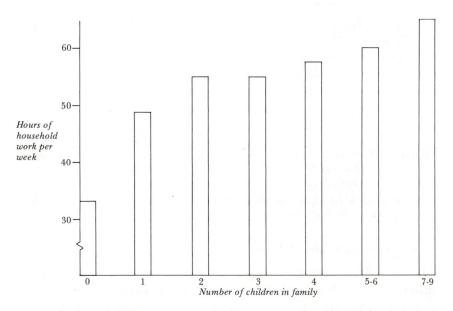

FIGURE 4.1 *Hours of household work used by homemaker per week by number of children in the family (1296 husband-wife families, Syracuse area, 1967–1968).*

Source: Kathryn E. Walker, "Homemaking Still Takes Time," *Journal of Home Economics* 61 (October, 1969): 623. (Hours per day converted to hours per week.)

11. Ann Smith Rice, "An Economic Life Cycle of Childless Families," Florida State University, Ph.D. dissertation, 1965.
12. Frances M. Magrabi and W. H. Marshall, "Family Developmental Tasks: A Research Model," *Journal of Marriage and the Family* 27 (November 1965): 456.

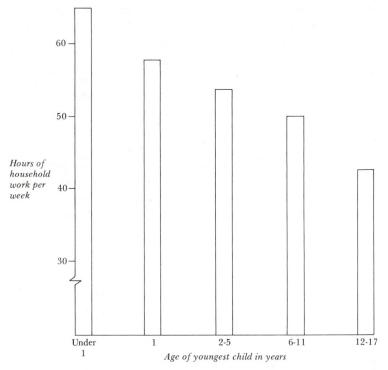

Hours of
household
work per
week

Under 1   1   2-5   6-11   12-17

Age of youngest child in years

FIGURE 4.2 *Hours of household work used by homemaker per week by age of youngest child (1128 husband-wife families with children, Syracuse area, 1967-1968).*

Source: Kathryn E. Walker, "Homemaking Still Takes Time," *Journal of Home Economics* 61 (October, 1969): 623. (Hours per day converted to hours per week.)

Family Size and Child Spacing

Family size, children's ages, and spacing affect home management through increased goal and event demands in relation to resources. These increased demands can be considered indirectly through resource use (output from system). The time spent on household work by families of varying sizes generally increases as the number of children increases, although not proportionately (Figure 4.1). The age of the youngest child rather than the number of children is more closely related to the use of time for household work (Figure 4.2). Total time used for household work is 65 hours per week for families with a child under one year old (regardless of number of children) and 42 hours per week for families with the youngest child 12-17 years old.

TABLE 4.2

Median income of families with related children under 18 years old, by race and number of children.

Number of related children	Median 1971 income (in dollars)	
	White	*Black*
All families	$10,672	$6,439
No children	9,803	6,414
One child	10,808	6,297
Two children	11,451	6,841
Three children	11,547	6,008
Four children	11,150	7,067
Five children	10,934	6,505
Six or more children	10,300	5,808

U.S. Dept. of Commerce, Bureau of the Census, "Money Income in 1971 of Families and Persons in the United States," Current Population Reports, Series P-60, No. 85 (Washington, D. C.: U.S. Government Printing Office, 1972), pp. 53–55.

The number and ages of children significantly affect community welfare activities. In one study of women's college graduates, participation in community affairs was low for homemakers with preschool children, and homemakers with more and older children had higher participation rates. Those who participated more also had household and child-care help. Older homemakers were the most involved in community welfare activities.[13]

Money income, as a resource input to the managerial system, is not directly related to family size (Table 4.2). According to one theory of family size, if all families received contraceptives equally, families with higher incomes would choose to have more children than would low-income families.[14] Several points, however, do not support this idea. Among non-Catholics, the white-collar workers want fewer children than do the blue-collar workers, even when incomes are similar. Blue-collar workers with higher incomes desire fewer children than do blue-collar workers

---

13. Laura G. Searls, "Leisure Role Emphasis of College Graduate Homemakers," *Journal of Marriage and the Family* 28 (February 1966): 81–82.
14. Gary Becker, "An Economic Analysis of Fertility," in National Bureau of Economic Research, *Demographic and Economic Change in Developed Countries* (Princeton, N. J.: Princeton University Press, 1960), pp. 209–40.

TABLE 4.3

Hours per day contributed by children for household work, by mother's employment and number of children (792 husband-wife families with school-aged children, Syracuse area, 1967-68).

Family composition	Children 6–11 years		Children 12–17 years	
	Mother		*Mother*	
	not employed	*employed*	*not employed*	*employed*
	Average hours/day			
All families	1.1	1.0	2.0	2.2
One child	.4	.6	1.2	1.1
Two children	.6	.6	1.1	1.6
Three children	1.0	1.5	2.2	2.9
Four children	1.5	1.0	2.2	3.2
Five to six children	1.6	1.1	2.8	3.6
Seven to nine children	2.6	*	3.4	*

Kathryn E. Walker, "How Much Help for Working Mothers?" *Human Ecology Forum* 1 (Autumn 1970): 14.
* Fewer than five cases.

with lower incomes.[15] For families as a whole, larger-size families do not have proportionately more income.

Children often help with household work. Help from young children increases with family size when the mother is not employed, and with age of children regardless of the mother's employment (Table 4.3). Help from the husband in household work should be viewed in terms of the total work day for both husband and wife in relation to the family size. The total work time for wife and husband generally increases with the number of children in the family (Table 4.4). When household work was examined separately in another study, the involvement of the husband in household tasks decreased until the birth of the fourth child, at which point his involvement increased.[16]

Family size seems to influence the decision-making patterns in families. As families increase in size, husbands increase their role in decision making about children's responsibilities, habits, and the expenditures made for the children. However, as family size increases wives take a more active

15. Judith Blake, "Income and Reproductive Motivation," *Population Studies* 21 (November 1967): 205.
16. Frederick L. Campbell, "Family Growth and Variation in Family Role Structure," *Journal of Marriage and the Family* 32 (February 1970): 49.

TABLE 4.4

Hours per week used by husband and wife for all work, by number of children (1296 husband-wife families, Syracuse area, 1967–68).

Number of Children	Total work	
	Wife	Husband
	Average hours/week	
All families	63	64
No children	55	57
One child	59	64
Two children	65	66
Three children	65	64
Four children	66	67
Five or more children	69	71

Kathryn E. Walker, "Time-Use Patterns for Household Work Related to Homemakers' Employment," U.S.D.A. Agricultural Research Service, 1970 National Agricultural Outlook Conference, Washington, D. C. (February 18, 1970), p. 3.

part in decisions related to social life of the family, such as going out for the evening or visiting.[17] Generally, the larger the family, the more the likelihood that the father will dominate the household.[18]

Family planning makes it possible for couples to control both the number and the spacing of children. Having children close together can contribute to increased goal demands for resources, which the family may or may not have. In one study, spacing affected the economic conditions of families to such an extent that the author proposed the following:

Those who have their children very quickly after marriage find themselves under great economic pressure, particularly if they married at an early age. Opportunities for education or decisions involving present sacrifices for future gains, are difficult. They are less able than others to accumulate the goods and assets regarded as desirable by young couples in our society. They are more likely than others to become discouraged at an early point and to lose interest more quickly than others in the competition for economic success. If such a syndrome does exist, it would be of considerable importance for the economy and for programs concerned with family planning.[19]

17. Campbell, p. 48.
18. F. Ivan Nye, John Carolson, and Gerald Garrett, "Family Size, Interaction, Affect and Stress," *Journal of Marriage and the Family* 32 (May 1970): 217.
19. Ronald Freedman and Lolagene Coombs, "Childspacing and Family Economic Position," *American Sociological Review* 31 (October 1966): 631–48.

INDIVIDUAL AND FAMILY CHARACTERISTICS

Health

The health of family members is important in home management. Health is defined as a "state of complete physical, mental and social well-being, and not merely the absence of disease or infirmity."[20] In this section, we shall consider the effect of extended illness on the families financial resources and the effect of chronic illness or disability on the operation of the household.

Extended and chronic illness can make formidable managerial demands at any stage of the life cycle. In the United States, one-half of the population has one or more chronic physical or mental-health conditions; these figures also have implications for social well-being. Among those families with annual incomes under $3,000, 18.2 per cent have members with one or more chronic conditions and are limited in ability to carry out activities; while for familes with over $15,000 income, only 7.9 per cent have members so limited in activities. These percentages take into account any effects due to lower incomes of older people.[21] A relatively small group of those chronically ill is actually limited in activities.

Families who have members with illness or chronic conditions often experience a strain on financial resources. The economic impact of illness on a family is related both to the family's earning ability and to its demands on income. In 1965, more than two-fifths of the household units with a disabled member had incomes under $3,000.[22]

In one study, families with a member hospitalized in semi-private and ward accommodations had more severe economic hardships than those with patients in private rooms.[23] The median income of families with a

20. United Nations, "World Health Organization Constitution," *Basic Documents* 21st ed. (Geneva, Switzerland: United Nations World Health Organization, April 1970), p. 1.
21. U.S. Dept. of Health, Education, and Welfare, Public Health Service, "Chronic Conditions and Limitations of Activity and Mobility, United States—July 1965–July 1967," Public Health Service Publication No. 1000, Series 10, No. 61 (Washington, D. C.: U.S. Government Printing Office, 1971), p. 7.
22. U.S. Dept. of Health, Education, and Welfare, Social Security Administration Office of Research and Statistics, "Sources and Size of Income of the Disabled," Report No. 16 (Washington, D. C.: U.S. Government Printing Office, 1971), p. 3.
23. Raymond S. Duff and August B. Hollingshead, *Sickness and Society* (New York: Harper & Row, Publishers, 1968), pp. 94, 359.

member in a private room was twice that of families with patients in semi-private accommodations.

The financial impact of illness is illustrated by the case of the Saxon family, in the "severe hardship class, who used their assets to meet expenses and who readjusted their living standard. Mr. Saxon was a semi-skilled factory worker who earned $100 weekly. He and his wife had two children who did well in school. Mrs. Saxon had a series of illnesses and was hospitalized for an extended period. The insurance plus $220 from the Saxons paid the hospital costs. Convalescent costs were $2,000, with $200 not covered by insurance. Mr. Saxon could not pay the bill. His car had broken down and cost $100 for repairs; they were behind in mortgage payments on the house, which needed repairs. Their son got a part-time job, and the 12-year-old daughter did most of the household chores. Mrs. Saxon improved, and upon her return the family began to recover emotionally and financially. Since Mrs. Saxon's disease is recurring, uncertainty exists for the future.[24]

The first potential effect of a chronic disease or disability on the operation of the household is the manner in which the input to the managerial system can differ from other households. One study found that parents of a diabetic child have lower goal agreement and greater parental role tension than parents of nondiabetic children.[25] Less agreement between the parents on the goals that enter the managerial system can increase the difficulty of managing a home in a manner consistent with the family goals.

Another effect that appears to be both task and role related is the difference among families in their acceptance of a disabled person into the family and the rehabilitation of that person. The acceptance of disability varies, too, among disabled persons. Acceptance of disability of a mother is often easier than for a disabled father, since her role and the tasks involve the home, and remaining at home is more compatible with social expectations.[26] Men who can no longer fill the role of main wage earner often have a more difficult time in rehabilitative efforts.[27]

24. Duff and Hollingshead, pp. 355–56.
25. Alan J. Crain, Marvin Sussman, and William B. Weil, "Effects of a Diabetic Child on Marital Integration and Related Measures of Family Functioning," *Journal of Health and Human Behavior* 7 (Summer 1966): 122–27.
26. Constantina Safilios-Rothschild, *The Sociology and Social Psychology of Disability and Rehabilitation* (New York: Random House, 1970), pp. 271–72.
27. Safilios-Rothschild, pp. 230–31.

Family members—children in particular—give help to chronically ill or disabled mothers.[28],[29] However, almost no physical or structural changes are made in homes to accommodate the ill or disabled mother.[30] For example, homes with hard-of-hearing mothers have few adjustments, such as a telephone amplifier, to assist the mother.[31] Compared to "normal" families, decision-making patterns differ little in families with a chronically ill or disabled mother,[32] including one who is hard-of-hearing.[33]

A study of time use in household tasks in Indiana had several disabled homemakers in the sample. As might be expected, they spent less total time on household tasks and less time in physical care of others or in financial management than did well homemakers.[34]

In another study of middle-income families with children under 18 years of age, the health of the homemaker contributed to differences in home management. For a household task, homemakers with poorer health were less realistic in their standards and sequence; the sequences of tasks were less flexible, and the standards were more complex (involved more persons and tasks) than those of homemakers with better health.[35]

Stresses related to role may occur with disability. In one study, disabled husbands dependent on wives for personal care were less involved in making decisions—such as those that involved car repair, or car purchase, or the computation of income tax—than were husbands who were disabled but not dependent for personal care.[36]

---

28. Ruth E. Deacon, Francille Maloch, and Ann S. Bardwell, "Relationship of Maternal Health to Family Solidarity Among Low-Income Families in 28 Appalachian Counties," The Ohio State University Research Foundation Project 2072 (Columbus, Ohio: The Ohio State University School of Home Economics, 1967), p. 46.

29. E. Jane Oyer and Beatrice Paolucci, "Homemakers' Hearing Losses and Family Integration," *Journal of Home Economics* 62 (April 1970): 260.

30. Deacon, Maloch, and Bardwell, p. 46.

31. Oyer and Paolucci, p. 259.

32. Deacon, Maloch, and Bardwell, p. 47.

33. Oyer and Paolucci, p. 260.

34. Sarah L. Manning, "Time Use in Household Tasks by Indiana Families," Research Bulletin No. 837 (Lafayette, Ind.: Purdue University Agricultural Experiment Station, 1968), pp. 5–6.

35. Francille Maloch and Ruth E. Deacon, "Components of Home Management in Relation to Selected Variables," Research Bulletin 1042 (Wooster, Ohio: Ohio Agricultural Research and Development Center, 1970), p. 8.

36. Edward G. Ludwig and John Collette, "Disability, Dependency and Conjugal Roles," *Journal of Marriage and the Family* 31 (November 1969): 739.

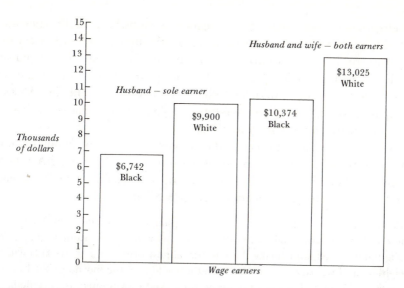

FIGURE 4.3 *Median family income by race, husband only and husband and wife working.*

Source: U.S. Dept. of Commerce, Bureau of the Census, "The Social and Economic Status of the Black Population in the United States, 1972," Current Population Reports, Series P-23, No. 46 (Washington, D. C.: U.S. Government Printing Office, 1973), p. 22.

Race

The effects of race and differential conditions associated with race appear early in the life of a child.[37] Infant mortality among black babies is almost twice that for white babies.[38] Further, a white male can expect to live almost 68 years, compared to 61 years for nonwhite males; for white females, the life expectancy is 75 years and for nonwhite females, 69 years.[39] Differences in mortality affect the resource situation of families through the woman's loss of productive time in bearing children who do not live, and through the reduced years of earning.

Money income is an indicator of the financial resources available to families. Marked differences in income exist between white and black men for the same level of education. In 1970, the median earnings for college

---

37. Although references to members of the Caucasian, Negroid, and Mongoloid races have differed from source to source, we have standardized the variations in usage for this text.
38. U.S. Dept. of Commerce, Bureau of the Census, *Statistical Abstract of the United States: 1972* (Washington, D. C.: U.S. Government Printing Office, 1972), p. 57.
39. *Statistical Abstract*, p. 55.

graduates (4 or more years) 25–34 years of age was $11,212 for white and $8,715 for black men.[40] For black husband-wife families, it is necessary for both husband and wife to work to achieve a median family income similar to that of white families (Figure 4-3). The median income of families in 1969 was lower for American Indians than for black families, $5,832 compared to $6,308. About one-third of American Indians and blacks were below the poverty level in 1972.[41]

We can more fully appreciate the resource situation of families below the poverty level when we examine the impact on the family. A report from a mother living in a low-income urban area in a northern city reveals the lack of resources permeating day-to-day living:

I don't know what to do. There's the city hospital, but it's no good for us. I went there with my husband, no sooner than a month or so after we came up here. We waited and waited, and finally the day was almost over. We left the kids with a neighbor, and we barely knew her. I said it would take the morning, but I never thought we'd get back home near suppertime. And they wanted us to come back and come back, because it was something they couldn't do all at once—though for most of the time we just sat there and did nothing. And my husband, he said his stomach was the worse for going there, and he'd take care of himself from now on, rather than go there.

Maybe they could have saved him. But they're far away, and I didn't have money to get a cab, even if there was one around here, and I thought to myself it'll make him worse, to take him there.[42]

With fewer financial resources, on the average, black families also have greater demands in terms of larger families. For husband-wife families, for women 15 to 44 years old blacks averaged 3.85 children ever born and whites averaged 3.10 children ever born in 1972; for families with husband absent, the averages were 4.34 for blacks and 3.34 children for whites.[43]

---

40. U.S. Dept. of Commerce, Bureau of the Census, "The Social and Economic Status of the Black Population in the United States, 1972," Current Population Reports, Series P-23, No. 46 (Washington, D. C.: U.S. Government Printing Office, 1973), p. 25.

41. U.S. Dept of Commerce, Bureau of the Census, "American Indians," Final Report PC(2)-IF (Washington, D. C.: U.S. Government Printing Office, 1973), p. 120.

42. Robert Coles, "Like It Is in the Alley," in *Life at the Bottom*, ed. Gregory Armstrong (New York: A Bantam Book, 1971), pp. 126–27.

43. U.S. Dept. of Commerce, Bureau of the Census, "Birth Expectations and Fertility: June 1972," Current Population Reports, Series P-20, No. 248 (Washington, D. C.: U.S. Government Printing Office, 1973), pp. 39–40.

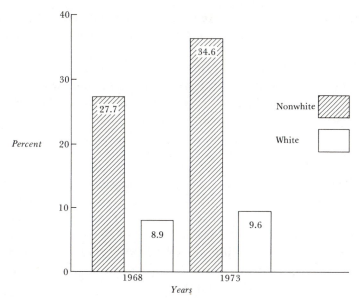

FIGURE 4.4 *Percent of families headed by women, by race.*

Source: U.S. Dept. of Commerce, Bureau of the Census, "The Social and Economic Status of the Black Population in the United States, 1972," Current Population Reports P-23, No. 46 (Washington, D.C.: U.S. Government Printing Office, 1973), p. 58.

The majority of both black and white families have a husband and wife present at home. However, families headed by a female are increasing among blacks and other races, more than in white families (Figure 4.4).

Consideration of differences in values between races is complicated by stereotypes of low-income black families from the viewpoint of middle-income white families. However, in a national study of values of men, social class was the most important factor in differences, more important than "race, or religion, or area of the country, or national background; larger (correlations), in fact, than for all of them together."[44]

Decision-making patterns differ by race. When a black wife is employed, the working-class black man is less active in decisions about what bills to pay and how much to spend on clothing. Black men whose wives are not employed are more active in decision-making. This is similar to

---

44. Melvin L. Kohn, *Class and Conformity, A Study in Values* (Homewood, Ill.: The Dorsey Press, 1969), p. 85.

working white men whose involvements are not as influenced by whether the wife is employed (Table 4.6). For both races, husbands are influential in the decision that the wife not be employed.

Working class black men report performing more household tasks when they are the sole breadwinner than when their wives are employed.[45] Involvement in tasks is influenced by factors other than the man's availability for participation.

Personality

Personality encompasses a person's characteristics, traits, and patterns of adjustment to his environment and to others.[46] Personality is rather stable over time, although individuals can change their personality. An individual's personality reflects fulfillment of needs or his response in certain ways or patterns of adjustment.[47] Maslow considered needs as a hierarchy, with individuals working to satisfy the most pressing need and then moving to the next highest need. Maslow's order of needs follows:

physiological—food, drink, sex
safety—security, stability, protection, structure, order
love and belonging—acceptance, giving and receiving love
esteem—self-respect and respect for others
self-actualization—self-fulfillment, reaching one's potential[48]

Maslow characterized a self-actualizing person as follows: perceives reality well; accepts self, others, and nature; is spontaneous and natural; centers problems outside of self; remains detached, needs privacy; is autonomous, independent of culture and environment, is "self-contained"; appreciates basic experiences; experiences life with intensity; feels affection and sympathy in relations with others; has deep interpersonal relations; has democratic nature; discriminates between means and ends, good and evil; has philosopical, benign humor; and is creative.[49]

---

45. Joan Aldous, "Wives' Employment Status and Lower-Class Men as Husband-Fathers: Support for Moyihan Thesis," *Journal of Marriage and the Family* 31 (August 1969): 474.
46. Blair J. Kolasa, *Introduction to Behavioral Science for Business* (New York: John Wiley & Sons, Inc., 1969), p. 242.
47. Henry A. Murray *et al., Explorations in Personality* (New York: Oxford University Press, 1938), p. 728.
48. Abraham H. Maslow, *Motivation and Personality* (New York: Harper & Row, Publishers, 1970, 2d ed.), pp. 35–46.
49. Maslow, pp. 153–74.

A study made of a group of home managers suggests that family participation in economic activities is associated with the degree to which home managers are self-actualizing.[50] Non-self-actualizing home managers listed more goals of self-development, while those who were more self-actualizing gave more goals related to social values.[51]

Related to one of Maslow's "safety" needs is the need for order, which has been studied from the organization aspect of home management. Order may be defined as placing "special emphasis on neatness, organization, and planning in one's activities."[52]

Organization is creating and maintaining order in household tasks and includes sequencing in planning and in all of implementing.[53] A study of

TABLE 4.5
Decision making as reported by lower-class husbands, by race and wife's employment status.

Decisions	Black husband		White husband	
	Wife		*Wife*	
	employed	*not employed*	*employed*	*not employed*
	Average score[1]			
Amount to spend on clothing	1.1	1.9	1.3	1.2
What bills to pay	1.7	2.5	2.2	1.8
Whether wife should work	1.1	2.3	1.1	2.5
Whether to have children	0.9	1.6	1.8	1.6

Joan Aldous, "Wives' Employment Status and Lower-Class Men as Husband-Fathers: Support for Moyihan Thesis," *Journal of Marriage and the Family* 31 (August 1969): 473. Copyright (1969) by National Council on Family Relations. Reprinted by permission.
[1]Score: 0=wife all the time
    1=both decide, but the wife most of the time
    2=both decide together
    3=both decide, but the husband most of the time
    4=husband all the time

50. Verda M. Dale, "An Exploration of the Relationship of Home Managers Self-Actualization to Participation by Family Members in Home Activities," Michigan State University, Ph.D. dissertation, 1968, p. 64.
51. Dale, p. 70.
52. Harrison Gough and Alfred B. Heilbrun, *The Adjective Check List Manual* (Palo Alto, Calif.: Consulting Psychologists Press, 1965), p. 8.
53. Nancy Ann Barclay, "Organization of Household Activities by Home Managers," The Ohio State University, Ph.D. dissertation, 1970, p. 19.

Canadian homemakers in Winnepeg revealed that the importance attached to sequencing and checking (a part of control within implementing) was related to a person's need for order.[54] Sequencing, checking, and facilitating were related to other personality traits, indicating that personality influences several phases of organization.

In another study, the group high in the need for order used high task standardization ("I try to avoid clutter by putting things away as soon as I have finished them,") and high task regularization ("I follow a regular routine for my work" and "I set a regular time for doing household chores.").[55] The study determined characteristics of homemakers with high and low need for order as follows:

Homemakers with *High Need* for Order
  were routinized, planful, and conventional

  sought stability and continuity in environment

  were diligent, practical, and persistent

  tended to be shrewd and calculating

  were intelligent and hardworking

  were thinkers rather than doers in goal seeking

Homemakers with *Low Need* for Order
  were perceptive, alert, spontaneous, often impulsive

  were action oriented

  preferred complexity and variety

  disliked caution and deliberation

  depended on others for support

  avoided decision-making situations

  were self-critical and anxious

  were outgoing

  were less certain about rewards of effort and involvement[56]

---

54. Barclay, pp. 45–47.

55. Catherine R. Mumaw, "Organizational Patterns of Homemakers Related to Selected Predispositional and Situational Characterisitcs," The Pennsylvania State University, Ph.D. dissertation, 1967, p. 81.

56. Mumaw, pp. 98–100.

A high degree of order may not mean a high degree of organization or of competent management—it may merely satisfy one's need for order for oneself or others. Other needs, such as the need for achievement, may affect the working toward success in an occupation, and may consequently affect the income level. Further, these needs may affect consumer choices of products and services. But research on the effects of personality on consumer behavior has yielded little consistency in results. Techniques of measuring personality variables, particularly those that use gross personality variables to predict specific consumer behavior and that have limited theoretical bases for hypotheses, complicate the research efforts. Expecting personality to affect specific consumer behavior may be unrealistic.[57]

Education

The effects of education of family members on home management are of three types: (1) the long-run effect of the extent of education on life chances for income and accompanying life style expectations; (2) the capacity for application of managerial processes; and (3) the short-run effect of educational institutions on the daily living patterns of families.

Long-run Effects on Resources and Orientation to Life. Formal education has an influence on the amount of an individual's lifetime earnings. Persons with limited education have a likelihood of lower earnings than those with more education. Male college graduates, white and black, earn about one-third more than male high-school graduates. White female college graduates earn about one-half more and black females who are college graduates earn 90 per cent more than high-school graduates (Table 4.7). One analysis found that completion of high school does not result in increased earnings for all occupations.[58] Earnings and education combine to influence management through availability of resources and knowledge in the use of resources.

Another long-run effect of education on resources is the relationship to family size. Women with more formal education have fewer children. In 1972, women 30–34 years of age who were not high-school graduates had

57. Harold H. Kassarjian, "Personality and Consumer Behavior: A Review," *Journal of Marketing Research* 8 (November 1971): 415–16.
   David T. Kollat, James F. Engel, and Roger D. Blackwell, "Current Problems in Consumer Behavior Research," *Journal of Marketing Research* 7 (August, 1970): 327–32.
58. Stuart O. Schweitzer, "Occupation Choice, High School Graduation, and Investment in Human Capital," *The Journal of Human Resources* 6 (Summer 1971): 321–32.

an average of 3.4 children; those with 1 or more years of college had an average of 2.2 (Figure 4.5). The difference in family size probably reflects a difference in orientation to life, with more education influencing a concern for having only those children who can be supported in a manner important to the family.[59]

Increased formal education of the family head is associated with increased volunteer work for women and a somewhat declining participation in volunteer work by men (Figure 4.6).

Educational attainment directly influences the wife's participation in the labor force—the higher the education, the higher the employment rate.[60] Many shifts occur in management with employment outside the home, including the obvious change in time spent on household activities.

Education affects the geographic mobility of families. Two types of geographically mobile groups have been proposed—those highly educated who move to localities that need their special skills and those poorly educated who must move because of limited local opportunities.[61]

TABLE 4.6
Money income in 1972 for persons 25 years old and older, by education, sex, and race.

	Level of education completed		
Sex and race	*Elementary*	*High school*	*College*[1]
	Median money income in dollars[2]		
Male			
White	$5,152	$9,584	$12,838
Black	3,685	6,767	8,940
Female			
White	1,859	3,390	5,068
Black	1,590	3,297	6,270

Source: U.S. Dept. of Commerce, Bureau of the Census, "Money Income in 1972 of Families and Persons in the United States," Current Population Reports, Series P-60, No. 90 (Washington, D. C.: U.S. Government Printing Office, 1973), pp. 124, 128.
[1] 4 or more years
[2] Based on persons having income

59. Blake pp. 185–206.
60. Elizabeth Waldman, "Marital and Family Characteristics of the U.S. Labor Force," *Monthly Labor Review* 93: (May 1970), 25.
61. James N. Morgan, Ismail A. Sirageldin, and Nancy Baerwaldt, *Productive Americans* (Ann Arbor, Mich.: Institute for Social Research, The University of Michigan, 1966), p. 260.

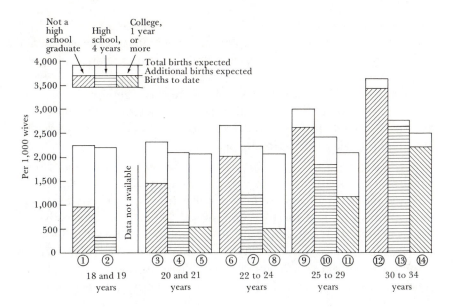

FIGURE 4.5 *Births to date, additional births expected, and total births expected per 1,000 reporting wives 18 to 34 years old, by age and educational attainment, June 1972.*

Source: U.S. Dept. of Commerce, Bureau of the Census, "Birth Expectations and Fertility: June 1972," Current Population Reports, Series P-20, No. 248 (Washington, D. C.: U.S. Government Printing Office, 1973), p. 3.

In either case, mobility introduces changes in family and friendship patterns and creates managerial problems: besides doing all that is involved in the move itself, the family must locate housing, select new services, and find new supply sources.

Effect of Education on Managerial Processes. Formal education is often related to sharpened ability to think abstractly—an ability that is particularly important in planning. Education affects housing choices by increasing income stability (regardless of lifetime earnings), the capacity to plan ahead, and the "willingness to make contractual commitments."[62]

Planning thoroughness and decision-making efficiency are associated with consumer satisfaction. Among families in three generations, these consumer qualities were found among the young and better educated.

---

62. James N. Morgan, "Housing and Ability to Pay," *Econometrica* 33 (April 1965): 306.

85

These younger married people with low-accumulated earnings and high residential mobility shared an optimistic, prudent, and developmental outlook and had good family organization, communication, and agreement on roles.[63]

Creativity and resourcefulness of home managers increase with education. Resourcefulness is an ability to deal effectively with things and people in household situations; creativity emphasizes fluency, flexibility, and originality in imaginative actions.[64]

Short-run Effects of Participation in Educational Systems. Decisions to participate in educational programs often involve the investment of time and money in anticipated long-run benefits at the current cost of additional pressures and the foregoing of satisfaction from alternative activities. These short-runs costs are more prohibitive at least in terms of money, at lower-income levels. "In 1970 a youth of 18 to 24 years old from a family earning above $15,000 was nearly five times more likely to be enrolled in college than a youth 18 to 24 from a family with income less than $3,000."[65]

The day's structure is affected if a family member is enrolled in an educational system. College students who operate a household attest to the challenge of fitting schedules together at each term's beginning. Colleges and universities offer classes at a wider range of hours than do secondary, middle, or elementary schools, but some local schools have two shifts of classes. Steidl and Bratton describe the impact of schools on the timing of household activities:

The hours when children are in school—the start and the end of the school day—contribute another set of inflexible time periods. For those families whose children must be ready for the school bus, the start of the school day is actually signaled by that moment when the children must leave for the pickup place. When children live close to school and come home for lunch, another set of inflexible time units is added to those which influence the homemaker's timing of other events.[66]

---

63. Reuben Hill, "Judgment and Consumership in the Management of Family Resources," *Sociology and Social Research* 47: (July 1963), 458.
64. Doris Wetters, "Creative Aspects of Homemanager's Resourcefulness," The Pennsylvania State University, Ph.D. dissertation, 1967, pp. 14, 51.
65. "Toward Equal Opportunity for Higher Education," College Entrance Board, New York, 1973, p. 11.
66. Rose E. Steidl and Esther C. Bratton, *Work in the Home* (New York: John Wiley & Sons, Inc., 1968), p. 87.

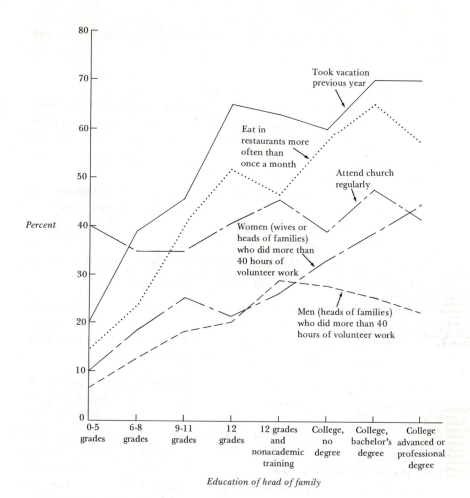

FIGURE 4.6 *Participation in various activities, by education of head of family.*

Source: James N. Morgan, I.A. Sirageldin, and Nancy Baerwaldt, *Productive Americans* (Ann Arbor, Michigan, Institute for Social Research, The University of Michigan, 1966), p. 297. Reprinted with permission of the publisher, Survey Research Center, Institute for Social Research, The University of Michigan, Ann Arbor, Michigan.

Other regular educational activities of family members (clubs, lessons, Scouts, etc.) affect the family's planning, especially sequencing. Sequence adjustments occur when there are changes in activities or school due to holidays, bad weather, illness of leaders, or suspension of a child from school. Each change contributes to the frustrations of family members who arrange for getting a child or family member to an activity. The situation is especially difficult for persons who, themselves, have a restricting time structure.

Occupation

Traditionally the family's lifestyle has been significantly influenced by the husband's occupation. For the middle class, the women's role has been to participate vicariously in her husband's occupation through support functions—typing, entertaining, and sometimes through acting as a receptionist or assistant.[67]

The sharp difference is fading between man as the breadwinner and woman as the nurturant, one who bears and rears children. In some families the man's occupation is no longer the major determinant of where to live and in what style.

The effect of the occupation of husband or wife on the family and its management depends on several factors:

1. the relative importance of the occupation compared to the importance of the family;
2. degree of synchronization of occupational and familial responsibilities;
3. degree of overlap in occupation and family setting.[68]

The compatibility of occupation and family is determined in part by interest in the job; if the job holds special interest, it may compete with the family or be a major concern. Jobs that require a high commitment and involvement are often those over which the job holder has some control, in that he can set the pace and the schedule. Jobs that have a variety of activities, jobs that require special education or training, jobs that include many contacts with other workers or customers or clients are also aspects of occupations that may compete with the family for the breadwinner's time. "Professions and positions in the higher echelons of business, highly skilled blue-collar occupations such as printing, or dangerous jobs such as mining are examples of high salience occupations."[69]

Society and paternalistic employers have expected certain modes of living for occupationally mobile men at high-income levels. However, many wives of high-level executives now commonly reject the idea that their ac-

---

67. Hanna Papanek, "The Two-Person Career," *American Journal of Sociology* 78 (January 1973): 90–110.
68. Joan Aldous, "Occupational Characteristics and Males' Role Performance in the Family," *Journal of Marriage and the Family* 31 (November 1969): 710.
69. Aldous, pp. 708–709.

tivities as a wife and as an individual must conform to a particular pattern of behavior to insure their husband's success.[70] Only 16 per cent of suburban housewives, whose husbands held a variety of jobs, mentioned entertainment as a form of influence on the husband's job.[71] In the case of executives' wives, 40 per cent gave entertaining business associates as an expectation of the husband's company.[72] The executive's wife may increase the compatibility of her husband's work with his family by recognizing the importance he places on his occupation and involving the family in achieving occupational goals. Modifications in the family's pattern of living and consumption can reduce stress or conflict.

An intensive study of dual career families in which both the husband and wife were career oriented found modification of the work involvement one way of reducing strain.

If one travels or gets deeply involved with complex relationships at work it is likely to impinge more on the other's capacity to function at work. Thus, most of the couples made choices that attempted to avoid unnecessary involvements of this kind so as to optimize participation of both partners in work and family spheres.[73]

While increasing numbers of women are working outside the home in the United States, women's career orientation is limited. In a study of wives professionally employed as practicing physicians, college professors, or attorneys, the majority of the women expressed the priority of the wife and mother role over professional obligations. Many indicated they did not want "career" responsibilities. As one academic person stated:

I have succeeded in doing what I want to do—in fact, having achieved academically an assistant professorship, I am rather sure that I do not want any more responsibility. When I was asked to be chairman of our department I decided this was the kind of thing that would be very difficult for me to balance with my home and marriage responsibilities, so I turned it down.[74]

---

70. Margaret L. Helfrich, *The Social Role of the Executive's Wife* (Columbus, Ohio: Bureau of Business Research, The Ohio State University, Monograph No. 123, 1965), p. 76.
71. Lopata, 1971, p. 97.
72. Margaret L. Helfrich and Barbara J. Tootle, "Economic Profile of the American Business Executive," *Bulletin of Business Research* 46 (November 1971): 6.
73. Rhonda Rapoport and Robert N. Rapoport, "The Dual Career Family," *Human Relations* 22 (February 1969): 13.
74. Margaret M. Poloma and T. Neal Garland, "The Married Professional Woman: A Study in Tolerance of Domestication," *Journal of Marriage and the Family* 33 (August 1971): 536.

These comments lead us to the next factor contributing to the effect of occupations on management in the home; that is the degree of synchronization of occupational and familial responsibilities.

This dimension encompasses such aspects of the job as its hours, the amount of geographical mobility it requires, and the stage of the family life cycle at which the occupation makes its peak demands. Occupations that have irregular hours or require night work as well as those that take the man away from home for days at a time, all limit his opportunity to assist with family decisions and tasks as well as to become acquainted with his children.[75]

Husbands employed professionally are an exception to the general relationship of higher occupational levels with higher decision-making power of the husband.[76] The professional man's lesser involvement in decisions seems consistent with the suggestion that synchronization of occupational and familial responsibilities can be more difficult for persons with irregular hours or night work, which professional occupations often require.

Synchronization is difficult for shift workers and probably most difficult for rotating shift workers. Interference in coordination of activities is an apparent cost of shift work. Participating in decision making is relatively low for rotating shift workers. A study of over 650 couples indicates that their difficulty in decision making is significantly greater than for non-rotating shift workers.[77]

Differences in household operation may occur when the husband travels or is away from home at meal time, for example. Meal preparation was less complex in Appalachian families when the father was absent than when he was present.[78] Synchronization of occupational and familial roles is important for the wife employed outside the home and for the husband. The full-time employed wife (30 or more hours per week) averages 34 hours in household work per week, while the full-time employed husband spends 53 hours in paid and volunteer work per week and 11 hours in home activities per week.[79] The total time involved in productive activities

75. Aldous, p. 709.
76. Richard Centers and Bertram H. Raven, "Conjugal Power Structure: A Re-Examination," *American Sociological Review* 36 (April 1971): 274.
77. Paul E. Mott *et al.*, *Shift Work* (Ann Arbor, Mich.: The University of Michigan Press, 1965), pp. 53, 135.
78. Marguerite Steele, "The Effect of a Selected Group of Variables on the Meal Type," The Ohio State University, Plan B Report for the M.S., 1970, p. 22.
79. Kathryn E. Walker, "Time-Use Patterns for Household Work Related to Homemakers' Employment," Speech, 1970 National Agricultural Outlook Conference, February 18, 1970, pp. 2, 5.

appears to be similar. One "solution" to synchronization of the two roles for women is part-time work. One writer describes this approach:

Part-time employment is this generation's false panacea for avoiding a more basic change in the relations between men and women, a means whereby, with practically no change in the man's role and minimal change in the woman's, she can continue to be the same wife and mother she has been in the past with a minor appendage to these roles as an intermittent part-time professional or clerical worker.[80]

The more time women spend in outside employment, the less time they spend in household work. When not employed outside the home, the average woman spends eight hours a day in homemaking, seven hours when employed 1–14 hours per week, and almost 5 hours a day when employed

TABLE 4.7
Median income and distribution of employed men, by major occupation groups for 1972.

Occupation group	Median income	Per cent distribution
White-collar workers		
Professional and technical	$13,029	13.7
Managers, officials, and proprietors	13,741	13.1
Clerical workers	9,656	6.9
Sales workers	11,356	6.2
Blue-collar workers		
Craftsmen and foremen	10,429	20.6
Operatives	8,702	18.6
Nonfarm laborers	7,535	7.8
Service workers	7,762	8.2
Farm workers		
Farmers and farm managers	2,684	5.0
Farm laborers and foremen	4,461	

Source: U.S. Dept. of Commerce, Bureau of the Census, "Income in 1972 of Families and Persons in the United States," Current Population Reports, Series P-60, No. 90 (Washington, D. C.: U. S. Government Printing Office, 1973), p. 148.
U.S. Dept. of Commerce, Bureau of the Census, *Statistical Abstract of the United States: 1973* (Washington, D. C.: U.S. Government Printing Office, 1973), p. 233.

---

80. Alice S. Rossi, "Barriers to the Career Choice of Engineering, Medicine, or Science among American Women," in *Women and the Scientific Professions*, eds. J. A. Mattfeld and C. G. Van Aken (Cambridge, Mass.: M.I.T. Press, 1965), p. 53.

30 or more hours per week.[81] The husband's time spent in household work remains constant at 1.6 hours per day regardless of the varying hours of the wife's employment.

A third factor contributing to the effect of occupation of either the husband or wife on management in the home is the degree of overlap in occupation and family setting. In the United States, business or professional offices are normally separate from the home. But in self-employed situations such as farming, and other situations in many parts of the world, the setting for the occupation and the family are the same. In these cases, meshing occupational and household work is important, and family desires and activities may have to be secondary to the occupational demands most of the time.

Another effect of employment is the impact of resources available to the family. Median income for men varied in 1972 from under $4,000 for farm related occupations to $13,029 for managers, officials, and proprietors (Table 4.7). See also Chapter 2. To some extent, educational choices limit occupational choices, particularly in professional categories. One cannot decide to enter a profession without the necessary educational background. Thus the effect of occupation on resources, as reflected by income, is rather constant once a commitment to an occupation has been made. For the future, instead of a career, a person will likely have a series of careers, by choice or by continuous technological changes, which make some jobs obsolete.[82]

Social Position

Social status indicates a perceived relationship of a person or a group to other persons or groups.[83] Social status accounts for some of the differences which exist in families' values, attitudes, expenditure patterns, decision making, and lifestyles. We shall first consider the strong influence of social status on values.

Values, input to the personal system, affect child-rearing practices. Values differ by social status. Fathers in lower social-class positions, as measured by their education and occupation (Hollingshead's Index of Social Position)[84], value conformity to externally imposed standards for chil-

---

81. Walker, pp. 4, 5.
82. Alvin Toffler, *Future Shock* (New York: Random House, Inc., 1970), p. 110.
83. Thomas E. Lasswell, *Class and Stratum* (Boston: Houghton Mifflin Co., 1965), p. 69.
84. August B. Hollingshead, "A Two-Factor Index of Social Position" (New Haven, Conn.: Hollingshead, 1957), 11.

dren. Fathers in high social-class positions value self-direction for their children.[85]

Mothers in a high social group responded to similar questions in a Washington, D. C. study and placed importance on respect for the rights of others. Middle-class mothers valued happiness, consideration, self-control, and curiosity for their children. Consistent with the study of fathers just described, the working-class mothers valued neatness and obedience and other evidences of behavioral conformity.[86]

In the managerial system, social class affects investment expenditures. Such an effect may be due to basic value differences as revealed through social position. With the same income, blue-collar families invest less in education, medical care, and insurance than do white-collar families. Unskilled workers prefer household durables more than other investments such as education, medical care, or insurance.[87]

TABLE 4.8
Family decision making, by family life stage and social class.

| | Family life stage | | | | Family |
| | *Younger couples*[1] | | *Older couples* | | decision |
Social class	No children	Children	Children	No children	making
		Per cent			
Upper middle	100	90	90	77	joint
	0	10	10	23	separate
Lower middle	100	85	80	31	joint
	0	15	20	69	separate
Upper lower	100	44	59	6	joint
	0	56	41	94	separate

Richard H. Evans and Norman R. Smith, "A Selected Paradigm of Family Behavior," *Journal of Marriage and the Family* 31 (August 1969): 514. Copyright (1969) by National Council on Family Relations. Reprinted by permission.

[1] Husband's age of 45 is cutoff point for younger and older couples.

85. Kohn, p. 52.
86. Kohn, pp. 20–22.
87. Kathleen H. Brown, "Social Class as an Independent Variable in Family Economics Research," *Journal of Consumer Affairs* 3 (Winter 1969): 133.

Questions continue to arise concerning the usefulness of social position or income as predictors of buying behavior.[88] For a wide variety of furniture and appliances, children's wear, women's wear, and men's wear purchases, and for travel, income, rather than social position, determined whether or not a family purchased a good or service within the last year. Exceptions were black-and-white television sets and a passport, which were more closely related to social position than to income.[89]

Among young couples with no children in three social classes, the husband and wife made joint decisions regarding interior housing materials. Upper middle-class families reported joint decisions throughout the life cycle, while upper lower-class families had more separate decisions (made by either husband or wife). Lower middle-class families had a joint decision-making pattern until the later stage in the family cycle when there were no children, at which point the majority of decisions were separate (Table 4.8).

Lifestyles are associated with social position. Participation in voluntary associations is an expectation for upper middle-class families. Participation in associations has increased slightly since the 1950's; the participation increases with social position. During 1955–1962, membership increased more among families with low income and limited education than among the higher levels.[90]

In the late 1950's, working class wives expressed feelings about involvement in associations, putting their concern for child-rearing obligations before "clubs." "I'll take care of my kids before I'll let clubs come into the picture. I have a young baby and just don't have time. I think a home and husband should come first, anyway. I won't join as long as I have to hire a baby sitter. The baby is the mother's first responsibility, I figure."[91]

The husband was a central figure in the reports of workingmen's

---

88. John E. Slocum, Jr. and H. Lee Mathews, "Social Class and Income as Indicators of Consumer Behavior," *Journal of Marketing* 34 (April 1970): 69–74.

89. James H. Myers and John F. Mount, "More on Social Class vs. Income as Correlates of Buying Behavior," *Journal of Marketing* 37 (April 1973): 71–73.

90. Herbert H. Hyman and Charles R. Wright, "Trends in Voluntary Association Memberships of American Adults: Replication Based on Secondary Analysis of National Sample Surveys," *American Sociological Review* 36 (April 1971) : 98–99.

91. Lee Rainwater, Richard P. Coleman, and Gerald Handel, *Workingman's Wife* (New York: Oceana Publications, Inc., 1959), chap. 7.

wives[92] in a 1972 study of 410 women from eight cities across the United States.[93] He had somewhat displaced children as a source of satisfaction. "Social changes and pressures seem to be converging to point the workingman's wife in directions which are more self-centered and self-indulgent."[94]

ENVIRONMENT

Location

Location in urban, suburban, and rural areas affects value orientations, standards, task performance, time expenditures and schedules, and community participation. Few differences exist at the macro level in education, family income, fertility, and age distribution, but there are differences in attitudes at the micro level, specifically for urban and rural areas.[95]

Value differences exist in degree; in an Ohio study, urban dwellers were more highly committed to formal education than rural dwellers, but both were highly committed. Rural respondents were more modernistic in outlook than urban respondents in the same study, with data collection in 1969 and 1970.[96]

In another Ohio study, differences in standards, a value related concept, were examined. Flexibility of a standard for a household activity increased with population density. The most flexible standards were held by urban, then by suburban, and then by rural homemakers.[97]

---

92. Social Research, Inc., Division of the Fry Consulting Group, "Working-Class Women in a Changing World," (Study: #287/07), May 1973 (New York: Macfadden-Bartell Corporation), p. 22.

93. Social Research, Inc., Division of the Fry Consulting Group, "A Study of Working-Class Women in a Changing World," undated news release, pp. 1, 2.

94. Social Research, Inc., "Working-Class Women in a Changing World," p. 14.

95. Ted L. Napier, "Rural-Urban Differences: Myth or Reality?" Research Bulletin No. 1063 (Wooster, Ohio: Ohio Agricultural Research and Development Center, 1973), p. 13.

96. Napier, pp. 6, 8.

97. Maloch and Deacon, 1970, p. 8.

TABLE 4.9

Household task performance for urban and rural families.

	Who performs task					
	Wife more than husband		*Husband and wife equally*		*Husband more than wife*	
Task	Urban[1]	Rural[2]	Urban	Rural	Urban	Rural
			Per cent			
Household repairs	9	14	7	24	83	63
Handling money and bills	40	55	23	29	38	16
Shopping for groceries	57	79	25	13	19	8
Putting children to bed	76	85	8	15	3	1

Urban Frederick L. Campbell, "Family Growth and Variation in Family Role Structure," *Journal of Marriage and the Family* 32 (February 1970): 47. Copyright (1970) by National Council on Family Relations. Reprinted by permission.

Rural Eugene A. Wildening and Lakshmi K. Bharadwaj, "Aspirations, Work Roles and Decision-Making Patterns," Research Bulletin 266 (Madison, Wis.: University of Wisconsin, 1966), p. 10.

[1]Percentages calculated by adding "mostly" and "always" ratings together for each spouse; percentages rounded after combining. Families were just married, or had first, second, or fourth child; there were 1,242 in the sample.

[2]Farm families with husband less than 65 years of age; there were 510 in the sample.

Distances to services and supplies and community activities may add to the complexity of planning. For those who not only live in a rural area but also farm, distances involved in completing farm errands make a difference in sequencing of the day. Farm errands are often scattered throughout the homemaker's day as events occur.

Time spent on household tasks is greater for rural farm families (55.4 hours/week) than for urban families (52.9 hours/week) and slightly more than for rural nonfarm families (54.7 hours/week).[98] Differences in percent of time spent on major household tasks follow:[99]

	Rural		Urban
	Farm	*Nonfarm*	
	Per cent of time of household tasks		
Food preparation	20	18	18
Child care	10	16	13
Dishwashing	14	11	13
Regular care of house	13	14	16

---

98. Manning, pp. 1, 5.
99. Manning, pp. 7, 18.

The patterns of time use differ relatively little and even less when family size and children's ages are accounted for. Urban families spent a proportionately greater time in regular care of the house, perhaps influenced by the predominance of new one-floor houses, which often expose more areas for public view.[100]

Husbands and wives differ in the tasks they do in rural and in urban settings. The category "wife performs task more than husband" has a higher percentage of rural than urban wives for each of the four categories shown in Table 4.9.

The size of the community affects volunteer work and involvement; more such activity occurs in small towns than in urban places.[101] It may be that small towns are not able to hire professionals for many needed services and consequently volunteer participation there is more extensive, or perhaps community members expect more participation in small towns than in metropolitan areas. Mobility is high in some urban areas and therefore the community roots may not be so strong as in small towns.

Housing

A dwelling is the outer shell which provides space for the activities of living as well as safety and protection. The cost of this space is generally high. Housing represents the largest single expense for most families.

The relationship of housing to the personal subsystem is the provision of a setting that encourages or inhibits the impact of other variables in the total social environment on the growth and development of family members.[102] Housing can provide a climate of privacy for family members; psychological stimulation, creativity, a sense of place, a self-concept, and feelings of relatedness to other systems.[103]

Privacy afforded by housing separates family members from other systems such as the political and the economic. The consequences of privacy on families are not clearly known. Privacy within the family system is

---

100. Manning, p. 35.
101. Morgan, Sirageldin, and Baerwaldt, p. 149. ,
102. Robert R. Rice, "The Effects of Project Head Start and Differential Housing Environments Upon Child Development," *The Family Coordinator* 18 (January 1969): 38.
103. James E. Montgomery, "Impact of Housing Patterns on Marital Interaction," *The Family Coordinator* 19 (July 1970): 267–75.

affected by allocation of space to family members and by living patterns accompanying family life cycle stages.[104]

Crowding makes privacy difficult, yet there is no convincing evidence "that crowding in a dwelling unit contributes materially to mental disorder or to emotional instability. Nor is there evidence as yet that crowding (or other housing deficits) interferes with a promotive style of life; that because of crowding, family roles and rituals cannot satisfactorily be carried out; or that the development of infants and children is severely impaired."[105] Nor is there evidence that crowding is beneficial to a promotive life style.

Some individuals adapt to crowded, noisy conditions, such as the child growing up "among a steady backdrop of high-intensity TV signals, rattling subway trains and yells from neighbors." He may adapt to these noises, but he may do it by also shutting out awareness of speech.[106]

Individual needs, desires, or values for privacy, sense of place, and self-concept vary considerably. A housing project requirement of separate bedrooms for two children of opposite sex is an unnecessary rule to some residents. One case is described:

In her previous quarters, her son had slept on the living room sofa and she had wanted to continue this practice since she could not afford to furnish another room. However, although she had to take the additional bedroom it remained empty and was used as a playroom. Meanwhile, her son still slept on the sofa and Mrs. Queen continued to protest that she was having to pay rent for a room that she did not need and could not afford to furnish.[107]

Although the housing environment is primarily a setting for the personal subsystem, the environment often reflects the family's values and at-

---

104. Ruth H. Smith, Donna Beth Downer, Mildred T. Lynch, and Mary Winter, "Privacy and Interaction Within the Family as Related to Dwelling Space," *Journal of Marriage and the Family* 31 (August 1969): 559–66.

105. D. M. Wilner and W. G. Baer, "Sociocultural Factors in Residential Space," mimeo., prepared for Environmental Control Administration of the U.S. Dept. of Health, Education, and Welfare and the American Public Health Association, 1970.

106. J. Sonnenfeld, "Variable Values in Space and Landscape: An Inquiry into the Nature of Environmental Necessity," *Journal of Social Issues* 22 (October 1966): 74–75 and Joachim F. Wohlwill, "The Physical Environment: A Problem for the Psychology of Stimulation," *Journal of Social Issues* 22 (October 1966): 36.

107. Camille Jeffers, *Living Poor* (Ann Arbor, Mich.: Ann Arbor Publishers, 1967), p. 25.

titudes. In an urban study, traditional behavior, religious attitudes, and marital role definitions were found in homes with traditional decor.[108]

Values, activities, and, consequently, space needs differ with the life cycle:

Family Life-Cycle Stage	*Primary Housing Value*
Families with preschool children	Family as a whole
Families with school-age children	Individuality, privacy, and equality of members
Families with retired husband, no children at home	Personal and social orientation of parents.[109]

Provision for and use of space to promote goals of the family are functions of the managerial subsystem. However, changes in space needs due to changes in the life-cycle stages do not necessarily bring about a change in the family housing.

. . . the "lumpiness" of changes in family size and the lack of concomitant increases in family income necessitate households making a number of tradeoffs between space and other necessities such as food, clothing, household location, and even time (doing without adequate space in the present so as to improve one's space circumstances in the future).[110]

Living space may be inadequate for family and individual activities. Lack of space may force family members to seek locations outside the home for these activities. Children, for example, may play on their neighbor's larger lawns or use community facilities (spaces and equipment) for hobbies and recreation. The effect can be a highly dispersed family.

Predictions for the future have varying implications of the relation of housing to managerial processes. Increased centering of activities in the

---

108. Edward O. Laumann and James S. House, "Living Room Styles and Social Attributes: The Patterning of Material Artifacts in a Modern Urban Community," *Sociology and Social Research* 54 (April 1970): 321–42.

109. Donna Beth Downer, Ruth H. Smith, and Mildred T. Lynch, "Values and Housing—A New Dimension," *Journal of Home Economics* 60 (March 1968): 173–76.

110. Daniel M. Wilner and William G. Baer, "Sociocultural Factors in Residential Space," abstract of position paper, *Proceedings of the First Invitational Conference on Health Research in Housing and Its Environment*, Arlie House, Warrenton, Virginia, March 17–19, 1970, p. 106.

home has been suggested in relation to the education of children and adults which would be made possible through computer assisted learning and utilization of computers in the home. Other trends relate to a transfer of activities from the home to other locations such as day-care centers and shared recreational facilities within living complexes. Even though actual impacts for the future are uncertain, housing affects the way in which managerial processes are directed to meet the needs of the individual or group.

Housing provides safety and comfort for families, but in widely varying degrees. Low-income families often find that their housing is unsafe, with both human and nonhuman sources of danger (Table 4.10).

Problems with safety and lack of comfort in homes may affect the management in homes through the constant meeting of unexpected events related to housing, or living with the results of ignoring these events.

What I dislike is when people mess up the hallways, when they don't cooperate, and when the elevator is broken I have to carry the baby upstairs. What I do like is that I have the type of kitchen and bath that I can keep clean. It's easier to keep these apartments clean except the dust that comes in from having so many windows. They also just put these new locks on which are sturdier than the old ones,

TABLE 4.10
Sources of danger in housing.

Human	Nonhuman
Violence to self and possessions	*Structural*
Assault	Deteriorated or poorly designed
Fighting and beating	buildings
Rape	Insufficiently protected heights
Objects thrown or dropped	*Utilities*
Stealing	Faulty electrical wiring
	Poor plumbing
Verbal hostility, shaming,	Dangerous and inadequate heating
exploitation	equipment
	Housekeeping
Attractive alternatives that lure	Trash (broken glass, sharp cans, etc.)
away from a stable life	Fire and burning hazards
	Poisons
	Rats and other vermin

Adapted from Lee Rainwater, "Fear and House-As-Haven in the Lower Class," *Journal of the American Institute of Planners* (January 1966), 32:27.

and you can't lock yourself out as easy as you could with the others. You know when I lived over on Waterman Street, the apartments used to get so cold in the winter time that you had to put the baby's blankets into the oven to warm them up so he wouldn't be too cold. You could talk to the landlady all of the time and complain about there not being enough heat, but she never turned it up. That is one thing you don't have to worry about here in the project, because in winter time it's always warm in these apartments. [111]

SUMMARY

Family life and role stages are gradually evolving periods marked by changes in individual and family responsibilities. Economic behavior and household tasks are particularly related to family life stages, and are reflected most clearly through evidences on family composition.

The effects of family size on home management are summarized more definitively in the following relationships: for resources, income does not increase directly with family size; help from children on household work generally increases with family size; help from husband on household work does not increase directly with family size. Resource use is affected in the following ways: total work time for husband and wife increases with family size; use of time for household work decreases as the age of the youngest child increases; and participation in community welfare activities increases with age of children and increased hired help. Decision-making patterns are modified for husband and wife with increased family size. Family spacing appears to have a strong relationship to economic status of families. Closely spaced children born during the early years of marriage place a family at a financial disadvantage.

Individual and family characteristics, such as health, race, personality, education, occupation, and social position, further influence home management. Illness in a family may create severe economic problems, depending on the economic circumstances prior to the problem; agreement on goals may be less when someone in the family is chronically ill; and the time spent on household tasks may be less for homemakers with ill health, their standards more complex, their standards and sequence less realistic, and their sequence of tasks less flexible than for well homemakers.

---

111. Lee Rainwater, *Behind Ghetto Walls* (Chicago: Aldine Publishing Co., 1970), p. 18.

Much remains to be known in describing and understanding differences in home management by race. Race makes a difference today in family income, even within the same educational levels. Black families are, on the average, larger than white families, and the number of families headed by a woman is higher for the black than the white family. Lower-class black men report doing more household tasks and making more decisions when they are the sole breadwinner, compared with families in which the wives are also employed.

Personality as a factor influencing home management is not consistent in its effect, probably due in part to the measures that are too gross for predicting specific managerial behavior. Maslow's work on the self-actualizing person has given research direction. There is evidence that the need for order is related to household task standardization and regularization.

Education has a long-run effect on life chances for income and accompanying life style expectations; education is associated with planning, decision making, efficiency, creativity, and resourcefulness. The educational system affects the family system through giving structure to the day and to the seasons.

The husband's occupation has traditionally been the influential factor in decisions related to mobility of the family. Today's emphasis on choice for men and women means that both the husband's and wife's occupation can influence managerial behavior. The importance of the occupation or career, the synchronization of occupation and family responsibilities, and the degree of overlap in occupational and family settings affect the impact of the occupation on management.

Social position has an effect on management of families through a difference in values held and in decision-making patterns. There is apparently greater conformity of lower-status families to externally imposed standards and less joint decision making of husbands and wives, compared to greater self-direction at higher levels and more joint decision making. Differences in expenditure patterns occur that are not due to income, suggesting the importance of social position in influencing economic behavior. Evidence of these differences is somewhat inconsistent.

The environment in which the individual or family system operates influences the managerial behavior. Chapter 2 described the interactions with other systems. Here, the potential effect of the location of the household, in rural or urban areas, was discussed. Rural farm families spend more time on household tasks, although the effect of family size and children's age is considerably more important. Patterns of volunteer work differ, with families in small towns participating more than in urban areas. Flexibility of standards increases with urbanization.

The effects of space and housing on individuals appear to be highly variable; adaptation by individuals makes generalizations difficult. Changing housing needs through the family life cycle present a challenge to the managerial system.

Decision Making and Communicating

5.

Decision making and communicating are discussed as processes underlying, but not limited to, home management. Both decision making and communicating are fundamental to all dynamic, social processes, including home management. Their significance to home management is emphasized in the following sections.

The interrelation of problem solving and managing is considered first. Then, steps in the decision-making process and types of decisions are discussed to clarify their relation to home management. Basic to the communication process in the systems context is the openness of the system members to sending and receiving various types of messages. Implications for home management are recognized throughout the section.

DECISION MAKING

Decision making is an increasingly important aspect of daily living—beginning with what to wear in the morning, what food to take in the cafeteria line, what to do when an appointment is cancelled, and ranging to what to give as a birthday present or what gasoline to buy for the car. Not only are we confronted with a wide range of problems, but we are also aware of the extensive possibilities for solutions within each problem area. A popular columnist comments on this situation: "Personally, I think people are on the brink of aggravation and despair because we are plagued by decisions. I go to buy a box of crackers. The clerk says, 'Soda, saltine, cheeseflavored, smoked, butter, round, square, triangle, garlic, pizza, chicken, taco, or onion?' 'Just a plain cracker,' I say. 'Lady, there is no such thing as a plain cracker.' "[1]

Predictions about available choices in the future range from minimal ones because of standardization to "overchoice," a condition in which a consumer's decisions become so complex that they outweigh the advantages of diversity and individualization.[2] An increase in both standardization and diversity seems likely in the future, with overchoice also occurring to some degree.

Decision making is sometimes equated with management,[3] but its use here is neither synonymous with nor unique to home management. Decision making is the choice or resolution of alternatives.[4] Alternative consideration can take place throughout the managerial system: in the input phase (both in setting goals and in surmising available resources); in standard setting and sequencing within planning; and in checking and adjusting within the controlling phase (Figure 5.1).

The decision-making process may be stated in various ways but it generally contains these steps: (1) recognizing that a decision is needed; (2) identifying and weighing appropriate alternatives; and (3) choosing among or resolving alternatives. This process is the basis for a rational approach to decision making.

Decisions may also be made intuitively. *Intuition* yields an immediate decision, bypassing well-defined, conscious steps.[5] Intuitive decision making is aided by experience, but does not necessarily result from it. The intuitive person focuses on a total conception of the problem and does not consider the elements of decision making singly. More things appear to be taken into account than can be verbalized. But there is a sense of comprehending the total situation and a general satisfaction with results. All

---

1. Erma Bombeck, "Life Isn't Simple Any More," *Columbus Dispatch,* April 5, 1972, p. 3B.
2. Alvin Toffler, *Future Shock* (New York: Random House, Inc., 1970), p. 239.
3. Herbert A. Simon, *The New Science of Management Decision* (New York: Harper & Row, Publishers, 1960), pp. 1,3.
4. Francille Maloch and Ruth E. Deacon, "Proposed Framework for Home Management," *Journal of Home Economics* 58 (January 1966): 33.
5. William T. Morris, "Intuition and Relevance," *Management Science* 14 (December 1967): B-158.

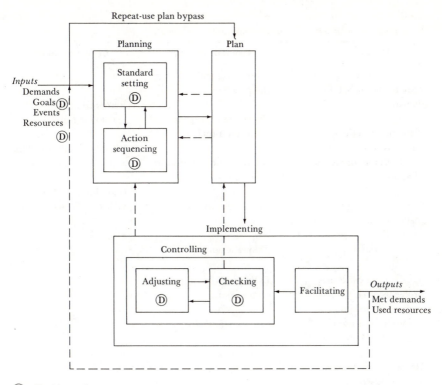

(D) Decision points
— — Feedback

FIGURE 5.1 *Decision-making points in a managerial system.*

or parts of decisions may be intuitive. Facts or experience may provide some insight, but an interrelating of unknowns may occur and result in a conscious sense of rightness or wrongness about some situation. Other less intuitive persons in the same situation would review the important factors considered beyond the facts and make estimates of their importance. Decisions as varied as a new business venture or a leisure activity may be approached through intuitive or rationalizing processes.

Relationships of Decision Making, Problem Solving, and Managing

Home management is broader than either decision making or problem solving, since home management includes the totality of managerial functioning (Table 5.1). Problem solving, as defined here, excludes

TABLE 5.1

Managing, problem solving, and decision-making elements.

Managing	Problem solving	Decision making
Planning and controlling resource use to satisfy demands	Identifying and defining the problem	
		Recognizing that a decision is needed
	Collecting information about the problem	
Planning—a series of decisions concerning standards and/or sequences of action		Identifying and weighing appropriate alternatives
	Innovating or producing alternatives	
		Choosing or resolving available alternatives
Controlling—regulating planned behavior	Choosing a course of action	
Includes	Taking action	
Total system concerns— problems in relation to each other; habitual actions, repeat use plans for meeting demands	Evaluating consequences of an action	
	Excludes	
	Habitual actions	
Decisions about goals, standards, sequences, checks, adjustments, and feedback (Figure 5-1)	Relationship of the problem to the total situation or system	

habitual actions. It excludes any situation or circumstance that does not threaten a family's values, or that does not require cognitive effort and interaction of its members to resolve the situation in a manner compatible with family values.[6] Day-to-day household management may or may not include problem solving.

Decision making includes recognizing a need for a decision, identifying and weighing appropriate alternatives, and choosing or reaching a resolution among alternatives. Decision making does not imply action and,

6. Joan Aldous, "A Framework for the Analysis of Family Problem Solving," in *Family Problem Solving,* eds. Joan Aldous, Thomas Condon, Reuben Hill, Murray Straus, and Irving Tallman (Hinsdale, Ill.: The Dryden Press Inc., 1971), p. 269.

therefore, does not encompass either problem solving or managing from this viewpoint, but is, instead, part of both.

Decisions occur throughout the managerial system. Many goal-setting and standard-setting decisions with long-run implications evolve gradually. In making decisions about goals, individuals and families may mediate their values by deciding in favor of a given goal direction in the personal system. A family may choose individual privacy over leisure by deciding on more living space in preference to a family trip. Having selected the goal, the family may then need to clarify it further through managerial planning. Considering resources, housing location, and other general factors, the decision may be to add a room to the present dwelling rather than to move to a new one. This is a goal-setting contribution of management. The operational goal for total management then becomes clear. Specific plans and actions for house expansion can be undertaken, that is, quantitative and qualitative standards for developing the addition can then be set and carried out.

In solving problems, families may become committed to certain actions that entail outcomes which were previously only vaguely perceived, if at all. As the outcomes become apparent, they are evaluated. If an outcome fails to meet the family's objectives, the family may search for other solutions or revise its goals.[7]

Families do not often fit the rational model, that is, they do not necessarily outline specific alternatives and consider or weigh each alternative to make a decision in problem solving or in management. Instead, families probably have a wide range of approaches, from rational approaches of developing alternatives to "falling into" alternatives or changing standards and goals to fit readily available solutions better.

The various elements of the decision-making process will be discussed in the order described.

Recognizing That a Decision Is Needed

The variations in recognizing a need for a decision are probably very great, even among families that have similar goals and resources. Educational and sales programs try to alert families to needs for decisions. An insurance salesman may ask about life insurance for a young mother or about educational insurance for the child. Until the salesman brings the

---

7. Aldous, p. 267.

questions to the attention of the couple, there may be little or no recognition that a decision is needed. Other informal episodes alert us to situations. A neighbor may consult us about lawn care or request our support in a campaign for better lighting in the parking lot. Some persons seem to have a heightened alertness to needs for decisions. One spouse may recognize needed decisions before the other spouse wants to consider a decision.

Identifying and Weighing Appropriate Alternatives

Identifying or generating alternatives varies with individuals, although the specific reasons for the differences, such as intelligence or personality, are not known.[8] However, in a simulated decision-making situation, the personality factors of dominance, capacity for status, sociability, social presence, self-acceptance, and well-being were correlated significantly with the time used in decision making under two sets of alternative conditions.[9] In this study, the weighing of objectives was measured by the amount of time spent for making decisions.

Studies show that the number of alternatives considered in decision making vary with the importance of the decisions to be made or with the individual's capacity to generate alternatives. In one study, Michigan farm families who were younger and more highly educated than other families and who had a higher net worth seriously considered alternatives to the preferred decision more often in making financial decisions than the other families did.[10] In two other studies, a majority (60 per cent) of home economics students and home economics graduates considered more than one alternative in making their decisions.[11]

Decision making which follows the format of the rational model promotes objectivity in weighing alternatives in home management. An individual who is faced with a decision situation that has different possible

---

8. Fred W. Ohnmacht, "Personality and Cognitive Referents of Creativity: A Second Look," *Psychological Reports* 26 (February 1970): 336.
9. Richard W. Pollay, "The Structure of Executive Decisions and Decision Times," *Administrative Science Quarterly* 15 (December 1970): 459–71.
10. Peggy K. Schomaker and Alice C. Thorpe, "Financial Decision-Making As Reported by Farm Families in Michigan," *Quarterly Bulletin* 46 (November 1963): 344–45.
11. Nancy A. Barclay, "Decision-Making by Students in the Home Management Residence Course," Pennsylvania State University, M.S. thesis, 1963, p. 30. Sharon F. Wood, "Day-to-Day Decision-Making of College Educated Homemakers," The Pennsylvania State University, M.S. thesis, 1966, pp. 53–54.

solutions is rational if he (1) evolves available alternatives, (2) considers consequences, (3) orders the alternatives by some rule or preference relationship, and (4) chooses the best or most preferred consequence.[12]

In most family or household systems, however, application of rational decision making is more likely a "bounded rationality." The principle of bounded rationality assumes that the human mind's capacity for analyzing and solving problems is very small compared with the complexity of problems that must be solved. The boundary lines for rational choice are, in a practical sense, limited by the human capacity to analyze as well as to generate possible solutions.[13]

Consistency in rationality of decision making may be related to education, according to evidence from a study of college-level cooperators. The young mothers who were more rational in technical decisions were also more rational in affective decisions. Mothers with a rational approach in decision making also felt they had more control over their environment than those with a less rational approach to decision making.[14]

The alternatives and outcomes of many decisions in the family system are simply not known. Nor is the relationship between alternatives and outcomes defined well enough to offer clear evidence about the amount of consideration given to alternatives.

Decision rules are "a uniform directive indicating a clear choice among properly specified alternatives."[15] Rules frequently given as being important bases for the preference ranking of choices are (1) the economy rule that results in the "cheapest alternative that does the job, even if performance is just barely satisfactory"[16] and (2) the optimizing rule that strives for the "best buy" or for getting the most for the expended resources. The relative benefits are greater for the optimizing alternative, that is, the ratio of benefits to costs is higher, even though actual costs may be greater than for the economizing one.

Individuals and families often simplify decision making by not going far

---

12. Marcus Alexis and Charles Z. Wilson, *Organizational Decision Making* (Englewood Cliffs, N. J.: Prentice-Hall, Inc., 1967), pp. 149–50.

13. Herbert A. Simon, *Models of Man: Social and Rational* (New York: John Wiley & Sons, Inc., 1957), p. 198.

14. Jean R. Halliday, "Relationships Among Certain Characteristics of a Decision Event: Decision Procedure, Decision Context, and Decision-Maker," Ph.D. dissertation, 1964, p. 52.

15. James R. Miller III, *Professional Decision-Making, A Procedure for Evaluating Complex Alternatives* (New York: Praeger Publishers, 1970), p. 28.

16. Miller, p. 30.

enough to find the best alternative. Instead, they select the first one good enough to meet the anticipated outcome.[17] The decision rule for this approach is called satisficing, which assumes that alternatives are sought only until an acceptable aspiration level can be met.[18] For example, in one study, non-college-educated homemakers commonly tried one or two alternatives before finding a sufficiently satisfactory one.[19]

In a hypothetical situation that provided full information on four relevant characteristics affecting the choice of a second car, university students applied satisficing and preference-ranking rules. Although a higher portion of the responses than would be expected by chance fit the tests for both the satisficing and preference-ranking rules, the less rigorous satisficing response was considerably more common. Even so, there was more use of both the satisficing and preference-ranking tests in relation to more than one characteristic than would have been expected by chance. These findings indicate that both rules are meaningful in decision-making situations.[20]

Decisions are made under varying circumstances, with different amounts of information about alternatives and consequences. *Certainty* is complete knowledge of consequences of a decision,[21] and uncertainty is the lack of this knowledge. Between the known or probable estimates of the degrees of certainty or uncertainty is the element of risk. Knowledge of a decision's consequences can come from experience, experimentation, a search for information, or a combination of these approaches. Decisions are frequently made under uncertain conditions because "probabilities of future outcomes cannot be equated to frequencies of past outcomes, either because such information is too meager or nonexistent, or because present and future circumstances are believed to be significantly different from the past.[22] *Risk* is the hazard or chance of a loss.

Knowledge of either *objective* or *subjective probability* forms the basis for making decisions with known risk. Objective probability is based on past

17. David I. Cleland and William R. King, *Management: A Systems Approach* (New York: McGraw-Hill Book Company, Inc., 1972), p. 225.
18. Herbert A. Simon, "Theories of Decision-Making in Economics and Behavioral Science," *The American Economic Review* 49 (June 1959): 277.
19. Reta R. Lancaster, "Case Studies of the Decision-Making of Ten Non-College Educated Homemakers," University of Kansas, M.S. thesis, 1966, p. 43.
20. Frances M. Magrabi, "An Empirical Test for Decision Rule," *The Journal of Consumer Affairs* 3 (Summer 1969): 48–51.
21. Alexis and Wilson, p. 151.
22. Samuel Eilon, "What Is a Decision?" *Management Science* 16 (December 1969): B-185.

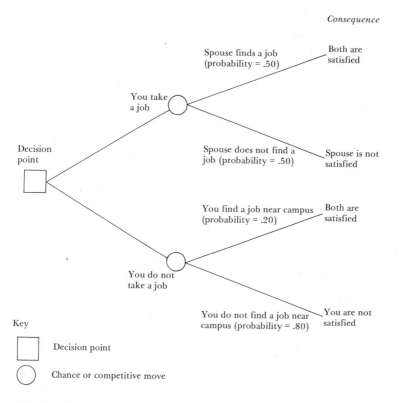

FIGURE 5.2 *A decision tree.*

Source: John F. Magee, "Decision Tree for Decision Making," *Harvard Business Review* 42 (July-August 1964): 127.

experience, repeated experiments, or the outcome of large samples. Weather forecasts, based on the present and predicted atmospheric situation, include an objective probability of certain weather conditions. Planning a party outdoors can be done with known weather risks as the party date draws nearer.

Subjective probability is a measure of the decision maker's belief in an outcome.[23] Subjective probability is probably far more prevalent in decisions concerning the household than is objective probability. The measure of the belief in the outcome may be quite inexact, that is, one alternative

23. Gerald J. Hahn, "Evaluation of a Decision Based on Subjective Probability Estimates," *IEEE Transactions on Engineering Management* EM-18 (February 1971): 12.

may be thought of as having a much greater likelihood of meeting the desired outcome than others.

A "decision tree," as shown in Figure 5-2, offers one way of visualizing alternatives and the probablity of predicted outcomes. Not every possibility is considered in decision making, and therefore only important decisions and consequences are isolated in the tree. A decision tree combines choices of actions and consequences of action that are affected by "chance or uncontrollable circumstances";[24] it provides a systematic approach for examining alternatives and their consequences. The requirements for making a decision tree, as suggested for business and industry, follow:

1. Identify the points of decision and alternatives available at each point.
2. Identify the points of uncertainty and the type or range of alternative outcomes at each point.
3. Estimate the values needed to make the analysis, especially the probabilities of different events or results of action and the costs and gains of various events and actions.
4. Analyze the alternative values to choose a course.[25]

"The tree is made up of a series of nodes and branches . . . . Each branch represents an alternative course of action or decision. At the end of each branch or alternative course is another node";[26] this node is a chance event or competitive move. "Each subsequent alternative course to the right represents an alternative outcome of this chance event. Associated with each complete alternative course through the tree is a payoff, shown at the end of the right-most or terminal branch of the course."[27]

Decision trees were originally used for investment decisions; so the consequences were stated in terms of yield over a period of time. When decision trees describe alternatives and consequences for decisions of a household, the complexity of the tree is increased, since the consequences cover a variety of factors, not just investment yield.

The example in Figure 5.2 is for a person ready to graduate from college with a job opportunity in another state. The person's spouse is em-

---

24. John F. Magee, "Decision Trees for Decision Making," *Harvard Business Review* 42 (July-August 1964): 128.
25. Magee, p. 130.
26. Magee, p. 128.
27. Magee, p. 128.

ployed on the college campus, but is willing to seek employment else-where. Only one decision point is considered, thus yielding a simple deci-sion tree. The probability is subjective; the outcomes are predicted on the basis of personal perception.[28] By assigning subjective probability, the ra-tional approach yields a decision to take the job that involves moving, with a fifty per cent chance that the spouse will find a job nearby.

This subjective probability could have been based on the experiences of acquaintances and on employment records for the past few months. Ex-perience is often used to weigh alternatives without commitment to a specific estimate of probability. In using experience to weigh alternatives, the present situation should be checked to see if it approximates the past experience. Decisions that are based on past experience without consider-ation for changed situations can be costly. "If experience is carefully analyzed rather than blindly followed, and if the *fundamental* reasons for success or failure are distilled from it, it can be useful as a basis for deci-sion analysis."[29]

Experimentation can be a revealing basis for making decisions. In choosing a carpet, a large sample on the floor in the room may be helpful for making a decision. Living in a furnished apartment provides ex-perimentation with furniture and other furnishings, which can be helpful in making later purchasing decisions.

Choosing or Resolving Available Alternatives

In weighing alternatives, a search for information about the al-ternatives and the possible consequences is another approach to increase certainty and reduce risk. Sometimes specific information is unavailable for decisions, but readily available facts are often unused. Information is more advantageous than experimentation for some kinds of problems, such as those involving costly or bulky items. For some small consumer items, however, experimentation with one or two products might be less costly, frustrating, or time consuming than getting information about sev-eral products.

Searching for information is best done when the problem is clearly defined and separated into parts so that the search can be directed to necessary areas. In two different studies, married home economics

---

28. Alexis and Wilson, p. 154.
29. Harold Koontz and Cyril O'Donnell, *Principles of Management: An Analysis of Managerial Functions* (New York: McGraw-Hill Book Company, 1972), p. 180.

graduates[30] and home economics students[31] reported information seeking in about 45 per cent of the decisions recorded. In a simulated decision-making situation, search for new information increased when the proportion of group members with a high conceptual level increased.[32] Individuals who have a high conceptual level typically see many information dimensions and use several methods of seeking information.[33]

Experience, experimentation, and search for information can form the bases for assigning *trade-off values* to various alternatives before selecting an alternative.

Table 5.2 presents available information for choosing credit sources for buying a house. The interest rates favor first borrowing the cash value of life insurance at 5 per cent, then borrowing from a family member at 6½ per cent, and getting the remainder from a mortgage loan at 7 per cent. Other factors, however, should be considered. If the family does not have term insurance or some other savings to cover the decrease in the protection value of the life insurance, borrowing against the life insurance is questionable. If the family member who can loan the money is one who will constantly remind the family of its indebtedness, the 6½ per cent interest rate may not be worth the nagging. If the family has other credit needs, the credit choice for the house purchase should be compatible with the other needs.

FIGURE 5.3. *Relationship of risk, certainty, and knowledge.*

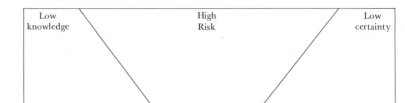

Low knowledge		High Risk		Low certainty
High knowledge		Low Risk		High certainty

---

30. Wood, p. 56.
31. Barclay, p. 32.
32. Paul Stager, "Conceptual Level as a Composition Variable in Small-Group Decision Making," *Journal of Personality and Social Psychology* 5 (February 1967): 159.
33. Stager, p. 152.

TABLE 5.2

Decision making under relative certainty of information; sources of $30,000 credit for a house purchase.

Possible source of credit	$ limit for borrowing	% of interest rate	Terms of repayment	Consequences of choice
Cash value of life insurance	$ 2,500	5	Lump sum or monthly installments. No limit on years.	Decreases protection value.
Family member	9,000	6½	Lump sum or monthly installments. No specified years.	Family might need the money back soon.
Loan secured by stocks and bonds	20,000	7½	Lump sum or monthly installments. Limited number of years.	Prevents selling at advantageous market time.
Mortgage loan	30,000	7	Monthly installments for 20 years	No penalty for repaying early option available.

The family may choose to trade the lower interest advantage of the loan from a family member for the independence gained in using a commercial source of money. Or, since the amount available from a life insurance loan is relatively small, the family may exchange the lower interest rate for the convenience of having only one loan to repay. Considerations that extend comparisons to include trade-offs of nonmoney factors as well as money factors often give a better picture of the relation of anticipated costs to benefits. The most limited constraint may have an overriding influence. Often the constraint is money, but patience may be also.

Orientation to risk differs among individuals; age is one factor that accounts for the difference. In a study of managers from 22–58 years of age, older persons were less willing to assume risks.[34] Two explanations that have not been tested are (1) that as people increase in age, their responsibilities increase and (2) sociocultural experiences in early years strongly affect the willingness to assume risks. Persons who live through a depression or other economic difficulties may be less likely to assume risks.[35] The relationship of risk, knowledge, and certainty is summarized in Figure 5.3.

Types of Decisions

Decisions can be categorized in a number of ways—as nonprogrammed or programmed, as social or economic, and as central or satellite. The decision types can help clarify the role of decision making in home management.

Nonprogrammed and Programmed. "Decisions are nonprogrammed to the extent that they are novel, unstructured, and consequential."[36] Setting goals, determining available resources, setting standards, and adjusting decisions are often of a nonprogrammed nature.

A decision about a car furnished an example of one aspect of a nonprogrammed decision, with an illustrative set of considerations:

1. Owner recognizes that a decision is needed:
   a. Present car requires frequent service.
   b. The time for most auto manufacturers to change models is approaching.
   c. Present car is paid for.
2. Owner identifies and weighs appropriate alternatives related to service. — Probability of reduced service costs and reliable transportation
   a. If used car is bought, the dealer offers a 30-day warranty. — Middle
   b. If new car is bought, manufacturer offers a one-year warranty. — Higher
   c. If present car is kept, it will need continued service. — Lower

34. Victor H. Vroom and Bernd Pahl, "The Relationship Between Age and Risk-Taking Among Managers," *Experimental Publication System* Issue 9 (December 1970): 5.
35. Vroom and Pahl, pp. 11–12.
36. Simon, 1960, p. 6.

3. Owner chooses among or resolves alternatives relative to service.
   Choice: Alternative b.

After making this nonprogrammed decision, the car owner will have to make other decisions and perhaps modify this one since the decision did not take into account other needs or the resource situation. If the choice among alternatives relating to other characteristics or needs (perhaps size) support buying a new or used car, the reconciliation of the goal with the resources will now lead to setting standards. This step may finally determine the choice between a new or a used car. The sequence for purchasing the car will be part of the planning.

Decisions about task sequencing to complete a plan and checking in the controlling aspect are primarily programmed ones. "Decisions are programmed to the extent that they are repetitive and routine, to the extent that a definite procedure has been worked out for handling them so that they don't have to be treated *de novo* each time they occur."[37] *Programmed decisions* can be seen most clearly in repeat-use plans.

Some decisions, such as reflex actions, appear to be completely unconscious, but evolutionists suggest that behavior of this type has been learned over millions of years. At first, instinctive or impulse reactions were not automatic or programmed but required deliberate consideration. Repetitive reactions to similar stimuli reduce the amount of thinking required for decisions, and habits or other programmed decisions are formed.[38]

In repetitive, programmed decisions, two steps are suggested as occurring:

1. a number of generally acceptable alternatives is maintained and
2. a choice is made from this stable set of alternatives.[39]

Grocery shopping is an example: The shopper has a stable set of alternatives for meats, and selects from the alternatives of meats during any one shopping period. The stable set of alternatives is referred to here as a

---

37. Simon, 1960, pp. 5–6.
38. Fremont E. Kast and James E. Rosenzweig, *Organization and Management, A Systems Approach* (New York: McGraw-Hill Book Company, Inc. 1970), p. 345.
39. David L. Rades, "Selection and Evaluation of Alternatives in Repetitive Decision Making," *Administrative Science Quarterly* 17, (June 1972): 196.

repeat-use standard. Repeat-use plans are discussed in the chapter on planning.

   Social and Economic Decisions. "Social relations are patterns of shared action and feeling. Each participant in a relation has . . . a feeling which is attached to the other person and which is expressed in action. Social actions are given pattern by cultural roles, which include expectations, obligations, and ideals. A system of cultural roles is a social system."[40] A definition suggested for *social decisions* is a focus on selecting "the types of roles an individual will play, the specific content he will choose to put into these roles, and how he will integrate these roles into a consistent self."[41]

   Social decisions within a family system are more personal and interpersonal in nature than the term may suggest to many people. Decisions pertaining "to the life, welfare, and relations of human beings in a community," (a dictionary definition of "social") fit the internal responsibility and relations as well as those that are external if the definition is interpreted specifically.

   A primary interest with respect to social decisions in the family setting is to keep values, goals, and standards in home management adequately consistent with, yet responsive to, members' current needs. Through social decisions, potential conflicts between members' values and goals are anticipated and/or resolved by selecting among or reorienting alternative directions that are more consistent with the total interests of the family and significant groups. Social decisions often relate to the definition of roles.[42]

   Decisions focusing on roles are of special concern today since the social role of wife and mother are under reconsideration. A social role of wife and mother, including both family and societal interactions, as perceived by 571 respondents, is presented in Figure 5.4. As an individual becomes involved in relations that form his social role he establishes contact with potential circle members, he tests and is tested for required role qualifications, and he acquires the knowledge and other tools necessary to perform the duties and receive the rights of his role. The process usually af-

---

40. Paul Diesing, *Reason in Society* (Urbana, Ill.: University of Illinois Press, 1962), p. 74.

41. Dorothy Z. Price, "Social Decision-Making," in *The Family: Focus on Management*, Proceedings of a National Conference (Washington, D. C.: American Home Economics Association, 1969), p. 14.

42. Diesing, pp. 14–64.

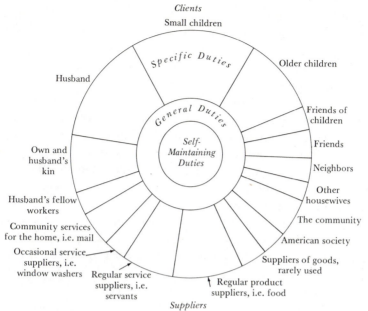

Clients

Small children

Specific Duties

Older children

Husband

General Duties

Friends of children

Self-Maintaining Duties

Friends

Own and husband's kin

Neighbors

Husband's fellow workers

Other housewives

Community services for the home, i.e. mail

The community

Occasional service suppliers, i.e. window washers

American society

Regular service suppliers, i.e. servants

Suppliers of goods, rarely used

Regular product suppliers, i.e. food

Suppliers

The size of the area represents its relative significance to the role.

FIGURE 5.4 *Social role of wife and mother.*

Source: Helena Z. Lopata, *Occupation: Housewife* (New York: Oxford University Press, 1971), p. 138.

fects the personality, changes perceptions of self, alters behavior, and shifts other roles into new patterns.[43]

The decision for a wife and mother to be employed outside the home may bring about shifts in other roles. The importance of social interactions in comparison with general and self-maintaining duties may be changed; specific duties will change.

Social decisions about role are important in home management because they can influence the *interface* of the personal and managerial subsystems within the family and the interface between the family system and other systems. The example in Figure 5.4 suggests specific duties that are a part of the managerial subsystem, but the figure does not illustrate the

43. Helena Z. Lopata, *Occupation: Housewife* (New York: Oxford University Press, 1971), p. 138.

changes in interface that may occur. As the interface between the family system and the economic system is extended from the previous situation (employment of the husband, constant transactions by family members) to the wife's employment, conflict may occur in roles, particularly between the wife-and-mother role and the employed-woman role.

Economic decisions are based on allocation and exchange processes relating to resource use; that is, economically oriented decisions are concerned with how resources are allocated to meet various goals and how they are exchanged. These processes also occur within and between personal and other societal units. At the societal level, allocation distributes values (economic) among alternative economic ends, while exchange transfers values among economic units.[44] At the personal or household level, resources within are allocated to various personal needs or goals, and exchanges with other economic units occur to make this possible. Within the allocation processes, the resources need to be utilized effectively to achieve goals. These decisions are identified as technical ones.[45] Rational economic choice occurs when alternatives are selected to maximize desired ends under these conditions: when there is economic scarcity, that is, when achieving one end means sacrificing another end, and when problematical alternatives can be compared.[46]

As in the case of economic decisions, which follow the rational model and are facilitated by accompanying decision rules, social decisions may apply neutral ground rules such as norms, principles, or other guidelines to resolve or avoid conflicts or otherwise facilitate social decisions. In the larger society, these rules or laws are made and subject to interpretation or evaluation (legal) within a decision-making structure (political). Such processes also occur within the family on a less formal basis. Rules evolve which are held as neutral and binding until changed on accepted authority, which may be democratic and/or authoritarian, depending on the group or the nature of the situation or decision. For example, hours when teenagers must come home from a date may be determined at first on parental authority and may later be relaxed or set more democratically as the children grow older and as mutually recognized criteria evolve.

Economic and technical decision processes were combined in two studies because of the similarities in the types of decision processes. For rural homemakers, the combined processes were used primarily for deci-

---

44. Diesing, p. 43
45. Diesing, p. 4.
46. Diesing, pp. 44–45.

sions in the areas of education, finances, family organization and relationships, and work of the home.[47] For urban affluent homemakers, the combined processes were used in financial matters, family organization and relationships, and work of the home.[48]

Economic (including technical) and social decision-making processes were used in two-thirds of the decisions for both rural and urban homemakers. Legal processes were also analyzed separately and accounted for a quarter of the responses, while political processes (making decisions by compromise, voting, giving in), occurred in about five per cent of the decisions for the rural and urban homemakers.[49]

Central and Satellite Decisions. Central and satellite decisions of planning are considered here from the decision-making viewpoint. They are further discussed in Chapter 7. *Central decisions* are the decision maker's crucial choices; *satellite decisions* follow to complete the action of central decisions.[50] Satellite decisions can be classified by type and may be further grouped under planning and implementing.

Satellite planning decisions

Tactical—an instrumental decision that initiates and implements action on the central decision.

Policy—a plan for making anticipated decisions when and if they are needed.

Program—changing the routine of a recurring activity.

Satellite implementing decisions

Control—regulating, adjusting, or facilitating any satellite decisions.[51]

Satellite decisions for three central decisions have been investigated. The percentage of occurrence of the satellite decision types is shown in Table 5.3. The satellite planning decisions—tactical, policy, and program—were reported more than satellite implementing decisions for the three central decisions. Differences exist between each central decision in the importance of satellite decision types; control decisions were more

47. Harriet Salome Babin, "Four Dimensions of Ten Decisions Made by Rural Families," Louisiana State University, M.S. thesis, 1971, p. 66.

48. Mildred F. Tribble, "Relationships Among Five Dimensions of Twenty-five Home and Family Decisions," Louisiana State University, M.S. thesis, 1970, p. 49.

49. Babin, p. 64 and Tribble, p. 47.

50. Martha A. Plonk, "Exploring Interrelationships in a Central-Satellite Decision Complex," *Journal of Home Economics* 60 (December 1968): 790.

51. Plonk, p. 790.

TABLE 5.3

Frequency of satellite decisions for three central decisions.

	Satellite planning decisions			Satellite implementing decisions
Central decision	*Tactical*	*Policy*	*Program*	*Control*
	Per cent			
Retirement housing	59	22	11	8
Wife's employment	22	40	13	25
Student's summer occupation	45	17	37	1

Addreen Nichols, Catherine R. Mumaw, Maryann Paynter, Martha A. Plonk, and Dorothy Z. Price, "Family Management," *Journal of Marriage and the Family* (February 1971), 33:115 and Anna Mae Myers, "Class and Interrelatedness of Decisions Ensuing from the Decision of Wives to Seek Employment," Virginia Polytechnic Institute, M.S. dissertation, 1967, p. 31.
Nancy M. Bean, "Decision Class, Linkage, and Sequence in One Central-Satellite Decision Complex: Students' Summer Occupational Choice," Michigan State University, M.S. dissertation, 1968, p. 56.
Martha A. Plonk, "Exploring Interrelationships in a Central-Satellite Decision Complex," *Journal of Home Economics* 60 (December 1968): 791. Copyright by the American Home Economics Association, Washington, D.C.

prevalent in the central decision of wife's employment than in the other two decisions.

Satellite decisions are by definition linked to central decisions; satellite decisions may also be linked to each other. Some decisions are linked together dependently and others independently; with independent linkage, one decision may occur before or after another.[52]

Decision-Making Patterns

There is much research on who makes certain decisions and on how many decisions are made within the household setting. Discussion precedes many decisions and the influence of either spouse may not be clearly defined; the research focuses on who makes the final decision.[53] Because the wife has been the one interviewed in many studies, often as a matter of expediency and cost, questions have been raised about the wife

---

52. Plonk, p. 790.
53. Robert O. Blood, Jr. and D. M. Wolfe, *Husbands and Wives: The Dynamics of Married Living* (Glencoe, Ill.: The Free Press, 1960), p. 20.

as the only source of information about decision making and other aspects of family life.[54]

Following a 1960 Detroit study, a number of cross-cultural studies in Tokyo, Louvain, Paris, and Athens found many similarities, even with sampling differences and modifications in questions about decisions due to cultural differences:

"The husband's job is conspicuously his business; whether the wife should leave home and go to work is more of mutual concern. Life insurance is a question of high finance with a masculine cast. Food budgets, clothes, and the children's spending money, on the other hand, are questions of low finance, which fall in the wife's domain along with child-rearing questions generally. The overall pattern suggests a division of labor between husband and wife in decisions relevant to their roles in the household structure. However, the family vacation and the family home affect both partners heavily and are essentially joint decisions."[55]

A number of factors influence husband-wife decision making: husband's power or role in decision making generally increases with his educational level, occupational prestige, and the family size.[56] Buddhists, other non-Judeo-Christian religions, and Catholics are above average in husband's decision power. Among races, the husband's power is greatest in Oriental couples and least in black families.[57] The husband's decision power decreases with his age (except for 60–69 years) and, therefore, with length of marriage.[58]

Where the *decision power* is about equal for husband and wife, the wife's health and health behavior are positively affected, according to one study. Regardless of the family's socioeconomic status, the lifetime health level,

54. Constantina Safilios Rothschild, "Family Sociology or Wives' Family Sociology? A Cross-Cultural Examination of Decision-Making," *Journal of Marriage and the Family* 31 (May 1969): 290-301.

55. Robert O. Blood, Jr. and Reuben Hill, "Comparative Analysis of Family Power Structure: Problems of Measurement and Interpretation," in *Families in East and West,* eds. Reuben Hill and Rene Konig (The Hague: Mouton & Co., 1970), p. 534.

56. Frederick L. Campbell, "Family Growth and Variation in Family Role Structure," *Journal of Marriage and the Family* 32 (February, 1970): 48; Richard Centers, Bertram H. Raven, and Aroldo Rodrigues, Conjugal Power Structure: A Re-examination," *American Sociological Review* 36 (April, 1971): 273-274. Robert O. Blood, Jr., and D. M. Wolfe, *Husbands and Wives: The Dynamics of Married Living* (Glencoe, Ill.: The Free Press, 1960), pp. 30–31.

57. Centers, Raven, and Rodrigues, p. 273.

58. Centers, Raven, and Rodrigues, p. 273.

present health level, health-care practices, the use of preventive services, and total use of services are higher for wives with equal power than for wives with unequal power—whether the power is stronger or weaker than the husband's. Where there is equal decision power, the husband's total use of health services and health knowledge are the only positively associated factors of those considered.[59]

The types of decisions and number of major decisions vary with the length of marriage. The average number of major financial decisions decreases with length of marriage, from .97 decisions per year for 0–4 years of marriage to .27 for 40–44 years of marriage, with an upturn to .48 decisions yearly in marriages of 45 and more years.[60] Decisions concerning the husband's occupation constitute the major portion of decisions in each of the groups by years of marriages.

Couples interviewed every six months since 1968 have changed who looks after the payment of bills, who keeps track of expenditures, and who decides on the use of money at the end of the pay period. The shift was predominantly from joint action to the wife.[61]

If accompanying satellite decisions could be investigated, this pattern of major, or perhaps central, decisions might reflect a clearer picture of total decisions.

On the whole, patterns of decision making of husbands and wives are remarkably similar in different countries and under given circumstances. Major financial decisions tend to be the husband's or joint decisions, and those relating to household operation tend to be the wife's. The husband's power increases with his education and occupational status (except professional), but decreases with years of marriage. The number of major financial decisions decreases over the years of marriage. Within these general patterns there is wide variation, however, and many additional evidences of equality and/or nonpatterning of decision roles. Growth in managerial decision making suggests that roles based on internal

---

59. Lois Pratt, "Conjugal Organization and Health," *Journal of Marriage and the Family* 34 (February 1972): 89.
60. Cleo Fitzsimmons, Dorothy A. Larery, and Edward J. Metzen, "Major Financial Decisions and Crises in the Family Life Span," North Central Regional Research Publication No. 208 (Lafayette, Ind.: Purdue University Agricultural Experiment Station, 1971), p. 24.
61. Robert Ferber and Lucy Chao Lee, "Husband-Wife Influence in Family Purchasing Behavior," *The Journal of Consumer Research* 1 (June 1974): 43–45.

factors—skills, available time, workload, and interest—will reduce such patterning.

COMMUNICATING

Our daily lives are filled with communicating, just as they are with decision making. Effective communicating, in fact, precedes and contributes to effective decision making. We convey verbal and nonverbal messages and receive messages from other people and other systems through many different channels. *Communication* is the process of transmitting messages from a source to a receiver.[62] *Messages* are stimuli flowing from a source to a receiver.[63] For an individual's response, such messages may be stimulated from within or from external sources. Messages direct from other persons are the focus of the discussion that follows.

Interpersonal communication is "the process of an individual stimulating meaning in the mind of another through a message."[64] The simplified diagram of interpersonal communication shown in Figure 5-5 illustrates an involvement of two persons, their internal consideration of a message,

FIGURE 5.5 *Communication at the interpersonal level.*

Source: Ronald G. Havelock, *Planning for Innovation* (Ann Arbor, Mich.: Institute for Social Research, The University of Michigan, 1969), pp. 2–8. Reprinted with permission of the publisher, Center for Research on Utilization of Scientific Knowledge, Institute for Social Research, The University of Michigan, Ann Arbor, Michigan.

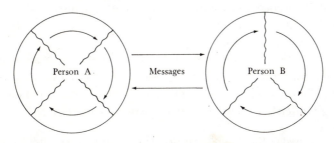

62. Everett M. Rogers with F. Floyd Shoemaker, *Communication of Innovations* (New York: The Free Press, 1971), p. 23.
63. James C. McCroskey, Carol E. Larson, and Mark L. Knapp, *An Introduction to Interpersonal Communication* (Englewood Cliffs, N. J.: Prentice-Hall, Inc., 1971), p. 4.
64. McCroskey, Larson, and Knapp, p. 3.

message barriers, and message transmittal. The message encounters internal barriers which must be permeated if the message is to get through. Individuals differ in recognizing needs, in isolating problems, in searching for solutions, and in actions and experiences leading to solutions.[65] Persons, therefore, receive messages differently.

Differences can form barriers, as in the following report by a resident visitor to a commune:

Elaine played the guitar, singing the melancholy Gordon Lightfoot song, "Early Morning Rain." I could empathize with her but the gap between us was so great that there seemed no way to tell her that I felt the same way she did. I tried to build intellectual bridges between us. We talked. Of her ambivalence toward men, of Christian ritual, carnal love, community, but I was always driving her into some . . . intellectual corner and she was always dodging me. I still pressed on, boring into her brain to get a photograph of it and match it with mine so that the differences could be analytically reconciled.[66]

The illustration mentions gaps or barriers "so great that there seemed no way to tell her that I felt the same way she did." *Barriers* prevent messages from getting through and divide the "inside" from the "outside" of a system.[67] Specific interpersonal barriers are differences in self-image and values, discrepancies in situation and role perception, and discrepancies in age, sex, status, or language. Each of these is included in Figure 5.6.

The familiar "generation gap" has been questioned, with the proposal that differences within one generation can be as wide or wider than between generations with divergent social classes.[68] High-school class reunions reveal differences in experiences, values, status, and situation perception, which form barriers even in a homogenous age group that shares common early experiences.

Idea communication occurs most frequently between senders and receivers who have similar beliefs, values, education, social status, and other attributes. If a person is free to interact with any of several persons, there is a strong tendency to select someone most like himself.[69]

---

65. Ronald G. Havelock, *Planning for Innovation* (Ann Arbor, Mich.: Institute for Social Research, The University of Michigan, 1969), pp. 2–12, 2–13.
66. Robert Houriet, *Getting Back Together* (New York: Coward, McCann & Geoghegan, Inc., 1971), p. 67.
67. Havelock, p. 2–14.
68. Gus Tyler, "Generation Gap or Gap Within a Generation?" *Dissent* 18 (April 1971): 145–54
69. Rogers with Shoemaker, p. 14.

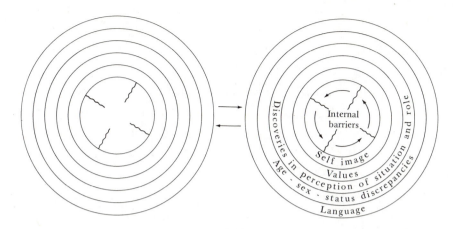

FIGURE 5.6 *Interpersonal communication barriers.*

Source: Ronald G. Havelock, *Planning for Innovation* (Ann Arbor, Mich.: Institute for Social Research, The University of Michigan 1969) pp. 2–18. (Slight modification) Reprinted with permission of the publisher, Center for Research on the Utilization of Scientific Knowledge, Institute for Social Research, The University of Michigan, Ann Arbor, Michigan.

The communication process has been defined as the process by which messages are transmitted from a source to a receiver. Interpersonal barriers, technical problems, and the reasons to communicate and receive affect message sending and receiving. When the individuals concerned have little motivation to either send or receive, communication becomes difficult. Figure 5.7 shows the communication process. An important feature of the illustration is the feed-back or effect of communication. Communication is a decidely two-way occurrence.

Technical problems, such as noise, may interfere with communication and are noted in Figure 5.7. *Noise* is communication interference. Noise can be separated into three types—syntactic, semantic, and pragmatic.

Syntactic noise is a structural disparity between a sent and a received message.[70] An intended compliment may be taken as a criticism when an instructor says that a student's paper is better than expected.

Semantic noise is ambiguity in denotation or connotation of a message.[71] A student, the sender, may seek "help on his files," intending to arrange

---

70. Russell L. Ackoff and Fred E. Emery, *On Purposeful Systems* (Chicago: Aldine-Atherton, 1972), p. 182.
71. Ackoff and Emery, p. 182.

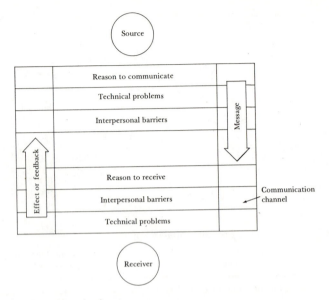

FIGURE 5.7 *The communication process.*

Source: Ronald G. Havelock, *Planning for Innovation* (Ann Arbor, Michigan: Institute for Social Research, The University of Michigan, 1969), p. 1–13 (Source of concepts only.) Reprinted with permission of the publisher, Center for Research on the Utilization of Scientific Knowledge, Institute for Social Research, The University of Michigan, Ann Arbor, Michigan.

and categorize papers in his study room; another student, who is the receiver, and accustomed to working with hand tools, may anticipate a job of "replacing handles on a file or repairing a drawer in the file."

Pragmatic noise has been called anything not produced by a sender in his message or by the environment surrounding the message, but that nevertheless interferes with communication.[72] For example, if a person smells burning cookies while receiving a telephone message, he may not hear or understand what the sender is saying.

Effective communication is important in the personal and managerial subsystems of the family system. The significance of verbal and nonverbal interpersonal communication in a small system such as the family is no less than in large systems such as the university. The proportion of verbal and nonverbal communication may change with the size and age of the system. Families in existence for some time "know" what the other family member

---

72. Ackoff and Emery, p. 182.

wants before he asks. Perhaps many years of meeting common problems also lessen the need to communicate.[73]

Nonverbal communication includes body movements and the use of space.[74] Nonverbal communication in the form of hugs or pats or ruffling of the hair may have particular meaning in a family or group. At the conclusion of the exchange between the visitor to the commune and Elaine, they read together some lines by Thomas Merton. "What was there to say? We hugged and it was said."[75]

Within families, communication can be particularly challenging because of discrepancies in age, in status (between parent and child), and in value differences (as children become teenagers). The amount and quality of communication within families vary widely. Married couples have revealed good and poor communication traits in listening habits, understanding, tone of voice, self-disclosure, and in their handling of anger and differences.[76] The variation probably results from basic differences or barriers such as self-image and values.

Family communication patterns are related to social class, with more communication in families with higher social positions.[77] However, in another study of better-educated families, satisfaction with communication lessened with years of marriage.[78] Increases in father's affective communication in low socioeconomic families were related to increases in education and per capita income.[79] Mother's communication behavior in these families increased with the unemployment of the father. Communication within families is also related to race, with blacks communicating least and Oriental and Caucasian families communicating more (Figure 5.8).

Increases in communication are associated with families of higher social positions, higher education, higher income, and Caucasian and Oriental races.

73. Reuben Hill, *Family Development in Three Generations* (Cambridge, Mass.: Schenkman Publishing Co., Inc., 1970), p. 50.
74. Edward T. Hall, *The Hidden Dimension* (Garden City, N. Y.: Doubleday, 1966).
75. Houriet, p. 67.
76. Millard J. Bienvenu, Sr., "Measurement of Marital Communication," *The Family Coordinator* 19 (January 1970): 26.
77. Mary C. Regan, "Family Patterns and Social Class," Research Monograph #5 (Davis, Calif.: University of California, 1967), p. 29.
78. Mirra Komarovsky, *Blue-Collar Marriage* (New York: Random House , Inc., 1962), p. 204.
79. Sister Madeleine Wheeler, "Communication Behavior and Task Collaboration in Families of Low Socio-economic Levels," The Pennsylvania State University, Ph.D. dissertation, 1971.

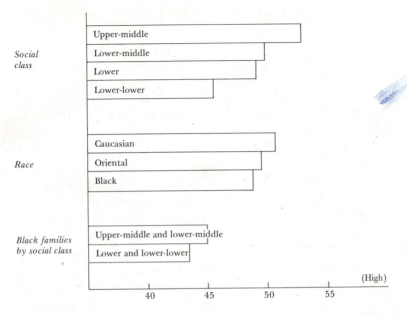

Mean standard score for communication

FIGURE 5.8 *The effect of social class and race on communications.*

Source: Adapted from Mary C. Regan, "Family Patterns and Social Class," Research Monograph #5 (Davis, Calif.: University of California, 1967), pp. 66–67.

Certain situations provide a setting for increased communication. Family interaction has been studied as the time and number of people in shared activities in relation to the number of family members.[80] The total interaction score increased, and therefore the potential for communication increased as follows:

1. on weekends compared to weekdays,
2. during mornings and afternoons compared to evenings,
3. during school vacation compared with other seasons,
4. with decrease in the time children spent in school,
5. with increase in social activities.[81]

---

80. Alice J. Davey, "Relationship of Family Interaction to Family Environment," Michigan State University, Ph.D. dissertation, 1971, p. 9.
81. Davey, pp. 50–58.

Effective communication is particularly important in family problem solving in situations where solutions are not immediately apparent.[82] Two proposals about problem solving stress the importance of communication:

1. "Effective family problem solving requires open channels of communication for all family members competent to contribute to a problem solution." A corollary to the first proposal is:
   "Effective family problem solving requires that the group remain sufficiently flexible so as to admit additional members into critical communication networks at such stages in the family life cycle—when they are able to make appropriate contributions."
2. "Effective family problem solving requires the ability of families to communicate and evaluate conflicting ideas without regard to the status of the persons initiating the communication."[83]

In a study comparing working-class and middle-class families of three societies, the "lack of communication interferred with the pooling of information and hence accounts for part of the working-class families' difficulty in solving the problem."[84]

Communication can affect the type of decision making in a family. Three types of decision making are considered here—consensual, accommodation, and de facto (Figure 5.9). *Consensual decision making* involves communication which concludes with all family members giving equal assent and all feeling equally committed to the decision.[85] For some families, consensus in decision making is rare.

The second type of decision making, for which communication has special implications, is *accommodation.* Agreement comes through accepting the desire of a dominant person when all the views are not reconciled.[86] Two effects of accommodated decisions are that commitment to the decision may be conditional and that there is a dominant role of one member, specifically the person whose desires were most closely followed in the decision.

---

82. Irving Tallman, "The Family As a Small Problem Solving Group," *Journal of Marriage and the Family* 32 (February 1970): 95.
83. Tallman, p. 97.
84. Murray A. Straus, "Communication, Creativity, and Problem-solving Ability of Middle and Working-Class Families in Three Societies," The *American Journal of Sociology* 73 (January 1968): 429.
85. Ralph H. Turner, *Family Interaction* (New York: John Wiley & Sons, Inc., 1970), p. 98.
86. Turner, p. 98.

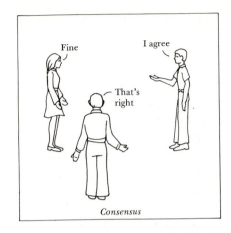

FIGURE 5.9 *Communication in consensus, accommodation, and de facto decision making.*

De facto decisions tend to follow from lack of effective consideration or communication of alternatives: ". . . agreement is by the absence of dissent rather than by active assent, and more important, commitment is by the course of events rather than by acceptance."[87] Sometimes the decision not to attend a class is de facto—a student looks at the clock and sees that she has overslept and will be late for class anyway. Or, in the case of a family, discussion of whether to go to the hockey game, as the sons want to do, or

---

87. Turner, p. 99.

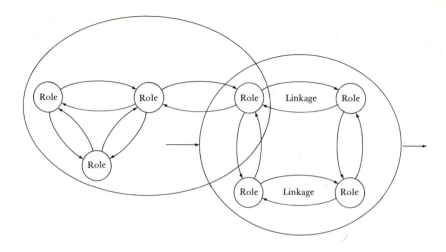

FIGURE 5.10 *Communication linkages between roles within systems and between systems.*

Source: Adapted from Ronald G. Havelock, *Planning for Innovation* (Ann Arbor, Mich.: Institute for Social Research, The University of Michigan, 1969), pp. 1–3. Reprinted with permission of the publisher, Center for Research on the Utilization of Scientific Knowledge, Institute for Social Research, The University of Michigan, Ann Arbor, Michigan.

to go to the movies, as the rest of the family wants to do, goes on until it is past time for the start of the hockey game. De facto decision making has taken place, and the family can only go to the movie.

Communication between social systems is important to the family because of the complex, overlapping social structures to which the family is related (Figure 5.10). The illustration shows one person in two systems. An example is a woman who is both a teacher in a county school system and a wife and mother in the family system. Individuals are shown as the systems' components, another approach to the managerial and personal functions of family subsystems already emphasized.

Some persons and systems develop *linkages* or fixed interaction patterns forming bonds among the systems.[88] Linkages develop between persons with different roles in the system—husband and wife, mother and child, doctor and patient, teacher and student. Communication flows at each linkage point.

Communication, whether interpersonal or between social systems, involves *interface,* the common boundary of two systems. The interface between systems exists "whether the two are interrelated or not, whether

---

88. Havelock, pp. 2–14.

they are in conflict or not, and whether or not messages are passing between them."[89] (The openness of systems was described earlier—regulations, hostility, financial requirements, or physical conditions may form barriers to openness. Communication with other systems is influenced by these barriers at the interface.

In the case of interpersonal communication, the interface may be the common boundary between two individuals in the same family. The interface between families and other systems varies widely with the family. To a low-income family a bank or a savings and loan institution in the financial system may seem to have an almost impenetrable boundary and be inaccessible. A higher-income family is not likely to sense such a limitation.

Communication within the family and between the family and other systems is important in meeting the demands placed on the family and taken on by them. Communication seems particularly facilitating in problem solving. Patterns of communication vary among families by social class, education, income, and race. The level and nature of communication can influence all aspects of management and can contribute limiting or expansive potentialities for managerial activity.

DEFINITIONS

Decision making is the choice or resolution of alternatives.

Intuition is an unconscious or subconscious process that yields an immediate decision, bypassing well-defined, conscious steps.

Decision rules are "a uniform directive indicating a clear choice among properly specified alternatives."[90]

Certainty is complete knowledge of consequences of a decision; *uncertainty* is the lack of this knowledge.

Probability is the relative possibility that a particular situation will occur.

Objective probability is the ratio of the number of actual occurrences to the total number of possible occurrences.[91]

Subjective probability is a measure of the decision maker's belief in the outcome.

Risk is the hazard or chance of a loss.

---

89. Havelock, pp. 2–9.
90. Miller, p. 28.
91. *The Random House Dictionary of the English Language,* ed. Jess Stein (New York: Random House, Inc., 1966), p. 1146.

Nonprogrammed decisions are novel, unstructured, and consequential.

Programmed decisions are repetitive and routine to the extent that a definite procedure has been worked out for handling them each time they occur.

Social decisions focus on the types of individual roles, content of the roles, and the integration of the roles into a consistent self.

Economic decisions are based on allocation and exchange rules and processes, relating to resource use.

Central decisions are decision maker's crucial choices.

Satellite decisions follow central decisions to complete the action of the initial decision.

Decision power is a measure of the relative authority in specific decisions and the degree of authority shared equally between husband and wife, in the same decisions.

Communication is the process of transmitting messages from a source to a receiver.

Messages are stimuli flowing from a source to a receiver.

Interpersonal communication is "the process of an individual stimulating meaning in the mind of another through a message."[92]

Barriers prevent messages from getting through and divide the "inside" from the "outside" of a system.

Noise is communication interference.

Syntactic noise is a structural disparity between a sent and a received message.

Semantic noise is ambiguity in a message's denotation or connotation.

Pragmatic noise is anything not produced by a sender in his message.

Linkage is a fixed interaction pattern forming bonds among the systems.

Interface is the common boundary of two systems.

---

92. McCroskey, Larson, and Knapp, p. 4.

Values, Demands, and Resources

6.

The simplest definition of any managerial activity is the "judicious use of means to accomplish an end," [1] or, more personally, "using what you have to get what you want." [2] Both definitions identify the necessary essentials: goals and resources plus a way to interrelate them so that the end results coincide with the objectives. The system components provide the framework for management, and values provide the underlying meanings and continuity for managerial decisions and actions. The first section of this chapter deals with values and their contributions to both resources and demand considerations in management.

Goal and event demands, inputs that elicit managerial responses, are discussed after the overview of values. Goals, as value-based objectives that provide specific direction for management, are further clarified. The significance of unanticipated events as sources of demands of the managerial system is then considered.

Properties of resources and the ways they interrelate and complement each other to meet demands are topics of the concluding section. The role of resources in the valuing process is a fundamental consideration. In short, this chapter focuses on the interrelation of meaning and means.

1. *Webster's Third International Dictionary* (Springfield, Mass.: G. C. Merriam Company, 1965), p. 1372.
2. Ella M. Cushman, *Management in Homes* (New York: The Macmillan Company, 1945).

VALUES

Values encompass all areas of human thought and action and are strategic in the interrelationships of the family system with its environment. Values provide the underlying meanings that give continuity to all decisions and actions. In the managerial context, values are meanings that indicate what is desirable and has worth to the manager. Management contributes to value clarification as we respond to and affirm worth in day-to-day personal affairs. The concept of values may be further clarified by a consideration of their nature, characteristics, and content.

Nature of Values

The values held by persons may be either relative or absolute in nature. The opportunity for a relevant response to new situations increases with a preponderance of relative values. *Absolute values* remain independent of surrounding conditions, while *relative values* depend on their context for interpretation. Individual and group values are more responsive to a new situation if they are more relative than absolute, because relative values are open to new alternatives. However, relative values are more difficult to identify and clarify.

The more relative a person's values, the broader his managerial potential. Conversely, the person who maintains absolute values rather than relative ones reduces alternatives and narrows the managerial potential. Absolute values also simplify responses to many demands. Some individuals and groups choose simplified lifestyles through high commitment to certain absolute values. An example is the Amish "religious ways of life dedicated to nonconformity to all worldly things."[3] Formal schooling beyond the eighth grade is rejected. The vocational training of boys for farming and of girls for homemaking is an unchanging pattern.

Fletcher's opposite position from the theological perspective suggests that love is the only absolute, or ultimate, value on the relative-to-absolute scale. All other values are relative and subject to love.[4] He acknowledges a common preference for absolute values to simplify personal decisions: "Many people prefer to fit reality to rules rather than vice versa."[5]

---

3. Stephan Arons, "Compulsory Education," *Saturday Review* 55 (January 15, 1972): 52.
4. Joseph Fletcher, *Moral Responsibility* (Philadelphia: The Westminister Press, 1967).
5. Fletcher, p. 25.

In reality, changing situations may foster a shift from an absolute position on the continuum to a more relative one. Less-developed societies have more absolute values and stable frameworks for decisions and actions. Richard Erdoes relates an example among the Sioux Indians:

I think of a young Sioux I know whose family was preparing a giveaway feast. He went to the trading post for enough bread, meat, and coffee to feed 50 or 60 people. "We'll pay you when we get the lease money in two months," he told the trader.

"You'll pay me now," said the trader, who was a new man in the area.

"You know I can't pay you now," said the Sioux. "The trader before you always gave us credit."

"He went broke," said the trader.

"This is a religious ceremony," said the Sioux. "I'll have to take the stuff, whether you like it or not. Watch what I take and write it down. I'll pay you when I can." And the Indian took what he needed and loaded it onto his old pickup.

The trader called the police, and now my young friend is doing time for robbery. He can't understand. Neither can his family.[6]

The value of the religious ceremony with the food for guests was unwavering and gave no alternative solution.

Situations change with increasing technology and industrialization and values have to be reexamined. Predictions of changes in values by the year 2000 anticipate the influence of societal factors and the relative nature of values (Table 6.1).

A relative approach to value interpretation does not minimize the need for value clarification. Clear values promote consistent choices and adaptation to changing situations;[7] they can help eliminate undesirable alternatives and give meaning to important ones.

Values generally held to be important may not be important in every situation; there is some relativity in most general values. Value rankings for the selection of a family living environment, for example, may differ from the general rankings of a group of families.[8]

---

6. Richard Erdoes, "My Travels with Medicine Man John Lame Deer," *Smithsonian* 4 (May 1973): 36.
7. Alvin Toffler, *Future Shock* (New York: Random House, Inc., 1970), p. 369.
8. Carol B. Meeks and Ruth E. Deacon, "Values and Planning in the Selection of a Family Living Environment," *Journal of Home Economics* 64 (January 1972): 15.

TABLE 6.1
Societal factors and predicted value changes.

Societal factors	Predicted value changes	Societal factors	Predicted value changes
Urban crowding	Devaluation of privacy Strengthening of small-group values Upgrading of physical security, stability, public order Upgrading of tolerance Upgrading of beauty, heightening of esthetic values	Improved transportation and communication	Upgrading of mankind-oriented values Growth of cosmopolitanism and strengthening of internationalism
Political-economic equalization	Downgrading of equalitarian values Erosion of idealism	Advance of automation	Downgrading of progress and material values Upgrading of handicrafts, workmanship, skilled and unskilled services Explosion of the "problem of leisure" myth and the "spectre" of mass technological unemployment
Expansion of welfare	Devaluation of economic security Erosion of initiative Flight from responsibility Growing ambivalence to authority Rising expectations for public economic support Ambivalence about physical comfort Reappraisal of public service	Onset of the "big brother" state Advances of medical techniques	Upgrading of democratic values Ambivalence to authority Weakening of defenses against physical discomfort in human life Weakening of family values—less dependence on husband and wife for procreation
Proliferation and sophistication of mass destruction weapons	Downgrading of traditional national pride Upgrading of mankind-oriented values	Educational advances	Disillusionment with education Intensifying of value stresses due to gap between educational fitness and "life"

Value rank	
General	*Housing*
1. Economic	1. Social
2. Personal	2. Economic
3. Social	3. Personal
(tie)	
Esthetic	

Values may be absolute for some situations and relative for others. For example, an absolute value for sharing may mean an unvarying portion of income is allocated to organized charities, but there may be openness to sharing funds with roommates or acquaintances. The values held to be important and their absolute or relative interpretations represent the meanings that guide an individual's thoughts and actions. The basic internalized values evolve over time. The greater their relative nature, the more they give general, rather than specific, directions to actions.

Because basic values are rooted in one's evolving personality, they are identified with the personal subsystem of the family system. From this perspective, values guide managerial behavior since they provide the orientation for goal development. Management is an exercise in evaluation in response to external and internal influences. Decisions continually influence the relative stability or change in an individual's basic values.

Characteristics of Values

Value characteristics significant to management are those that help to clarify the interactions of demands and resources. Their intrinsic-extrinsic meanings, their general or specific scope, and their subject-object-relational qualities are important in explaining how values give direction and promote internal consistency in managerial behavior.

Intrinsic-Extrinsic Meanings. Intrinsic value is the desirable and self-sufficient quality of an experience: the joy of watching a beautiful sunset or seeing a flower bloom. Intrinsic values are an aspect of the personal system since they are ultimate in their meaning or they are ends in themselves. Extrinsic value is the meaning or worth derived from the relation of one thing to another. An extrinsic value depends on or is instrumental to a purpose. Because of management's functional role, extrinsic values are related more to managerial processes.

A potential source of confusion about values in relation to management is that they are guides to decisions and actions, and, as met demands, they are also the essence of the decisions and actions. Values are circular in this

143

sense. Management processes lead to extrinsic values by meeting as nearly as possible the goals that are value based.

Examples of intrinsic and extrinsic values and goals interrelationships are given in Table 6.2. Goals help direct specific actions consistent with either extrinsic or intrinsic values. The goal to be employed part time may be consistent with the extrinsic value of helping to earn a desired level of living, which in turn contributes to the intrinsic value of pleasure of achievement. Goals reflect intrinsic or extrinsic values in the objectives to be met and promote extrinsic values as objectives are met.

General-Specific Scope. Values that are fulfilled or satisfied in a single action are specific. Values prevailing over time and requiring a number of actions, each inadequate in its ability to satisfy, are general in scope. Intrinsic or extrinsic values may be general or specific. On a bright spring day, a desire to see forsythia in bloom (intrinsic) is specific. The need to remain on a job for two years to receive full retirement is specific and extrinsic. Both needs are satisfied by specific acts.

An example of a general, more pervasive value is knowledge, which is not fulfilled by the accumulation of certain facts or the achievement of a given level of education. A sense of security is not fulfilled by the purchase of a new set of tires or a new insurance policy, although either purchase may help to promote feelings of security. A general value may encompass an extensive series of activities, as in the case of a medical missionary

TABLE 6.2
Examples of intrinsic and extrinsic values and goals.

Intrinsic values	Extrinsic values	Goals
Pleasure in achievement	Earning or helping to achieve a desired level of living	To be a foreman To be employed part time To be a gourmet cook
Sense of security	Having assets to meet needs	To have life insurance To own some mutual fund shares To have a savings account
Sense of trustworthiness	Maintaining good credit rating	To meet financial commitments

144

whose preparation for service may require many years of study, experience, and personal growth. General values are sometimes called higher-order value because so many actions build toward them.

A managerial activity may serve one or more values at any level of generality or specificity. A decision may be complex because more general or underlying values influence the goal choices. The selection of a university may be very complex when a number of important general values influence the choice.

Subjective-Objective Components. The subjective and objective components of values parallel the management concepts of goals and resources. The subjective component is indicated by a person's needs, wants, interests, aims, or purposes: his or her goals. Accompanying each goal is a set of intrinsic or extrinsic value criteria which need to be met (Figure 6.1). The objective component is represented by anything capable of meeting the criteria.[9] Available resources are relevant to the extent that their attributes or properties coincide with the criteria that are prescribed. The evaluative criteria are matched with the attributes or properties of the

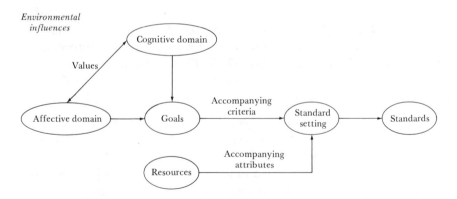

FIGURE 6.1 *Relation of cognitive and affective domain, goals, standard setting, resources, and standards.*

9. D. W. Gotshalk, *Patterns of Good and Evil* (Urbana, Ill.: University of Illinois Press, 1963), pp. 66–81.

145

resources as advantageously as possible in the standard-setting function in planning, and to some extent the checking function in implementing.

A student who wishes to play a musical instrument illustrates the subjective-objective aspects of values. The interest in learning to play is a long-range goal, perhaps leading to a more specific goal of being in the band. The chance to be with friends, the prestige, the enjoyment of music—all may be values underlying the goal of band membership.

Accompanying considerations, such as a preference for a given instrument and certain musical sounds, are part of the subjective component in specifying what instrument will be purchased. The material, style, or size of the instrument are properties that are aspects of the objective component. By relating the subjective and objective components, the standards are set for the instrument by the student. In addition, the parents may try to balance the cost with an estimate of talent and interest. The final choice is an instrument with desired qualitative and quantitative characteristics, reflecting as fully as possible the standards determined in planning, considering the available resources.

Content of Values

Value content is the substantive meaning of value judgments in the affective and cognitive domains. The affective content of values is the positive or negative feelings about something. The cognitive content is the perception of values, goals, and related criteria as bases for interpretation of situations and their potentialities. The affective domain of values is associated most directly with the personal system and cognitive domain with the managerial system, although both are present in each system.

Affective Domain. The evolution of values in the affective domain is an internalizing process. Evidences of incomplete or tentative adoption of desired behavior comes first, then there is a more complete adoption. Early experiences through which values are internalized include those of receiving and responding to situations with expressive or affective overtones. Through continued evaluations, leanings toward particular value orientations occur. Gradually the basis for an organized value system emerges and grows into an integrated value complex as the internalization process is completed.[10]

---

10. David R. Krathwohl, Benjamin S. Bloom, and Bertram B. Masia, *A Taxonomy of Educational Objectives: Handbook II: The Affective Domain* (New York: David McKay, 1964), pp. 29, 37.

To illustrate, a couple married for eight years and with two children review their lifestyle and values. He is a civil-rights lawyer and she works in an architect's office. They now have a combined income of over $35,000. The wife, Judy, says that she and Sandy "have only recently realized and accepted their different backgrounds and different values about money."

> I have felt with some justification that he thought that I was materialistic. . . . But now I think, yes, I am materialistic and I'm going to continue to be materialistic. . . .

> I mean it does matter to me to feel secure. It matters to me, not to have the things that other people do not necessarily think are the important things, but things that are lovely. The things that I really like, I like to have them, and I no longer choose to feel ashamed to have them, or to want them.[11]

Such recognition and clarification of one's values approach an internal, integrated value system, the highest meaning in the affective domain.

Cognitive Domain. The cognitive domain is based on a hierarchy of concepts from simple to complex: knowledge, comprehension, application, analysis, synthesis, and evaluation.[12] Evaluation is making (value) judgments in relation to some purpose.

Knowledge is acquaintance with facts and principles, but does not include all possible uses or application of levels of cognitive interpretation. Factual knowledge is used in making judgments. The bases for judgment vary with the situation; different situations require different facts.

Facts from an objective study are reliable for specific conditions, changing the situation may alter their usefulness. Knowledge of the values of Zuni Indians who have stayed with their tribe in New Mexico cannot be ascribed to those who have left the tribe.

Managerial processes require a cognitive, or conscious, dimension. As higher levels of cognitive insight and interpretation are reached, information can be used creatively in varying situations, implications can be drawn with increasing accuracy, and possibilities for reformulations into new options are more readily recognized. At the higher levels, the capacity to make satisfactory (value) judgments in relation to underlying purposes and their accompanying criteria becomes well developed. This evaluative

---

11. Tom Huth, "$30,000 a Year 'Permits' Dissatisfaction," *The Washington Post,* May 13, 1973, pp. A1, A20.
12. Benjamin S. Bloom and a Committee of College and University Examiners, *A Taxonomy of Educational Objectives: Handbook I: The Cognitive Domain* (New York: David McKay, 1956).

capability is shared at the higher levels of both the affective and the cognitive domains.

Management can take objective account of the affective dimension in a demand situation, but managerial components do not explain the processes by which experience takes on positive or negative content. Most values have both affective and cognitive content, somewhere between the extremes of a continuum, and involve continuous interaction between the personal and managerial subsystems. Solely affective behavior is likely to involve the managerial subsystem only to a limited extent, as in self-fulfilling interpersonal relationships; likewise, factors that are solely cognitive are unlikely to involve the personal subsystem extensively in a managerial choice.

Management can, however, enhance the expressive response to intrinsic values. For instance, managerial activity may create a sumptuous meal by planning and implementing its preparation and serving. Management's function is instrumental in attaining goals based on either intrinsic or extrinsic values. Extrinsic values are probably the most common bases.

The emphases of the two interacting subsystems on values may be characterized as follows:

Value quality	*Personal subsystem*	*Managerial subsystem*
Meaning	Intrinsic	Extrinsic
Content	Affective	Cognitive

In summary, the overview of value relations to management has had three major purposes: to indicate the importance of their relative nature to managerial considerations; to identify their characteristics important to managerial decisions about the use of resources to meet demands; and to identify the interactions of the personal and managerial subsystems in the changing affective-cognitive dimensions of value content. Values give stability and continuity to management decisions in the face of change; through management, values respond meaningfully to change. A more specific discussion of resource and demand inputs to the managerial system follows this background on the pervasive role of values throughout management.

GOALS AS DEMANDS

Goals give direction and purpose to values. Goals as input to the managerial subsystem are anticipated ends; fulfilled goals as output come from a series of value judgments in the managerial subsystem. Goals are guidelines for planning, but they do not include specific resource allocation.

For families, value-based objectives arise in the personal subsystem for action in the managerial subsystem. Goals develop from values through reactions, insights, new knowledge, and information feedback from the managerial subsystem and the environment. The value of health becomes a goal to increase physical excercise when one knows the importance of physical fitness for health. The insight may have been gained through friends with health problems.

Fulfilled goals permit changes in values emphases. Acquiring an advanced degree (a met goal demand) allows one to shift emphasis from formal education to economic security. Shifting value emphases after meeting goals may not be easy. Writers describe this difficulty in the Western goal-oriented society:

The worst thing for the individual in such a goal-focused social system is not so much the pains of struggle toward some special aim but the apprehension of bewilderment upon reaching it. Existence, then, amounts to the incessant pursuit of goals which never turn out to be ends but merely the means to continue the competition. It's as if nothing is of value in itself. The sense of always going somewhere (and never actually getting there) is so ingrained into the traditional Western life-pattern that people learn to create obstacles for themselves to overcome . . .

To arrive at some goal and stop the contest is unthinkable; for to stop eternally "becoming" is to begin "being," and simply "to be" isn't in our heritage. To people who are always drawing on the past for traditions and forever focusing on the future as a field for even grander contests, the concept of simply living in the present moment—of "being" in an existential sense—is disorienting and plainly uncomfortable.[13]

Goals are clarified through planning for specific action, especially in setting standards for meeting the goal. The goal to buy a car with air condi-

---

13. William Hedgepeth and Dennis Stock, *The Alternative: Communal Life in New America* (New York: The Macmillan Company, 1970), p. 182.

tioning is sharpened by the standard of having a six- or eight-cyclinder engine. Another way to clarify goals is to examine available resources in relation to the desired objective. The goal of a vacation in Acapulco may have to be revised in favor of a nearby trip after a comparison of the vacation costs with the available money.

Choices among alternative goals can be considered managerially: to rent or buy a house; to go to a movie or take a motorcycle ride; to be an extension worker or a teacher. Goal alternatives are examined during the planning process when the balance between resources and demands is considered. Information obtained during the clarification of goals returns to the personal subsystem for verification or redefinition of values.

Nature of Goals

Understanding the nature of goals helps interpret their influence on other managerial subsystem components. Goals concern resources and actions and are integrally related to values. Three qualities of goals are important: duration, continuity, and independence.

Duration.   Long- and short-term goals differ in the length of time required to reach the goal. Goals are long-term when resources must be accumulated. (A father intends to buy a lathe for his workshop "when his ship comes in.") Goals are long-term when accomplishing the goal takes a long time regardless of resources; (to specialize in radiology requires several years' work beyond the M.D. degree). Short-term goals help increase goal tangibility, "bridging the gap between hopes and expectation, and providing benchmarks for measuring progress."[14]

In achieving long-term goals, short-term goals are often developed. A long-term goal of getting ahead in a career may lead to a short-term goal of attending a workshop for career development. A long-term goal of maintaining the family dwelling may precede a short-term goal to replace the front steps with the specific standard of four concrete steps.

Are some families or individuals oriented primarily to short- or long-term goals? For many years, the middle-class American subordinated gratification in sex, marriage, and material goods to educational achievements and occupational pursuits. Much has changed. Technology has mass produced material goods including contraceptive aids; economic gains permit parental assistance to children; and credit makes purchases

---

14. William H. Newman, Charles E. Summer, and E. Kirby Warren, *The Process of Management* (Englewood Cliffs, N. J.: Prentice-Hall Inc., 1967), pp. 476–77.

readily available for many. Waiting to gratify wants is increasingly open to question.

Present-time orientation, short-term goals, immediate gratification, and concreteness of goals are reported to be characteristics of part of the United States low-income population.[15] Present orientation can be an outcome of inadequate resources for facing the future with confidence. Most persons in the United States probably have a mixture of short- and long-term goals. Personality, family life stage, and economic well-being influence the balance between goals of long and short duration.

Continuity and Change. Some goals require almost continuous effort and attention, such as preparation for classes and attendance, while other goals involve only sporadic (although recurring) attention, such as that given a class project. Meeting goals that require continuous attention can become routinized, an aspect discussed more fully in the chapter on planning.

An event or shifts in resources can change goals, requiring either continuous or sporadic attention. A man injured in intramural sports (an event) faces lifetime wheelchair confinement that may severely alter his career goals.

A young family with an unplanned child may replace former asset accumulation goals with aims for the child's growth and development. Resources available for savings and investment are altered when the wife quits her job to give birth and when child-raising costs are encountered. A family whose child has special problems may replace goals for his educational achievement with goals for the child's self-functioning and independence in daily living.

Independence and Optimization. Although some goals are relatively independent of other goals, many are intermeshed so that the pursuit of one goal affects another. The effect of interdependent goals is similar to a jigsaw puzzle: the puzzle is incomplete without all the interlocking pieces (Figure 6.2).

With interdependent goals, the best solution for one goal may be less than optimal[16] for another goal. The goals of a husband and wife to find satisfying and rewarding work in the same commuting area are

---

15. Lola M. Irelan and Arthur Besner, "Low-income Outlook on Life," in *Low-Income Life Styles,* ed. Lola H. Irelan, U.S. Dept. of Health, Education, and Welfare, Welfare Administration Publication No. 14 (Washington, D. C.: U.S. Government Printing Office, 1968), pp. 1–12.

16. David W. Miller and Martin K. Starr, *The Structure of Human Decisions*(Englewood Cliffs, N. J.: Prentice-Hall, Inc., 1967), p. 48.

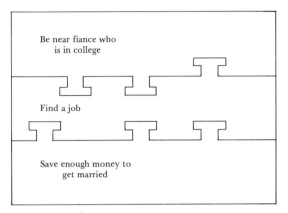

Be near fiance who
is in college

Find a job

Save enough money to
get married

FIGURE 6.2 *Interdependent goals.*

interdependent. The best living location for the husband's work may not be the best for the wife.

An optimal solution can be sub-optimal over time because knowledge of the future is limited. A person who takes a liberal arts college program because of wide interests (an optimal solution at the time) may find the solution sub-optimal upon graduation when available work is in specialized fields.

Goal priorities

Individuals, families, and institutions face multiple goals with similar priorities. In a university setting, both undergraduate and graduate teaching, research, and continuing education may have similar priorities. But obviously no individual, family, or institution can strive for all goals at the same rate of endeavor. When priorities for goals of similar importance cannot be formed, one approach is to compartmentalize decisions related to one goal and to deal with one goal at a time as though the other goals of similar priority did not exist. People who separate career goals from family goals are compartmentalizing. Under some conditions, compartmentalization may be the only method of dealing with goals that have similar priorities, but the interdependence of many goals may sometimes make compartmentalization difficult.

Over the years, goal priorities for families and individuals change, even though values remain relatively stable. Family needs and resources affect aims. Early years of marriage are times of intensive goal setting[17] when there is major emphasis on financial security, education and housing-environment goals. Couples in developmental years having responsibilities for their children's well-being report a high incidence of level of living, education, financial security, housing-environment, family relations, and management goals. Level of living and housing-environment goals continue high in the early and middle years of marriage and into the retirement years when health and family relations and management goals are also high.[18] Goals themselves and priorities as set by individuals and the family differ due to age disparities and the involvement of family members in other systems.

TABLE 6.3
Combinations of goal agreement by family members.

Number of persons agreeing on goal	Family member			
	Mother	*Father*	*Son 16 years*	*Daughter 7 years*
Two	X	X		
Two	X		X	
Two	X			X
Two		X	X	
Two		X		X
Two			X	X
Three	X	X	X	
Three	X	X		X
Three	X		X	X
Three		X	X	X
Four	X	X	X	X

X denotes persons agreeing on a goal.

17. Cleo Fitzsimmons, Dorothy A. Larery, and Edward J. Metzen, "Major Financial Decisions and Crises in the Family Life Span," North Central Regional Research Publication 208 (Lafayette, Ind.: Purdue University Agricultural Experiment Station, 1971), p. 48.
18. Fitzsimmons, Larery, and Metzen, p. 15.

The family's many goals with each member's separate priorities make "family" goal consensus difficult. Some families never agree on goals, but work toward goals important to individual members or combinations of individuals. Table 6.3 gives combinations of goal agreement among four family members on one goal. Agreement between particular family members may be considerably more likely—for example, agreement between mother and father may be more likely than agreement on a goal by the son (16 years) and daughter (7 years).

Lack of family-member consensus on goals and goal priorities can lead to conflict. If a father can meet his goal of a new position in his firm only by moving to another city, all family members may not agree on goals and goal priorities. The children's objectives may be to continue in the same school system with their current friends; the mother's goals may be to keep the family intact under one roof and, at the same time, to increase their level of living. These objectives may or may not have high priority for other family members. If the father's personal achievement goal is accompanied by a goal to meet his family's needs, he might be more open to a review of the family's varying objectives than if achievement were his primary goal.

For long-term goals, one study shows that consensus among young couples was higher for families with a professionally employed husband than among middle- and working-class families. The goals and values of families with professionally employed husband are reported in Table 6.4, by order of importance for both husband and wife.

EVENTS AS DEMANDS

Events are pertinent, unanticipated, or unforeseen occurrences that require action. Events are of two types: those with no prior expectations and those which contradict prior expectations.[19] Having a baby, whether planned or not, is an expected occurrence, but an unanticipated premature birth contradicts prior expectations. Most accidents are events, since no conscious prior expectations exist.

Families with differing values and resources vary in their recognition of events. The frequency and severity of events they experience also may

---

19. Thomas Mathiesen, "The Unanticipated Event and Astonishment," *Inquiry* 3 (Spring 1960): 3.

TABLE 6.4
Importance of goals and values for families with professionally employed husband.

Goal*	Value	Rank in importance for husband and wife
Satisfy each other's needs Be deeply in love	Affection	1
Have many interests in common Do a lot of things together	Inclusion	2
Know how to make decisions Agree on who does what	Control	3
Have a good income Have a good reputation	Achievement	4

Alan C. Kerckoff, "Status-Related Value Patterns Among Married Couples," *Journal of Marriage and the Family,* 34 (February 1972): 107. Copyright (1972) by National Council on Family Relations. Reprinted by permission.
*Designated by Deacon and Firebaugh as goals; Kerckhoff reported as value items.

vary. Observations suggest that some individuals and families do not anticipate recurrent, predictable occurrences. Other families are skillful in predicting occurrences. These families are aware of the high probability of certain occurrences and manage preventively before they happen.

Families' responses to illness show differences in event recognition. Middle-class families report concern over illness and want to see a doctor in reaction to a symptom, while lower-class families may react in a rather casual manner.[20] Certainly the differences in resources could affect these responses.

Minor events create a need for quick managerial reactions. Having someone accept a last-minute invitation for dinner may elicit hurried planning. The event may be a pleasant one; some persons, in fact, may enjoy " creating" an event to which they must respond.

Many events can be unpleasant—when a person's health or safety is threatened, when a valuable or sentimentally valuable object is damaged or destroyed, and so on.

_____

20. John A. Ross, "Social Class and Medical Care," *Journal of Health and Human Behavior* 3 (Spring 1962): 39.

When an event causes more than one specific response to one situation and is actually a turning point in direction, it is a crisis. A plane crash in a residential area, unpredicted and of low probability, is a crisis event.

Whatever problems the crisis may bring, the family must manage in relation to the changed situation and must react rapidly to the most pressing events. During crisis the family's sense of commitment may be stronger than it is in less dramatic events. Families respond to crises with disorganization, recovery, and reorganization (Figure 6.3). The rate and effectiveness of recovery could vary with such factors as how family members perceive their role, the family life cycle, family composition, and the levels of functioning prior to the crisis.

When a storm damages homes, shopping areas, and schools, actions must be taken quickly to provide shelter and a safe food and water supply. The families who are involved respond to events as demands, just as if they were goals. The sureness of daily living is affected, and action taken is intended to return the family to some order or sureness—to reorganize. Some families may not return to their previous level of organization, as indicated by the broken lines in Figure 6.3. The "angle of recovery" is thus increased.

Events are demands in the family system, occuring inside and outside the system; they are unanticipated or unforeseen, but the consequences are made tolerable through management.

Perhaps the realistic stance for a manager is to:

1. recognize that both goal and event demands elicit managerial responses;
2. be alert to situations that may precipitate an overbalance of event demands which affect direction toward important goals;
3. approach events as positively as possible to maintain flexibility in a changing world; and
4. avoid a feeling of management failure that hinders the exercise of the desired control or progress toward desired goals.

RESOURCES

Thus far in the valuing process, we have emphasized the meanings that values hold for persons, the goals derived from values, and the direction that the goals dictate. This is the subjective side of the valuing

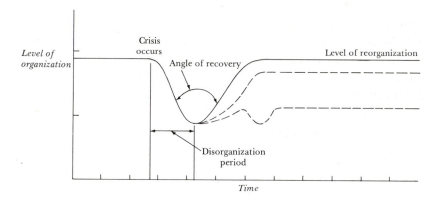

FIGURE 6.3 *Common patterns of family adjustment to crisis.*

Source: Adapted from Donald A. Hansen and Reuben Hill, "Families Under Stress," in Harold T. Christensen (ed.), *Handbook of Marriage and the Family,* ©1964 by Rand McNally and Company, Chicago, Figure 1, p. 810. Reprinted by permission of Rand McNally College Publishing Co.

situation. The object, or resource, side of the valuing process makes it possible for any goal or event to be met. *Resources* are the supply reservoir for use in the system's specific actions,[21] and are necessary in some form to solve every management problem. Resources vary in kind and in potential for meeting complex and unique needs.

The input of resources into the family system and the output from the managerial decisions and actions involve a continual resource flow as the family acts within and interacts with external systems to meet demands. In the process, the balance of resources retained within the boundaries of the family is continually undergoing change. At any one point in time, the combination of available resources summarizes what has accrued from past activity that can contribute to meeting future demands. While insight into the stock of resources can be useful as a measure of security or rate of getting ahead, it is the continuous flow that occurs in relation to system demands which clarifies the dynamics—the special conditions that make a difference. If every available resource is directed toward a handicapped child's health care, resources are then limited for other system goals such as another child's education. To understand the total effect of resource commitment, one must weigh the family's total resource and demand situation.

---

21. C. West Churchman, *The Systems Approach* (New York: Delacorte Press, Rutgers University Press, 1968), p. 39.

To promote this understanding, the next section focuses on the nature of resources as inputs to the family system, to supplement the attention directed earlier to the nature of demands. Human and material classifications of resources, resource attributes, and resource measures are also considered.

Resource Classification

Resources for individual and family management are classified in different ways—human and material, economic and noneconomic, and tangible and intangible. Each classification is limited in some ways and suggests different aspects of problems of interpretation that overlap. Fundamental differences are not necessarily clarified by classification, since naming something does not necessarily explain it.[22] But, since classifying is a practical way to distinguish members of a class, the material and human category is used here because it relates more than do the other categories to the nature of resources and the properties that make them useful as means for meeting demands.

In reality, all means that contribute to the meeting of goals and that yield satisfaction in use have utility as resources, regardless of their arbitrary classification as economic, noneconomic, tangible, or intangible. Goals have more and less tangible dimensions, as do resources. One of our efforts is to make intangible dimensions of goals and resources more explicit. At the same time, we need to avoid emphasis on the more tangible decision situations, which may be relatively unimportant, at the cost of less tangible decision situations, which are important.[23]

For our discussion then, individual and family resources are divided into material and human categories. Material resources are everything that serves as a means and that are external to persons; human resources are all means vested in persons.

Material. Material resources are all those things that belong to or are otherwise available for use by the household in meeting goals and events that are not part of persons. They are the tangible goods of consumption or investment and the cash or liquid savings that are kept available for potential claims on resources. Savings and items owned also have,

22. Karl E. Scheibe, *Beliefs and Values* (New York: Holt, Rinehart and Winston, Inc., 1970), pp. 50–51.
23. Kenneth E. Boulding, "The Ethics of Rational Decision," *Management Science* 12 (February 1966): B-165.

respectively, fixed and variable dollar values as assets. All contribute to the individual or family lifestyle.

At a given point in time, resource assessment is subject to an understanding of the nature of the resources to be measured. Since available family resources may be owned, rented, borrowed, or shared through some community or other social process, measuring household resources is complex.

For example, a recognition of the time dimension of household resources is an important factor with respect to durable goods as consumption and investment assets.[24] The utilities to be realized from a major portion of nondurable household goods are short-term since these goods are consumed soon after purchase. The utilities from purchases of durable consumption goods continue to flow over an extended period of use, although their value as an asset usually depreciates in some relation to the utility value already consumed. (In some instances, a durable good appreciates in value due to market price fluctuations or to years of survival when the good becomes an antique.) A carpet is a durable good that is consumed gradually. Other durable goods contribute to household production processes as household capital or investment items. As such, they are involved in the flow of utilities through the production of current consumption items (such as meals) or more durable consumption items (such as clothing). Their asset value also depreciates in relation to their contribution to production. Further consideration is given to the time dimension of resources in Chapter 10.

A household's net stock of resources describes the state and condition of its managerial potential at any time. When a household exchanges resources internally or with an outside system, there is resource flow. A listing and evaluation of a household's assets and liabilities show the net worth or material resource position—that is, the household's available material means. The value of the stock of material goods can be estimated since material goods are measurable in money terms.

Human. Human resources are characteristics or personal attributes used as means for meeting goals and events. Human resources, like material resources, are objects of value, but they are less tangible.

Cognitive and psychomotor aspects of human resources are significant in managing. The cognitive domain, as noted in the discussion of values,

---

24. Gwen J. Bymers and Mabel A. Rollins, "Classification Systems: Household Expenditures Data and Household Accounts," Bulletin 1014 (Ithaca, N. Y.: Cornell University Agricultural Experiment Station, 1967).

progresses from knowledge, comprehension, application, analysis, and synthesis, to evaluation. Knowledge is an important part of the human resource stock. Use of the knowledge resource can simplify activities. Information about the bookstore location and layout, class policies on book buying, and used-book sources can facilitate book acquisition.

In today's rapidly changing environment, knowledge applied to new situations is a significant cognitive resource. Recognizing the relation of existing knowledge to the present situation is imperative in avoiding mistakes or in using knowledge that is inappropriate to the situation. For example, highly mobile individuals or families can make better decisions about the selection of a new apartment when they apply knowledge acquired through experience and study. The ability to analyze, synthesize, and reformulate these varied insights and experiences creatively into new approaches to situations is indicative of the highest level of human capacity—resourcefulness.

Cognitive resources are used to analyze alternatives in decision making, to identify pertinent resources for a situation, and to evaluate the realistic possibilities for meeting goals.

Psychomotor resources are used in physical reactions to mental stimuli. They are the capacity for producing movement and doing physical work. With ever-changing equipment, products, and processes that alter the necessary skills, psychomotor resources remain important in home management. Persons with poor manipulative skills or infants in the process of maturation may demonstrate the value of psychomotor resources. The effort and adaptations necessary for a physically handicapped person exemplify the role of psychomotor resources. Manipulating equipment dials, reaching stored items, cleaning surfaces, or caring for an infant require psychomotor resources. For the person with motor limitations, each of these tasks may be difficult and may require mechanical aids for assistance.

Cognitive and psychomotor resources are closely interrelated human resources. Receiving, processing, and storing information (cognitive skills) are a part of adapting motor skills to new and varying situations. Using new products, whether paint, food mixes, or correction tape for typing, often require information that differs from that required by past products. Both cognitive and psychomotor resources help accomplish a task that involves a new product.

The total (or stock) of human resources is the human capital of a household. Economists define human capital as people resources which affect future income. People investing in themselves enhance their production and consumption capabilities.[25] Education is the largest investment in human capital.

A significant part of human capital development is the unconscious learning and conscious training carried out by household members. A parent who takes time to teach a child to perform an everyday task may contribute to the child's human capital, perhaps at a cost to the adult's progress. Home training, as well as formal education, may contribute to differences in the abilities of individuals as consumers and as producers.

Resource Attributes and Measures

Resources have "want-satisfying power," and utility is the satisfaction derived from them. Consuming one unit of an item gives a certain amount of satisfaction or utility; consuming more units yields more total utility but less utility per unit. Marginal utility is the consumer's added satisfaction from the last unit used. When a consumer reaches the point that equal satisfaction is derived from the last unit across many categories of items, the greatest total satisfaction is achieved.

Utility is an economic concept and is meaningful in relation to human or material resources as they contribute to meeting demands. For example, use of the cognitive capacity to analyze situations in order to arrive at a successful solution to a problem yields satisfaction or utility. Other resources are also likely to be involved in the solution. The returns as utility are the intrinsic and extrinsic values gained from resource use.

Certain characteristics are often used to identify the status of resources as economic means—scarcity, utility, neutrality, and divisibility.[26] Money functions in special ways to make these attributes meaningful in an exchange economy. The scarcity of certain resources in relation to other resources and the usefulness of all tend to make the limited resources relatively more valuable, at least temporarily. Neutrality about how something might be used and the possibility of dividing available means into various-sized units permit them to be put to alternate uses, in whole or in part. Where relative values may be measured and reflected through price, choices among alternative uses are facilitated. Such choices may include selecting the most economical resource to meet a goal, directing a given

---

25. Marguerite C. Burk, "On the Need for Investment in Human Capital for Consumption," *Journal of Consumer Affairs* 1 (Winter 1967): 124

26. Paul Diesing, *Reason in Society* (Urbana, Ill.: University of Illinois Press, 1962), chap. 2.

resource to a higher goal priority, or utilizing the most advantageous combination of resources.

Management makes resource measurement necessary for comparing complex goals. Some decisions require precise measurements; others may be appropriately made with an intuitive sense of amounts. A family on a trip, for instance, may consider eating at a cafeteria, but then choose to buy hamburgers at a fast-food chain. The exact amount of money for a cafeteria meal may not be known when the family decides between the two alternatives, but the time involved may be guessed more readily.

A complex goal, such as purchasing a condominium, may require a careful comparison of (1) dollar costs, (2) the accessibility to work and shopping areas, and (3) the quality of neighborhoods. Balancing these conditions in decision making is difficult because equivalent measures of each factor are not always available.

Money is both a resource and a measure of resources. To accomplish objectives, money must first be exchanged for goods and services. Considering money as a resource means that its potential claim on goods and services is recognized. As a measure of market value, money facilitates comparisons by serving as a common denominator for the measurement of varied resources.

Material goods exchanged in the marketplace have a clear value, but human resources are not so readily evaluated. The degree of necessary skill or knowledge may be measured, but the ability to apply knowledge or other cognitive skills is not so identifiable. Tests, educational levels, and performance records help to show human potential and may be translated into money terms for the paid worker.

In the household, tests and performance records are generally not available for measuring skills. Furthermore, skills such as child care are useful during one family life stage and minimally useful at other stages. Changes in the stock of human resources, particularly skills, are difficult to show.

Time is often the intermediate measure in assigning economic worth to human resources. Number of sales per week or typing speed per minute are examples of how time helps to objectively determine human resource values. Time may be the ultimate constraint for human resource use since it cannot be increased as goods can be. "Paying" attention reflects a sense of cost when there are multiple demands. Services purchased to replace the use of some human resources can increase available time. Like money, time as a measure makes comparison of unlike activities possible on a similar basis.[27]

Unlike material resources, time cannot be accumulated. In our affluent society, time becomes scarcer with increasing consumption. Chapter 2 notes Burenstam Linder's "partial affluence" view of the time cost of earning more money to purchase more goods, which take time for their use, care, and maintenance.

The calorie, another measure of human resources, helps compare energy costs of various activities. The lack of readily available information on energy use for activities limits its usefulness in decision making. The same tasks use varying amounts of calories, depending on individual work methods and habits, posture, environmental conditions, and other individual physiological aspects.

SUMMARY

This chapter emphasizes the various roles of values, goals, events, and resources as managerial inputs. Values are shown to have pervasive relations to other system inputs. Values are products of value judgments and experience. While they are not specific in defining action, values set the criteria for decisions such as goals, which specify proposed actions.

Although goals are purposeful and represent expected or anticipated outcomes, the possibilities for their successful fulfillment depend on the available resources. Resources provide the means by contributing the properties necessary to match the criteria of the goal.

Events confront the manager with unanticipated demands for action. Like goals, events call for value judgments in making purposeful responses. The processes for translating resources and demands into purposeful actions are analyzed as managerial system throughput in the next chapter.

---

27. Diesing, p. 48 (footnote).

DEFINITIONS

Values are meanings relating to what is desirable or has worth.

Absolute values are independent of surrounding conditions.

Relative values depend on their context for interpretation.

Intrinsic value is the desirable and self-sufficient meaning of an experience.

Extrinsic value is the meaning derived from the relation of a purpose or thing to another.

General values prevail over time and are met through a variety of actions.

Specific values are fulfilled or satisfied in a single action.

Subjective components of values provide the criteria which are to be met to achieve satisfaction.

Objective components are the attributes or properties of resources capable of meeting the evaluative criteria.

Affective domain is the positive and negative feeling or affect from experience leading to the internalized adoption of a value system.

Cognitive domain is the perception of values, goals, and related criteria as bases for creative interpretation of situations and potentialities.

Goals are value-based objectives; anticipated outcomes.

Events are pertinent, unanticipated occurrences which require action.

Resources are means for meeting demands.

Material resources are means external to persons for meeting goals and events.

Human resources are personal capacities and attributes for meeting goals and events.

Planning

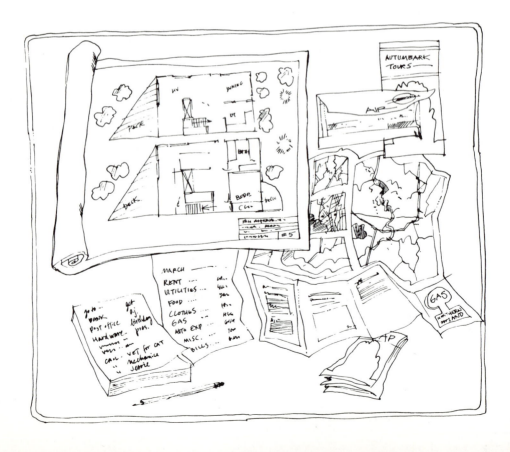

7.

In transforming inputs to desired outputs within the home management boundary, planning has the strategic function of determining the possibilities and the procedures. Man's capability to plan consciously is suggested as his most distinctive feature.[1] Planning is possible because of the ability to store and process information in relation to the future, whether the future is years ahead or only hours or minutes away. Through planning, decisions for future actions are made—decisions about whether demands can be met, how well they can be met, and when they will be met.

In this chapter, we define the role of planning in meeting demands. Then, the concepts of planning and of plans (the output of the planning subsystem) are elaborated in terms of the dimensions of plans, the factors that affect planning, and the planned facilitators which can influence the overall effectiveness of the planning function.

ROLE OF PLANNING

Since management cannot occur unless there is a plan of some nature—written or unwritten, general or specific—planning is a necessary function for guiding actions in meeting the demands of the family. Planning includes setting standards to reconcile demands with resources, and

---

1. Martin K. Starr, *Management: A Modern Approach* (New York: Harcourt Brace Jovanovich, Inc., 1971), p. 300.

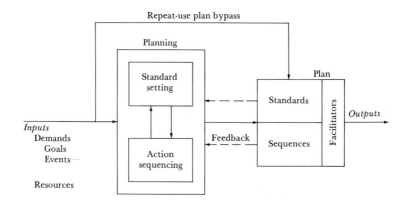

FIGURE 7.1 *The planning system.*

sequencing actions to meet the standards. *Planning* is a series of decisions concerning future standards and/or sequences of action. Standards establish the quantitative and qualitative properties of a plan, and sequences of action determine the order among tasks or of parts of a task. Planning, then, is comprised of standard setting and action sequencing, whether for a single, specific task or for a lifetime goal.

In systems terminology, resources and demands are inputs of planning. Plans are the output of planning and become input for the implementing component of management (Figure 7.1). Resources and demands come both from the personal subsystem within the family and from systems in the environment that are external to the family.

Planning differs from making decisions since decisions need not involve action or the future.[2] A decision to take no action on something does not provide a plan for future action, although the decision may influence future plans. Decision-making skills are important in planning; both standards setting and sequencing of actions involve decisions.

---

2. Fremont E. Kast and James E. Rosenzweig, *Organization and Management, A Systems Approach* (New York: McGraw-Hill Book Company, Inc., 1970), p. 436.

DIMENSIONS OF PLANS

Four interrelated dimensions of plans are considered here
—generality, time, scope, and repetitiveness. General plans are concerned
with the main elements rather than the details, and specific plans contain
details of standards and sequence. The time dimension of a plan is its time
length. Long-range plans often cover careers, marriage, a house purchase, or retirement; short-range plans may be completed in brief time
periods.

The scope of plans describes their extensiveness. A series of related, interdependent plans and decisions calls for extensive plans. Plans may have
a repetitive dimension; some may be used repeatedly, while others are
used only once. Limited research is available on interrelationships of the
plan dimensions, but a number of propositions merit further exploration:

1. Plans for short time periods can be more specific than those for long
   periods of time.
2. Plans that are more limited in scope can be more definite than plans
   that are extensive in scope.
3. Plans that are extensive in scope can incorporate specific repeat-use
   plans.

Generality

Plan generality depends on the definiteness of the information
input and the nature of the persons who are doing the planning. When
the resources, goals, or event demands are relatively certain, specific
standards and action sequences can be developed. General information
can lead to indefinite standards or several contingency plans to accommodate the general information, although persons with unclear goals could
make indefinite and general plans even though they had detailed information.

Specific plans, based on definite input information, are sometimes
called "Cook's Tour" plans, containing specific details of standards and
sequences.[3] On a typical Cook's Tour, the breakfast hour is specified, the
tour of the city, lunch details and free time are designated, and the plan

---

3. Clay Thomas Whitehead, *Uses and Limitations of Systems Analysis* (Santa Monica,
   Ca.: Rand Corp, 1967), p. 39.

for dinner includes a specific standard (dining room in the hotel, number of courses, type of entree, wine, or other beverage). Such specific plans use definite information for development: available resources, the tour agent's goals (purchased by the tourist), and the hotel manager's goal for making a profit.

Plans differ in generality, depending on the topic of the plan. In a study of long-term planning, planning for housing was more detailed than was planning for family communication and financial security.[4]

Definite plans for a specific time are more frequently carried through to completion than are indefinite plans.[5] In a study of three generations of families, definite plans were important to completion of plans for durable-goods acquisition, home improvements, changing residence location, and altering financial holdings.[6]

Input information about indefinite conditions can lead to contingency planning. *A contingency plan* contains alternative standards and sequences for indefinite conditions. *If* the first restaurant is overcrowded, there is a second one to go to in the vicinity; *if* the landlord demands rent on time this month, there is someone to borrow from at the neighborhood center. Increased information can increase specific planning and minimize contingency plans; for example, the restaurant can be telephoned and perhaps a reservation can be made.

Individuals and families may prefer to make general plans. Instead of making specific plans to purchase durable goods, many families have a general willingness to spend money, a desire to have new things —an attitude, rather than specific intentions to buy a particular item.[7] General plans are sometimes used to deal with indefinite goals, resources, and environments. Such plans give general direction to avoid major pitfalls in case circumstances turn out on the low, rather than the high, level of the range of possibilities. Self-employed families often experience uncertain incomes, which make detailed planning difficult. Other families may prefer general plans in order to exercise a degree of spontaneity

---

4. Judith A. Dawson, "An Exploratory Study of Long-Range Planning by Families," The Pennsylvania State University, M.S. thesis, 1970, p. 53.
5. Reuben Hill, *Family Development in Three Generations* (Cambridge, Mass.: Schenkman Publishing Co., Inc., 1970), p. 172.
6. Hill, pp. 118, 141, 164.
7. James N. Morgan, "Some Pilot Studies of Communication and Consensus in the Family," *Public Opinion Quarterly* 32 (Spring 1968): 118, and George Katona, *The Mass Consumption Society* (New York: McGraw-Hill, Inc., 1964), chap. 9.

within prescribed limits. These are referred to as "Lewis and Clark" plans.[8] Some individual and family plans are for uncharted areas, with unforeseen complications constantly arising. The first planning experience for a cross-country move may seem uncharted for some. After the first experience, a second plan can be more of a "Cook's Tour" type since more input information is either known or can be obtained from previously unknown sources.

Time Span

Plans vary considerably in the length of time they cover. A plan may extend over a number of years or it may apply to something that lasts only a short time. Specific plans with short time spans are more likely to be fulfilled than longer-range plans.[9] Plans vary in their time span by the subject of the planning. In an exploratory study, homemakers said that they planned for longer periods in the areas of housing and financial security and for shorter periods in the area of family communication.[10]

Confusion arises if one associates long-term plans with those of lasting significance, or short-term plans with those having ephemeral significances. A plan with a very'short span may have lifetime significance for an individual or a family. A quickly evolved plan to take a child with facial injuries to a plastic surgeon in a distant city may be completed within a few hours, but the effect on the child's appearance may be long lasting.

A plan to care for a mentally retarded child may extend to the time of his independence. A plan for such a lengthy period cannot be developed with precision. The effects of certain programs are unknown, the family situation may change considerably, or the child may develop other problems and capabilities. Plans in such a situation are probably the contingency type: if the child does not respond to classes offered in his home area, the parents may plan to explore opportunities at a mental retardation center some distance away.

Scope

Extensiveness of plans may vary with the breadth of the goal or event, its importance, and its certainty. A goal of such breadth as

---

8. Whitehead, p. 39.
9. Hill, p. 172.
10. Dawson, p. 53.

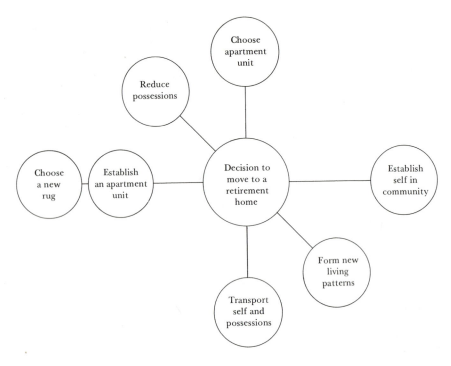

FIGURE 7.2 *Central and satellite decisions and actions basic to a plan for retirement living.*

Source: Adapted from Martha A. Plonk, "Exploring Interrelationships in a Central-Satellite Decision Complex," *Journal of Home Economics* 60 (December, 1968): 790. Beatrice Paolucci, "Managerial Decision Patterns," *Penney's Fashion and Fabrics* (Fall/Winter 1963), p. 13.

retirement may require many interrelated plans. The plan for housing depends on the plan for location during retirement; the plan for a specific housing choice limits the alternatives for furnishings. These interrelated plans can be thought of as resulting from central decisions and satellite decisions (Figure 7.2).[11] Plans of a general nature more likely accompany central decisions, while specific plans accompany satellite decisions.

A plan's scope is related to its certainty or uncertainty; the more inclusive or extensive the plan, the less certain are the facts available for plan-

_____

11. Martha A. Plonk, "Exploring Interrelationships in a Central-Satellite Decision Complex," *Journal of Home Economics* 60 (December 1968): 789.

ning; the narrower a plan, the more certain the environment and related facts may be.[12] The importance of a plan may contribute to its extensiveness; plans for a bar mitzvah may become quite extensive because of its importance.

Repetitiveness

Plans may be for one time or for repeated uses. Plans can be developed and reused for a recurring task, or called upon for a similar situation when an existing plan appears appropriate. Generalized *repeat-use* plans provide policies about when to invoke the plan in response to similar situations that recur. Families can also use repeat-use policies to control changes in their lives, even though they cannot predict when or if they will need to use them. A plan for practicing home fire drills regularly can make a difference in an emergency although the emergency may never arise. Families with well developed policies seem more content with changes in their lives.[13]

When repeat-use plans or policies are used, the planning process is bypassed (Figure 7.1). Repeat-use plans are often modified to apply them to current situations. A change in both standards and sequences calls for a new plan, even if the skeleton of the repeat-use plan or policy is used as a basis for the new plan.

Single-use plans are used only once or as part of the development of repeat-use plan. Plans to purchase a particular house or car, to rent an apartment with certain persons, or to celebrate a twenty-fifth wedding anniversary are examples of plans likely to be used only once. Single-use plans can involve detailed standards and sequences, depending on the nature of the activities.

The value relation of standards may tend to intensify their repeated use; however, there are many established patterns of work, meals, children's bedtime, and so on that tend to promote repeat-use sequences. A risk of repeat-use plans, either standards or sequence or both, is that the plan or part of it may become the goal. The original intent of the plan is lost, and it may be inappropriate in a changed situation. For example, a sequence can itself take on value if a plan becomes so routinized that the very lack of variation is valued. A person with a morning routine may

---

12. Kast and Rosenzweig, p. 448.
13. Hill, p. 329.

value its sameness, and a change in sequence may prove disturbing. If an event frustrates the routine, it can be upsetting.

Continued use of a repeat-use plan in changing situations can result in inappropriate actions. The mother of young children who continues to hold the same standards for appearance of the house that she held in pre-child days and who tries to follow the same sequence as before the birth of the children needs to evolve standards and sequences appropriate for the current situation. This is the essence of the situation-specific planning concept.

FACTORS AFFECTING PLANNING

Family Qualities

Wide variety exists in planning among individuals and families. Of the families included in a three-generation study—grandparent, parent, and married child—those successful in identifying needs, deciding courses of action, and taking planful actions had many of these characteristics:

1. higher education of husband and wife,
2. higher occupational and social status,
3. gainfully employed wife,
4. high social participation of wife,
5. role allocation flexibility,
6. higher marital communication,
7. fewer undesirable role attributes, and
8. expanding family life cycle stage.[14]

Urban, middle-class wives used planning more than rural, low-income wives when compared on meal-planning frequency, shopping from grocery lists, trying out new foods, subscribing to consumer magazines, and budgeting for family expenses.[15] Wives who had more frequent contacts

---

14. Hill, p. 237.
15. Murray A. Straus, "Social Class and Farm-City Differences in Interaction with Kin in Relation to Societal Modernization," *Rural Sociology* 34 (December 1969): 476, 485.

with relatives planned less and were less innovative in planning, when location and social position were statistically controlled in the study.[16]

In a study of planning, information seeking, and product choosing, middle-income earners spent more time in acquiring information before buying consumer goods than did low- or high-income earners.[17]

In the future, will careful planning, including information searching, be more or less prevalent than it is today? No one really knows, of course, and different prognosticators forecast in opposite directions. With the many choices available for goods and services, one could propose that increased planning and information searching will be necessary.

Another view suggests a reduction in planning for some income levels. As incomes increase, an increase is felt in the scarcity of time, and time scarcity may affect planning.[18] As time becomes scarce, "we can expect a decline in the quality of decisions." In the future, "instead of possessing complete knowledge, we shall be acting on increasingly uncertain grounds."[19] Consumers can trade the time necessary for making wiser decisions in the use of income for some other benefits. At some point, it may pay to make more mistakes in expenditures than to use income-acquiring time to plan purchase decisions carefully.[20]

Another anticipated dimension of the information problem is that of information overload. Consumers are seen as having more information available than they can adequately process. One way of coping with the overload is to clarify useful consumer information so that decisions are not encumbered by unrelated data.[21]

Individual Qualities

Planning is affected by differences in individual orientation and abilities. Little is known about attitudes toward planning, internal-external control, or present-future time orientation. More is known about planning abilities, particularly creativity, foresight, elaboration, and ordering.

16. Straus, p. 489.
17. George Katona and Eva Mueller, "A Study of Purchase Decisions," pp. 30–36 in *Consumer Behavior,* vol. 1, ed. Lincoln H. Clark (New York: New York University Press, 1955), p. 79.
18. Staffan Burenstam Linder, *The Harried Leisure Class* (New York: Columbia University Press, 1970).
19. Burenstam Linder, p. 67.
20. Burenstam Linder, p. 67.
21. V. H. Brix, *You Are A Computer, Cybernetics in Everyday Life* (New York: Emerson Books, Inc., 1970), p. 44.

Persons who believe they can control their own destiny have internal control;[22] those with external control perceive events as being unrelated to one's own behavior or as unpredictable because of complex forces and, therefore, beyond personal control.[23] A strong orientation to external control, such as belief in astrological power or influence, can affect one's planning. On auspicious days in the East, many weddings take place; on ordinary days, few or no weddings occur.

The individual who strongly believes that control of one's destiny is possible will likely be more aware of parts of the environment that provide useful information for future behavior.[24] If one believes in controlling the course of events, then knowing about limited selections of fresh meats, fruits, and vegetables at some stores on late Saturday afternoons can influence planning of future grocery shopping.

Time orientation, either present or future, seems to be a relative term. A Brazilian woman's experience in a *favelado* (slum) of Sao Paulo illustrates a time orientation: "It's been two weeks that I haven't washed clothes because I haven't any soap. I sold some boards for 40 cruzeiros. The woman told me she'd pay today. If she pays I'll buy soap."[25]

The woman lives a day-to-day existence, but she anticipates a way to meet a need, and is therefore planning. Is she present- or future-oriented? How far ahead do future-oriented persons plan? The limits of future orientation depend on the situation and on the possibilities for looking ahead. With a relative approach, we can avoid characterizing those with low incomes as present oriented and those with middle and upper incomes as future oriented. For effective functioning, one probably needs a mixture of present and future orientation. Concerns only for the future, which may be operable in the short run, can leave many day-to-day things undone; eventually, day-to-day matters must be attended to.

From a number of planning abilities, four seem particularly meaningful in home management: creativity-originality, foresight, elaboration, and ordering. The abilities vary in importance, depending on the situation surrounding a plan and on whether the planning activity is standard setting or sequencing.

---

22. Julian B. Rotter, "Generalized Expectancies for Internal Versus External Control of Reinforcement," *Psychological Monographs* 80, Whole No. 609 (1966): p. 1.
23. Rotter, p. 1.
24. Rotter, p. 25.
25. Carolina Maria De Jesus, *Child of the Dark* (New York: E. P. Dutton & Co., Inc., 1962 and New York: The New American Library), p. 45.

Creativity-originality in planning is important where new procedures must be devised or old procedures must be applied to new situations.[26] College students may be interested in the finding that students who live at home are less creative than other students. Parental ties may be detrimental to creative functioning.[27] Creativity is not necessary in many tasks. In fact, automatic equipment is designed to minimize the need for it. Unless equipment is new and unfamiliar or is only in partial working condition, little creativity or originality is even desirable. If something mechanical fails in the car, however, creativity may be needed to use available resources to repair the car enough to make it mobile. Creativity is not to be confused with flexibility, which equipment is commonly designed to serve.

The planning ability of *foresight* is awareness of possible future events relating to a present situation.[28] Foresight has at least two facets —perceptual and conceptual. Perceptual foresight is the ability to explore possible alternatives and select the most effective ones for solving problems.[29] Conceptual foresight involves anticipation of needs or consequences of problem situations.[30] Perceptual foresight involves an ability to project to the future from the present, while conceptual foresight is the ability to relate anticipated future situations to the present. Conceptual foresight is more abstract and idea related,[31] but both perceptual and conceptual foresight are apparently interrelated.[32]

Elaboration is a planning ability to produce ideas or alternative methods for an adequate solution.[33] Such an ability seems related to a person's level of ability to process information. As information relating to given situations is used more fully, more alternatives are evolved from the possibilities presented, and given characteristics are combined in different ways. More complex rules for comparison are needed in order to evaluate the possibilities within these situations. An organizing structure is then

---

26. J. P. Guilford, R. M. Berger, and P. R. Christensen, "A Factor-analytic Study of Planning," Reports from the Psychological Laboratory, No. 12 (Los Angeles: University of Southern California, May 1955), p. 19.
27. Russell Eisenman and Diane J. Foxman, "Creativity: Reported Family Patterns and Scoring Methodology," *Psychological Reports* 26 (April 1970): 619.
28. R. M. Berger, J. P. Guilford, and P. R. Christensen, "A Factor-analytic Study of Planning Abilities," *Psychological Monographs* 71 Whole No. 435 (1957): 28.
29. Guilford, Berger, and Christensen, p. 15.
30. Guilford, Berger, and Christensen, p. 17.
31. Stanley Kaye, "Ego Identity, Time Perspective, Time Conceptualization, and Planning," New York University, Ph.D. dissertation, 1968, p. 12.
32. Kaye, p. 32.
33. Berger, Guilford, and Christensen, p. 2.

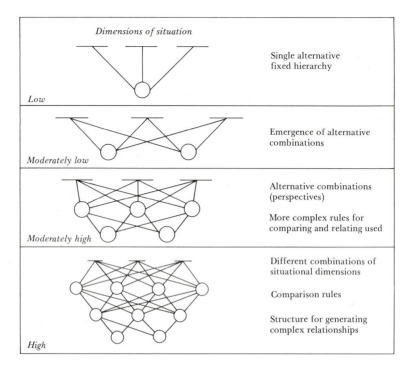

FIGURE 7.3 *Level of information processing.*

Source: *Human Information Processing: Individuals and Groups Functioning in Complex Social Situations* by Harold M. Schroder, Michael J. Driver, and Siegried Streufert. Copyright © 1967 by Holt, Rinehart and Winston, Inc., pp. 15-23. Adapted and reprinted with permission of Holt, Rinehart and Winston, Inc.

needed for meaningful interpretations. The most concrete level of information processing involves compartmentalizing and a relatively fixed hierarchy of rules or parts (Figure 7.3). At this level, persons think in categories, with minimal conflict, since few alternatives are generated. Their behavior is anchored outside themselves, and whatever changes they make are abrupt.[34]

Persons at the next level have alternative ways of organizing the dimensions of situations, but they may lack organizing rules.[35] Their behavior moves away from absolutism; yet their thinking is inflexible and their outlook is negativistic.

---

34. Harold M. Schroder, Michael J. Driver, and Siegfried Streufert, *Human Information Processing* (New York: Holt, Rinehart and Winston, Inc., 1967), pp. 16–17.
35. Schroder, Driver, and Streufert, p. 18.

At the moderately high level, there is an ability to combine perspectives and use rules for matching, comparing, and relating pairs. Persons who plan at this moderately high level are more internally oriented. Their behavior is less deterministic. Their rules are minimally fixed, and they can view alternatives simultaneously.[36]

At the high conceptual level of information processing, persons effectively adapt to complex, dynamic situations. Their ability to discover and use information from a set of stimuli makes possible a structure that is not dependent on external conditions for forming rules and on past experiences for forecasting events.[37]

The fourth ability of importance in planning is *ordering*—an ability to define an arrangement of objects or events in a meaningful sequence of time, hierarchy, or cause and effect.[38] This ability is used most in the sequencing aspect of planning. Sequencing is defined as ordering parts of a task or specifying successions among tasks. The ordering, however, may vary considerably in its effectiveness. Some persons have the ability to combine a number of related activities into a meaningful sequence far more readily than others are able to do. A further part of ordering is the ability to arrange activities according to their importance, either to the individual, to a family member, or to some external system.

Each of these abilities or individual qualities can influence the planning, the plans, and the fulfillment of the plans. The extent of influence is not known, but future research should bring such information.

ASPECTS OF PLANNING

Standard Setting

Standard setting identifies the potential of available resources for meeting goal and event demands in a particular situation. In planning, values underlie goals and provide criteria for selecting standards to guide managerial activity. But goals and/or demands must also be reconciled with available or potential resources. During planning, standards are set that are compatible with both the goals and the available resources and

---

36. Schroder, Driver, and Streufert, pp. 20–22.
37. Schroder, Driver, and Streufert, p. 23.
38. Berger, Guilford, and Christensen, p. 26.

these standards are defined in qualitative and quantitative terms as criteria for the action to follow.[39]

Under conditions of changing values and dynamic managerial situations, standard setting is an especially significant aspect of planning. Situations and standards may remain unchanged for extended periods. But if conditions change and standards remain unchanged, then resources or other managerial processes need to respond accordingly. When prices rise or family size increases, one manager may "moonlight" to maintain a level of living, thereby putting forth more effort to meet the higher cost of the standard. Another manager who is interested in technological changes to reduce effort may not be prepared for the accompanying change in standard.

Some standards are said to be conventional or socially determined. Groups that share resources need to have consensus about standards to guide their activities or their acceptance of varying standards. Individuals who have much in common are likely to adopt similar standards. If an individual accepts and uses conventional standards meaningfully, the source of these standards is unimportant; but if they are adopted without thought, they may limit adaptability in changing situations. Standards must relate to the realities of a current situation if effective planning is to be promoted.

Quality and Quantity. The possible contribution of human and material resources in meeting goals may be explored, clarified, and defined in qualitative and quantitative terms. A goal to plant a flowering bush involves the need to consider criteria relating to size, hardiness, color, vulnerability to insect infestation, and so forth. Of these considerations, color is a qualitative consideration, and the goal may even specify a red bush. The particular color may need to be determined as part of the planning process in relation to the other criteria. The size of bush to purchase can be viewed quantitatively—current size in relation to cost and matured size in relation to need and the time that is needed to grow. *Quantity* is the definitive or estimated amount that meets the purpose, while *quality* is defined as the image (attractive, red) or property (tall) of what is desired.

"The human mind's capability of forming an image (standard) to check against is important. If one's activity is interrupted, a new image will be

---

39. Florence S. Walker, "A Proposal for Classifying Self-Imposed Housekeeping Standards," *Journal of Home Economics* 60 (June 1968): 456.

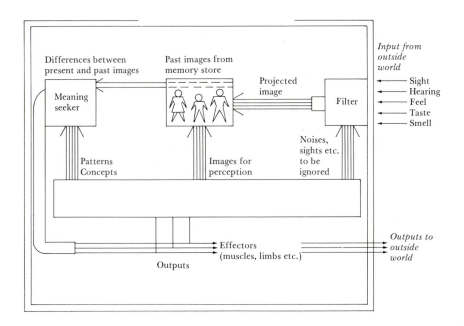

FIGURE 7.4 *Information processing, including present and past image comparison.*

Source: V. H. Brix, *You Are A Computer: Cybernetics in Everyday Life* (New York: Emerson Books, Inc., 1970), p. 45 (slight modification); and V. H. Brix, *Cybernetics in Everyday Affairs* (London: David Rendel, Ltd.)

formed for completing the task. Reflective thought rehearses the imagination—it compares, evaluates, and selects alternative ways to reach a goal. Mentality enables an individual to anticipate consequences of an action and to respond to them before committing himself to action."[40]

We are constantly receiving, filtering, and processing messages from the senses and relating them to images stored in the memory, which change through feedback (Figure 7.4). An open system grows through positive feedback, which supports deviation-amplifying behavior.

Measurement is useful in interpreting differences in properties, but is not often possible. Different images are more difficult to compare than are different design features because objects can be directly observed while images cannot. An individual may well perceive qualitative differences such as color, workmanship, or sweetness. Although these may seem quite tangible, they are not often readily measurable and comparable.

40. Tamotsu Shibutani, "A Cybernetic Approach to Motivation," in *Modern Systems Research for the Behavioral Scientist,* ed. Walter Buckley (Chicago: Aldine Publishing Company, 1968), p. 333.

181

Consumer tests and standards help make qualitative features more comparable through measurement.

As a definitive or estimated amount, the quantitative factor refers only to the amount of something and can usually be measured or estimated in a comparative way. The quantity of one thing may be compared with the quantity of another, but the comparison is usually meaningful only if the quality class remains constant.

Quantity should not be confused with measurement of a qualitative factor. A large head of lettuce may or may not weigh more than a small head because of differences in compactness. The amount of lettuce depends on weight; relative size—largeness or smallness—is a qualitative factor.

Judgments on qualitative-quantitative values may be made by ranking or grading. Ranking places items in a hierarchical order according to a set of criteria. If the criterion is size or distance, then ranking one item above another is determined by the appropriate quantitative measure—weight, length, and so on. Qualitative characteristics may also be ranked according to criteria that permit comparisons about whether one thing is better or worse than another. The ranking may proceed until the best or worst among a given group of items is determined.

Grading usually refers to the position of something in relation to all items of its kind. The criteria that are set need to be specified, with all items considered. The color of an apple may be graded "good" or "bad" relative to given criteria for other apples of its kind. Most people reflect their image of color in relation to their experience with apples when they say, "This is a good red apple." They may also be combining qualities to mean that it is a good apple in general but particularly with respect to color. Specific qualities for milk, eggs, and other foods are graded accordingly, by generally recognized standards. What is "good" in individual situations may vary.

If one were managing with full information in an ideal setting, alternatives could be identified and graded against a readily available scale of preferences. With unlimited resources, the highest ranked alternatives could be chosen. In the real world, however, the criteria may be complex; information is often incomplete; the capacities of alternatives for meeting needs are uncertain; and resources are limited. With these constraints, the prudent choice is often difficult and elusive and may be the acceptable alternative to evolve in the situation.[41] However they are selected, the alter-

---

41. Herbert A. Simon, "Theories of Decision-Making in Economics and Behavioral Science," *American Economic Review* 49 (June 1959): 262-63.

natives identify qualities and quantities to serve as guidelines for the actions to follow and determine their expected outcomes.

Attributes of Standards.   Four attributes of standards considered in this section are: clarity, flexibility, reality, and complexity. Each has an explanatory role in every situation, although generally not to the same degree.

Clarity of standard is defined as the specification of quality and/or quantity. Where qualitative and quantitative factors can be specified, the possibilities are greater for achieving the expected outcomes. Standards are guidelines for management activity, and the clearer the quality-quantity elements, the more it is possible to control resource inputs or to assure desired outcomes. If someone else is to carry out a plan, communicating clear standards can make the difference in the success of the plan.

Because of the variety of available selections in market situations, characteristics of standards may need more attention than they do in nonmarket situations. The responses to questions included in a management study of homemakers in Columbus, Ohio, indicate that a majority of the homemakers specified standards for market situations more often than they did for nonmarket situations.[42]

Flexibility in standards is the range of acceptable qualitative-quantitative factors for a situation. One might incorporate a range of acceptable variations around a preferred set of standards for a situation where some variation in conditions cannot be controlled. Such a range can also be useful in repeat-use plans because circumstances often vary over time. If variations reach outer limits, there may be a tendency to undercorrect or overcorrect until a more acceptable degree of variation returns (Figure 7.5). A changed demand, such as an increase in clothing needs or a defective washing machine, may lead to variations, which reach or exceed acceptable limits and require adaptations in the plan. Being alert to developing problems can avert irritation or drastic responses, such as replacing rather than repairing a washer. In some situations, widened acceptable limits may follow an appraisal. Several respondents in a study of two-career families noted that they could very easily tolerate untidiness in the house. One stated:

You must begin with what one does not do. I have a cleaning woman . . . and what she doesn't do, doesn't get done. My kitchen shelves are cruddy, but it doesn't

---

42. Francille Maloch and Ruth E. Deacon, "Components of Home Management in Relation to Selected Variables," Research Bulletin 1042 (Wooster, Ohio: Ohio Agricultural Research and Development Center, 1970), p. 9.

Limit of acceptable   Desired variation   Limit of acceptable
variation   variation

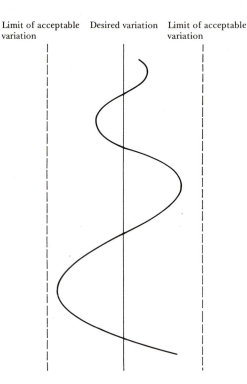

FIGURE 7.5 *Flexibility in standards.*

> Source: Adapted from *The Theory and Management of Systems* by Richard A. Johnson, Fremont E. Kast, and James E. Rosenzweig, p. 65. Copyright 1963. Used with permission of McGraw-Hill Book Company, Inc.

bother me. Dust sits around. It doesn't bother me that everything isn't shipshape. . . The way a house is kept is not the most important thing in the universe.[43]

A study of managerial components included flexibility in standards for the task of bedmaking. Homemakers were shown photographs and asked which beds were acceptable if they or their children had made them. Flexibility was measured by the number of beds deemed acceptable (Figure 7-6). Urban homemakers employed at higher skill-level occupations were more flexible than those employed at lower skill-level jobs.

---

43. Lynda Lytle Holmstrom, *The Two-Career Family* (Cambridge, Mass.: Schenkman Publishing Company, 1972), pp. 70–71.

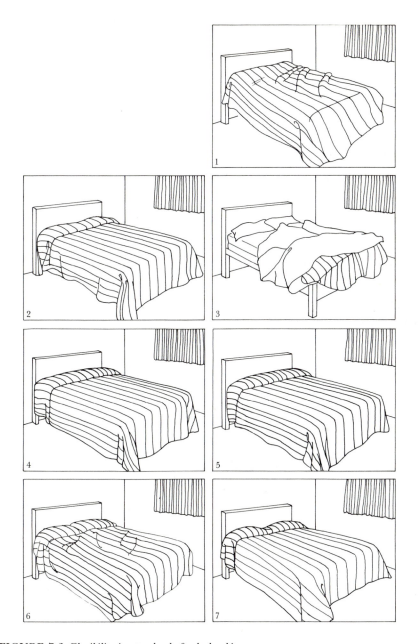

FIGURE 7.6 *Flexibility in standards for bedmaking.*

Source: Francille Maloch and Ruth E. Deacon, "Components of Home Management in Relation to Selected Variables," Research Bulletin 1042 (Wooster, Ohio: Ohio Agricultural Research and Development Center, 1970), pp. 34–35.

Reality in standards is the feasibility of achieving the chosen quality and/or quantity. When tasks can be accomplished as planned, the standards for the task are realistic. Estimating a realistic solution is a problem, in part, of clarifying probabilities. We may know, for example, that under ordinary conditions a tank of gasoline will last during the drive from Cleveland to Cincinnati. We may also know a strong head wind reduces the mileage per gallon. We may believe that under today's conditions we will need to refill the tank along the way. Such beliefs are mixtures of certainty and doubt about an outcome and can be expressed as an estimate of probability. A person who arrives at a .50 probability (intuitively or mathematically) that the tank will need filling before Cincinnati is less likely to take a chance than the person who concludes that the probability is zero. The more factors considered (or the more dependable the gauge), the less uncertainty there is. But variable conditions make such gaming a rather common way to deal with uncertainty even though exact probabilities are not specified.

In the previous illustration, the effect of the type of gasoline (a qualitative factor) was assumed to have been considered in the mileage estimate, so that the quantity of gasoline needed could be the focus of the problem. In other problems, different qualities may be reflected in the different prices of an item. To this extent, the choice at the desired price can be reduced to the quantity that can be obtained with available resources. Or, if a given quantity is needed, the adjustment may need to be made in quality.

An image of color combinations to be used in a room illustrates how probabilities may relate to qualitative aspects of standards. In deciding on the color of paint or the choice of wallpaper for a room, one may look at paint chips or wallpaper samples and still be uncertain about the effect of the paint or paper in the room. Yet, one may be certain enough and sufficiently confident to make a choice without actually applying the paint or wallpaper. If there is not an acceptable level of certainty, advice or further evidence may be sought. The latter evaluations lack the precision possible for more measurable factors, but there is evidence that the human brain continually makes probability estimates of this nature.

Homemakers have been reported to be more realistic than unrealistic in their standards. However, the presence of young children in the household or the state of health can make a difference in her ability to plan standards for household tasks that can realistically be accomplished.[44]

---

44. Maloch and Deacon, p. 10.

TABLE 7.1

Illustrations of possible interactions of factors affecting complexity of standards.

Examples of combinations	Level of complexity of standards
1. Goal criteria—clear Resources—adequate Scope of task—limited Number of persons—one	Simple
2. Goal criteria—unclear Resources—adequate Scope of task—limited Number of persons—two or more	Moderately complex
3. Goal criteria—unclear Resources—inadequate Scope of task—extensive Number of persons—two or more	Complex

Goal criteria—clear; unclear
Resources—adequate; inadequate
Scope of task—limited; *extensive
Number of persons—one; *two or more
*The complexity of standards increases with these factors.

Also, according to wives, the frequency of meeting expectations on standards is related to the degree of agreement with their husbands on the standards to be met.[45]

Complexity in standards is the interrelationship of persons, tasks, and standards. More specifically, complexity includes the qualitative-quantitative interactions within or between tasks involving one or more persons. Some important complexity factors that affect standard setting are the scope of the choice to be made, the clarity of ordering the goal criteria, the adequacy of resources, and the number of persons involved. An illustration of how these factors can compound to affect levels of complexity is shown in Table 7.1, which shows three of the sixteen possible combinations of varying complexity for the four factors.

---

45. E. Carolyn Ater and Ruth E. Deacon, "Interaction of Family Relationship Qualities and Managerial Components," *Journal of Marriage and the Family* 34 (May 1972): 262.

With constancy in the scope of the task, the goal criteria, and the involvement of persons, an increase in resources would ordinarily simplify standard setting. Yet, if more information is available than can readily be processed (information overload), complexity is increased. Either vague goal criteria or vague information could thwart effective selection of pertinent information and could reduce its adequacy. In controlling complexity, there is apparently a growing need for clear information and a better capability on the part of families or individuals to use only that which is applicable to the solution of a problem.

An illustration of how complexity increases when resources are reduced relates to health. More persons are likely to participate in tasks in households where the homemaker's health is lower than average.[46] In other cases, higher complexity occurs in terms of suggestions and help, when agreement in standards between husbands and wives (as perceived by the wives) is lower.[47] Whether lesser agreement is affected more by the positive or negative nature of the suggestions is not clear, but greater involvement of persons and factors to be considered increases complexity.

Sequencing

Sequencing, the ordering of parts of a task or specifying successions among tasks, contributes to the structure of day-to-day living.[48] The way tasks are ordered interrelates with standards in important ways. A homemaker who has invited guests for dinner has standards about the food she serves and the appearance of her family. If she plans to serve fresh vegetables, which she does not want to hold too long before cooking she must do her shopping within a given period. Certain clothing may need to be washed and appropriately dried and/or ironed to be ready for the special occasion. The order and times for working these tasks into a day affect the eventual standards. Standards affect sequence, and both are necessary to complete a plan.

---

46. Maloch and Deacon, p. 11.
47. Ater and Deacon, p. 262.
48. See also: Rose E. Steidl and Esther C. Bratton, *Work in the Home* (New York: John Wiley and Sons, Inc., 1968). Timing is "the spacing of time use or time inputs—within a given task and among tasks," p. 85.
    Nancy Ann Barclay, "Organization of Household Activities by Home Managers," The Ohio State University, Ph.D. dissertation, 1970. Sequencing is part of organizing, along with checking and adjusting (controlling).
    Addreen Nichols, "Person-centered and Task-centered Styles of Organization," Michigan State University, Ph.D. dissertation, 1964, pp. 3–4.

The balance between structured and unstructured activity and sequence will vary from situation to situation. The degree to which structured activity takes on a regular patterning will also vary from household to household. But routines do help stabilize our lives. "When we have certain routines worked into a structure or framework, we reduce some of the element of change in our life . . . Rhythms help us to perceive change and permanence and let us respond to the varying and enduring content of our lives.[49]

Structure and order take on importance in situations such as communes which appear outwardly to be unstructured. Many communes fail because they lack structure. "Nobody gets the sudden overpowering inspiration to take out the garbage. Everybody says, you know, that it's a compromise if you get structured . . . The common thing is if you try to structure you're on an ego trip. Maybe the guys that are trying to keep it unstructured are the ones on the ego trip. And the guys that are trying to structure something for survival are the ones that really care."[50]

Households often have relatively structured days, with eating patterns, school and work schedules, and activities forming a core sequence for weekdays. Part of the daily sequence need not be reconsidered each day. A certain amount of structure for minimizing sequence decisions probably contributes to mental health.

Each of us has an "internal clock," which may give a sense of uneasiness if we deviate to any great extent, such as in long-distance air travel when daily activities are moved backward or forward a few hours. Some persons have a continuing awareness of their clock; they may be distinctly early-morning persons or night persons. Social activities are designed and scheduled for economic efficiency and convenience; a person needs to detect his own cycles and schedule for his own health, rather than accept external sequencing.[51] Our mass education systems and many work situations do not allow for individual preferences in scheduling; the largest area for choice is in discretionary activities. The full-time homemaker may be able to sequence according to personal preference, depending on the ages of the children and the nature of other demands.

Mumaw examined task regularization, which is a part of sequencing; she found that homemakers belonging to the Mennonite denomination

---

49. Steidl and Bratton, p. 83.
50. William Hedgepeth and Dennis Stock, *The Alternative: Communal Life in New America* (New York: The Macmillan Co., 1970), p. 188.
51. Gay Gaer Luce, "Biological Rhythms in Psychiatry and Medicine," U.S. Dept. of Health, Education, and Welfare, Public Health Service Publication 2088 (Washington, D. C.: U.S. Government Printing Office, 1970), p. 151.

were higher in regularization than non-Mennonite affiliates. Statements included in the measure of regularization were: "I follow a regular routine for my work," "I set a regular time for doing the household chores," "I assign certain jobs to certain days of the week," "I work at two or more jobs at the same time," and "I plan for flexibility in my daily schedule of activities." The latter two statements were rated negatively by the Mennonites.[52]

There are external restrictions to choice in sequencing which include business hours, in addition to the work, school, and activities already mentioned. The limited business hours of speciality shops, some financial institutions, and services increase the importance of careful sequencing. Some metropolitan areas are easing restrictions by having supermarkets open twenty-four hours a day, seven days a week, and by including services such as a post office, check cashing, and a wide selection of nongrocery items. Specialized businesses have added after-hour telephone recording services, but these are inadequate when personal choices of style must be made. The potential for shopping by computer seems bright, with choices flashed on a home screen for selection. Wherever the standard for products or service is primarily qualitative in nature, shopping by computer will be slow in acceptance. Since efficient computer operations will require a high degree of standardization, ways to provide optimum choice and to accommodate desired changes in style will need to interrelate with the advantages in sequencing if the total planning of consumers is to be facilitated.

Coordination of Tasks. Sequencing of tasks may be done separately, or two or more tasks may be coordinated. In either manner, sequencing is strongly influenced by the nature of the sequenced tasks and the nature of the individuals involved. Sometimes the sequence that is chosen depends on the standard to be met. The appearance standard for a house painted by teenagers in a family may require that work be done after office hours or on weekends when someone is home to supervise and help.

Separately sequenced tasks are planned so that one task is completed before the next task is begun. Some persons may prefer much separateness in sequencing to reduce the frustrations of complexity. Tasks to be performed separately may require one's full attention for the duration of the task.

---

52. Catherine R. Mumaw, "Organizational Patterns of Homemakers Related to Selected Predispositional and Situational Characteristics," The Pennsylvania State University, Ph.D. dissertation, 1967, p. 83.

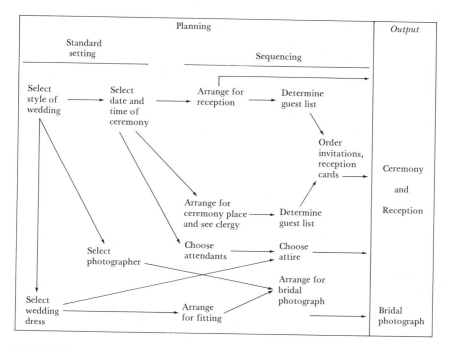

FIGURE 7.7 *Sequencing for "traditional" wedding ceremony and reception.*

Tasks that are dependent on one another are sequenced separately. A dependent task can be started only after another task is completed. For a complex series of tasks, identifying the dependent tasks precedes the planning of sequences. Task dependency in preparation for a bridal photograph is illustrated in Figure 7.7, showing a chain of decisions and actions. The photograph depends on the wedding-dress selection and acquisition. The dress is selected after the wedding style is chosen. Task dependency increases the complexity of sequencing; when *dependent tasks* are scheduled too closely together, a delay in one is felt in succeeding tasks. Tasks may be flexible or inflexible in their time requirements. In the illustration of wedding plans, the bride-to-be or someone in charge must order invitations in time to address the envelopes and mail them at the desired time. Flexibility can be increased if the envelopes can be secured even before the invitations are printed.

Several tasks in the same vicinity may be scheduled for completion within a certain time period. Each task may be approached and completed separately from the others, even though their sequencing is interrelated. In going to the library, returning a book, checking out a reserve book, and reading the book, one may complete each task separately; no task is scheduled to take place while another is being processed, although they are dependent on sequence. However, if the reserve book is already checked out to someone else, a rapid shift to an alternate sequence (or the development of a new one) may require coordinating two tasks. In the latter case, one may request the reserve book, study something else a little while, and check back for the reserve book intermittently.

Task coordination that provides for intermittent attention to two or more tasks until they are completed is called *dovetailing*. Many household tasks are discontinuous and thus appropriate for dovetailing.[53] Food preparation tasks require intermittent attention. While the meat is cooking, the salad can be made and the vegetable put on to cook. The sequencing of food preparation is altered by the microwave oven, which reduces the cooking time formerly used.

Doing the laundry in an apartment utility area may be dovetailed with getting the mail and seeing the manager about a necessary repair. The tasks are unrelated except for the general location where they are to be accomplished. Coordinating tasks by location may be important to a person with limited physical capacity. The equipment and supplies used for tasks also create possibilities for coordinating otherwise unrelated tasks. When the vacuum cleaner is brought out of storage, the equipment may be used in several rooms for different purposes—dusting or vacuuming the blinds or floors. The locations may be fairly close together, but the primary relating factor can be the equipment. Errands may be combined, not because of proximity, but because sequencing the car or cycle within a given trip is easier than rescheduling.

A second type of coordination is *overlapping of tasks,* or concurrent attention to two or more tasks. This coordination is particularly appropriate for relatively simple household operations where activities have high continuity. Village women in India can give simultaneous attention to two separate tasks while making chapatis (pancake type bread) in a seated position. The women can combine child care, including child nursing, with preparing the chapatis.

Overlapping of tasks is possible because of differences in the attention levels required for the tasks. If one is highly skilled in knitting, or if the

---

53. Steidl and Bratton, p. 195.

pattern is not difficult, combining knitting with watching TV may be quite workable. Primary attention may be switched from task to task even if they are concurrent.

Attributes of Sequencing. Clarity of sequence is the degree of specified order within or among tasks, and is important when someone else is to follow the sequence, when accuracy is necessary for completing tasks within one's minimum standards, and when completion of tasks is important.

A plan for a holiday dinner may be successful if the task sequences are clear to the other family members helping with the preparations. A plan for refinishing the living room floor is clear if it includes the steps needed to attain the desired quality of finish.

The need for detailed sequencing is increased by the importance of deadlines and the priorities of tasks. Priorities are clear for dependent tasks, but they may be less clear for independent tasks. The importance of some tasks may establish clear priorities, but other factors may have overriding influences.

A study of managerial components indicates that clarity of sequence, in contrast to clarity of standards, is higher for nonmarket than for market tasks. In terms of the household, two factors have different relations to clarity of sequence. When there are more children under 6 years of age, there is less clarity of sequence, but if the house is more crowded there is more clarity of sequencing. "Perhaps as the home becomes more crowded the homemaker is forced to be more clear in specifying order within or among tasks."[54] It may also be that with younger children in the household, sequencing plans are especially difficult to make and follow.

Sequence flexibility is the range of acceptable order of tasks. Flexibility in sequence appears to be related to the social position and lifestyle of families. A study of managerial components indicates that the lower the family's social position, the lower the sequence flexibility.[55] Another study of working-class women reports rather inflexible meal schedules due to employment patterns of the husbands. To accommodate shift work, the main meal may be served at 2 P.M., prior to the shift. Other working men want to have the main meal ready for them when they return in the late afternoon—at 4 or 5 P.M. Working-class women described the sequence of their days including the sameness of weekends, as dull and routine,

---

54. Maloch and Deacon, p. 12.
55. Maloch and Deacon, p. 8.

while middle-class women report few "typical" days, even though they plan to accomplish certain things each day.[56]

The weekends of working-class and middle-class families differ because of the type of work: many workers hold public service, transportation industry, or extra jobs that involve weekend work. One homemaker notes: "Saturday is different from Sunday because my husband brings home all his work clothes, and I wash them."[57]

Jobs of middle-class men and women often allow greater flexibility in scheduling over weekends, even though a school teacher may grade papers or do professional reading during the weekend. One middle-class homemaker noted: "We never have a set routine for the weekend. We do whatever we feel like on the spur of the moment. I don't worry about the work as much. I spend more time with my family—and we just enjoy loafing around the house and get more relaxation out of it. We may have some extra-good things to eat.[58]

A lifestyle involving nonemployment activities outside the home makes a rigid sequence of household tasks impractical. Committee meetings, organization activities or nonroutine social activities necessitate flexibility in sequencing of household responsibilities.

Sequence reality is the feasibility of order within or among tasks. The work of a school secretary provides examples of the need for realistic sequencing: duplication of materials requires a certain amount of time; the mail is to be picked up at a given time; an examination must be ready for a certain hour; and students stop by between classes. A realistic order of the work must be determined within and among tasks to reach the desired ends.

Realistic sequences are highly related to the situation. Some situations have predictable periods of interruption because of the nature of the tasks: machine processing, such as clothes washing, requires a person's intermittent attention; and a baking or simmering process requires time, but often no attention. A realistic sequence allows for the necessary processing time and for attention at the proper time.

If interruptions external to the tasks are probable, a sequence planned without consideration for interruptions is unrealistic. Planning to study in the dormitory just before dinner may be quite unrealistic if there is much

---

56. Lee Rainwater, Richard P. Coleman, and Gerald Handel, *Workingman's Wife* (New York: Oceana Publications, Inc., 1959), chap. 2.
57. Rainwater, Coleman, and Handel, p. 36.
58. Rainwater, Coleman, and Handel, p. 37.

visiting and idea exchanging at that time. Enough clock time may exist, but the sequence choice is poor if interruptions are not allowed for.

Sequencing for outdoor activities lacks reality if alternative sequences are not made for inclement weather. The probability of rain or snow given in weather forecasts has increased the information base for realistic decision making about sequencing.

A realistic order is particularly important for dependent tasks when one must be completed before another is begun. Letters about a political candidate must be duplicated and folded before the envelopes can be stuffed, and that must be done before the envelopes can be sealed and mailed. If several groups are going to help with the mailing process, a compatible sequence must be established.

Sequence complexity is the degree of interrelationship between persons and tasks. As with complexity of standards, complexity of sequence affects the relative complexity of the total plan. In terms of sequence, the number of persons and the number of tasks are major factors that contribute to complexity. The basic assumptions are that if two or more tasks are planned together, the sequence is more complex than for separate tasks, and if a person plans tasks for others, the sequence is more complex than if the same person planned and executed the task(s).

Level of complexity [59]	Number of persons	Number of tasks
Simple	1	1
Somewhat complex	1	2
	2	1
Complex	2 or more	2 or more

Task assignment, which reflects sequence complexity, is less complex with more efficient and task-centered persons.[60] Other studies indicate that "when home managers had positive feelings about the worth of others and were willing to accept the work standards of other family members they were more likely to receive help."[61]

---

59. Nichols, pp. 3-4, uses the term "levels of organization"; we have used and adapted her ideas in terms of level of sequence complexity.

60. Mumaw, p. 105.

61. Addreen Nichols, Catherine R. Mumaw, Maryann Paynter, Martha A. Plonk, and Dorothy Z. Price, "Family Management," *Journal of Marriage and the Family* 33 (February 1971): 116.

By definition, sequence complexity is related to the number of persons in a household old enough to participate in activities.[62] Sequence complexity also seems to be related to the type of task. When homemakers were questioned about sequence complexity, they reported that market tasks were complex more often than nonmarket tasks.[63] Perhaps when the tasks to be sequenced are outside the home, complex sequencing is needed.

Planned Facilitators

Facilitating is assisting the progress or flow of actions by capitalizing on individual or environmental potential, as defined in Chapter 2 and as further discussed in Chapter 8. *Planned facilitators* are an output planning, as indicated in Figure 7.2. Such factors may facilitate a current plan or continue to facilitate over a period of time. Facilitating factors affect the flow of action, but they are not central to the action. Planned facilitators as a result of planning are important to recognize because individuals and groups can affect their own flow of actions.

Actions can be facilitated in the planning stage in several ways. One important way is to include mechanisms in a plan that promote carrying out a given order. A second way to introduce the facilitation of action into the plan is by delegating responsibility for overseeing or providing the planned procedure. A third approach to planned facilitation is to anticipate environmental distractors or inhibitors that could affect the flow of action. A fourth contributor to the flow of action that can be anticipated is recognizing the role of motivation.

Mechanisms that promote a given order include a timer to remind one of a planned action for a certain time. A grocery list made in the order of the floor plan of the store promotes an even flow of actions. Or, in financial management, a weekly or monthly budget also serves as a planned facilitator.

Delegating responsibility for procedure facilitates a task when the expectations are compatible with the skills, capabilities, and willingness to accept responsibility. Leaving a house key with the water department can be a facilitating solution to providing access to the meter when no one is home during the day, by delegating the responsibility to the company for seeing that the meterman has the means of access. Assigning a job to a

---

62. Nichols *et al.,* p. 116.
63. Maloch and Deacon, p. 13.

child that is within his capabilities is facilitating compared to assigning a job that is too complex for the child.

Tasks can be facilitated by being planned in relation to environmental distractions or other conditions. A mother may plan to do certain jobs while the children are asleep in order to give the jobs her full attention and accomplish them more easily. Students who plan to study when suite mates are gone or who schedule two related subjects during the same term are using situations to facilitate the tasks to be done.

Anticipating inhibitors to the progress of work can be important in sequencing tasks. Avoiding interruptions can increase the flow of actions. Some tasks are made more enjoyable with interruptions, but other tasks need continuity in attention for a good flow.

When there is a choice, doing tasks when one is in the mood commonly gives a sense of smoothness in carrying them out. Knowing the motivations and interests of family members is an aspect of assessing human resources in planning. Using this insight in determining who will do what can contribute to the facilitating of plans. The related aspect of how people interact can often help to organize a more advantageous flow of work. Also, recognizing times when repeated tasks are most satisfying and planning to do them then can be a way to promote overall satisfaction.

Planned facilitators are often planning projects in their own right. The purchase of household appliances or the arrangement of a convenient work area may be carefully planned. After the plan is implemented, appliances or work arrangements can facilitate the current implementation of tasks, usually indirectly through built-in convenience. That is, actions programmed by the automatic washer do not need to be considered in detail except for choosing the program.

SUMMARY

Man's capacity for planning allows him to anticipate resource use to achieve goals. The dimensions of planning are generality, time span, scope, and repetitiveness. The information available for planning partially determines the specificity or generality of a plan. Included in the concept of generality is the definiteness of plans; with indefinite information, contingency plans may be made with alternate standards and sequences, depending on the way the situation develops.

Individuals and families make short-term and long-term plans, with the greater likelihood that they will accomplish the short-term plans. The scope of the plan may include the effects of a central decision and many plans for satellite decisions surrounding important central decisions. Plans may be used repeatedly or just once. It is important to gear plans to current family needs, particularly during times of changing life-cycle stages or during changing lifestyles.

Planning is affected by the family situation and by individual qualities. A belief in the potential for controlling one's destiny is an internal control, which can affect the planning ability of an individual. Creativity in planning is necessary to deal with new situations; foresight, both perceptual and conceptual, is another planning ability that is needed to deal with future situations.

Elaboration, as a planning ability, appears to be influenced by a person's information-processing skills. Ideas or alternative methods for dealing with a situation are stimulated by the use of information. The capacity for ordering objects or events is the last planning ability of particular importance to sequencing.

Standard setting and action sequencing are basic components of the managerial subsystem of planning. The standards, which reconcile resources with demands, and the sequences, which order the task to be accomplished, are integral to plans that are adequate bases for effective action. Standards are quality-quantity characteristics, which provide the criteria for what the action will be and how it will be carried out to achieve the desired outcome. Sequences indicate when and where the action is to take place.

Both standards and sequences may be analyzed in terms of common attributes—clarity, flexibility, reality, and complexity. These factors may be identified with either new plans or repeat-use plans, which serve recurring situations. Facilitating possibilities may be considered during the managerial process of planning.

DEFINITIONS

Planning is a series of decisions concerning future standards and/or sequences of action.

Contingency plan is one with alternative standards and sequences for indefinite conditions.

Decision making is the choice among or resolution of alternatives.

Single-use plan is a plan used only once or as part of the development of a repeat-use plan.

Repeat-use plan is a plan used more than once.

Foresight is awareness of possible future events relating to a present situation.

Elaboration is the process of producing ideas or alternative methods for an adequate solution.

Ordering is the process of defining an arrangement of objects or events in a meaningful sequence of time, hierarchy, or cause and effect relationship.

Standard setting is defining a measure of quality and/or quantity that reflects the reconciliation of resources with demands.

Quality is the property or image of what is desired.

Quantity is a definitive or estimated amount.

Clarity of standard is the specification of quality and/or quantity.

Flexibility in standards is the range of acceptable qualitative-quantitative factors for a given situation.

Reality in standards is a feasible quality and/or quantity.

Complexity in standards is the interrelationship of persons and standards.

Sequencing is ordering the parts of a task or specifying successions among the tasks.

Separately sequenced tasks are tasks planned so that one task is completed before the next task is begun.

Dependent tasks are tasks that can be started only after another task is completed.

Coordinated tasks are those tasks performed together, either overlapping or dovetailing.

Dovetailing is intermittent attention to two or more tasks until they are completed.

Overlapping of tasks is concurrent attention to two or more tasks.

Clarity of sequence is the degree of specified order within or among tasks.

Flexibility of sequence is the range of acceptable order of tasks.

Reality in sequence is the feasibility of order within or among tasks.

Complexity in sequence is the degree of interrelationship between persons and tasks.

Planned facilitators assist the progress or flow of actions by capitalizing on individual or environmental potential.

Implementing

8.

For all the plans made by individuals and groups, obviously some action must be taken by someone or something if the plan is to become a reality. The managerial term commonly used for the activation of plans is "implementing." Implementing is defined as putting a plan into effect. Implementing is comprised of both controlling and facilitating actions. Controlling is checking the actions against the plans and adjusting the standards or sequences; facilitating is assisting the progress or flow of actions by capitalizing on individual and/or the environmental potential. The relation of implementing to planning and plans can be seen in Figure 8.1.

Implementing is based on plans that follow from wide variations in planning behavior. Plans may have very explicit standards and sequence, while very general plans may provide only a framework for regulating behavior. Some persons begin activities with only generalized plans and then develop specific standards and sequences during the activity. Others plan explicitly and control the plan carefully by frequent checking and adjusting. The actions of either explicit or general plans may be facilitated.

CONTROLLING

In order for *controlling* to occur (the checking and adjusting of actions in relation to a plan) several of the following conditions must exist:

1. a plan with defined limits and/or acceptable variations,
2. a procedure for getting information about the current status in relation to the planned status, and

201

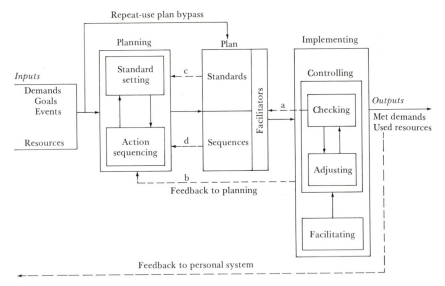

Key

a   feedback from checking to the plan
b   feedback from implementing to planning
c   feedback from standards to planning
d   feedback from sequences to planning

FIGURE 8.1 *Implementing in the home managerial system.*

3. an adjustment in behavior if there are deviations from planned behavior.[1]

The existence of a plan, regardless of the generality, time dimension, scope, or repetitiveness, is clearly necessary if planned behavior is to be controlled. The second condition for controlling may be less obvious, and that is a procedure for information exchange on the status of actions in relation to the plan. Information exchange, which compares the plan to the actions that are taking place, is generally accomplished through internal feedback (arrow "a"). When checking reveals a deviation from the plan both in planning and in sequencing, the information is fed back to the planning subsystem to reconfirm or adapt the original plan (arrow "b"). If

---

1. Sarah Jane Smith, "Personality Traits, Values, Expectations, and Managerial Behavior," The Pennsylvania State University, M.S. thesis, 1971, p. 32.

only one individual is involved in both planning and implementing, the feedback necessary for controlling is not a complex procedure. If the person implementing the plan is different from the planner, getting information about the current status in relation to the planned status adds complexity to implementing. The person implementing a plan checks with the planner who, in this case, controls the actions even though someone else is carrying out the plan.

For some persons, it can be frustrating to have the responsibility for defining and carrying out what needs to be done after someone else has both planned and controlled the actions. Sometimes women who change from employment in the labor force to working in the home full time experience such anxiety:

Some (homemakers) feel that the whole shift from a work role into that of a housewife increases responsibility, which is not necessarily welcome. They miss the time and work controls and systems of the job, and women not accustomed to being self-motivating or (to taking) initiative in their behavior have to undertake major personality changes in the way they handle themselves, their duties, and their relations with others. Passive stances, awaiting the initiative of others, may be effective and even desired of secretaries to charismatic and ever-present bosses, but the modern housewife generally cannot afford such an approach to her roles. This stage (expanding circle) requires a great deal of work to be planned, organized, and executed by the same person.[2]

If the actions are deviating from the plan, corrective procedures may take place as a result of feedback or the exchange of information. Corrective measures are taken to align the actions with the plan or to change the plan so that the output will coincide as nearly as possible with the original demand. Another important effect of feedback can occur. Information on deviation of actions from a plan and information about a rapidly changing environment may lead to a far greater variety of actions than was previously envisioned. With a repeat-use plan, for example, the effect may be the relaxation of formerly stringent standards (arrow "c") or a change in some aspect of the sequence (arrow "d"). The original plan may be broadened or narrowed, but not reoriented. For instance, when the city puts in new traffic lights, one may have to allow a few more minutes to get to work because of the extra stops to be made. In other cases, the produc-

---

2. Helena Z. Lopata, *Occupation: Housewife* (New York: Oxford University Press, 1971), p. 36.

tion of whole new standards and sequences may be needed to more nearly fit the reality (arrow "b").

The many decisions that lead to the wife's employment outside the home illustrate change, which is both expansive and realistic. For example, a husband-wife family with five children had the goal that the husband would earn money to support the family and the wife would care for the children and all household matters. When they checked the expenses of the family against the plan for spending, it became obvious that some change would have to be made. Cutting down on expenses (corrective action) no longer seemed possible, and the couple decided the wife should go to work outside the home. After her employment, the husband changed his standards and sequences since he saw that he would have to help care for the children and with other household matters. The new plans that developed were more consistent with the reality of resources and demands. Controlling can lead to corrective actions and to expanded or changed plans to accommodate deviations.

Checking

Checking is the examination of actions, which may be carried out by the planner or by the person or machine implementing the plan. When clothes are brought to the dry cleaner, they are checked for spots and decorations that need special attention and for other potential problems. Then they are checked afterward for appearance, for missing buttons or decorations, and so on. As a customer, you may also check on these last items when you pick up the dry cleaning; but if you use a reliable dry-cleaning establishment, you may completely transfer the checking to them.

Transferring the responsibility of checking is widely practiced in family financial management. Withholding from paychecks provides a way to control plans, whether the money is withheld for taxes, for united giving, for retirement, for health or automobile insurance, for stock-option plans, or for savings bonds. The implementing may be transferred completely to the employer, including the checking against the planned withholding. In a study of families whose goal was to finance their children's college educations, controlling was primarily effected by contractual savings.[3]

---

3. Julia Mae Schriver Hahn, "Families' Control of the Allocation of Financial Resources for the College Education of Their Children," M.S. thesis, The Pennsylvania State University, 1968, p. 89.

When property is bought, checking on the payment of taxes and insurance can be transferred to the lending agency. An escrow account is set up, and the amount due on insurance and taxes is accumulated regularly with the mortgage payment. The lending agency then pays the insurance and taxes when they are due.

Checking by either the planner or the person or machine to which the checking is transferred is accomplished by subjective and objective methods. Objective methods include measuring devices such as thermometers, scales, and receipts; subjective methods use visual, auditory, tactual, or other sensory means. Testing the springiness of a cake to see if it is completely baked is subjective checking.

In a consumer purchase, such as the purchase of a desk lamp, specific standards of quality and quantity can be established and checked both objectively and subjectively. When selecting a lamp, one can compare the lighting capacity (objective), the height (objective), the sturdiness and design of the base (subjective), and other important qualities with preferred standards for the lamp.

Checking actions against a standard have been found to be prevalent in both market and nonmarket situations.[4] In relation to marketing, almost three-fourths of the homemakers who were asked these two questions reported checking actions: "How were you sure you had the kinds and quality of frozen and canned foods you wanted?" and "While you were shopping, how did you know you had the right amount of a certain product?"

Checking on a variety of factors has been reported in observations of grocery shopping. The process of selecting packages involves, "putting them down, fondling them, reading them, dropping them, picking them up and putting them back in the wrong place, etc.," and people sometimes look at weight, price, and what premiums are offered and read the fine print.[5] This observation of a shopper in the cereal aisle of a grocery store was recorded during such a study:

When she sees the cereals, she immediately stops and picks up a large box of H. O. Quick Oats. She looks the box over entirely (apparently looking at the price and weight content). While still holding this box in her hand, she picks up a box of

---

4. Francille Maloch and Ruth E. Deacon, "Components of Home Management in Relation to Selected Variables," Research Bulletin 1042 (Wooster, Ohio: Ohio Agricultural Research and Development Center, 1970), p. 16.

5. William D. Wells and Leonard A. LoSciuto, "Direct Observation of Purchasing Behavior," *Journal of Marketing Research* 3 (August 1966): 231.

Mother('s) Oats. She then looks this box over entirely and compares the two boxes. She looks at the H.O. Quick Oats and then at the Mother('s) Oats (apparently comparing their prices). After comparing the two, she puts the box of Mother('s) Oats back on the shelf and puts the other box in the cart. After making this decision she remains where she is and continues to look at the cereals. She then notices the smaller box of H. O. Quick Oats, which is on the upper shelf. She picks up this box and looks at it, again reading the panels. She puts the box down and turns around to her carriage. She then stops, turns around, picks up the box again and places it in her cart. She replaces the larger box on the shelf, in the wrong place, and continues down the aisle not looking at the rest of the cereals.[6]

The shopper apparently intended to purchase cereal, but she had no specific brand preference and was checking against rather general standards. In the same study, clear evidence of product and/or brand intentions was found for the three product purchases observed: 55 per cent of the cereal purchases, 38 per cent of the candy purchases, and 72 per cent of the detergent purchases.[7]

Grocery shopping specifications formed prior to shopping were categorized in another study as follows:

Planned
Product and brand—both are known before the shopper enters the store.
Product only—product purchase is planned but not by a specific brand.
Product class—product type only, for example, bakery dessert, is specified.
Need—generalized standard is known, for example, something for children's lunches or something for dinner.

Unplanned
Need not recognized—no plan has been made at any of the other levels of specification; the need may be latent and unrecognized before in-store stimuli.[8]

About half the purchases made by almost 600 shoppers were categorized as unplanned.[9] Controlling activity depends on having a plan; checking is made against a planned standard and/or sequence. Further examination of the "unplanned purchases" in the grocery-shopping study

---

6. Wells and LoSciuto, p. 231.
7. David T. Kollat and Ronald P. Willett, "Customer Impulse Purchasing Behavior," *Journal of Marketing Research* 4 (February 1967): 21.
8. Kollat and Willett, p. 21.
9. Kollat and Willett, p. 23.

showed that a large percentage (64) of the purchases was for items needed to restock the household inventory. The shoppers replenished their inventory with the same brands that they had previously stocked. Only six per cent of the shoppers bought items to restock their inventory that were not the same brand as previously purchased.[10]

"In-store stimuli usually remind shoppers of present or future needs rather than evoking new needs."[11] In grocery shopping, checking is more likely to involve testing against a generalized standard or against a plan for a certain size inventory, rather than against criteria relating to a specific intention for a shopping trip.

A written shopping list is concrete evidence of a plan that can be used for checking. Thirty per cent of 3,200 shoppers in thirteen stores had a shopping list, according to another study.[12] Shoppers with a prepared list shopped longer and spent about 5 cents more per minute than those without a list.[13] Perhaps a planned trip is a major rather than a fill-in trip and may require more time for the shopper to choose and check the items against the plan. Or, locating specified items may require more involved checking; less specification may mean that a broader range of items is acceptable.

In another study of almost 600 grocery shoppers, those with a list who purchased more than fifteen products purchased a smaller portion of unplanned products than those without a list who purchased the same amount of groceries. If fewer items were purchased, a list did not affect the percentage of unplanned purchases.[14] A list thus appears to help in checking against a plan for purchasing for major grocery shopping trips.

Fewer homemakers report that they sequence in nonmarket situations compared to market situations.[15] Perhaps because of the familiarity of a less structured environment such as the home, checking the sequence does not seem as important as in an away-from-home setting.

---

10. Kollat and Willett, p. 29.
11. Kollat and Willett, p. 30.
12. Nick Havas and Hugh M. Smith, "Customers' Shopping Patterns in Retail Food Stores," U.S. Dept. of Agriculture, Economic Research Service, Marketing Economics Division ERS-99 (Washington, D. C.: U.S. Government Printing Office, 1962), p. 13.
13. Havas and Smith, p. 13.
14. Kollat and Willett, p. 27.
15. Maloch and Deacon, p. 16.

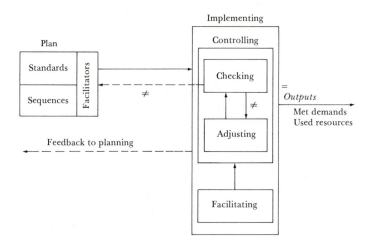

FIGURE 8.2 *Controlling in implementing.*

Adjusting

Adjusting is changine a planned standard, a sequence, or their underlying processes to increase the chances of the desired output. When there is deviation from planned behavior, as identfied through checking, plans must be adjusted. The TOTE unit (Test, Operate, Test, Exit)[16] describes the concept of checking and adjusting. If the plan is being met after it has been tested against the planned standard and-or sequence, there is an exit (output). This is noted in Figure 8.2 by the = sign above the output from checking. If checking reveals a discrepancy between what is desired and what is being accomplished, adjusting takes place. This is indicated by the = sign from checking to adjusting. After adjusting takes place, whenever what is desired is met, (=), there is output from checking in the form of met demands and used resources. When adjusting involves changes in both standards and sequences, a new plan results.

The real world contains many situations that require adjusting. A college student plans to buy a relatively new car soon after graduation. A course being offered next term requires field work away from campus, and a car would be helpful. What is the possibility of getting the car before

---

16. George A. Miller, E. Galanter, and K. H. Pribram, *Plans and Structure of Behavior* (New York: Henry Holt and Co., 1960), pp. 17, 21–39.

graduation (a change in sequence)? What is the possibility of getting an older car now (a change in standard and sequence—therefore, a new plan)?

Apparently more adjusting is found in market than in nonmarket situations, although more new plans are generated in nonmarket situations.[17] Since a change in both the standard and the sequence is needed for a new plan, unplanned purchases are considered an adjustment in standards. Changes from the original plan in the time allowed for shopping and in the pattern of shopping are sequence adjustments. Almost two-thirds of the homemakers in one study did not adjust the sequence of time or the pattern of grocery shopping, while nearly two-thirds of the homemakers adjusted their standards for items at the store while shopping.

One of the studies previously discussed suggests that many "unplanned purchases" may be quite purposeful when in-store stimuli remind the shopper of gaps in her home inventory that need to be filled with certain items.[18]

In a household work situation such as baking a cake, if the cake does not spring back to the touch (a deviation from the desired standard), it will probably be left to bake a little longer (a corrective action, or change in the standard for length of time for baking given by the recipe). If the oven thermostat is faulty or if the cake is left in the oven longer than was planned, a change in the standard (accepting an overdone cake) or a change in both standard and sequence might occur.

FACILITATING

Facilitating is assisting the progress or flow of actions by capitalizing on individual and/or environmental potential. Plans may include facilitating actions, and facilitating may originate while the plan is being implemented (Figure 8.3). The individual potential relates to the planners themselves and the environmental potential involves other persons and things in the situation. Conditions that promote achieving the standards or sequences of plans facilitate their implementation.

Facilitating processes may be evolved in the implementing subsystem. While implementing a task, a person may intuitively see an easier way to

---

17. Maloch and Deacon, p. 16.
18. Kollat and Willett, p. 30.

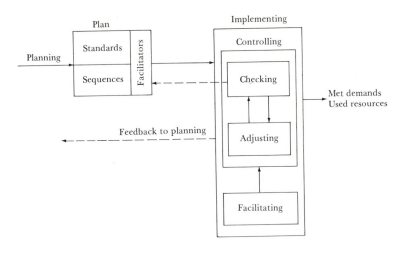

FIGURE 8.3 *Facilitating actions originating during planning and implementing.*

do the task, allowing the work to flow more continuously or more smoothly. While implementing a plan, a clerk-typist may discover an easier work method for doing a task. Assembling more sheets of paper may be made easier by putting brads through the paper in a certain manner. The typist may have had a general sequence in mind for putting the paper together, but not the specific method of putting brads in the paper. Facilitating of this type usually involves an adjustment of sequences.

The physical environment can help homemaking work in some instances and can hinder it in others. In one study, respondents recognized both the positive impact of good physical environment and the negative impact of poor physical environment.[19] Of the things affecting work difficulty, the homemakers most often mentioned specific features of the house and contents, such as equipment adequacy, supplies, space, and room.[20]

For grocery shopping, physical aspects, such as store arrangement or layout, location or type (small neighborhood store, chain supermarket, etc.), and store policies, contributed to making the task easier or harder

---

19. Rose E. Steidl, "Difficulty Factors in Homemaking Tasks: Implications for Environmental Design," *Human Factors* 14 (October 1972): 476.

20. Steidl, p. 476.

according to an Ohio study.[21] The impersonal structure of modern stores has been described as a system designed to facilitate logical deduction of probable locations of items (even in unfamiliar stores). The customer is left free to make decisions, with no one to question the selections or recommend anything based on personal knowledge about the shopper or his family.[22] Although these features may be facilitating to some shoppers, they may be frustrating to others who would prefer more personal attention and assistance—a more humanized environment.

Technology has had a major impact on the environmental potential. For example, the use of heating fuels other than coal and oil has eased cleaning in homes. Technology's effect on families has been uneven; to enjoy its benefits, the family must have adequate resources available. In low-income homes, household equipment often functions poorly or is not available. Doing laundry by drawing water from an outdoor source, heating it on the stove, washing with a wringer washer, and hanging the clothes up to dry can use large blocks of time,[23] and the flow of work is not enhanced. If the environment inhibits a person or unnecessarily increases the workload, it reduces opportunities for creativity and satisfaction with the output quality.[24]

Whether a task is facilitated by plan or by intuitively developed action probably does not affect the satisfaction with output or even the satisfaction of doing the task. For example, at a large party, one may discover early that changing the location of the refreshment area will move the crowd through more quickly, but the fact that the first location was less successful probably will not add to or detract from the satisfaction with the party.

Facilitating should not be confused with efficiency or the quickest way to accomplish a task; it is the flow of action. One can make a few trips with heavy loads and accomplish the task quickly, but facilitating actions for such a task would be those that actually make the task progress more

---

21. Maloch and Deacon, p. 18.
22. Lopata, p. 167.
23. Janet M. Fitchen, "The People of Road Junction: The Participant Observer's Study of a Rural Poverty Area in Northern Appalachia, with Particular Reference to the Problems of Employment of Low-Income Women," in *A Study of the Effects on the Family Due to Employment of the Welfare Mother,* Volume III, Report to Manpower Administration, U.S. Dept. of Labor (no date), p. 88.
24. Steidl, p. 481.

smoothly. One senses a lack of facilitating actions in the description by a professionally employed woman:

The difficulty most apparent to anyone who walks into our house is the fact that I have never been able to keep house the way my husband and I would like to have our house kept. It is seldom that the niceties are accomplished and it is not always that the necessities can be counted upon. Nor is it possible to keep up with all the various errands that wives and mothers usually take care of for their husbands, children, households, and themselves. Things get done after a fashion, but usually behind time and then, only when really necessary. Furthermore, they must be done in the quickest way, which is often not the best way.[25]

FACTORS AFFECTING IMPLEMENTING

Family, individual, environmental, and task qualities affect implementing, both in controlling and in facilitating. Some of the factors may be considered in planning, while other qualities are not usually considered each time a plan is formed.

Family Qualities

The family-related variables that seem to make a difference in implementing plans are the family life cycle, ages of the children, and family size—all interrelated factors. Having preschool children present may make some household tasks more difficult to control, but this situation may or may not be prominent in a person's analysis of the job to be done. Some mothers are acutely aware of trying to accomplish certain plans while the children are asleep, while others seem to carry on oblivious to interruptions.

Family life-cycle stage affected implementation of plans in a study of three generations.[26] The fulfillment of plans and the extent of planned actions were considered together and represent what is viewed here as implementing. Four types of families emerged from the analysis, and in

---

25. Sidney Cornelia Callahan, *The Working Mother* (New York: The Macmillan Company, 1971), pp. 116–17.
26. Reuben Hill, *Family Development in Three Generations* (Cambridge, Mass.: Schenkman Publishing Co., Inc., 1970).

each of the family types one or two of the generations predominate, that is, a higher percentage of grandparent, parent, or child generation appears in a type.[27]

Family type	*Predominant generation*
High plan-fulfillment and many unplanned actions	Child; Parent
High plan-fulfillment and many planned actions	Parent
Low plan-fulfillment and many unplanned actions	Grandparent
Low plan-fulfillment and many planned actions	Child

The child generation dominates the low plan-fulfillment and many planned actions group (fruitless planners) probably because they verbalize plans (risking lower plan-fulfillment) and undertake actions without prior plans.[28]

Significant differences were found in a study of marketing practices for families in different stages of the family life cycle. More older couples and couples with infants had changed marketing practices in the past five years than had others. Since family composition changed within the time, the differences might have been expected. It is also probable that controlling was limited if marketing practices did not change with the family situation.[29]

The impact of family planning, including child spacing, is beginning to be recognized in home management. Most of the research on the difference in desired and actual family size has been done in areas other than home economics. Future emphasis on both planning and controlling family size and child spacing will likely increase. "Clearly the major labor-saving device benefitting the housewife in industrial societies is the contraceptive."[30]

---

27. Hill, p. 221.
28. Hill, p. 222.
29. Carol B. O'Brien and Dorothy Z. Price, "An Investigation of The Traditional Concept of Management," *Quarterly Bulletin* of the Michigan Agricultural Experiment Station 44 (May 1962): 719.
30. Wilbert E. Moore, *Man, Time, and Society* (New York: John Wiley & Sons, Inc., 1963), p. 32.

Family size and child spacing indicate a controlling to meet plans when both the desired family size and the actual family size are known. Religious affiliation formerly played an important part in family-size decisions. "Catholics in the United States do not practice contraception so much for child spacing as for limiting family size, whereas non-Catholics use it to control both the spacing and number of births."[31]

Family planning has been theorized to have passed from the higher socioeconomic women to lower socioeconomic women. "The urban women of highest socioeconomic status were the first to resort to family limitation practices and hence were the leaders in the trend toward small families. Family planning practices eventually filtered downward through the socioeconomic classes and outward to rural areas. The rural women of lowest socioeconomic status, according to this theory, are the last to accept family planning."[32] The theory reflected reality until 1960, when trends appeared that were apparently inconsistent with the theory. Differences in birth rates by farm status and race are in the opposite direction: greater declines among nonwhites than whites, and among farm than nonfarm women.[33] Other evidence since 1960 supports the earlier observation. High-school graduates now have lower birth rates than women with less education.[34]

Individual Qualities

Individual qualities that may affect implementing are skills for controlling and facilitating, personality and orientation, health, education, and employment.

Skills for controlling are suggested as being particularly important in checking and adjusting; successful checking may depend on skill in receiving and interpreting information. Knowing, predicting, and deciding are helpful in adjusting. Facilitating may require all the skills of receiving and interpreting information, knowing, predicting, and deciding.[35]

Personality traits that affect organizing, controlling, and facilitating are

---

31. N. Krishnan Namboodiri, "The Wife's Work Experience and Child Spacing," *The Milbank Memorial Fund Quarterly* 52 (July 1964): 75.
32. Clyde V. Kiser, "Changing Patterns of Fertility in the United States," *Social Biology* 17 (December 1970): 306.
33. Kiser, p. 313.
34. Kiser, p. 314.
35. Nancy I. Hungerford, "An Approach to the Study of Managerial Control," Cornell University, M.S. thesis, 1970, p. 88.

summarized in Table 8.1. Organizing, which is defined as a structure of relationships formed for or during planning and implementing, includes some aspects of controlling.[36]

The dominant personality traits related to control are persistence, order, lack of impulsiveness, and planfulness. Some individuals may aspire to be free and impulsive in their actions; they may not wish to control the situation. The artist is stereotyped as a creative and, to some extent, impulsive person, without order and routine; but when his actions in pursuit of important goals are examined, the stereotype does not always fit. The steady painting, practicing, or drilling in technique toward creating desired effects may demonstrate a strong controlling emphasis.

An individual's orientation to a situation can affect performance in a task. Individuals who are in situations where personal competence can affect the outcome tend to perform more adequately than when the situation is less controllable.[37] Persons in public housing may feel that they have little or no opportunity for affecting outcomes, and they may perform less and less effectively over the years.

In one study of managerial behavior of homemakers, health influenced adjusting—the poorer the health, the more adjusting became necessary.[38] Another study of organizing, which included checking, adjusting, facilitating, and sequencing, found a relationship between health and the homemaker's concept of her organizing ability.[39]

Apparently less adjusting occurs among those with more education. Fewer homemakers with more formal education reported adjusting decisions in the market.[40] Significantly higher percentages of homemakers with college education made lists in a logical order and checked the completeness of their purchases.[41]

Relatively little is known about the impact of the wife's employment on controlling actions. In the three-generational study previously cited, the

36. Catherine R. Mumaw and Addreen Nichols, "Organizational Styles of Homemakers: A Factor Analytic Approach," *Home Economics Research Journal* 1 (September 1972): 35.

37. Herbert M. Lefcourt, "Belief in Personal Control: Research and Implications," *Journal of Individual Psychology* 22 (November 1966): 188.

38. Maloch and Deacon, p. 17.

39. Nancy Ann Barclay, "Organization of Household Activities by Home Managers," The Ohio State University, Ph.D. dissertation, 1970, p. 50.

40. O'Brien and Price, p. 718

41. O'Brien and Price, p. 718.

TABLE 8.1
Personality traits associated with controlling, organizing, and facilitating.

Managerial component	Personality trait	Selected attributes or behaviorial patterns
Controlling-checking[1]	Orderliness (need for order)	Tidy, clean, and precise: arranges, organizes, puts away objects
	Sameness	Persistent in purpose, consistent in conduct, rigid in habits, likes familiar places and people
	Deliberation	Inhibited, hesitates, reflects before acting; not impulsive
	Placidity	Emotionally serene; shows little autonomic excitement or affection
Controlling-facilitating[2]	Conjunctivity	Coordinates action and thought; organizes purposes and behavioral patterns
	Resourcefulness	Uses technical and social knowledge
Controlling[3]	Responsibility	Dependable, thorough, progressive, conscientious, and efficient
	Tolerance	Enterprising, informal, clear-thinking
	Intellectual efficiency	Capable, intelligent, progressive, thorough, alert
	Flexibility	Informal, confident, idealistic, assertive
Organizational patterns[4]	Orderliness	Emphasizes neatness and organization
	Dominance	Seeks and sustains leadership in groups
	Endurance	Persists in tasks
	Achievement	Strives to be outstanding in socially recognized situations
	Heterosexuality	Seeks companionship and emotional satisfaction from interaction with opposite sex
	Less lability	Unable to tolerate consistency and routine

[1,2] Nancy A. Barclay, "Organizing of Household Activities by Home Managers," The Ohio State University, Ph.D. dissertation, 1970, pp. 17, 29, 46.
[3] Sarah Jane Smith, "Personality Traits, Values, Expectations, and Managerial Behavior," The Pennsylvania State University, M.S. thesis, 1971, pp. 29–30, 43–44.
[4] Catherine R. Mumaw, "Organizational Patterns of Homemakers Related to Selected Predispositional and Situational Characteristics," The Pennsylvania State University, Ph.D. dissertation, 1967, pp. 109, 146–47.

low plan-fulfillment and low planned-action families outnumbered the remaining family types.[42]

The fourth group in the listing below contained a disproportionate number of families where the wife was not employed outside the home. Perhaps the wives-at-home make wishful plans they are unable to fulfill.[43]

		All generations
1.	High plan-fulfillment with many unplanned actions	16%
2.	High plan-fulfillment with many planned actions	28%
3.	Low plan-fulfillment and many unplanned actions	37%
4.	Low plan-fulfillment and many planned actions	19%

A mother previously employed outside the home and now doing free-lance work at home states ". . . I find it very hard to work well with fragments of time, and almost impossible to think of more than one thing at a time. Paid work, with its organized chunks of time, fits my habit of mind, and makes me turn my lazy side to good use. Juggling the fragments of several projects, committees, housework leads to just one end: procrastination."[44]

Task discontinuity is the feature of household work that the mother found frustrating; apparently she was unable to control plans she had made. Many homemaking tasks consist of small units of action. Work needs to be sequenced to take advantage of active and inactive periods inherent in each task if the discontinuous nature of the work is to be less difficult to work within.[45]

Environment-Related Qualities

"Not only is the environment something that is outside the system's control, but it is also something that determines in part how the system performs."[46] The macro-habitat includes the structured and

---

42. Hill, p. 221.
43. Hill, p. 226.
44. Callahan, p. 178.
45. Steidl, p. 480.
46. C. West Churchman, *The Systems Approach* (New York: Delacorte Press, 1968), p. 36.

natural space and the biological contents of the surroundings; much of this environment is outside the system's control. The micro-habitat is the immediate surroundings of the family—its physical setting, the family members, the things directly impinging on the family. Families can exert control over some aspects of the micro-habitat.[47]

The impact of the environment, both the macro-and micro-habitats, is felt on facilitating. Facilitating is affected by the adequacy of equipment, supplies, space, and rooms.[48] Aspects of the micro-habitat that have been reported as making work more difficult include the following inadequacies and inconveniences:

space—insufficient work space;
   poorly located counter space;
   inadequate and poorly located storage space

equipment—poorly designed and poorly functioning equipment;
   insufficient refrigerator space;
   insufficient pots, pans, serving dishes, and silverware

supplies or utilities—insufficient hot water
   poor water quality.[49]

If using household equipment actually makes work less difficult, it might follow that equipment facilitates work and saves time. Evidence is difficult to gather, however, since work methods change when certain equipment is used. A vacuum cleaner may be used to clean draperies that were previously only drycleaned. The total time spent on household tasks may thus increase with equipment use. Since facilitating is the flow or progress of actions, equipment use can be very facilitating even though the time spent on a task increases. For most people, there is a different and an easier flow of actions with an automatic washer than with an apartment-size wringer-spinner washer, which requires the operator's presence during certain stages of the cycle. The flow of actions might be improved by use of community laundry facilities for washing several loads of clothes at one time.

---

47. Hungerford, p. 29.
48. Steidl, p. 476 and Maloch and Deacon, p. 18.
49. Steidl, p. 476.

Changing storage facilities can increase ease of work and bring feelings of better organization when functional storage is effected.[50] When the homemaker has improved storage space, the time spent on tasks may be lessened little, if any, but the increased flow of work can make changes in storage very desirable. Time is an inadequate measure of ease or flow of work.

Weather, a component of the macro-habitat, can affect both controlling and facilitating in many parts of the world. Inclement weather may interrupt or postpone activities, presenting problems in controlling and causing plan adjustments. Outdoor cooking, as practiced in many areas of India, is subject to weather disturbances such as dust storms. In a study of Indian village households, women reported that when a dust storm arose they simply moved the cooking inside. The intense heat of some seasons encourages cooking outdoors, and thus the households seem subject to the rigors of weather much of the time.

In the United States, alternate plans for drying clothes during inclement weather developed over the years. Clothes were dried indoors near a source of heat either in the attic or the basement. Today, many families use mechanical clothes dryers and thus are less affected by the weather. In the future, artificial weather controls may make families far less susceptible to weather changes.

The stage in the family life cycle may well influence the impact of weather on controlling and facilitating activities. Families with young children may be particularly affected by inclement weather when the children must remain indoors. The time set aside for working relatively uninterrupted is "lost," and work may become more difficult or "negatively facilitated." In a study of young homemakers, weather was not frequently mentioned as making work more or less difficult.[51] Possibly some of them did not mention weather because they felt they had little control over the situation.

Task Qualities

Young homemakers who were asked about tasks with high and low cognitive requirements, attention, judgment, and planning, reported

---

50. Rose E. Steidl and Esther Crew Bratton, *Work in the Home* (New York: John Wiley & Sons, Inc., 1968), p. 277.
51. Steidl, p. 476.

what made the tasks more or less difficult. Tasks that were ranked as the most liked, most complicated, and most difficult were almost always the highly cognitive tasks; those ranked as the least complicated and the least difficult were nearly always the low cognitive tasks and were very often the least liked.[52]

Complicated tasks need more controlling and greater attention to reach the desired standard. Food preparation and child care are tasks with reportedly high cognitive requirements. The complexity of food and meal preparation probably varies widely among families, and, for many, a great deal of concern about meals and nutrition contributes to the need for controlling plans and facilitating the work.

Emotional or affective aspects of child care make concern for accomplishing activities in a particular way very important to some families. If parents want their children nearby for supervision while other activities are undertaken, they must provide an area for both the work and the children's play. In such a situation, controlling is generally more complex by overlapping them with single tasks.

SUMMARY

Implementing plans involves controlling and facilitating actions. Checking the actions against the plan and adjusting standards and sequence as needed make up the controlling aspect.

Through checking, the qualitative and quantitative aspects of standards and the sequences of plans are examined for acceptability. Internal feedback is important for information on how well a plan is being met and to help determine when a new plan is needed.

Adjusting, another part of controlling, is a change in either the standards desired or the sequence to be followed. When both standards and sequence must be changed, a new plan is needed.

Facilitating plans, or assisting the progress or flow of actions, capitalizes on human resources, material resources, and other environ-

52. Steidl, p. 480.

mental conditions. The environment of a task can assist or inhibit the smooth flow of actions.

Implementing is affected by characteristics of the family, such as family life cycle, ages of the children, and family size. The individual factors of skills for controlling and facilitating—personality and orientation, health, education, and employment—may also affect implementing. Environmental qualities that can affect implementing include space, equipment, supplies or utilities, and weather. Qualities of the tasks themselves can also affect implementing.

DEFINITIONS

Implementing is putting a plan into effect. Implementing is comprised of controlling and facilitating actions.

Controlling is checking actions against plans and adjusting standards and/or sequences.

Checking is examining actions against planned standards and sequences.

Adjusting is changing a planned standard, sequence, or their underlying processes to increase the chances of the desired output.

Facilitating is assisting the progress of flow of actions by capitalizing on the individual and/or environmental potential.

Output and Input-Output Relations

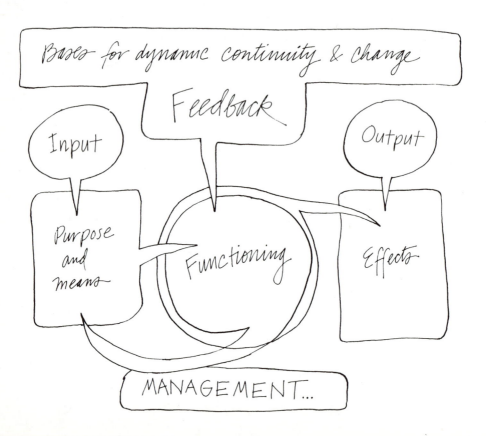

Bases for dynamic continuity & change

Feedback

Input

Output

Purpose and means

Functioning

Effects

MANAGEMENT...

9.

In judging the effectiveness of a system we may compare the actual outputs with the outcomes that we had anticipated, that is our demands. The more consistent the outputs are with what was anticipated, the more effective we may judge the management system to be, since anticipated outcomes are translated into expected outcomes through planning and into actual outcomes through implementing.

As part of a purposeful social system, however, household members do more than respond mechanically to the stimuli of goals when they manage.[1] Numerous decisions accompany the activity of the management processes as they are initiated by a goal and brought to fruition as output. And these decisions are continually monitored through feedback in terms of their relation to the system demands. To understand the effectiveness of a goal-directed management system, we must examine not only outputs, as such, but also their relationship to inputs.

Demands and resources, like inputs, may be viewed as separate output entities —met demands and used resources—and in the following sections we shall discuss these outputs first. We then consider input-output relationships and the ongoing influences of feedback.

---

1. Russell L. Ackoff and Fred E. Emery, *On Purposeful Systems* (Chicago: Aldine Atherton, 1972), p. 6.

OUTPUTS

Goals and events stimulate managerial action, and the system responds with two forms of output: met demands and used resources. Management translates anticipated and unanticipated demands into outputs that are as consistent as possible with the expectations.

The output of an open system is conveyed to its environment. The output of a household management system may remain within the family system or go to the external environment since such output may be either internal or external to the family system. Output that results from a disastrous event such as a flood is an example of internal and external output. The human resources used to clean up the silt and repair the damage to the family dwelling are internal to the family system. The money spent for materials to repair the flood damage, the human resources used to care for strangers or help neighbors and their housing, and the concern expressed are external outputs.

Met Demands

The value-related meanings or satisfactions that follow from the managerial activity represent the met demands component of output. The source and purpose of demands determine the nature of the satisfaction and whether it stays within the household or extends beyond the household boundary. Goals that evolve within the family system are likely to produce met demands that have their primary effect within the family system, although sharing with others may influence the goals. For example, the goal to fix up the basement for family activities may be motivated by the family's pleasure in being together or in their enjoyment of certain activities. The shared meaning attached to these effects when the project is finished will be of primary importance to the family members. Any enthusiasm conveyed to friends and neighbors that influences a similar goal for them may or may not change the family's sense of satisfaction. If the family was motivated to finish the basement as a means of "keeping up with the Joneses," the major sense of achievement would accrue from that source rather than from the enjoyment of shared activities within the family, although the latter satisfaction could also occur. In either case, the output as a met demand remains primarily internal to the family.

As illustrated above, the personal system is likely to determine the nature of the satisfaction from the goal-related activity of the management system. In a similar situation, the role of the personal system is further illustrated by a study of middle-income mothers who reported more satisfaction with the organization of their household work when they also perceived higher marital agreement.[2]

Societal rules and regulations are a common form of met demands that have external effects. Certain demands may be met with a recognition of their necessity and simple compliance, while the purpose of others may be strongly supported or opposed, as is often the case with taxes. The manner in which these demands are met is sometimes foreshadowed at an earlier date when, for example, a family either helped to bring the levy to a vote or tried to defeat its passage. This output to the political system is identified in Figure 2.3 (D^2), outputs expressed as formal or informal demands from the family system to the political system. The family system's tangible support of existing obligations (S^2) is output, which is a form of resource use, and is an aspect discussed in the next section.

Used Resources

Managerial decisions and actions underlie the household's resource flow. Current resource use represents a shift in the stock of available means for meeting demands. The effects of resource use may be retained within the household or conveyed to the external environment. Various managerial activities affect changes in the amount and kind of available resources.

Managerial activity	*Change in amount of available resources*
exchanging	no change
consuming	decreases
protecting	decreases
transferring	decreases
producing	increases
saving-investing	increases

Exchanging. As indicated above, an exchange is characterized as a shift in the inventory of resources without a change in the value of total available resources. Such exchanges may occur within the family system

---

2. E. Carolyn Ater and Ruth E. Deacon, "Interaction of Family Relationship Qualities and Managerial Components," *Journal of Marriage and the Family* 34 (May 1972): 260.

and between the family and other systems and may or may not involve money, although money is likely to figure in the facilitation of exchanges.

Output from many household managerial activities results in shifts in the resource inventory of individuals or household members who either share resources or who have understood rights of use and disposition. A father may purchase his son's car when the son cannot take it to college. For the father, the internal exchange of money for the car affects the composition of his total inventory, but probably not its total value. The same is true for the son. For the household, if the son is dependent, neither the amount of each resource nor the total has changed. For this reason, exchanges with the external environment are probably more significant to household management.

Exchanges inside or outside the system need not involve money. An exchange of garden tools by neighbors can be mutually beneficial. The common expectation is that an exchange will change the inventory make-up but not its value even though the new acquisition has preferred attributes over the exchanged one. If an unneeded radio is sold, the money is more desirable than the radio. When the money is spent for new records, they are obviously wanted more than the radio or the money.

Each type of managerial activity listed above that results in shifts in a household's stock of resources involves exchanges—except, of course, transfers, which are by definition one-way. Since the activity which follows the exchange is to be emphasized in its relation to effects on the resource stock of the household, each category will be discussed separately with only a passing reference to the exchange aspect. As external exchanges, these outputs from the household are inputs to other systems and have important effects, primarily on the economic system. Household consumption choices, for example, made in response to various household demands, contribute to the determination of market demand—the quantity of a product or service that will be taken at a price.

Time-related exchanges, such as services, are less amenable to measurement than are material resources because time is not exchanged but is used in exchange for something. It cannot be held or accumulated as can material resources. These difficulties are alerting both economists and home economists of the need to account more adequately for the time factor in exchanges.

A person who exchanges his skills and his time for pay finds the money more useful than if the time and skills were used in another way. Exchange relationships are not easily weighed if the value of each good or service is not readily measured in market terms. The total impact of returns from outside productive work, the consumption level, and the demands of household work must all be evaluated in order for households to maximize their work and consumption potential. If income and consumption increase in relation to outside employment, time demands then increase for consumption and household maintenance, leading to inclinations to decrease total work.[3] Time-related choices are complex and affect the various aspects of resources and their allocation.

Consuming.   The consistent effect of consuming is a reduction in resources and their available utility values. This occurs whether stocks of resources internal to the household are consumed or whether money is exchanged externally for a good or service.

Meaningful classifications are difficult because of the varied purposes for which consumption expenditures are made and the varying periods of time over which satisfaction from use continues. Reference in this context will be limited to the time period over which satisfactions from consumption are anticipated—currently, or in the near or far future.[4] Families currently consume about 70 per cent of their yearly expenditures; the proportion is higher for families that have below-average expenditures and it is lower for those that have above-average expenditures.[5] The other 30 per cent of the year's expenditures for durable goods have asset value as well as current and future utility value for consumption. This long-run impact of current spending needs to be recognized. Repairs to a TV set presumably extend its service life, but also imply future benefits along with current ones.

Protecting.   Insurance protection is the resource counterpart to protection against the effects of unforeseen contingencies (event demands). The output or resource allocation is for the private policy premium payment or the required contribution to a govermental insurance program. The accompanying met demand is the expectation of minimizing economic risks by sharing potential losses through insurance.

---

3. Staffan Burenstam Linder, *The Harried Leisure Class* (New York: Columbia University Press, 1970), p. 33.
4. Gwen J. Bymers and Mabel A. Rollins, "Classification Systems: Household Expenditures Data and Household Accounts," Bulletin 1014 (Ithaca, N. Y.: Cornell University Agricultural Experiment Station, 1967).
5. Gwen J. Bymers and Marjorie Galenson, "Time Horizons in Family Spending—A Study of Household Investment," *Journal of Home Economics* 60 (November 1968): 711.

If no contingency arises, the resources are reduced by the amount of the premiums. The sense of security in having protected life, health, job, or property is a form of consumption. If the contingency arises, insurance is expected to replace part or all of the economic loss. The cost of insurance coverage reduces resources, but avoids extreme resource losses when contingencies do arise.

Transferring. Managerial output may reduce available resources by one-way transfers to users outside the household through gifts, contributions, taxes, and so on. These alternatives to consumption are voluntary or mandatory commitments to individuals or to society. Individual benefits from publicly or privately supported community services are frequently unrelated to their cost.

For both families and individuals, obligatory tax outlays are balanced to some extent by such services as public education, recreation facilities, and police or fire protection. Voluntary transfers include support of community organizations and services, for which contributors may or may not have consumption opportunities. An example is the support for neighborhood settlement houses, which are not in one's neighborhood but which are designed for special area needs. Such contributions reduce individual assets and tend to increase social resources.

Gifts to individuals represent another form of transfer. The decrease in available resources usually brings a commensurate reduction in consumption opportunities. Average gifts over a ten-year period show a faster rate of increase than income,[6] illustrating that a willingness to give can increase as income increases. Gifts to individuals may be in the form of services, such as in times of severe illness. According to one study, relatives, friends, and neighbors gave help, while institutional and professional services, other than those of the physician, were used minimally.[7]

Transfers must be external to the household to effect a reduction in resources. A money gift to children in the household merely shifts the opportunity to make decisions about money use from adults to children and does not alter the system's total available resources.

Producing. Producing is creating added resources or utilities from existing resources. Earnings outside the home and household pro-

6. Kathryn R. Murphy, "Contrasts in Spending by Urban Families," *Monthly Labor Review* 87 (November 1964): 1250.

7. Sydney H. Croog, Alberta Lipson, and Sol Levine, "Help Patterns in Severe Illness: The Roles of Kin Network, Non-Family Resources, and Institutions," *Journal of Marriage and the Family* 34 (February 1972): 34–35.

duction are examples of productive output. Most resources of families and individuals arise from their productive activities.

Productive output that is internal to the household can occur in ordinary ways—when a household member assembles a set of shelves for the living room, paints a room, bakes a cake, or launders clothes. Purchasing the basic materials is an exchange, but through productive processes within the household the form or location or function of the materials is changed to make them more useful.

External output results from the use by household members of their time, abilities, and other resources for earning wages, salaries, or self-employment profits. Earnings from productive activity outside the household is output which directly affects household resource inputs. We can assume that there is some purpose behind the goal to earn: increasing security, meeting personal needs, providing for others. The actual productive activity, internal or external, represents the cost of earning or of making available resources more useable.

Saving-Investing. Through saving (or dissaving) and investment behavior, adjustments are possible in the availability of resources over time. According to the life-cycle hypothesis, families adjust their consumption in order to obtain optimum satisfaction from their available resources.[8] Although research has yielded only limited insight into the complicated role of savings over the life cycle, families do save in various ways and for various reasons. A family may set money aside in savings accounts, bonds, etc. for later spending—perhaps in ten weeks or ten years—with the expectation that delayed consumption will bring greater total satisfaction. Or, desired items may cost more than current resources allow at the moment. Or, the family may anticipate greater needs than future earnings are likely to cover when the needs occur. Uncertainties about unforeseeable contingencies may also motivate savings. Accumulated assets, including human capital, are part of the output which reflects such family choices.

A family's stock of resources, less credit obligations, represent the family's *net worth*. It includes assets of lower liquidity, such as housing, and assets readily available or of high liquidity, such as cash on hand or in a checking account. All assets are output from the standpoint that the family had to make some decision or take some action in relation to resource

---

8. Dorothy S. Projector, *Survey of Changes in Family Finances* (Washington, D. C.: Board of Governors of Federal Reserve System, 1968), pp. 33–37.

use in order to meet a demand—as with housing, recreation equipment, and so forth. Such actions and decisions, in turn, affect input by determining resource availability, those of low liquidity being less available. For example, a self-employed family often feels "pinched" even if there are greater total assets than in most families because it needs greater quantities of resources for the business. Income-producing assets, such as investments, are not as readily available for short-term needs as are the more liquid savings accounts, but they may be used as security for borrowing. This capability, combined with total available resources (including the negative side, debts), makes the net-worth concept most useful for analyzing household savings in a systems framework.

Dissaving is the output from borrowing which allows the use of anticipated future income for current needs and wants. Credit use is a way of life for many families; half the families in the United States use credit cards in daily household transactions, and their use increases as income increases.[9] For some families, credit accounts are mostly a convenience since they are not basically used to extend current spending beyond current income. For others, short-term credit is regularly used to extend resources beyond current income. About one-half of all families have installment debt, and the tendency is higher for younger families and for those with higher incomes.[10] Using extensive, long-term credit beyond current income usually requires assets for collateral to protect the lender's interests.

Although the term "savings" is often used to refer to all assets of low and high liquidity, investing is identified here with assets of low liquidity and savings with high-liquidity assets. From this perspective, savings characteristically maintain a fixed-dollar value with a relatively secure source of income, even though interest rates fluctuate with economic conditions. An *investment,* on the other hand, is an asset that varies with economic conditions both in dollar value and in earnings. Investing is a means of maintaining relative asset value during changing prices, an opportunity to hedge inflation and/or to increase total resources while, at the same time, assuming risks of declines in asset value should the reverse trend in economic conditions occur.

---

9. George Katona, Lewis Mandell, and Jay Schmiedeskamp, *1970 Survey of Consumer Finances* (Ann Arbor, Mich.: Institute for Social Research, The University of Michigan, 1971), p. 33.
10. Katona, Mandell, and Schmiedeskamp, p. 23.

INPUT-OUTPUT RELATIONS

General

Inputs and outputs of behavioral systems are identified generally and can be reduced to information, matter, and energy. These broad terms, however, do not characterize the inputs in their relation to particular systems. Demands and resources are the input terms that indicate the special relation to the home management system.

The idea of energy exchange helps us to understand the interdependence of input on output and of output on input for the maintenance of a system. Management's success depends on how well the outcome from planning and implementing activities coincides with the desired outcome or goals. Each activity has some cost or energy expenditure. This cost of transforming resources is ordinarily assumed to yield a more worthwhile product or result than was the case with the initial resources. The input "re-energizes" the system for continued activity. Exchanges of an open system with its environment renew the resources necessary to keep the system viable.[11]

Bardwell found a number of anticipated relationships of demand and resource-related inputs to managerial outputs in her study of adjustment of low-income families with chronically ill mothers. As the amount and number of nonrelief sources of income increased, for example, their degree of economic dependency declined.[12] Also, as the mother's limitation increased, children assumed responsibility for more household tasks.[13]

The reciprocal input-output relation may be illustrated for any purpose to which the managerial system responds. The output from a goal to paint the house is an expenditure for the desired color and type of paint. The purchase occurs in the environment external to the household, contributing to the market demand for paint and further generating production and income through economic processes. After the paint is purchased and applied, the house value may increase (an external outcome) or it may be enjoyed more (an internal outcome). One can also imagine that the paint

---

11. D. Katz and R. L. Kahn, *The Social Psychology of Organizations* (New York: John Wiley & Sons, Inc., 1966), p. 89.
12. Ann Skinner Bardwell, "Resource Use of Low-Income Families and Its Relationship to Family Patterns of Adjustment to Chronic Maternal Illness," The Ohio State University, Ph.D. dissertation, 1968, p. 116.
13. Bardwell, p. 122.

job might stimulate the owner or his neighbors to make other housing improvements.

Open systems must regenerate themselves to survive. A system may move to disorganization or death by a process called *entropy*. Chronic illness, apathy, compulsive spending, and divorce are evidences of the entropic process that affects families. Open systems can build up a base of human and material resources to carry them through crises. *Negative entropy* takes place when there is a positive balance of resources entering a system compared with those expended. Families who strive to get ahead exemplify the tendency of open systems to maximize this relation.[14] Effective management is one of the most important tools for countering the entropic process of individual and family systems.

Some means used to reverse entropic influences are clarifying values, increasing flexibility, improving skills and abilities, and acquiring financial reserves. These same means may also forestall the effects of potentially catastrophic events or a gradual depletion of resources.

Ongoing systems typically develop a self-perpetrating pattern of input-output activity. Meals provide a format for transforming income into food and food into health and physical energy for earning income. Mealtime may also provide an opportunity to communicate goals for the day, schedule activities, share experiences, or change plans. An activity other than meals can provide the needed basic patterning. Recurrent activities are characteristics of and useful to system survival, but undue dependence on them may stifle responses to changing situations. Families who experience a reduced income often retain spending habits that were established before the decline. When input shifts, output will eventually have to change.

The interdependent roles of input and output keep the system "energized," meaningfully patterned, and adequately responsive. The feedback mechanism helps to clarify input-output relations.

---

14. Katz and Kahn, pp. 94–95.

Feedback

Feedback is the portion of output that reenters as input to affect succeeding output. Feedback helps maintain the dynamic character of an open system; it is an information source for evaluating activities in pursuit of goals and for adapting to changing conditions. Feedback involves the system's evaluation of its own output, including information about the responses of other systems to the output compared with the intended responses.

The positive or negative nature of feedback promotes either continuity or change in the system. *Positive feedback* reveals any differences between expected and actual outcomes, acknowledges factors that support the deviation, and favors an increase in or continuation of the deviation—which is really a change in goal. Positive feedback is expansive in nature; for example, when a student finds that one required course cannot be scheduled during his last quarter at the university, he may reconsider his goals and decide to stay two extra terms and graduate with a double major.

Neutral feedback recognizes the compatability of output with input; the effect is also neutral.

Negative feedback indicates a difference between actual and desired output and influences the system to reduce the deviation so that the output stays within the limits established by goals.[15] Negative feedback is a monitoring function which may be used critically or defensively. A three-generation study shows some differences in the use of feedback: the youngest generation uses feedback most extensively—it is also the generation most likely to plan actions. Families with low incomes and low plan-fulfillment, "where the need for monitoring and negative feedback is greatest," apparently use the evaluation mechanism to mask the deficiencies of their chosen actions.[16]

In Figure 3.1, feedback lines extend from the managerial output to the input arrow of the managerial system and the personal system of the family. Feedback from output to the external environment may also return to the family system. Note that the external feedback supplies information

---

15. Walter Buckley, *Sociology and Modern Systems Theory* (Englewood Cliffs, N. J.: Prentice-Hall, Inc., 1967), p. 53.
16. Reuben Hill, *Family Development in Three Generations* (Cambridge, Mass.: Schenkman Publishing Co., Inc., 1970), p. 324.

about the family system's output to other systems. However, when the output of the family system enters another system as input and is processed by that system into its own output, any portion of that system's output that becomes input to the family system is a system exchange rather than feedback from the family system's output.

The feedback information sources for the family system are both internal and external. The information returning to the family system from external systems as a result of the family's own managerial output can be direct or quite diffused. For example, forgetting to sign a check in payment of a household service will result in immediate, direct information about the oversight (negative feedback). The check is not acknowledged by the recipient until it is signed. Planning to shop at a usual time, which has always been considered advantageous, but then being delayed and finding that the store is less crowded at a later hour can lead to a changed standing plan in favor of the new time (positive feedback).

Purchase behavior may also have feedback effects, and these may help to clarify feedback and intersystem input-output interactions. A decision on the part of one consumer not to repeat a particular purchase that did not fulfill expectations but to replace it with another item is behavior that is likely to continue if the new item proves satisfactory over time. If other consumers similarly reject the product, the manufacturer or processor may then change the product to bring it back in line with consumer expectations. Under these circumstances, the purchaser is encouraged to change purchases as an effective way of dealing with unsatisfactory products (positive feedback). If the family does not accept the new product or if use of the new product proves more complex, the feedback may signal a return to the original product and acceptance of minor limitations (negative feedback).

Information from external and internal experiences and situations combine to promote continuity along previously satisfactory lines or to seek new objectives and approaches. Feedback from managerial output to the personal system helps reinforce or redirect value orientations. The feedback influences the nature of the goals, which become input to the managerial system.

Output from the management system that returns to affect succeeding input to the management system is the most direct effect of feedback. For example, a family spends more money on a holiday weekend than they had anticipated. The available resources that have been diminished by overspending may alter plans for the following week. The information that resources have been reduced may make it necessary for the family to revise or postpone goals. This feedback line is outside the management system, but inside the family system from output back to goals.

Feedback from output of the management system is similar to the evaluation concept of home management presented in earlier home management texts which refer to evaluation as evaluating the desired results[17] and evaluating results for use in future planning.[18] In the systems approach, evaluation is considered integral to decision making and occurs throughout management. The broader concept of feedback includes knowledge of results as the activity progresses as well as evaluation after an activity occurs; the latter aspect is called learning feedback because it can affect future activity.[19]

The feedback that occurs within the management system is an action feedback[20] that helps to identify the internal shifts that must be made during the course of action. The internal feedback takes place between managerial subsystems and is consequently limited in scope compared to goal-directed feedbacks. The information loop of a goal-directed feedback may flow from output to reentry directly into the managerial system, or it may go by way of the external environment as input back into the family system. Through positive or negative feedback processes the ensuing output to the management system through the personal system may be either similar to or different from earlier output. Values, for example, may be reinforced or altered and may affect goals accordingly. Feedback complements the overall purpose of the system and is essential to an open, on-going, adaptive social system to maintain adequate stability in situations that require dynamic responses. Capability to correct internal deviations during an activity is important, but more is required. The goal-directed feedback loop permits output to affect directly the underlying purposes of a system. The loop may include learning, goal-seeking, expanding the system organization, and generally supporting continuation

17. Paulena Nickell and Jean Muir Dorsey, *Management in Family Living* (New York: John Wiley & Sons, Inc., 1967), p. 86.
18. Irma H. Gross and Elizabeth W. Crandall, *Management for Modern Families* (New York: Appleton-Century-Crofts, 1963), p. 90.
19. Irma H. Gross, Elizabeth W. Crandall, and Marjorie M. Knoll, *Management for Modern Families* (New York: Appleton-Century-Crofts, 1973), p. 263.
20. John Annett, *Feedback and Human Behavior* (Baltimore, Md.: Penguin Books, 1969), p. 29.

of the system.[21] Feedback makes a system "whole" by emphasizing its purposefulness as the system responds to the surroundings and keeps elements of continuity and adaptiveness intact.

DEFINITIONS

Met demands are the output from managerial action initiated by goals and events.

Resource use is the output from managerial action representing a shift in the stock of available means.

Consuming is the reduction of available resources through "using up" their utility value.

Protecting is minimizing potential economic losses at the cost of risk sharing.

Transferring is the reduction of available resources through voluntary or mandatory transfers to users outside the household.

Exchanging is a shifting in the makeup but not necessarily the value of the household resource inventory.

Producing is creating additional usefulness from available resources.

Saving-investing behavior anticipates improvement in resource availability and allocation over time.

Net worth is the stock of available resources less credit obligations.

Savings are fixed dollar assets.

Dissavings are the credit uses against anticipated future income.

Investment is an asset varying both in value and earnings with economic conditions.

Entropy is the tendency of all forms of organization to move to disorganization or death.

Negative entropy is the tendency, particularly of open systems, to maximize the ratio of resources that enter the system to those that are expended.

Feedback is the portion of output re-entered as input to affect succeeding output.

----

21. Buckley, p. 70.

Positive feedback acknowledges differences between expected and actual outcomes and supports an increase in the deviation.

Negative feedback acknowledges differences between expected and actual outcomes and promotes reduction in the deviation to established limits.

Part Three

Application of Home Management Concepts

Financial Management

*A*s the economy has grown, the family's managerial options have focused increasingly on money and have become more interdependent with the general economy. Money—one of many significant resources of individual and family management—is likely to be central to planning. The role of money is primarily indirect: It is a medium for value comparisons and claims on resources that are used directly as well as a mechanism for interchanges with the general economy and interactions with other individuals, groups, and institutions. Money has a strategic role when decisions are made about total resources. This chapter covers the opportunities and complexities of managing with and in relation to money.

The systems format of input-throughput-output continues in the following discussion of demand-resource relationships from the input perspective, where these questions are considered: How does money affect goals and aspirations? How do people perceive income adequacy? What changes have occurred in income amount and distribution? What effects have economic conditions had on prices? How is earning ability related to the family life cycle? What affects feelings of economic security or insecurity, and what are some financial alternatives? How is security related to income adequacy?

The second section, throughputs—planning and implementing, deals with managerial concepts and techniques useful for households in determining their unique aspirations and potential for achievement. Goals, resources, and managerial actions may vary with individual problems, but the basic managerial functions remain the same. The family's organization patterns and the nature of its income flow contribute to planning and implementing and are discussed along with the related processes of budgeting and record keeping. Economic risks and ways to minimize their effects also receive attention. The theme of the chapter is how the planning and implementing functions of management translate individual aspirations and resources into spending and saving patterns.

The long-run outputs of financial activity are presented. They include changes in standards and levels or styles of living, in financial and material assets and obligations, and in human capacities. The agreement of aspirations and outputs is related to management motivation and the success or satisfaction gained. The effects of long-run outputs on succeeding inputs through feedback are also discussed.

INPUTS—DEMANDS AND RESOURCES

Goals and Aspirations

An individual's or a family's sense of economic well-being is related to the realization of financial goals and aspirations. How different classes of families evolve and respond to economic goals is the subject of much study, but no one explanation prevails. Rather, fragmentary theories each contain a modicum of reality.[1]

In an evolving value system, the individual or family economic aspirations usually mirror the family's comparative economic position. That is, the current economic level of the family is compared with that of its peers, and past choices and achievements are related to the present situation and/or to future expectations.

Feelings of satisfaction or economic well-being are said to accompany fulfilled aspirations; yet, some observers contend that met aspirations are not so fulfilling at lower economic levels as they are at higher economic levels.[2] Many people agree that the gap between economic goals and accomplishments affects the degree to which economic well-being is perceived as adequate and also provides motivation for closing the gap.

Goals are "reality-bound" reflections of aspirations and expectations. Aspirations may be adjusted upward if experience and observation sug-

---

1. Burkhard Strumpel, "Economic Life Styles, Values and Subjective Welfare—An Empirical Approach," in *Family Economic Behavior: Problems and Prospects*, ed. Eleanor Bernert Sheldon (Philadelphia: J. B. Lippincott Company, 1973), pp. 69–125.
2. Richard S. Weckstein, "Welfare Criteria and Changing Tastes," *American Economic Review* 52 (March 1962): 133–45.

gest that more can be achieved, or they may be adjusted downward if the evaluation is opposite.[3]

Complex interactions of situations and judgments about them help shape financial goals. For example, a group of young heads of households ranked "a secure life" as their first goal more often than they ranked "a prosperous life", which emphasizes the level of living. They also ranked "a prosperous life" first more often than an "important or exciting life".[4] White men with higher education and in professional occupations, selected the "important or exciting life" more often than did other groups. Their current situations probably already offered relatively high security and prosperity. Preference for an important or exciting life under affluent circumstances supports Maslow's idea of a hierarchy of needs, where basic needs are met before more self-fulfilling or self-actualizing values and goals are sought.

Higher-status (socioeconomic position) persons have a relatively high optimism about the future and high confidence in their ability to improve their situation. Lower-status persons, by comparison, are more dissatisfied with their situation, are more worried, are less involved in the job, and are less confident in their ability to affect the situation.[5] Lower-status families do not generally have the satisfaction of fulfilled goals.

Whatever the aspiration level, a gap exists if the resource potential is perceived as inadequate. Families in poverty areas who perceive their income as less adequate experience more intense financial problems than do those who consider their income to be more adequate.[6]

A group of families was asked to identify both their expected and desired levels of living compared with their present ones. If the difference was large between present and expected or desired levels, well-being was judged low, and vice versa. More than 40 per cent indicated no difference in their aspired and expected levels. Younger families felt less economic well-being compared with their aspirations and expectations than did older families. Similarly, families that were more future-and achievement-oriented had relatively low feelings of economic well-being.

---

3. Strumpel, p. 74 and George Katona, *The Mass Consumption Society* (New York: McGraw-Hill, Book Company, Inc., 1964), p. 185.
4. Strumpel, p. 88.
5. Strumpel, p. 114.
6. Atje Pat Zwaagstra, "Factors Related to Family Financial Problems and Perceived Adequacy of Income," Purdue University, M.S. thesis, 1971, p. 107. Evelyn Sue Fowler, "Factors Related to the Economic Well-being of the Family," Purdue University, Ph.D. dissertation, 1972, p. 88.

Both their aspirations and their expectations were higher than for the present. Where aspirations exceeded expectations, more education was usually contemplated.[7]

It is probably more realistic for older families to expect less change in the future than for younger families. Younger families who anticipate changes are also realistic when they are motivated to strengthen their aspirations with more education. Education is one way to promote a closer long-range relation between the present and future aspiration levels.

Desired and actual living levels may have different relations to motivation and perceptions of economic well-being. Lower-status families find that a gap between what they have and what they consider adequate is more problematic than challenging, while the reverse is true for those families of average or higher status. Higher-income and higher-status persons who are aided by greater resource availability take corrective measures to seek fulfilling experiences.

Studies of United States and Western European consumers also illustrate the influence of perceptions on expectations and aspirations.

During the last decade a substantial proportion of Americans as well as West Europeans have perceived progress in their personal financial well-being; in this respect the differences are fairly small.

Americans are more confident about further progress than West Europeans; the proportion of individuals who believe that they are making progress—not only that they are better off than a few years ago but that they will be still better off a few years hence—is much larger in the United States than in Germany, Holland, or England.

Many more Americans than West Europeans attribute their progress to their own efforts rather than to any outside forces.

On both sides of the Atlantic, confidence in one's progress and optimism about the future stimulate discretionary consumer expenditures and make for high consumption aspirations.[8]

Income Trends and Price Effects

Most individuals achieve their economic position from their current economic activity. The information that follows on changes in income

---

7. Kristan Rinker Crosby, "Perceived Levels of Living and Family Welfare," The Ohio State University, M.S. thesis, 1970, pp. 58–59.

8. George Katona, Burkhard Strumpel, and Ernest Zahn, *Aspirations and Affluence* (New York: McGraw-Hill Book Company, Inc., 1971), p. 42.

TABLE 10.1 *Per capita personal income and median family income, in current and constant purchasing power, 1950–1972.*

Year	Per capita personal income			Median family income			Consumer Price Index	
	Current dollars	*1967 dollars*	*1972 dollars*	*Current dollars*	*1967 dollars*	*1972 dollars*	*1967 = 100%*	*1972 = 100%*
1950	1,496	2,075	2,602	3,319	4,603	5,757	72.1	57.5
1955	1,876	2,339	2,931	4,421	5,512	6,898	80.2	64.0
1960	2,216	2,498	3,130	5,620	6,336	7,941	88.7	70.8
1965	2,770	2,931	3,674	6,957	7,362	9,221	94.5	75.4
1970	3,933	3,382	4,238	9,867	8,484	10,617	116.3	92.8
1972	4,492	3,585	4,492	11,116	8,872	11,116	125.3	100.0
1972 as a per cent of 1950	300	173	173	335	193	193	174	174

U.S. Dept. of Commerce, Bureau of the Census, *Statistical Abstract of the U.S. for 1972*, 93rd ed. (Washington, D. C.: U.S. Government Printing Office, 1972), p. 319.
U.S. Dept. of Commerce, Bureau of Economic Analysis, *Survey of Current Business* 54 (April 1974), 17.
U.S. Dept. of Commerce, Bureau of Census, "Money Income in 1972 of Families and Persons in the United States," Current Population Reports, Series P-60, No. 90 (Washington, D. C.: U.S. Government Printing Office, 1973), pp. 32, 34.

levels, on prices and their effects on purchasing power, and on income distribution to individuals and families shows current trends.

Overall Trends. Personal income is the total amount received over a given time period by individuals. Per capita personal incomes were in actuality three (3.00) times as high in 1972 as in 1950, increasing 200 per cent from $1,496 to $4,492 (Table 10.1). In the twenty-two-year period, prices increased 74 per cent (174 minus 100), and per capita personal income purchasing power (income adjusted for prices) increased 73 per cent (173 minus 100).

Real income represents the available goods and services from productive activity in a given period, usually a year. The unpaid productive effort of households is part of their total real income. Since unpaid work is usually not evaluated in dollar terms, real income commonly refers to the purchasing power of current money income, adjusted for price changes in relation to a base year or period of years. Price indexes are ordinarily constructed or weighted so that a different base year or period of years for the index may be adopted by dividing all other index numbers by the desired year or years with which comparisons are wanted. The base time is then identified by an index number of 100. The adjustment of current income to real income is accomplished by dividing current income by the price index for that year, as in Table 10.1, where 1967 and 1972 are the base years. Income figures in constant 1967 or 1972 dollars (or any base period) convey the same comparative information. The 72-per cent increase in real per capita personal incomes over the twenty-two years, slightly over three per cent annually, is one of the clearest evidences of how an increased level of living has occurred.

Since per capita personal income is based on an aggregate figure for the total population, it gives information on income changes only if incomes were distributed evenly. Income distribution data are needed to identify income by groups.

The nuclear family or other combinations of living arrangements that involve shared resources are meaningful units for comparing income distribution. Definitions of living units and income can vary, depending on the purposes of data collection. Annual information of the Bureau of the Census is widely used; the median total money income of families from this source is given in Table 10.1. Families are commonly defined as units with two or more persons living together who are related by blood, marriage, or adoption.

Median income is the mid-point income for all family units, half receiving more than that and half receiving less. The mean, or average, income tends to be higher than the median because of the effect of very high incomes. The median family income in 1972 in current dollars was more than three times that of 1950. The real income of families increased 93 per cent compared to 72 per cent on a per capita basis. Families at the median income level fared relatively better over the years than the increments in per capita personal incomes show. Additional information is needed to understand trends in distribution of money to individuals and families.

Consumer Price Index. Income changes alone do not necessarily reflect changes in the level of living. What income will buy is a basic question, and changes in the general price level determine purchasing power. The Consumer Price Index, published monthly by the Bureau of Labor Statistics, alerts the public to changes in the general level of consumer prices. It reflects changes in the prices of representative items purchased by urban workers. The prices of the four hundred items included in the Index are checked regularly in fifty-six cities throughout the United

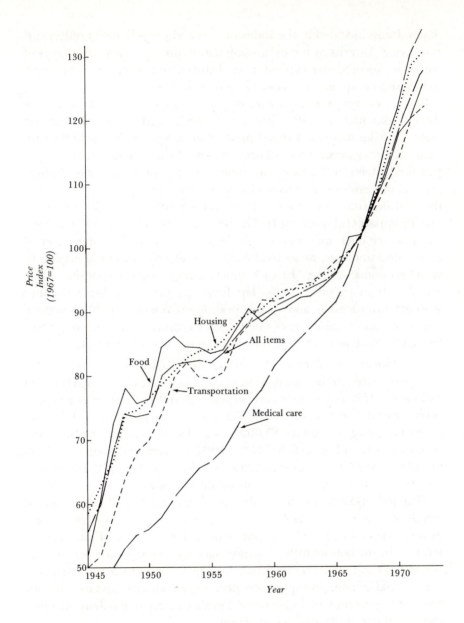

FIGURE 10.1 *Consumer Price Index for all items, food, housing, transportation, and medi-cal expenses, 1945-72.*

Source: U.S. Dept. of Labor, Bureau of Statistics. Reported in "Economic Report of the Presi-dent" (Washington, D. C.: U.S. Government Printing Office, 1973), p. 244.

States. Items included in the Index are revised periodically to reflect current living patterns of the urban population through national surveys of consumer income and expenditures. Information from the most recent survey should appear in a revised item list in the mid-1970's.

Consumers are certainly aware of price changes without an index, although they may not differentiate cost rises caused by increased quality from cost rises in an unchanged product or service. A change in the container size may make price adjustments less obvious unless unit pricing is practiced. Items in the Index are monitored to assure that price changes are real increases or decreases. Groups of items in the Index differ from the total and from one another in their rates of change, but general trends may be apparent (Figure 10.1). The medical-care index, with a large relative price change, indicates a high demand for available services. Food prices tend to follow the general pattern of all items except in periods of rapid economic change. In such times, food is more responsive to the economy than are other items. The food category in the Index contains seasonal, unprocessed, and volatile-price items as well as highly processed items with more stable prices due largely to contractual processing costs. In Figure 10.1 however, seasonal fluctuations are averaged out.

Income Distribution. According to Table 10.2, considerable change occurred in the distribution of families by income groups between 1950 and 1972. The incomes are adjusted to reflect constant purchasing power over the years in terms of 1972 dollars. The proportion of families in the two categories under $5,000 was under 20 per cent in 1972 compared with over 40 per cent in 1950. The 16 per cent of families with 1950 incomes of $10,000 and over increased to 56 per cent in 1972. Incomes of unrelated individuals also made major shifts upward.

Changed distribution among income levels (Table 10.2) and upward trends of average incomes (Table 10.1) are usually cited as evidence of a general rise in affluence in the population. But the share of total income received by the bottom fifth of families has changed only one per cent between 1950 and 1972 (Figure 10.2). The unchanging pattern of shares in the national income prompts many persons to seek new ways to either increase the earnings of low-income families or to redistribute incomes among groups by governmental action.

What are some differences in the composition of lower-and higher-income groups? Compared with the top fifth of families, the bottom fifth of families have younger and older household heads, more nonwhite and female heads of house, smaller families, fewer earners, more members in

TABLE 10.2 *Distribution of total money income to families and unrelated individuals, adjusted to constant 1972 dollars.*

Money income	1950	1960	1965	1970	1972
			Number in thousands		
Families	39,929	45,456	48,279	51,948	54,373
Income range			*Per cent of all families*		
Under $3,000	20.8	14.2	10.7	7.9	7.2
$3,000 to $4,999	19.4	12.8	11.3	9.4	9.4
$5,000 to $6,999	23.2	14.5	12.2	10.6	10.2
$7,000 to $9,999	19.9	24.8	21.5	18.1	16.8
$10,000 to $11,999	⎫	11.3	13.0	12.7	11.5
$12,000 to $14,999	16.4⎬	10.4	13.3	15.0	14.6
$15,000 and over	⎭	12.0	18.0	26.2	30.3
			1972 dollars		
Median income	5,757	7,941	9,221	10,617	11,116
Index of income change	100	138	160	184	193
			Number in thousands		
Unrelated individuals	9,366	11,081	12,132	15,357	16,811
Income range			*Per cent of all families*		
Under $1,500	43.3	35.1	26.9	20.7	17.9
$1,500 to $2,999	20.1	20.6	24.7	25.2	26.0
$3,000 to $4,999	19.2	16.6	15.9	17.6	18.5
$5,000 to $6,999	12.0	13.5	12.1	11.9	12.0
$7,000 to $9,999	3.9	9.9	11.8	13.2	13.2
$10,000 and over	1.7	4.2	8.6	11.3	12.3
			1972 dollars		
Median income	1,877	2,442	2,863	3,383	3,521
Index of income change	100	130	153	180	188

U.S. Dept of Commerce, Bureau of the Census, "Money Income in 1972 of Families and Persons in the United States," Current Population Reports, Series P-60, No. 90 (Washington, D. C.: U.S. Government Printing Office, 1973), pp. 34, 35.

service and operative occupations, fewer heads with full-time jobs, and less schooling.

Race has already been described as a factor that can affect the life chances for income. Black families and families of other minority groups had median incomes 54 per cent of those of whites in 1950, compared with 62 per cent in 1972.[9] While black families are generally improving

9. U.S. Dept. of Commerce, Bureau of the Census, "Money Income in 1972 of Families and Persons in the United States," Current Population Reports, Series P-60, No. 90 (Washington, D. C.: U.S. Government Printing Office, 1973), p. 37.

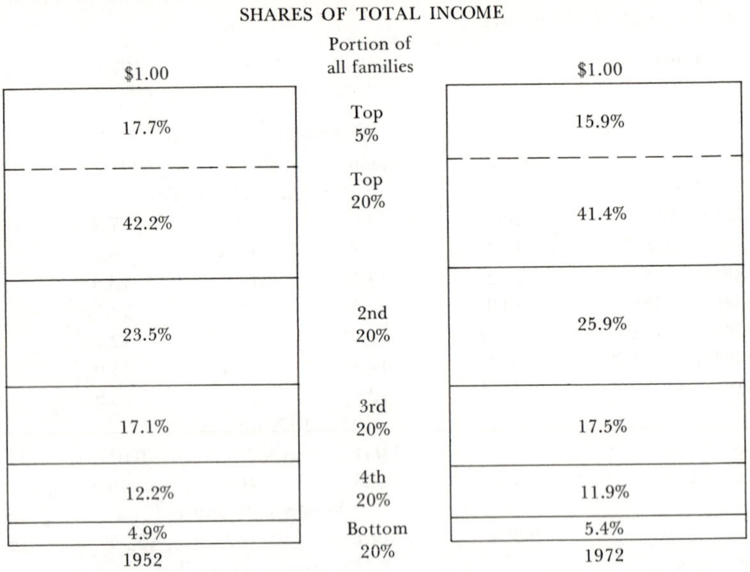

SHARES OF TOTAL INCOME

$1.00	Portion of all families	$1.00
17.7%	Top 5%	15.9%
42.2%	Top 20%	41.4%
23.5%	2nd 20%	25.9%
17.1%	3rd 20%	17.5%
12.2%	4th 20%	11.9%
4.9%	Bottom 20%	5.4%
1952		1972

FIGURE 10.2 *Distribution of family income for 1952 and 1972, by income rank.*

Source: U.S. Dept. of Commerce, Bureau of the Census, *Consumer Income* Current Population Reports, Series P-60, No. 90 (Washington, D.C.: U.S. Government Printing Office, 1973), p. 45.

their relative income position, those with female heads are not sharing in this improvement to the same degree.

Low-Income. The fixed-income-level concept currently used to define low income was developed by Orshansky. The poverty income level for 1973 was $4,450 for a nonfarm family of four. This is an estimate of the cost of a family's market basket of goods and services, based on the cost of the United States Department of Agriculture's minimal nutritionally sound food plan, multiplied by three.[10] Low-income families spend about one-third of their income for food. The method has several important characteristics: "It is absolute with reference to the income of the rest of the population; it is adjustable for price changes; and it is adaptable for family size."[11]

---

10. Mollie Orshansky, "Counting the Poor: Another Look at the Poverty Profile," *Social Security Bulletin* 28 (January 1965): 3–29.
11. Bruno Stein, *On Relief* (New York: Basic Books, Inc., Publishers, 1971), p. 6.

TABLE 10.3

Incidence of poverty under alternative definitions.

	Median family income, U.S. (nonfarm)	Poverty income		Poor population	
		Amount	*As per cent of median*	*Number (millions)*	*As per cent of total*
Fixed standard					
1959	$ 5,417	$2,943	54	39.5	22
1968	8,632	3,531	41	25.4	13
1972	11,116	4,275	38	24.5	12
Variable standard					
1968	8,632	4,661	54	34.6	18
1972	11,116	6,002	54	44.0	21

Adapted from Herman P. Miller, *Rich Man, Poor Man* (New York: Thomas Y. Crowell Company, Inc., 1971), p. 121. Copyright © 1971 by Thomas Y. Crowell Company, Inc., with permission of the publisher.

U.S. Dept. of Commerce, Buearu of the Census, *Consumer Income*, Current Population Reports, Series P-60, Nos. 90 and 91 (Washington, D.C.: U.S. Government Printing Office, 1973), p. 32 and p. 1.

a Four-person family with male head.

b Note that the relation of the poverty level in 1959 to median income is near the 50 per cent point suggested by Fuchs. This relationship is maintained for the comparative years for calculation of poverty income on the relative basis.

c Estimated.

But families and individuals want to improve their levels of living when others are improving theirs. "The poor will not be satisfied with a given level of living year after year when the levels of those around them are going up at the rate of about 3 per cent per year."[12] One approach that avoids this criticism is a variable standard for low income based on an established point in relation to an average family income. Fuchs suggests that any income less than one-half of the median family income identifies a poor family.[13] One advantage of a variable standard that is based on a commonly understood and continuing measure such as median family income is that adjustments for changes in price levels and living standards are made automatically with rises and falls in income. The difference between a fixed and a variable standard is illustrated in Table 10.3.

12. Herman P. Miller, *Rich Man, Poor Man* (New York: Thomas Y. Crowell Company, Inc., 1971), p. 120.
13. Victor R. Fuchs, "Toward a Theory of Poverty," in Chamber of Commerce of the United States, Task Force on Economic Growth and Opportunity, *The Concept of Poverty* (Washington, D. C.: Chamber of Commerce of the United States, 1965), p. 74.

Both the fixed and the variable standards can take the following factors into account: regional differences; location, such as farm and nonfarm; and characteristics such as race, age, sex of head of household, type of family, number of earners, occupation, and education of head. The fixed poverty line of Orshansky can be used for policy making since it accounts for differences in family needs to some extent, while the Fuchs approach can be used to evaluate policy decisions.[14]

Any definition of low income based on cash income is subject to at least two criticisms: It excludes both nonmonetary income and net worth. Nonmonetary benefits to low-income families include food stamps, Medicaid, public health services, school lunches, training programs, and so on. Such benefits are sometimes received at the same time, but they are often spread over time. The economic position of a low-income family receiving nonmonetary benefits in addition to financial assistance may exceed the economic position of ineligible low-income individuals and families.[15]

Net worth is the stock of available resources less credit obligations. Net worth can be converted to equivalent annuity value and added to supplement current income.[16] Equal net worths convert to higher annuities for older persons with fewer remaining years of life expectancy than for younger persons. Older families, in general, have greater assets. Planners have not used this alternative to refine low-income definitions because estimates of the number of persons who would move above the poverty line do not justify the added costs of administration.

Affluence. Definitions of affluence are almost as difficult to agree on as definitions of low income. Three definitions in use today are germane: families with incomes over $50,000; families with wealth of $100,000 or more; and those who die with a gross estate of $60,000 or more. Noteworthy among the affluent are those with estates of $1 million or more.[17]

14. Stein, p. 12.
15. James R. Storey, Alair A. Townsend, and Irene Cox, "How Public Welfare Benefits are Distributed in Low-Income Areas," Paper No. 6 in Studies in Public Welfare for Joint Economic Committee (Washington, D. C.: U.S. Government Printing Office, 1973).
16. Burton A. Weisbrod and Hansen W. Lee, "An Income-Net Worth Approach to Measuring Economic Welfare," *American Economic Review* 58 (December 1968): 1315–29.
17. Miller, pp. 149–50.

Families with incomes of $50,000 or more have heads who primarily work full time and have earnings and other income. Salaried managers and self-employed professionals make up almost two-thirds of the group. Most are well educated.[18]

Inherited wealth is not an important influence on the financial position of most families; seven out of eight families report no inheritance. Families who are wealthiest, however, are more likely to have inherited a large portion of their assets than is the average family. Of those units with total assets of $100,000 or more, 50 per cent report no inherited assets; with assets of $500,000 or more, 39 per cent report no inherited assets and 34 per cent report a large proportion of their wealth to have been inherited.[19]

Stocks are without a doubt the favorite investment of the rich. Exactly one-half of the assets of millionaires are tied up in corporate stocks, often stocks of businesses they directly control and operate. It is significant that this small group, which constitutes far less than 1 per cent of the population (2/10 of 1 per cent to be exact), own 7 per cent of all the privately held wealth and 21 per cent of all the stock in corporations.[20]

Tax-free state and local bonds and real extate are other important components of the investments of the wealthy, accounting for one-sixth of all assets held by millionaires.[21]

Family Life Cycle and Resources

One concern of individuals and families is to provide adequate resources over the life span to meet needs at all stages. A role of the managerial subsystem is to promote the optimum relation of demands and available resources. What are some evidences of the success of this role? If there is managerial success, do individuals and families adjust their resources to meet their needs, or vice versa, or both?

The relation of earning ability or current incomes to demands over the life span is an important consideration. If expected resources are consistent with needs, management may be made simpler. Decisions on current demands can be made with confidence in the future if income expectations are usually fulfilled.

---

18. Miller, p. 151.
19. Miller, p. 158.
20. Miller, p. 162.
21. Miller, p. 162.

Relatively few studies help reveal how goals and income are related over the life span. Inferences often come from information collected for other purposes. Two such studies provide life-cycle information to clarify answers to our questions; other sources will be used as appropriate. The life-cycle studies involve about nine hundred families in Missouri, Indiana, and Nebraska, with information on major financial decisions and crises during marriage[22] and an intergeneration study of about one hundred families, each in the grandparent, parent, and married child generations.[23] They will be called the regional and intergenerational studies.

In the regional study, goals changed in number and in topic as the years of marriage increased. Financial security, education, and housing –environment were dominant during the first 5 years of marriage. Income–occupation goals were particularly important from 5–9 years of marriage. Level–of–living goals were important over the cycle, but relatively more important after 30 years of marriage. Financial security, housing–environment, and education goals also ranged over the cycle, but were more important in the first 30 years of marriage. The major financial decisions throughout the cycle for meeting these goals were reported in this order of importance: husband's occupation, housing, consumer goods, and health–education–family relationships. Few major decisions were reported for the 10–19 years of marriage. The families' experiences prompted the following breakdown as a family financial model for the life cycle[24] (see also Chapter 4).

Family goal formation in the regional study depended on current income, net worth, years of marriage, and other factors. To generalize, financial goals during the life span depend on resources at hand and on anticipated income—that is, the realistic possibility for fulfillment affects the goals.

The income pattern from the intergenerational study shows an upward movement that may extend into the first 15 years of marriage, a 20-year leveling off, and a decline after 35 years of marriage (Figure 10.3.) The median income for beginning marriage was successively higher for each

22. Cleo Fitzsimmons, Dorothy A. Larery, and Edward J. Metzen, "Major Financial Decisions and Crises in the Family Life Span," North Central Regional Research Publication No. 208 (Lafayette, Ind.: Purdue University Agricultural Experiment Station, 1971), p. 9.

23. Reuben Hill, *Family Development in Three Generations* (Cambridge, Mass.: Schenkman Publishing Co., Inc., 1970). p. 24.

24. Fitzsimmons, Larery, and Metzen, p. 44.

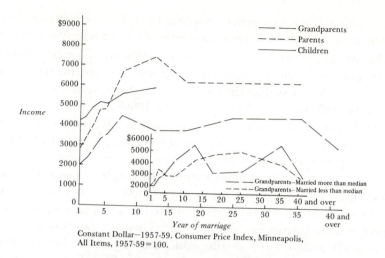

Constant Dollar—1957-59. Consumer Price Index, Minneapolis,
All Items, 1957-59=100.

FIGURE 10.3 *Median income by year of marriage and by generation.*

Source: Reuben Hill, *Family Development in Three Generations* (Cambridge, Mass.: Schenkman
Publishing Company, Inc., 1970) pp. 125-26.

Years of marriage	*Financial stage*
0 to 4 (may include 5–9)	*Foundation years:* Major goals are formed, and decisions on living levels and occupations are made.
5–19 (may include 20–24)	*Developmental years:* Decisions build on earlier ones, fulfilling goals of foundation years.
20–39	*Assessment, achievement, and readjustment years:* Level of living, housing, financial security, occupational, and retirement goals and decisions occur. These are more pronounced where husband's education and family income are low, where both husband and wife are employed, and where annual income changes are either small or great.
40 and more	*Retirement years:* Level of living, housing, and health goals most prominent, with accompanying decision making.

generation. Increasing general resource levels have permitted higher goal aspirations, which have promoted activities to provide more resources. The overall pattern of each generation is similar, although variation occurs in each. In the grandparent group, for example, for those married more and those less than the median years, the pattern is altered and reveals the effects of the depression of the 1930's.

Different income patterns by occupations are important. Both the potential income level and the point at which incomes begin to decline vary by occupation (Figure 10.4). In general, the lower-income occupations tend to reach peak earnings earlier than higher-income occupations. Within occupations, variations depend on differences in education, experience, location, and other situation factors. The general patterns, however, provide a basis for planning. Individual families may adjust by the husband's and/or wife's seeking education to prepare for jobs that will provide their preferred income; others may adjust their expectations by choosing alternate living patterns.

Young couples with expanding families frequently need to increase their inventory of goods and at the same time meet increasing day-to-day expenses. According to some observers, resources tend to be most scarce when consumption needs are greatest. One analysis of this situation proposes that a way be sought to distribute resources over the life span, making a larger portion available in the early marriage years.[25] Other analyses of young families' experiences have led observers to conclude that increasing financial needs can be consistent with increasing resources if there is time to make personal and financial adjustments before the first pregnancy and if there is time before the next pregnancy to move ahead. That is, incomes tend to rise fast enough to meet demands if the pressures are gradual enough.[26] Young low-income people with limited skills or other resource limitations are particularly vulnerable to expanding family demands.

Economic Security and Financial Alternatives

Security. To meet ongoing needs and to cover unforeseen contingencies, families use their continuous earning ability. A sense of se-

---

25. Lester C. Thurow, "The Optimum Lifetime Distribution of Consumption Expenditures," *The American Economic Review* 59 (June 1969): 324–30.
26. Joan Aldous and Reuben Hill, "Breaking the Poverty Cycle: Strategic Points for Intervention," *Social Work* 14 (July 1969): 3–12.

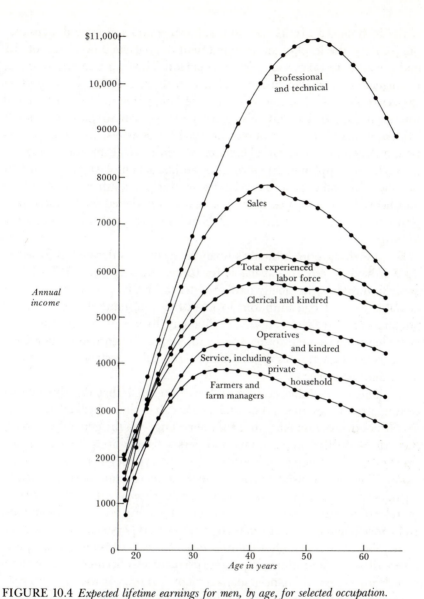

FIGURE 10.4 *Expected lifetime earnings for men, by age, for selected occupation.*

Source: U.S. Dept. of Commerce, Bureau of Census, "Present Value of Estimated Lifetime Earnings," Technical Paper No. 16 (Washington, D. C.: U.S. Government Printing Office, 1967).

curity in financial affairs has both subjective and objective dimensions. Subjectively, the level of and commitment to goals and awareness of risk and uncertainty vary from person to person. How earning and resource management capacities and confidence in them coincide are important subjective factors. Objective evidences of being able to meet known and unknown future demands also vary from person to person. Possible evidences include the level of income, the level of assets, insurance protection, maintenance of credit obligations within manageable limits, and the possibility of supplementing income by additional employment of a family member. For some, generous relatives or anticipated inheritances provide an underlying sense of security. For many, broadened government programs reduce the concerns about being able to cope with future unknowns.

For this discussion, a family's financial security is defined as its assurance of having resources available for future financial needs.[27] Economic security indicates the ability and confidence one has to maintain an acceptable level of consumption; to meet financial emergencies; to build adequate resources for retirement, disability, or loss of income; and/or to provide for an estate or other special interests.[28] A sense of economic security reflects a synthesis of actual and potential expectations for achieving economic goals.

A pioneering family economist has contended that dependence on common resources makes the family, rather than the individual, the more significant decision-making unit for interacting with the general economy. Kyrk divided risks into economic and personal categories.[29] *Economic risks* are those beyond individual control, affecting large segments of the population. They are caused by pervasive general conditions such as price changes, unemployment, and interest rates. *Personal risks* reflect hazards of individual events and are independent of general economic conditions. In financial management terminology, uninsured personal risks make one vulnerable to events with accompanying effects on resources—property losses, disability and illness expenses, premature retirement, and premature death. A task of financial management is to remove the financial risks of events from the family. The nonfinancial demands on the family's time,

---

27. Fitzsimmons, Larery, and Metzen, p. 8.
28. Fitzsimmons, Larery, and Metzen, p. 9.
29. Hazel Kyrk, *The Family in the American Economy* (Chicago: University of Chicago Press, 1953), pp. 166–67.

energy, attention, and concern from such contingencies cannot be assuaged by financial management.

The event of premature retirement carries the unanticipated possibility of resources inadequate for the demands of the situation. Planned retirement is not an "event," although there is the uncertainty that resources will fully satisfy demands. Premature death, as a financial event, transfers financial responsibilities to dependents, but plans can be made to alleviate the financial effects of such an eventuality. Families with very limited resources have little opportunity to put any plan into effect because current expenditures equal or exceed their current incomes.

Shifting financial risks from events to anticipated contingencies is part of financial management's role to promote financial security. A capacity to meet emergencies also contributes to an overall assurance that consumption levels can be maintained and that gains will be protected. The availability of resources to meet event demands is the predominant variable of financial security. Alternatives for considering demands are discussed next.

Financial Alternatives. Aspects discussed in this section relate to resource inputs as means for minimizing risks: employment, private and social protection devices, credit availability, and asset position.

Persons may prepare themselves for varied employment-income patterns; stable employment may provide either a steady or a fluctuating income. Salaried professional positions provide a steadier income than does self-employment, but self-employed persons tend to have more opportunities to increase their gains in an expanding economy. The same opportunity to realize greater gains under favorable economic conditions (when risk is assumed) applies to wage earners. Those receiving wages in more stable occupations such as transportation and public utilities do not realize increments as readily in expansion periods as do construction workers; nor do reductions and job losses occur as soon during recessions. Individuals can choose to increase or lessen the risks, thereby affecting their alternatives accordingly. Some individuals accept more risks for the challenges and the potential for a greater gain that may evolve. One way individuals can decrease their risk of unemployment, in spite of vulnerability to economic conditions, is to provide themselves with an educational background that is flexible enough to allow movement to new occupational opportunities.

Health and safety practices may help one avoid undue personal risks. While risk can be reduced, it is nearly impossible to eliminate. One-third of all fires in the United States (more than one a minute) are residential; home accidents claim three lives each hour.[30] Insurance protection provides for sharing risks of economic loss. If a contingency occurs, the individual's economic loss is minimized while those who do not experience the loss share its cost; if the contingency does not occur, the nominal cost of sharing has purchased protection and an increased sense of security.

In recent decades, responsibility for at least minimal protection has shifted from the individual to society. Government, employer, and various group programs have broadened protection to the extent that personally initiated coverage is now largely supplemental. Dependents are frequently included in health, liability, and other insurance plans. Individuals and families can thus do much to protect themselves from the impact of a major financial loss from some occurrences.

The prepaid Social Security programs, which provide income and health benefits to employees or their survivors upon their retirement or disability are broad-based forms of insurance. Beneficiaries are taxed, but the benefits are set by law and are not necessarily commensurate with taxes. A recent law provides automatic increases in cash benefits to match each three-per-cent rise in the Consumer Price Index (unless Congress enacts an increase before the three-per-cent price rise is reached). This helps alleviate anxieties of retired persons who have seen their fixed income eroded by rising prices.

The public assistance aspects of Social Security are welfare programs, noncontributory by beneficiaries, to benefit those with inadequate resources who can establish their qualification for assistance. The programs are traditionally administered by the states, but recent changes provide for shifting administration to the federal level to minimize criticisms of administrative inequalities. Local governments and agencies also provide supplemental services.

As broad plans for minimizing major risks continue to evolve, coverage for risks that occur less frequently may be omitted. Or, insuring of risks by families may unknowingly be duplicated. The individual needs to be alert in order to have the best possible coverage for his insurance expenditure.

Consumer credit provides the opportunity to alter the timing of resource use—for a price. Consumer credit allows persons to acquire money, goods, or services by undertaking an obligation to repay from fu-

---

30. *Insurance Facts,* 1972 (New York: Insurance Information Institute, 1972), pp. 29–30.

ture income. The total available resources are not increased but, in fact, are decreased to the extent of the finance charges. Credit adds flexibility to financial management and adds a sense of security for some families. The advantages include the possibility of meeting emergency expenses when there are no other available means; the use of durable goods while payments on the loan are being made; the opportunity to buy on sale or when other advantageous situations arise; and the opportunity to repay the debt in cheaper, inflated money during times of rising prices. Using credit depends on the availability of credit according to an individual's credit rating and on the willingness of an individual or family to pay the cost of credit.

A consumer credit obligation is a short-term transaction, but it can be used over long periods of time. If credit obligations are built up to $1,000 and maintained there by the continual replacement of old obligations as they are paid off with new ones, the effect is to increase one's available resources by this amount. A number of families do this successfully and consider the costs worthwhile. Each family should question whether the continual use of its available credit for current consumption is worth the flexibility sacrificed for meeting emergencies.

A related aspect of coping with emergencies is the decision to use credit to finance major purchases even though there are available assets. One rationale often given is that savings are protected for emergency use and the commitment to repay the obligation will be honored, while one's own commitment to replenish savings may not be fulfilled. An assumption that better service accompanies credit use is not generally a safe one. Two reasons that disprove this belief are the wide use of credit and the practice of retailers to sell their outstanding credit obligations to collection agencies to reduce tying up funds in this aspect of their business.

Credit obligations are concentrated in the middle-and higher-income families; low-income families are not highly committed (Table 10.4). In many cases, credit is not available to low-income individuals and families, and, in other cases, older families with low incomes have other assets to call upon. Young families are more heavily committed to debt payments than are older families—that is, the percentage of families having annual debt payment of 10–19 per cent of their income decreases as the age of the family head increases.

Material assets are the owned resources that can be assigned an economic value and that may be used for protection, exchange, consumption, and/or investment-production. Their availability can simplify man-

TABLE 10.4
Installment debt of families by income and age of head, 1971.

Comparison	Having no installment debt	Making monthly payments $100 or more	Having total debt of $2,000 or more	Having annual debt payment 10–19 per cent of income[a]
	Per cent of families			
Income in dollars				
Less than 3,000	70	3	2	12
3,000–4,999	62	5	5	8
5,000–7,499	49	13	8	15
7,500–9,999	47	16	17	15
10,000–14,999	40	21	19	21
15,000 or more	54	20	19	7
Age of family head in years				
Younger than 25	34	18	19	26
25–34	35	19	15	15
35–44	38	21	14	14
45–54	49	19	9	16
55–64	64	8	4	8
65–74	82	1	3	7
75 or older	92	b	b	3

Lewis Mandell, George Katona, James N. Morgan, and Jay Schmiedeskamp, *Surveys of Consumers 1971–72* (Ann Arbor, Mich.: Institute for Social Research, University of Michigan, 1973), pp. 8, 10, 12. Reprinted with permission of the publisher, Survey Research Center, Institute for Social Research, The University of Michigan, Ann Arbor, Michigan.
[a] Previous year's disposable income.
[b] Less than 0.5 per cent.

agement of unforeseen events. Such assets may be part of a plan to provide the necessary resources to meet contingencies, especially those that cannot be insured against. Liquid assets, which can be readily converted into cash, can provide the needed quick response to a situation and makes one free of future commitments. However, resources may not need to be readily available to relieve the emergency situation. Equity in a tangible asset, such as housing, can also be used to obtain credit in emergency situations.

Larger portions of low-income than of high-income families are without liquid assets, life insurance, or equity in their homes (Table 10.5). The higher-median liquid assets among lower-income asset holders reflect the

TABLE 10.5

Family ownership of liquid assets, life insurance, and housing, by income and age of head, 1970 and 1971.

Comparison	No liquid assets 1971	Median liquid assets 1970[a]	Life insurance (employer and individually purchased) 1970	Home ownership of nonfarm families		
				Owners 1971	Median house value 1970	Median mortgage amount 1970
	Per cent	Dollars	Per cent		Dollars	
Income in dollars						
Less than 3,000	48	700	52 ⎫	50	10,000	3,100
3,000 – 4,999	34	1,080	⎬	54	11,300	2,700
5,000 – 7,499	24	570	78	51	13,700	6,200
7,500 – 9,999	18	720	88	65	15,000	8,100
10,000 – 14,999	5	1,300	94	73	19,000	10,000
15,000 – 19,999	4	⎫	⎫	⎫	⎫	⎫
20,000 – 24,999	3	3,700 ⎬	97 ⎬	84 ⎬	28,500 ⎬	12,200 ⎬
25,000 or more	b	⎭	⎭	⎭	⎭	⎭
Age of family head in years						
Younger than 25	20	350	78	17	c	c
25 – 34	18	580		51	c	c
35 – 44	16	1,300	88	71	c	c
45 – 54	14	1,650	90	78	c	c
55 – 64	25	3,100	83	74	c	c
65 – 74	19	5,000 ⎫	61 ⎫	76 ⎫	c	c
75 or older	27	⎬	⎬	⎬	c	c

George Katona, Lewis Mandell, and Jay Schmiedeskamp, *1970 Survey of Consumer Finances* (Ann Arbor, Mich.: Institute for Social Research, University of Michigan, 1971), pp. 42, 100, 117.

Lewis Mandell, George Katona, James N. Morgan, and Jay Schmiedeskamp, *Surveys of Consumers 1971-72* (Ann Arbor, Mich.: Institute for Social Research, University of Michigan, 1973), pp. 28, 67.

Reprinted with permission of the publisher, Survey Research Center, Institute for Social Research, The University of Michigan, Ann Arbor, Michigan.

a Of those having savings accounts, certificates of deposit, checking accounts, or government savings bonds.

b Less than 0.5 per cent.

c Not available.

presence of older persons with available assets but with limited current income. Although younger family heads are almost as likely to have some savings as older family heads, the median amount is much lower. The importance of savings in a family's total plan varies with the life-cycle stage and with its vulnerability to unforeseen situations.

SUMMARY

In financial management as in other areas of management, family interactions with the environment are apparent through their financial activity. Feedback from one's own activities, experiences, and satisfactions affects the demand input over time by reaffirming goals or promoting goal changes.

An individual's or a family's economic aspirations may be relatively high or low for many reasons. At any aspiration level, the sense of economic well-being varies widely, perhaps because of the relation of resources or living level to aspirations. Younger families may have a wider gap and a lower sense of economic welfare than other age groups, but other factors may increase the width of the tolerable gap. A young husband with few resources, but with high skills, a promising job, and available family support, may more realistically accept a wider difference between his long-range expectations and his current economic situation than a young man with limited skills, no job, and no available source of emergency support.

The purchasing power of families has generally increased over time. Lower-income families and individuals have not generally benefitted, however. Low-income families are identified by two methods—a fixed income level, based on food costs, and a variable standard, comprised of all families with less than half the median family income. Neither income measure takes into account nonmoney income or net worth of families in identifying these low-income individuals and families.

In contrast to low-income families, affluent families have large assets and are composed of well-educated individuals; the family head often works full time in an upper-level occupation.

Financial goals vary by family life cycle although resources are often inconsistent with the goals in the early years of family formation. Young families who are at a particular disadvantage financially are those who have children soon after marriage and who have them close together.

Subjective and objective factors influence an individual's sense of financial security. Expectations, economic capacities, and performance all converge to define the degree of assurance that resources will be available for future needs. Family or group members may or may not share the same degree of confidence or sense of security.

Economic risks are of two types: those related to general economic conditions and those that strike more personally. While individuals cannot control the general impact of economic factors, they can prepare themselves to be in a strong employment situation either in their occupation, by improving their skills, or among occupations, by developing multiple skills.

Personal economic risks of ill health, property losses, premature retirement, or death may be shared through private and through social means. Both social and private insurance programs seek to reduce the critical resource impacts.

Consumer credit can be a useful resource. If it is excessively used, credit can contribute to vulnerability to risks. Its basic security contribution is the opportunity to alter the timing of resource use, at a price.

Assets contribute to overall financial security by allowing consumption over the life cycle or by increasing the family's financial resources through investment. They minimize the impacts of emergencies. Low-income families are less likely to have this source of security.

THROUGHPUTS—PLANNING AND IMPLEMENTING

Most people develop a lifestyle consistent with their financial means, whether by trial and error or by design. For persons to have a sense of financial well-being, ways of handling affairs must have evolved that seem adequate to get along and to get ahead. The methods may be partly unconscious and supplemental to more formal planning activities, serving to facilitate resource use to achieve desired ends.

Planning

Budgeting. In financial management, a budget is a plan—mental or written, and general or specific—that indicates how and/or when to allocate available financial resources among various needs and wants. The budget is a planned facilitator to the extent that the plan has repetitive or organizing features, built-in reminders for action, and similar aids.

Budgeting may provide highly detailed and complete plans for action, but this is ordinarily not the case. Often a budget simply identifies the resources that are expected to be available in a time period and provides the amounts for general allocation. Such a budget provides only broad outlines; it may tell how much can be spent for food, but may not specify the quantities and qualities of individual items. Even the allocation of amounts to each category does not help to sequence the total over the year or allow for periods of greater or lesser need.

TABLE 10.6
Lee and Lori Young's first annual budget.

Income		
Husband	$2,500	
Wife	5,200	
		$7,700
Living expenses		
Food $2/day/person + $80	$1,540	
Rent and utilities	1,680	
Clothing	350	
Shoes $100 Coat $80		
Underclothing $100		
Shirts, blouses, etc. $70		
Transportation	1,100	
Insurance $400 Other $700		
Medical care	400	
Reading, recreation	360	
Personal care and supplies	320	
Gifts, insurance	450	
College expenses	1,500	
		$7,700

A budget with guidelines for available resources and their broad allocation is, in essence, a general, preliminary plan that defines the inputs to
which major attention will be given during the budget period. This is part
of the quantitative aspect of standard setting.

As an illustration, consider the situation of Lee and Lori Young who are
in their first year of marriage. They must plan carefully to reach their goal
of staying within their income. Lee is a college junior and Lori worked one
year in her home town after completing high school. When they were
married, she was able to get a secretarial job in the university town that
pays $5,200. He works in a lab 10–15 hours a week, earning an average of
$25. During the three summer months, he works full time at a print shop
in the same city for $100 a week. They do not expect to save nor do they
want to incur debts during the year; they want to be independent. They
have not yet set their long-term money management goals. Their wedding
gifts help to eliminate many costs of getting started. To stay within their
income during the year, they made an overall budget (Table 10.6). It is a

general plan that represents what they feel they should allocate to make optimum use of their available resources.

Both general and specific plans are useful. Persons who know their regular spending patterns within a comfortable range can often visualize the flow as they take stock of special needs for the year. People with different wants who are sharing the same resources may need to project spending by convenient time periods, such as per month or per pay period, to clarify possibilities. This can also start the evolution of a realistic, overall summary, approaching the long view from the realities of the present.

The annual allocations by expenditure categories worked out in Table 10.7, show that the Youngs would need a $700 reserve early in the year for tuition and insurance for Lee's automobile. With little time to accumulate savings before marriage and with the wedding expenses, cash savings may not exist. If not, their parents may advance the needed funds, credit may be used (for tuition, as an example), or some adjustment might be possible in their food and housing allocations. The food budget approaches a moderate-cost diet, assuming that most meals are prepared at home[31] and that only an occasional meal is eaten out. Even with possible adjustments, additional resources are required now for next semester's tuition. They have included the cost of a group health plan available through Lori's work, and Lee has some health services available at school. Lee continues a life insurance policy that his parents started for him.

If goals and resources are anticipated in a general way, they can serve as realistic guidelines for planning. The purposes to be served by the plans will dictate the form and amount of budgeting detail most likely to facilitate financial management. Sequencing allocations by projecting income and outflow throughout the year (Table 10.7), helps to operationalize the overall guidelines of an annual budget (Table 10.6).

Income and other factors can influence planning and controlling expenditures. Compared with middle-income earners, persons with low incomes may have difficulty in planning expenditures because they continually have to adjust expenditures to make ends meet. High-income families may function well with a very generalized plan for expenditures.

In order to set up an expenditure plan as detailed as in Table 10.7, the

---

31. U.S. Dept. of Agriculture, Agricultural Research Service, Consumer and Food Economics Research Division, *Family Economics Review,* "Cost of Food at Home," ARS–62–5 (Summer 1973): 27.

TABLE 10.7

Lee and Lori Young's first annual budget and anticipated resource flow by months.[a]

Category	Annual budget	Jan.	Feb.	Mar.	Apr.	May	June	July	Aug.	Sept.	Oct.	Nov.	Dec.
							Dollars						
Income (after taxes)													
Husband	2,500	100	100	100	100	100	500	500	600	100	100	100	100
Wife	5,200	433	433	434	433	433	434	433	433	434	433	433	434
Total	7,700	533	533	534	533	533	934	933	1,033	534	533	533	534
Expenses													
Food	1,540	120	120	130	120	130	120	130	150	120	130	130	140
Rent and utilities	1,680	140	140	140	140	140	140	140	140	140	140	140	140
Transportation	1,100	50	50	250	100	50	50	50	50	250	100	50	50
Clothing	350	0	25	20	80	10	0	50	0	85	10	30	40
Medical care	400	20	20	30	20	20	80	60	20	40	30	30	30
Reading, recreation	360	30	30	30	30	30	30	30	30	30	30	30	30
Personal, other	320	25	25	25	25	35	25	25	25	25	25	35	25
Gifts, life insurance	450	15	80	15	15	30	35	20	80	20	15	15	110
College expenses	1,500	650	50	50						700	50		
Total	7,700	1,050	540	690	530	445	480	505	495	1,410	530	460	565
Monthly net		-517	-7	-156	3	88	454	428	538	-876	3	73	-31
Accumulated net		-517	-524	-680	-677	-589	-135	293	831	-45	-42	31	0

a To conserve space, a monthly comparison is used. Weekly and bi-weekly pay periods would probably make an easier comparison for this family.

couple would at least have to arrive at general standards for their needs in specific categories. For example, perhaps they decide that the clothing allowance should allow for two pairs of shoes each for Lee and Lori, a winter coat for Lee, a dress for Lori, and miscellaneous small articles. From this point, plans for actual purchases may readily evolve because specific standard setting and sequencing alternatives can be realistically determined.

The extension of the overall budget into a "flow chart," helps identify vulnerable periods during the year. Lee and Lori have a number of months in which they would have real problems if an unexpected expense, such as a major car repair, occurred. A new budget would have to be developed in such a case.

If a more convenient due date for fixed commitments such as insurance, would make it easier to meet them, changes can sometimes be made. When regular expenditures settle into a pattern and credit obligations leave no surplus, the only flow chart some families find useful is one that emphasizes fixed commitments. A combined plan-record for fixed commitments is discussed later.

Individual family expenditures are likely to differ from the average expenditures of families because resources, values, and situations differ. Lower-, intermediate-, and higher-level standard budgets have been developed by the Bureau of Labor Statistics from information on family expenditures to provide a basis for comparison. The budgets represent expenses of an urban family of four (husband 38 years old, employed full time, wife not employed outside the home, girl of 8 and a boy of 13).[32]

At the lower budget level in 1971, the portion of the budget used for personal consumption was greater than at the higher budget level, largely due to a greater allocation of money to food and medical care (Table 10.8).

For families with a different composition, equivalent levels of living are included in Table 10.9. To live at an equivalent level a husband and wife under 35 years of age with no children need only half the income than does an older family with two children of 8 and 13 years.

The cost of equivalent levels of living varies by location. At the intermediate level, the same family of four living in Boston needs 40 per cent more income than a family living in nonmetropolitan areas of the South. This information can be helpful in planning expenditures, especially when a family is changing locations.

Standards of Living. Individuals living alone, families, and groups translate their aspirations and values into goals or expectations regarding

---

32. U.S. Dept. of Labor, Bureau of Labor Statistics, "Three Standards of Living for an Urban Family of Four Persons, Spring 1967," Bulletin 1570-5 (Washington, D. C.: U.S. Government Printing Office, 1969).

TABLE 10.8

Annual budget summaries for 4-person families at three levels of living, urban United States, autumn, 1972.

Item	Budget amount			Per cent of total		
	Lower	*Intermediate*	*Higher*	*Lower*	*Intermediate*	*Higher*
	Dollars			Per cent		
Total budget	7,386	11,446	16,558	100.0	100.0	100.0
Total family consumption	6,029	9,013	12,462	82	79	75
Food	2,058	2,673	3,370	28	23	20
Housing	1,554	2,810	4,234	21	24	25
Transportation	546	979	1,270	7	9	8
Clothing, personal care	864	1,217	1,770	12	11	11
Medical care	629	632	659	9	6	4
Other	378	702	1,159	5	6	7
Other: gifts, contributions, life insurance, occupational expenses	365	576	967	5	5	6
Taxes [a]	992	1,857	3,129	13	16	19
Social Security (OASDI)	397	482	482	5	4	3
Personal income	595	1,375	2,647	8	12	16

Jean Brackett, "Urban Family Budgets Updated to Autumn 1972." *Monthly Labor Review* 96 (August 1973): 70.

a Taxes not listed are included in consumption and other items, for example, excise, sales, and use.

a "standard" that represents their preferred lifestyle. Although individual standards may be similar to or different from those of others within the group that one identifies with, they are likely to be influenced to some extent by the larger group. Standard of living is the generalized term for the complex of goods and services that reflect the goals and aspirations of individuals and/or groups. The clarification of standards involves planning with foresight to promote consistency and change in actions which relate goals and events that have long- and short-term effects.

TABLE 10.9

Annual consumption budgets at equivalent levels for selected family composition, urban United States, autumn 1972.

Family size, type, and age	Budget amount [a]		
	Lower	*Intermediate*	*Higher*
		Dollars	
Single person under 35 years	2,110	3,150	4,360
Husband and wife under 35 years:			
No children	2,950	4,420	6,110
1 child under 6	3,740	5,590	7,730
2 children, older under 6	4,340	6,490	8,970
Husband and wife, 35–54 years:			
1 child, 6–15 years	4,940	7,390	10,220
2 children, older 6–15 years [b]	6,029	9,013	12,462
3 children, oldest 6–15 years	6,990	10,460	14,460
Husband and wife, 65 years and over [c]	3,070	4,600	6,360
Single person, 65 years and over [d]	1,690	2,520	3,490

Jean Brackett, "Urban Family Budgets Updated to Autumn 1972." *Monthly Labor Review* 96 (August 1973), : 70.

[a] For details on estimating procedures, see: U.S. Dept. of Labor, Bureau of Labor Statistics, "Revised Equivalence Scale," Bulletin 1570-2 (Washington, D. C.: U.S. Government Printing Office, 1968).

[b] Estimates for the BLS 4-Person Family Budgets.

[c] Estimates for the BLS Retired Couple's Budgets, 51 per cent of the base (4-person) family.

[d] Estimated by applying a ratio of 28 per cent of the base (4-person) family.

Record Keeping. Many families record current information they otherwise might not retain in order to document allowable tax deductions. In the process, they may gain insights into their overall financial situation that are economically more useful than the tax information.

Useful records for overall planning include those on: asset aquisition, income and current consumption expenditures, interest payments, health expenditures, and charitable contributions. Informal records such as checkbook summaries, which show cash on hand and chronological payments, are probably less meaningful for planning future allocation of resources than are other classified records. From a managerial perspective, records are a tool that provides information to exercise control by checking the allocation of expenditures according to plan.

Long-Range Planning. How can resource projections be made to cover the family life cycle? They can only be tentative, but the projection efforts can help forecast major periods of opportunity and pressure, making optimum preparation possible.[33] The previous section presents the income pattern for average families: a 15-year period of rising levels, a 20-year plateau, and a decline after 35 years of marriage. A family financial life cycle of four stages of goals and decisions is also discussed.

A resource projection for these periods is shown in Table 10.10 for Lee and Lori Young. A number of factors related to individual circumstances need to be clarified for each case and are omitted to avoid further complexity. Broad outlines are nevertheless apparent. Two children are anticipated, in the third and sixth years of marriage.

Lori's employment provides a financial lift for three years before and between births while Lee is finishing school and getting established. Their plan for her to earn money after the youngest child has completed the elementary grades adds the most potential for building an estate or sizeable cushion for retirement years. Lee's income might be higher or, for some reason, he might develop a decreased earning ability. Lee's income is projected as adequate for current consumption at increasing levels even if Lori does not earn outside income after their fourth year of marriage. This income level will allow them to invest in housing and to meet college expenses of the two children; it would also support a third child, with some adjustments in their consumption.

They could maintain their level of consumption during retirement through Social Security benefits, estimated to be between $4,000 and $5,000 in current purchasing power, and income from investments. If investments are not possible at the level projected, they feel they could live on Social Security and use capital from modest investments as needed, but particularly for emergencies.

Price changes have not been projected; if prices go up, incomes will probably rise accordingly. Social Security benefits are now tied to the price level, as well.

The annual and accumulated net cash summaries show how current earnings meet current consumption and housing mortgage payments. Anticipated short-term credit obligations are included in the total for current consumption along with interest on them and on the mortgage. The cumulative asset value reflects housing and durable goods purchases only

---

33. Glen A. Mumey, *Personal Economic Planning* (New York: Holt, Rinehart and Winston, Inc., 1972).

TABLE 10.10
Summary of family life-cycle resource projections for Lee and Lori Young.

Financial cycle	Foundation					Developmental		Achievement, reassessment		Retirement
Income cycle	Rising income						Income plateau		Declining income	Declining income
Marriage Year	1	2	3	4	5	6-15	16-20	21-35	36-40	41+
Resource item					Current resource flow in Dollars					
Annual after-tax income H	2,500	4,500	8,200	9,000	10,000	13,000	16,000	17,000	15,000	10,000
W	5,200	3,000	5,500				6,000	7,000	7,000	(Soc. Sec. and investment income)
Total	7,700	7,500	13,700	9,000	10,000	13,000	22,000	24,000	22,000	10,000
Annual living expenses	6,200	7,200	9,000	11,000	9,200	12,000	15,000	16,000	14,000	10,000
College expenses	1,500	800						2,250 (8 yrs.)		
Annual net cash	0	-500	4,700	-2,000	800	1,000	1,000 (3 yrs.) 7,000 (2 yrs.)	8,000 (7 yrs.) 5,750 (8 yrs.)	8,000	
House mortgage				22,000		12,000 (year 11)				
Down payment				3,000						
Cumulative net cash		-500	4,200	-22,800	-22,000	-24,000 (year 15)	-7,000 (year 20)	95,000 (year 35)	135,000 (year 40)	
					Net worth in Dollars ⟶					
Cumulative asset value	1,000	1,500	2,000	29,000	29,000	44,000	47,000	170,000	235,000	?
Net worth	1,000	1,000	6,200	6,200	7,000	20,000	40,000	170,000	235,000	?

TABLE 10.11
Fixed dollar commitments of George and Jean Knight[a] for 1973, by months.

Commitment	Jan.	Feb.	Mar.	Apr.[b]	May	June	July	Aug.	Sept.	Oct.	Nov.	Dec.	Year Total
	Due:Pd	Due:Pd	Due:Pd	Due:Pd	Due:Pd	Due:Pd	Due:Pd	Due:Pd	Due:Pd	Due:Pd	Due:Pd	Due:Pd	Total
Mortgage Date	31:26	28:26	31:29	30:29	31:	30:	31:	31:	30:	31:	30:	31:	
Amount	$142.00	142.00	142.00	142.00	142.00	142.00	142.00	142.00	142.00	142.00	142.00	142.00	1704.00
Real estate taxes		15:12						15:					
		$212.00						212.00					424.00
Insurance						8:							
						65.00							65.00
Utilities[c]	20:15	20:15	20:15	20:19	20:	20:	20:	20:	20:	20:	20:	20:	
	$26.00	26.00	26.00	26.00	26.00	26.00	26.00	26.00	26.00	26.00	26.00	26.00	312.00
Life insurance Husband				5:1						5:			
				154.00						154.00			308.00
Wife	10:8						10:						
	$45.00						45.00						90.00
Mann's Auto Mart	20:15	20:15	20:15	20:19	20:								
	$80.00	80.00	80.00	80.00	80.00								400.00
Long's Department Store	10:8	10:8	10:9	10:9	10:	10:	10:	10:	10:	10:	10:	10:	
	$20.00	20.00	20.00	28.00	28.00	28.00	28.00	28.00	28.00	28.00	28.00	28.00	312.00
Church	1:7	1:4	1:4	1:1	1:	1:	1:	1:	1:	1:	1:	1:	
	$25.00	25.00	25.00	25.00	25.00	25.00	25.00	25.00	25.00	25.00	25.00	25.00	300.00

United Way

	31:26	:	:	30:29	:	:	31:	:	31:	:	:	31:	
United Way													60.00
Fixed commitments:	15.00			15.00			15.00		15.00			15.00	
Total	$353.00	505.00	293.00	470.00	301.00	286.00	281.00	433.00	221.00	390.00	221.00	221.00	3975.00
Total withheld	$190.00	190.00	190.00	190.00	190.00	190.00	190.00	190.00	190.00	190.00	190.00	190.00	2280.00
Total commitments	$543.00	695.00	483.00	660.00	491.00	476.00	471.00	623.00	411.00	580.00	411.00	411.00	6255.00

[a] 3 children, ages 4, 7, and 9.
[b] Payments illustrated through April only.
[c] Budget plan, cost is spread across the year, taking out seasonal variations.

until the achievement-reassessment period (after 20 years of marriage) when returns from other investments are also possible.

Net worth is the stock of available resources less credit obligations. This net figure illustrates how current resource flows result in changes in net worth, a summary of how the family is getting ahead. The net worth projections in the last line on Table 10.10 are the difference between cumulative asset values and cumulative net cash. Changing economic conditions affect asset values over time and would also need to be considered in financial planning.

Budgeting and long-range planning may be unsuccessful either because the estimates are unrealistic or because the expense totals carry no sense of commitment or understanding about how the overall guidelines can be used in daily spending decisions. Tying plans to important goals can increase a commitment; this is often the effect of purchasing on credit. A credit obligation often provides the commitment that a plan to save for the item would not provide. When credit is used in this way, the item needs to be worth the additional expense.

Budgeting is probably undertaken during a transition period or a time of emergency when changed patterns of spending are necessary. Information from records that can add reality to the planning are often not available. An expectation that an overall budget for a year or a month will magically become an effective plan for handling daily financial affairs is even more problematical for the person or family beginning to budget their expenses. Long-term budgeting cannot be expected to provide details for day-to-day action; more detailed planning is needed to define the standards and sequences of a specific plan.

Implementing

Planning is only part of financial management. Implementing —controlling and facilitating—is an important aspect which is the focus of this section. Records provide information on allocation of financial resources to control spending; they may also form a basis for new planning. Record keeping, a tool for a variety of purposes, may be simple or detailed. The most direct form of record keeping is the combined budget and record. Table 10.7 can easily become such a form. Space can be alloted to enter individual expenditure items for each category. Actual monthly totals can be compared with planned expenditures and a monthly net figure can be calculated. If the net amount is close to the planned amount, small variations from the planned expenditures (part of the standard) are probably unimportant. If, when checking planned and actual expenditures, one finds that the difference is significant, a new plan may be needed or closer control of expenditures may be needed. Inexperienced persons or anyone who is in a period of stress or transition can benefit from developing a plan for spending (a budget) and from following through by checking actual expenditures against it.

For meeting fixed commitments, a plan may become the actual record (Table 10.11). The amounts to be allocated are knowns, and the due-date schedule is essentially a reminder of sequence. Meeting fixed obligations is important for most persons; when their obligations are actually paid, the plan can become a record by noting any change in the amount and date of payment. The fixed commitments of the Knights (in Table 10.11) claim over half their income. February, April, and August are particularly heavy months for which to plan. Some families may find it worthwhile to readjust due dates to help equalize committed amounts throughout the year.

A number of years ago, an observer of the American scene noted a tendency for many families to be uncomfortable unless all discretionary income was committed in fixed obligations. He called this budgetism an opiate of the American people.[34] If one obligation was met, another was needed soon to avoid uncertainty about using the uncommitted funds. He suggested that the tendency to undertake regular credit commitments could also be applied to saving by treating savings as a commitment. Resource allocation by fixed commitment may direct resources to important uses and avoid dissipating uncommitted funds for less important uses. When fixed obligations limit the leeway to absorb emergencies, however, the risk of this approach may outweigh its advantages. The degree of patterning that is most effective for helping to direct resource allocation will vary with each family.

Because controlling expenditures can be facilitated by record keeping, stress has been placed on the role records can play in planning for future expenditures. The reason for keeping the records will determine the type, categories, specificity, and accuracy. Traditional categories for recording resource activity have been food, clothing, housing, and other types of goods and services plus assets and credit use. The items within categories are similar although their underlying use may vary. Although food items are generally intended to satisfy hunger and provide nourishment, dif-

---

34. William H. Whyte, Jr., "Budgetism: Opiate of the Middle Class," *Fortune* 53 (May 1956): 133–37, 164, 166, 171–72.

ferent underlying purposes may affect the kind of food purchased. Some food has recreational, psychological, or social purposes in addition to the physiological needs. Trying to record in relation to an underlying purpose is complicated by the variety of purposes for which many purchases are made.

One alternative for classifying expenditures is to recognize the duration of anticipated benefits, rather than to group by commodity class.[35] On a current-future time continuum, food, gasoline, and movies provide short-term benefits; sheets, clothing, or stereo tapes are enjoyed over a somewhat longer time span; returns from houses and education are indefinite. The time orientation to spending is related to the planning horizon, but the focus is on the relative present-future returns from current spending rather than on the timing of the spending. In a time-of-benefit grouping, purposes other than present or future orientations may be as diffuse as with the more traditional classifications. A given automobile, for example, may be selected because it is expected to operate well and have inventory value for a longer time than some other car. Other reasons for the choice, such as the car's suitability for commuting versus long trips, are not clearer than with traditional classifications.

The current-future basis for classifying, however, does recognize that current spending and investing may affect the future and may determine how well families get ahead. Categorizing by the time-of-benefit does help to clarify why there are higher annual gains in net worth than are reflected by the net flow of assets and liabilities of traditional classifications.[36] But when either the interest or opportunity for orienting to the future is limited, gains in the economic position will probably also tend to be limited.

An advantage of traditional categories for records (food, clothing, and so on) is that they focus on specific items for which quantity and quality decisions need to be made. Persons or families with the present-future perspective are more likely to identify and perhaps emphasize items related to economic progress—housing maintenance, durable goods purchases, and education expenditures, for example, than do families who use more traditional classifications.

35. Gwen J. Bymers and Mabel A. Rollins, "Classification Systems: Household Expenditures Data and Household Accounts," Bulletin 1014 (Ithaca, N. Y.: Cornell University Agricultural Experiment Station, 1967).

36. Ruth E. Deacon and Janet A. Krofta, "Economic Progress of Rural Nonfarm and Part-time Farm Families," Research Bulletin 976 (Wooster, Ohio: Ohio Agricultural Research and Development Center, 1965), p. 21.

Categorizing expenditures on a current-future basis can also relate to the nature of the shift in the stock of available resources that result from managerial choices, as discussed in Chapter 9. Although the discussion of resources as output related to the broader question of the reallocations of all resources, as managerial decisions are made, the categories are applied in this section to the use of current money receipts. Since exchanges are usually an interim step in reallocations, they are identified, where possible, with the intended purpose.

The purposes or uses of the information from record keeping on a current-future continuum will determine the time period. In the allocations listed on pages 280—81, the only categories that require special decisions regarding time of use are those of consumption and production. A short term-long term division of less than or more than a year can be made. Or, "current consumption" may mean within a month, "intermediate term" may be one month to three years, and "longer term" may be over three years.[37]

Planning and implementing financial plans within families is important to children because the setting provides an opportunity to learn about money management. Family practices in distributing money to members can facilitate learning.

In an exploratory intergeneration study, sharing financial situations with their children and allowing the children to be present for family financial discussions was prevalent among the grandparent generation.[38]

Several patterns of distributing funds to children exist—allowances, money doled out as needed, and payment for work done around the house. The methods may or may not be facilitating factors for the children's financial management. An allowance facilitates a child's assuming responsibility for certain decisions and planning within definite resource limits. The extent of his use of the allowance as a distribution method probably varies with the age of the child, among other factors. Of 1,300 teenagers, about one-sixth received a regular allowance.[39] In the exploratory study just mentioned, only two-fifths of the grandparents gave allowances to their children, but nearly three-fourths of their children were giving or planning to give allowances to their offspring.[40]

37. Bymers and Rollins, pp. 24–25.
38. Karen Schnittgrund, Marilyn Dunsing, and Jeanne Hafstrom, "Children and Money . . . Attitudes and Behavior of 52 Grandparent and Parent Families," *Illinois Research* 15 (Spring 1973): 12-13.
39. Lenora G. Smith, "High School Youth and Their Money Management, "Purdue University, M.S. thesis, 1971, p. 35.
40. Schnittgrund, Dunsing, and Hafstrom.

Purpose of allocation	Time-of-benefit	Scope of category or explanation
1. Consumption; related production	Current	Exchanges for direct consumption or for related production at home are included where benefits are anticipated in the short run, say, within a year.
		Examples: groceries, cold tablets, gasoline, utilities.
2. Production; income earnings outside the home	Current	Exchanges made in pursuit of current earnings if useful for tax or other purposes; otherwise include in above category.
		Example: professional or union dues.
3. Protection	Current	Benefits are available from exchanges from premium payment only (any with savings features belong under that category).
		Examples: term life insurance, fire insurance.
4. Transferring	Current	For the grantor, the claim is immediately relinquished; the time perspective of the recipient is unknown.
		Examples: cash gift for a nephew's college expense; taxes.
5. Consumption	Future	Exchanges for durable goods and their maintenance where long-run consumption benefits are anticipated.
		Example: furniture.

6. Production at home	Future	Exchanges include home production goods, home improvements (including maintenance) having long-run consumption benefits.
		Examples: household appliances; house painting.
7. Savings-investment	Future	Included are current resources diverted into assets of fixed or variable dollar value or into development of human capacities, e.g., health or education, having long-run effects.
		Examples: college expenses; surgery; permanent life insurance; stocks and bonds.

The dole method of giving money upon request or demand does not facilitate the child's financial management since each situation is considered on its merit. If used advantageously, doling can be mutually beneficial in developing financial insight; but the child's chances to make decisions about resource use are often reduced. In the study of teenagers, about one-third received money most often by asking as they needed it, with the amount varying for each situation.[41]

Being paid for work done around home is another means of distributing funds to children. Many parents feel that children should do some jobs around the house for no pay. Some children feel they are expected to do too much without pay.[42] The value of the method for learning financial management depends on the regularity of the work, on whether the work opportunity varies with need, and on the certainty of being paid for work.

---

41. Smith, p. 35
42. Schnittgrund, Dunsing, and Hafstrom, p. 13.

Factors Affecting Planning and Implementing

The nature of income flow, the organization patterns, and the changing price level influence how allocations are made and when spending is done. These factors influence the processes by which decisions are made or how responsibilities are designated.

Nature of Income Flow.   Either individually or in combination, stability, frequency, and amount are components of income flow that affect financial planning and implementing. A stable income allows either long-term or short-term planning, while a fluctuating income requires a relatively longer planning period. During a year, two families may receive the same total income: one, stable in amount and timing and the other, fluctuating. The fluctuating income requires careful planning with a relatively low commitment to current spending since the time of income is unknown. The steady income allows for income-expenditure relationships to be brought into balance more quickly than the fluctuating income.[43]

Income frequency is the time between pay periods. Expenditures are more highly related to the payday with shorter pay periods: that is, a higher portion of expenditures cluster around payday.[44] Food, household operation, personal, and total expenditures are especially oriented to payday.

Wage contracts increasingly emphasize weekly pay periods; apparently families find planning and controlling expenditures easier with shorter pay periods. For families paid more than once a month, portioning wages over the month limits the money available in any pay period and thus simplifies control. With pay periods more nearly a month apart, large obligations are more likely to be assumed near payday.[45]

The amount of income is a major factor affecting the planning and control of finances. While younger and lower-income families may reflect less satisfaction with outcomes, they generally do more planning.[46] With very

---

43. Sarah L. Manning and Ethel L. Vatter, "Financial Management Practices of Families with Steady or Fluctuating Incomes," Bulletin 997 (Ithaca, N. Y.: Cornell University Agricultural Experiment Station, 1964), pp. 20–22.

44. Francille Maloch and C. R. Weaver, "Orientation of Expenditures to Day of Pay," *Journal of Consumer Affairs* 5 (Summer 1971): 140.

45. Maloch and Weaver, pp. 142-43, and Ruby Turner Norris, *The Theory of Consumer's Demand* (New Haven, Conn.: Yale University Press, 1952), p. 100.

46. Hill, p. 199.

low incomes and especially with larger families, planning and controlling were relatively limited in the intergeneration study.[47] The family unable to control its course apparently does not seek to do so, and the reverse is also true.[48] Planning becomes too problematical at some point where many demands meet too few resources. Higher income permits discretionary choices and makes a future orientation to spending possible.

Organization Patterns. Patterns or standing plans facilitate financial planning and implementing by specifying roles and/or procedures. Organization thus assists the flow of actions in financial affairs, influencing how allocations are made and when spending is done.

For families in general, neither the husband nor wife is more effective as the financial manager;[49] effectiveness seems to depend more on what the procedure is and not on who follows it. In a study of couples with professionally employed wives, it was usual for either the husband or wife to keep accounts, pay bills, and prepare tax returns.[50] The role may be for the financial manager to submit proposals or plans for spending and then implement them after mutual decisions are made.

Roles are less traditional in the younger generation.[51] Successful responsibility for a role depends on interests, experience, work schedules, and so on, rather than on traditional allocation of roles—that is, that the man make the decisions about large purchases such as automobiles. Determining patterns of organization is a major part of financial planning, especially for young couples.

Delegating responsibilities for meeting common financial goals assumes some prior consensus or knowledge. Delegation of responsibility does not necessarily mean that others are not involved in choices. Responsibility may be assumed for any aspect of the choice or for complete implementation, and the extent of role assumption may depend on the degree of consensus that has evolved. When greater consensus evolves with time, less

---

47. Hill, p. 206.
48. Alvin L. Schorr, "The Family Cycle and Income Development," *Social Security Bulletin* 29 (February 1966): 21.
49. Imogene Romino, "Financial Management Practices of 52 Couples with Teen-age Wives in Baltimore County, Maryland," Pennsylvania State University, M.S. thesis, 1970, p. 78.
50. Lois Hessacker Preisz, "An Investigation of Credit Usage Among Young Married Couples in Western Oregon," Oregon State University, M.S., thesis, 1971, p. 45.
51. Hill, p. 49

extensive planning is needed. Thus, in early marriage, a high degree of planning and consensus are related, but later there is a tendency toward less detailed planning with high consensus.[52]

Changing Price Levels

Changing economic conditions have an important effect on available financial alternatives for individuals and families. Risks in price-level changes are difficult to avoid because of the unknown direction and timing of changes, but the effect of fluctuating prices can be minimized. The longer trend in prices shows some downturns, as in the 1930's, but prices have trended steadily upward since 1940 (Table 10.1). Fluctuations of individual items in the Consumer Price Index have had problematic short-run effects for many families—the declines in housing of the mid-1960's, for example. In general, families whose planning anticipated rising prices have made more financial gains than families who hedged against rising and falling prices; yet, the past is no clear gauge for the future.

The following discussion concerns the individual household that seeks to protect the purchasing power of its savings. Under extreme economic conditions, the normally wise individual actions may unduly accelerate an abnormal economic situation. Many persons acting similarly at such a time may produce an economic overreaction that is not advantageous to individuals or society in general. The depression of the 1930's in the United States is one example; individuals withdrew their money from banks when they feared loss of their savings.

Under normal conditions, the economy is usually flexible enough to absorb a wide range of responsible, but self-serving, individual economic choices. The opportunity for such choices contributes to and is a function of a healthy, open economic system.

Major alternatives for families in their use of future-oriented funds under different price situations are given in Figure 10.5. When the general price level is rising, the value of goods increases in relation to the value of money. To hold their relative economic position, people who expect prices to rise or who want to protect themselves in this event seek places for their resources that take advantage of the increasing value of goods compared with money—stocks, real estate, and consumer durables that rise in value with the rise in prices.

---

52. Hill, pp. 216–19.

Rising prices	Uncertain prices	Falling prices
Characteristics	*Characteristics*	*Characteristics*
Goods increase in value	Goods change in value and money is uncertain	Goods decrease in value
Money decreases in value		Money increases in value
Appropriate actions	*Appropriate actions*	*Appropriate actions*
Invest in real estate	Buy balanced mutual funds	Maintain money savings
Invest in stocks	Have retirement plan that responds to price changes	Hold bonds
Buy consumer durables		Rent or postpone purchase of durables
Borrow money		Lend money

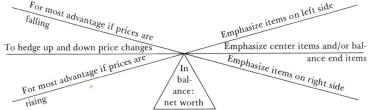

FIGURE 10.5 *Financial choices for strengthening net worth position during changing price levels.*

Source: Adapted from class notes from Dr. Jean Warren, New York State College of Home Economics (Human Ecology), Cornell University, Ithaca, New York.

Money may be borrowed with the expectation that the cost will be less now than later. A higher future price to be paid for durable goods is considered a primary justification for borrowing now; repayment of a loan in the future with cheaper dollars is additional incentive. However, if prices are expected to decline, the argument is reversed; dollars buy more as time passes. Renting items is advantageous if they can be purchased later with enough fewer dollars to justify the extra costs of rental.

Having savings in fixed dollar accounts or in investments such as bonds, interest accounts, life insurance equity, and annuities is desirable in times of price decline. Loaned money is expected to be repaid with more valuable dollars. The preponderance of funds is concentrated less on goods and more on dollars and their increasing purchasing power. Even during rising prices, some assets in a safe and liquid fixed dollar account provide the flexibility often needed for emergencies or to protect other investments.

As a basic plan, persons often wish to protect themselves from the extreme effects of both rising and falling prices and so choose to have items on both sides of the balance. Owning a house and having a savings account is an example of hedging against future price changes in either direction.

Few items are in themselves a hedge against both upward and downward price changes. Preferred stocks have elements of risk and safety to protect the dollar and its value. Mutual funds are oriented to this protection, although they vary by type. Funds composed of predominantly growth stocks favor rising price levels; funds that contain mostly corporate bonds emphasize security of the dollar investment; balanced funds, or those with both stocks and bonds, help offset either rising or falling prices. Regardless of the type of security emphasized, mutual funds offer the advantage of diversification of the portfolio to minimize risks.

Legislation to change Social Security benefits to be in line with changing prices has protected the level of living of persons dependent on Social Security by protecting the purchasing power of their income. Social Security benefits will decline if the duration and extent of a price decline is great enough to trigger the legislated response in benefits. The response of state, federal, and private retirement systems to changing prices varies with the system.

Individuals who have more than enough resources for current living have flexibility to use investments before retirement to increase financial security. Retirement usually requires a secure income from investments, but secure income investments give limited protection to price changes, particularly price rises. Many people hold growth investments during their working years to guard against inflation, shifting to more income-secure investments after their retirement.

Financial management to minimize the effects of changing prices involves awareness of general economic trends and a degree of maneuverability for advantageous resource shifts. Flexibility also helps in other risk areas of financial management. Management opportunities for minimizing risks depend heavily on inputs—an awareness of risk potential, evolving goals to reduce their effects, and the availability of resources to do so.

Those who are more affluent prefer investments with the opportunity for making capital gains. Saving for retirement or for children's education is important to the affluent, but less so in the high ranges of affluence.[53]

---

53. Robin Barlow, Harvey E. Brazer, and James N. Morgan, *Economic Behavior of the Affluent* (Washington, D. C.: The Brookings Institution, 1966), p. 43.

OUTPUT

Levels of Living

The expected outcome of financial management is to meet demands (whether long-term goals, short-term goals, or events) by effective use of the resources available to each managerial unit. A major output is the achieved level of living and the related sense of fulfillment of goals. Satisfaction of husbands and wives with their handling of finances is apparently sustained over the life cycle, except for a drop from the preschool to school stages (Figure 10.6).

Lee and Lori Young's level of living—their resource use—coincides with their aspirations if their plans for spending during the first year provide the wanted items and if their satisfaction from these items is as anticipated. Their management is inconsistent with their expectations if anticipated results fail to materialize. They may foresee their needs or wants inaccurately (more recreation may, in fact, be preferred over more per-

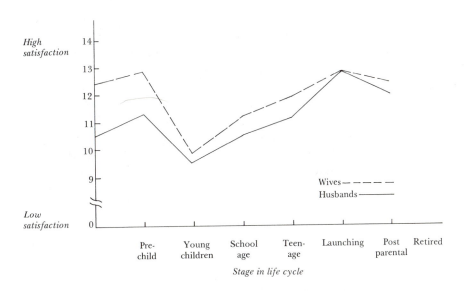

FIGURE 10.6 *Satisfaction with the way finances are handled, by family life cycle.*

Source: Wesley R. Burr, "Satisfaction with Various Aspects of Marriage Over the Life Cycle: A Random Middle Class Sample," *Journal of Marriage and the Family*, 32 (February 1970): 33. Copyright (1970) by National Council on Family Relations. Reprinted by permission.

sonal care or more clothing), or they may anticipate results that are not realistic (the food money may not cover all that was expected). Inconsistencies in resources and demands can be altered somewhat through more realistic appraisal of what the available resources will actually purchase —through information feedback or through an increase in resources and/or a decrease in demands. The level of living may more nearly reflect the standard of living desired by the family when a combination of these alternatives occurs.

Net Worth and Human Capital

Another area of output from financial management is the degree of satisfaction with the level and rate of change in the human and financial resource position of the family. Resource allocations may be grouped by their anticipated short-term and/or long-term benefits, as previously described. For most families, day-to-day living expenses and accompanying short-term benefits use most current resources. The family's relative orientation to the future affects its gains in material and human capital at all but the lowest income levels. Before expanding into assets of greater risk, the usual pattern is to invest in household equipment, an automobile, life insurance with an increasing cash value, and interest-bearing savings. Credit use is important for growth in assets and affects the net worth position. Income stability, or fluctuation, may affect planning processes, but need not affect rates of net worth increase.[54]

Net worth is the output of financial management over time. The net worth for the Young family was presented in Table 10.10 for each stage of the family life cycle. Detailed net worth statements for the third and fourth years of marriage for Lee and Lori Young appear in Table 10.12. While the net worth is the same for each of the years, the underlying assets and liabilities have changed considerably. These changes reflect a major shift in the family's financial goals and commitments for the future, a trait indicative of the foundation years in the family life cycle.

The net stock of assets at the end of each family life-cycle stage (Table 10.10) indicates that many current consumption outlays, along with long-term investments like housing, have asset value. Liquid assets are often invested and change in value by either capital appreciation or depreciation, by earnings of the principal, or by inflation that may erode the purchasing power.

---

54. Flora L. Williams and Sarah L. Manning, "Net Worth Change of Selected Families," *Home Economics Research Journal* 1 (December 1972): 108–109.

TABLE 10.12

End of year net worth statements for Lee and Lori Young.

Item	Marriage year	
	Third (end)	*Fourth (end)*
Assets		
Cash on hand	$4,200	$ 300
Automobile	600	500
Durable household goods		
TV	350	300
Camera	90	80
Furniture	750	1,300
Lawn mower	0	80
Appliances	0	1,120
House	0	25,000
Cash value life insurance	210	320
Savings accounts	0	0
Other investments	0	0
Accounts receivable	0	0
Total	$6,200	$29,000
Liabilities		
Mortgage	0	$22,000
Charge accounts		
Sofa	0	350
Range, refrigerator	0	450
Other accounts payable	0	0
Total	0	$22,800
Balance	$6,200	$ 6,200

Human capital assets, such as education and health, have long been recognized for their actual and potential contributions to the productivity of individuals and, therefore, to family income. Education influences the present or future consumption orientation of families. [55] Higher incomes

55. Jeanne L. Hafstrom and Marilyn M. Dunsing, "Satisfaction and Education: A New Approach to Understanding Consumption Patterns," *Home Economics Research Journal* 1 (September 1972): 8–12.

permit more discretionary spending and include more emphasis on future-oriented categories such as education.[56] Families with more highly educated heads of household spend more than average on formal and informal education—a fact that reinforces evidence of an interaction between opportunity and choice.

Bankruptcy results when net worth remains negative, that is, when liabilities exceed assets. One-fourth of the cases in one study of bankruptcy lacked "prudent financial management leading to spending beyond the capacity to repay," and one eighth of the cases had attitudes that were manifested "in part by lack of responsibility toward paying debts" The remainder of the cases of bankruptcy occurred because of events such as a catastorphic accident or illness.[57]

In another study of families who filed for bankruptcy or who had sought counselling to meet overextended debts, the families were above the poverty line on the average, but below the average income in their locality.[58] The average short-term or consumer credit used by the bankrupt families was about one year's income before taxes, compared with two-thirds of a year's income for families seeking other solutions to their credit difficulties. Short-term debt was three times higher than the total assets of the bankrupt families.[59] Consumer debts are claims against assets or future income. Such claims, when excessive, make these families highly vulnerable to unforeseen financial events. These families need planning and implementing that are related to realistic goals and potential events.

SUMMARY

The allocating role of budgeting in planning and the informational role of record keeping in controlling current plans and developing later ones have been illustrated in case situations. How different situations affect the

---

56. Gwen J. Bymers and Marjorie Galenson, "Time Horizons in Family Spending—A Study of Household Investment," *Journal of Home Economics* 60 (November 1968): 713.

57. H. Lee Mathews, "Causes of Personal Bankruptcies, Columbus, Ohio," Monograph No. 133 (Columbus, Ohio: The Ohio State University Bureau of Business Research, 1968), p. 53.

58. Mary Ellen Ryan, "An Analysis of Economic and Demographic Characteristics of Consumers Associated with Excessive Installment Debt," University of Minnesota, M.S. thesis, 1968, pp. 68–69.

59. Ryan, p. 69.

need for detail was described by plans with more and less detail, with accompanying differences in opportunities to exercise control.

Standards of living represent the preferred lifestyle of individuals, families, and their reference groups; included are the complex of goods and services representative of their goals and expectations. Average expenditures provide information for planning, although the differing values and actual resources of individual families usually require individual applications.

Plans for resource allocation may be projected over the family life cycle by major stages. Net worth expectations need to be included in such projections.

Attention was directed to possibilities of converting budgets into records to facilitate greater integration of planning and controlling functions. A plan for meeting fixed commitments (primarily a sequencing problem) and a recording system for checking payments were illustrated.

The idea to classify expenditures by the nature of their effect on total resources, present and future, of expected consumption of goods was introduced. A time continuum integrates expenditures and savings and focuses on their interrelation in the assessment of the financial progress of families over time.

Families may introduce their children to financial planning and implementing in many ways. The means for providing money to children —through allowances, doling, or providing opportunities for earning —may or may not promote the child's learning about the value of money.

Factors affecting planning and implementation include the nature of income flow, organization patterns, and changing price levels. The stability, frequency, and amount of income characterize the nature of its flow. In general, steady and frequent income payments facilitate sequencing and controlling, especially checking.

Organization patterns for financial management vary greatly; young families or newly formed groups have to evolve satisfactory plans for roles or procedures. Income flow and organization patterns do not determine the amount of resource allocation to any item or determine which item will be purchased. Instead, they influence decision-making processes and help designate responsibilities.

Changing price levels further affect financial planning and implementing. For maximum purchasing power and net worth growth, savings or investment alternatives should emphasize variable dollar assets during inflation and fixed dollar assets during deflation. The alternative of hedging price changes by spreading holdings over both fixed and variable assets provide basic security against major price effects.

Satisfactions of husbands and wives with their financial management accompany the more tangible effects of levels of living and net worth. The components of net worth reflect decisions affected by other systems, especially the economic system. Human capital increases often follow from financial outlays for education and training, although the cost may or may not be borne directly by the individual or family.

Bankruptcy is a negative output from financial management—when resources and demands have not been successfully balanced.

Managing Household Activities

11.

Through unpaid productive work and leisure activities, home managers use appropriate resources within the environment to meet various demands of household members. Management of financial and household activities may be viewed separately, but they are both a part of the total management of the household.

Household activities are identified with the repetitiveness of many aspects of daily living. Responding to this constant series of demands often fosters the development of routines that either limit awareness of their value or the opportunity for variation.

Household activities are traditionally interrelated in time spent and are not measured as productive activity contributing to real income. The relative returns from household activities in their long-run satisfactions tend to be obscured and often minimized. The women's movement has brought attention to household activities and has urged a sharing of the responsibility rather than adhering to sex-role stereotyping.

The first section of the chapter considers input factors of goals and events and of human and material resources. Planning and implementing were discussed as separate chapters, in which some emphasis was given to household activities. They are also discussed here, but only briefly. Used resources and met demands are presented, along with background on the micro-habitat, with emphasis on the influence of the situation, itself, on household activities.

INPUT

Demands

Goals. Recognizing important priorities clarifies how household activities need to be organized to achieve the quality of life desired. Many family and individual goals relate to household activities or task performance. The ratings for nine goals, according to their importance, follow:

1. Affection. Having family members satisfied with the amount of love they give to each other.
2. Companionship. Having family members enjoy doing things together and feel comfortable with each other.
3. Happy children. Helping the children become well adjusted and enjoy their lives.
4. Personal development. Giving each family member the opportunity to develop as an individual.
5. Religion. Living according to religious principles and teaching.
6. Economic security. Keeping up or improving the family's standard of living.
7. Attractive home. Having a place that is comfortable and attractive to live in.
8. Wise financial planning. Making sound decisions in budgeting for present and future purchases and making intelligent use of money.
9. A place in the community. Giving family members a respected place in the community.[1]

The goals—economic security, attractive home, and wise financial planning—are particularly related to task performance.

A number of factors in situations can influence goals. Among the important factors are role, social position, and the environment. Goals related to household activities are influenced by the roles assumed by family members. Many household activities are traditionally prescribed as women's work, and women inside and outside the women's movement continue to find that housework is regarded primarily as their responsibility. Men spend limited time in work around the house. There are case studies of equal household work contributions by men and women, but no

---

1. George Levinger, "Task and Social Behavior in Marriage," *Sociometry* 27 (December 1964): 441.

trend crosses widely different groups of families or units. Specific data is given in the section on resources.

Single-parent households may experience problems in setting goals for household activities and responsibilities since one adult must often care for the children, work outside the home, and manage all household activities.

Events. Specific household activities may be brought about by events. These pertinent and relatively unpredictable occurrences differ from interruptions to the flow of work. Interruptions represent a break in work being done, but do not require a change in activities; events involve some change in actions as a response to the event.

Households with children are vulnerable to unplanned and relatively unpredictable occurrences. Some of these events are accidents, which may or may not result in injury. Factors such as fatigue and stress, poor sight, and the physical condition of the area contribute to accidents. Data on accidents occurring in the home indicate that 94 per cent of the injuries are associated with unexpected or chance events.[2]

The location of home accidents, according to a study of emergency-room cases, is given in Table 11.1. The kitchen, dining area, yard or outdoor living area, and hallway are places where preventive measures might well be taken. Records from hospitals in the National Electronic Injury Surveillance System reveal that the home structure, furnishings, and fixtures are major categories in home-related injuries (Table 11.2).

Some practices that lead to home accidents and near accidents with a high degree of certainty are incorrect use of tools, unsanitary practices, and unsafe practices such as cutting bacon into a hot frying pan.[3]

The concept of accident proneness was supported by a study of kitchen accidents in which persons who had kitchen accidents were also more likely to have automobile accidents.[4]

Alcohol appears to be a factor in home accidents, although the relationship is relatively limited in the case of females. Breath analyzer tests given in an emergency room to 520 persons involved in home accidents revealed that almost one-third of the men had a blood alcohol concentration

---

2. Henry Wechsler *et al.*, "Alcohol Level and Home Accidental Injuries," U.S. Public Health Service Grant #UI 00022-02, Progress Report, 1967 (unpublished), p. 21.
3. Joan S. Guilford, "Prediction of Accidents in a Standardized Home Environment," *Journal of Applied Psychology* 57 (June 1973): 310.
4. Guilford, p. 306.

TABLE 11.1

Home accident location, in descending order of frequency.

Area	Per cent of cases
Kitchen or indoor dining area	17.8
Yard or outdoor living area	15.7
Hallway or hallway stairs	15.5
Living room	10.9
Bedroom	10.3
Bathroom	5.7
Basement	4.0
Occupational accidents in homes	1.7
Unknown	18.4
Number of cases = 580	

Henry Wechsler *et al.,* "Alcohol Level and Home Accidental Injuries," Research Progress Report, October 1967, p. 21 (PHS Grant #UI 00022-02).

TABLE 11.2

Frequency of injuries associated with consumer products reported July 1, 1972 – June 30, 1973 in 120 hospitals in the National Electronic Injury Surveillance System.

Description	Frequency
General household appliances	2,402
Kitchen appliances	3,459
Space heating, cooling, and ventilating appliances	2,238
Housewares	16,618
Home communications and entertainment appliances and equipment	1,787
Home furnishings and fixtures	50,953
Home workshop apparatus, tools and attachments	6,788
Home and family maintenance products	8,048
Packaging and containers for household products	9,369
Yard and garden equipment	6,576
Child nursery equipment and supplies	1,970
Personal use items	9,299
Other products	4,217
Home structures, construction materials	69,214

Consumer Product Safety Commission, Bureau of Epidemiology, "Fiscal Year 1973 Tabulation of Data from National Electronic Injury Surveillance System (NEISS), July 1, 1972 – June 30, 1973."

of .02 per cent or above. Fewer than 10 per cent of the women had a blood alcohol concentration of .02 or above.[5] In a study of life insurance policy holders who were 15–64 years old, alcohol was associated with one-seventh of 537 males and about one-fifth of 310 females who had had fatal accidents in the home.[6]

In a laboratory-simulated home kitchen, women who reported they never drank alcoholic beverages were less likely to have kitchen accidents than those who drank alcohol.[7]

Little is known of the effect of narcotics on accidents in the home or on the management of household activities.

Resources

Human Resources. Time, physical capacity, and cognitive resources are important human aspects of the resource base for accomplishing household activities.

Time. Total time as a resource input is "fixed" in the sense that each of us has twenty-four hours a day. The time allocated for a given situation can be highly variable, however, and depends on other inputs such as the importance of the activity (goal importance) and other resources since time in itself is never a sufficient resource input. Information on time used for activities reflects values and goals in interaction with resources in a special way: compared to money, which varies among users over a given time period, the total available time is the same.

A New York state time study (Table 11.3) shows that the total time used in all household work ranged from 7.2 to 17.4 hours per day when the wife was not employed outside the home and from 5.0 to 11.3 hours when the wife was employed outside the home. The major part of that time, in either situation, was spent by the wife.

The time spent on all household work is related to the characteristics of adult members, the family composition, and the micro-habitat (Table 11.4). The number and ages of children and the wife's employment are probably the greatest factors affecting total time use.

Benchmark information on time use and human physical capacity is useful for developing plans and implementing household activities, just as

---

5. Wechsler, p. 28.
6. "Alcohol and Home Accidents at the Working Ages," Metropolitan Life Insurance Company, *Statistical Bulletin* 48 (October 1967): 3–4.
7. Guilford, p. 311.

TABLE 11.3

Average hours per day used by homemakers and by all workers for all household work, related to number of children and employment of homemaker.

Number of children	Homemaker not employed+		Homemaker employed	
	Homemaker	*All workers*	*Homemaker*	*All workers*
	Hours			
None	5.7	7.2	3.7	5.0
One	7.4	9.7	5.1	7.7
Two	8.4	11.1	5.9	9.8
Three	8.1	11.6	6.0	10.8
Four–six	8.7	12.8	6.3	11.3
Seven–nine	9.4	17.4	*	*

Kathryn E. Walker, "Household Work Time: Its Implication for Family Decisions," *Journal of Home Economics* 65 (October 1973): 10-11.

*Fewer than 3 cases; total number = 1,296 cases.

+Homemaker worked 0-14 hours/week for pay; homemakers who worked 15 hours or more per week for pay.

TABLE 11.4

Summary of factors affecting total time used in household work.

Factor	Effect on household work time	
	Less time	*More time*
Characteristics of adult members		
Family head		
Sex*	Man	Woman
Marital status*	Single	Married
Education*	More	Less
Wife's employment†	Employed	Not em-ployed
Family composition		
Number in family*	Smaller	Larger
Age of youngest child at home†	Older	Younger
Micro-habitat		
Location of dwelling**	Urban	Rural farm

* James N. Morgan, Ismail Sirageldin, and Nancy Baerwaldt, *Productive Americans,* Survey Research Center Monograph 43 (Ann Arbor, Michigan: Institute for Social Research, The University of Michigan, 1966), p. 109. Reprinted with permission of the publisher, Survey Research Center, Institute for Social Research, The University of Michigan, Ann Arbor, Michigan.

† Kathryn E. Walker, "Homemaking Still Takes Time," *Journal of Home Economics* 61 (October 1969): 623.

** Sarah L. Manning, "Time Use in Household Tasks by Indiana Families," Research Bulletin No. 837 (Lafayette, Indiana: Purdue University Agricultural Experiment Station, 1968), p. 39.

average expenditures can be used as a reference point in financial management. For the families studied, the time used in separate household activities changed during the period from 1927 to 1967, and the total time spent in household tasks increased somewhat.[8] The decrease of thirty minutes in food preparation and cleanup was offset by an increase in marketing, record-keeping, and management time. Food activities continue to be the major time factor in the household (Table 11.5).

The time used for individual household activities is affected by family characteristics, the activity and its standards, and the micro-habitat (Table 11.6).

Time use in a particular household may vary weekly and seasonally. Week-to-week variations in time spent for individual household tasks may be expected if specific standards are used for a specific situation. For an occasion when a clean house is desired, the time used for housecleaning can be expanded, while in a period of regular family routine or in a time of crisis, housecleaning may take a minimal amount of time.

Seasonal differences do not greatly influence total time use in household activities, but several tasks are affected by season. In a study of Indiana families, marketing fluctuated by seasons, with peaks occurring

TABLE 11.5.
Time used for household work by urban homemakers.

	Homemaker	
Activity	*Employed* *	*Not employed* **
	Hours per day	
All food activities	1.6	2.3
Care of house	1.2	1.6
Care of clothes	.9	1.3
Care of family members	.8	1.8
Marketing and record keeping	.8	1.0
All household work	5.3	8.0

Kathryn E. Walker, "Homemaking Still Takes Time." *Journal of Home Economics* 61 (October 1969): 622.

*Number = 317 cases; worked 15 hours or more per week for pay.

** Number + 979; worked 0-14 hours/week for pay.

---

8. Kathryn E. Walker, "Homemaking Still Takes Time," *Journal of Home Economics* 61: (October 1969), 622.

TABLE 11.6
Factors predicting time used for household activities.

Task	Predictors
Family-member care	*Single best predictor* Number of children *Second* Age of youngest child
Food preparation and after-meal cleanup	Meal complexity
Machine-washing clothes	Number of loads
Ironing	Number of pieces
Cleaning	Number of rooms

Kathryn E. Walker, ARS Summary Report of "Time Used for Household Work," Department of Consumer Economics and Public Policy, New York State College of Human Ecology, Cornell University, June 15, 1971 (mimeo).

around July 4, Thanksgiving, Christmas, and Easter.[9] Sewing and mending work peaked between Labor Day and Thanksgiving and again before Easter. Food preservation peaked between June 1 and July 4, and twice between July 4 and Labor Day.

Physical—energy. Energy use in household activities is shown in Table 11.7. The values are average total energy expenditures, not energy above a resting base. Continuous expenditure of over 4 Cal/min can produce fatigue.[10] High-energy activities, however, are not likely to be continuous; for example, a person doing gardening will probably break the activity several times and may not continue the activity for long periods. Picking up items from the floor and climbing stairs are by nature discontinuous activities.

Energy expenditures are not additive. In one experiment, energy expenditures for separate tasks were added, and their sum was more than

9. Sarah L. Manning, "Time Use in Household Tasks by Indiana Families," Research Bulletin 837 (Lafayette, Ind.: Purdue University Agricultural Experiment Station, 1968), p. 14.
10. Rose E. Steidl and Esther Crew Bratton, *Work in the Home* (New York: John Wiley & Sons, Inc. 1968), p. 146.

TABLE 11.7

Approximate human energy costs for selected activities.

	Energy use in Calories per minute			
Activity	*1–2*	*2–3*	*3–4*	*4 or more*
Sedentary				
Hand sewing	x			
Machine sewing	x			
Knitting	x			
Standing				
Ironing	x			
Using a rotary beater	x			
Dishwashing	x			
Sweeping		x		
Dustmopping		x		
Applying floor wax with applicator		x		
Hanging clothes		x		
Playing piano		x		
Washing floor			x	
Waxing floor			x	
Changing sheets in bedmaking			x	
Cleaning carpeted stairs			x	
Going up or down stairs				x
Picking up items from floor				x
Gardening, weeding				x

Rose E. Steidl and Esther Crew Bratton, *Work in the Home* (New York: John Wiley & Sons, Inc., 1968), p. 144. (Slightly adapted.)

the total energy expended in performing the same tasks simultaneously.[11]

Standing requires about 16 per cent more energy than sitting,[12] but if an activity is performed while the worker is sitting and again while he is standing, the energy-use relationship changes. Energy expenditures are

11. R. B. Andrews, "The Additivity of Values of Energy Expenditure of Simultaneously Performed Simple Muscular Tasks," *Ergonomics* 9 (September 1966): 514.

12. Martha Richardson and Earl C. McCracken, "Energy Expenditures of Woman Performing Selected Activities," U.S. Dept. of Agriculture, Agricultural Research Service, Home Economics Research Report 11 (Washington, D. C.: U.S. Government Printing Office, 1960), p. 3.

slightly less for work done in a standing position than for work done in a sitting position. One study showed standing energy-use values range from 98 to 84 per cent of the sitting values;[13] other studies have produced similar results.[14] Available evidence gives little support to the recommendation that persons with cardiac limitations should sit while working to minimize their energy expenditures.[15]

The energy cost of climbing stairs with loads was examined for two age groups—women aged 26–36 and women aged 63–73. Each of the loads—a basket of clothes, an upright vacuum cleaner, and a doll weighing sixteen pounds—was carried up and down the stairs and was held differently. Energy use did not vary with the type of load for the younger women, but did affect the energy use of older women who required more Calories than did the younger women to carry loads upstairs.[16] For both groups, ascending stairs required more energy than descending. When the body weight must be lifted, energy expenditures increase.

The reduction of energy expenditure for healthy women in the United States is less important today than it was in the past. Substantial reductions in human energy use came with home central heating and hot water heaters that are directly connected to a water supply, but more recent changes primarily affect convenience, not energy use. Examples of these changes are lighter weight vacuum cleaners, self-defrosting refrigerators, and self-cleaning ovens.

Physical—heart rate. Heart rate varies with factors such as age, sex, weight, physical fitness, time of day, and emotions. Physically fit persons have lower heart rates during rest, exercise, and recovery activities than do those persons who do not exercise regularly.[17] Physical fitness did not affect the heart rate in a study of ironing, a nonstrenuous household

---

13. Martha Richardson and Earl C. McCracken, "Energy Expenditures of Women Performing Selected Activities While Sitting and Standing," *Journal of the American Medical Women's Association* 16 (November 1961): 864.

14. Steidl and Bratton, pp. 153–54.

15. Howard Rusk, E. Kristeller, J. S. Judson, G. M. Hunt, and M. Zimmerman, "A Manual for Training the Disabled Homemaker," Rehabilitation Monograph 8, 2d ed. (New York: New York University Institute of Physical Medicine and Rehabilitation, 1971), pp. 37–76.

16. Doris E. Elliot, Mary Brown Patton, and Mary Edna Singer, "Energy Expenditures of Women Performing Household Tasks," Bulletin 939 (Wooster, Ohio: Ohio Agricultural Experiment Station, 1963), pp. 34–35.

17. Donald K. Mathews and Edward L. Fox, *The Physiological Basis of Physical Education and Athletics* (Philadelphia: W. B. Saunders Company, 1971), pp. 155–56.

activity.[18] The heart rate-fitness relationship may be closer for a heavier task.

More heart rate information for home activities is being gathered. The heart rate for all daily home activities averaged 100 to 125 beats per minute for Swedish homemakers and 95 beats for English home-makers.[19] A group of United States mothers of a preschool child averaged 99.5 beats per minute for the task of ironing.[20] In a laboratory study a small group of mothers of preschool children had an average heart rate of 104 beats during ironing and 93 beats per minute when not engaged in a task.[21]

Most household tasks for English mothers of young children required within 5 heart beats per minute of the mean of 95.[22] The mothers engaged in heavy activities about an hour each day when the heart rate was as high as 110 beats per minute. Heavy activities included climbing stairs, shopping and carrying packages, pushing packages and a child in a cart, or walking the young children. Climbing stairs averaged twelve trips each day, and half the trips were made when the mother was empty-handed. The most frequent load was a child carried in the arms. The heaviest child weighed 40 pounds. A twenty-pound vacuum cleaner was another frequently carried item.[23]

Physical—body position. Posture for household activities is particularly important for lifting, carrying loads, and standing in one position. Suggestions for lifting include: keep the back relatively straight and bend the knees (Figure 11.1), spread feet apart for the support base, and hold objects close to the body.[24]

---

18. Reta Hamilton Richardson, "Stimuli in Homemaking Activities Associated with Heart Rate Changes in Women from Two Socioeconomic Levels," The Ohio State University, Ph.D. dissertation, 1969, p. 81.
19. June I. Grieve, "Heart Rate and Daily Activities of Housewives with Young Children," *Ergonomics* 15 (March 1972): 144.
20. Richardson, p. 89.
21. Jean Dearth Dickerscheid, "Development of a Method of Measuring the Effects of a Preschool Child on the Mother's Heart Rate," The Ohio State University, Ph.D. dissertation, 1967, p. 91.
22. Grieve, p. 141.
23. Grieve, p. 144.
24. Katherine H. Sippola, "Your Work and Your Posture," Cornell Extension Bulletin 1139 (Ithaca, N.Y.: New York State College of Home Economics, 1965) and Steidl and Bratton, pp. 234–37.

FIGURE 11.1 *Optimal body position for lifting.*

> Source: "Andy Capp," Columbus Evening Dispatch, February 12, 1969. (London: Publishers-Hall Syndicate and Daily Mirror). Reprinted by permission of I.P.C. Newspapers Ltd. and Publishers-Hall Syndicate.

Lifting and carrying a child is one of the frequent examples of lifting and carrying in the home. Studies for both farm and industry suggest working out an optimal load size for as low a metabolic (energy) cost as possible without overloading muscles and the cardiovascular system.[25] The nature of household activities precludes the use of such information since loads are variable and children continue to grow.

Many ways exist to minimize lifting and carrying loads for the person without physical limitations. For the person in a wheel chair, lifting and moving items can be a frustrating and tiring experience; but depending on the limitations, some persons in wheelchairs become quite adept at pushing or pulling items along.

Standing in a static position can be fatiguing and should be avoided because blood pools in the extremities. Household activities have many advantages over industrial activities because one can move around at will in the house; the many trips made in meal preparation suggest that static positions are infrequent in that task. Also, improved finishes and fibers have altered the patterns of ironing, and long periods of static work are also unlikely.

---

25. Eliezer Kamon and Harwood S. Belding, "The Physiological Cost of Carrying Loads in Temperate and Hot Environments," *Human Factors* 13 (April 1971): 161.

Cognitive. Information overload, the opposite of insufficient information, comes from an inability to process the available information effectively. For example, the spate of advertising and analyses from stock brokers can confuse the prospective buyer and cloud his investment objectives. Marketing may be the household activity most likely to involve information overload.

Filtering, pigeonholing, and categorizing are devices for dealing with too much information.[26] Through filtering, some information is processsed more intensely than other information. Pigeonholing is storing information in a previously learned category. One example is information on the energy consumption of an item of household equipment. The information can be stored for later comparison with the energy requirements of other brands.

Establishing new categories for information is a time-consuming process. Some of the information about the use, care, and safety of microwave ovens may need to be put into new categories by shoppers. Insights about children's behavior and responses to certain situations may be an overload until appropriate new categories are developed to receive the information.

Household activities that require a great deal of attention, judgment, and planning were identified by a group of young homemakers. The reasons why food tasks required these cognitive resources included:

Quality and quantity considerations: growth, health and nutrition factors; variety; aesthetically pleasing results; quantity and quality control of the product.
Timing considerations: careful timing required, decisions on when to do the task, the time span needed, and the time squeeze.
Procedural activities and preparatory work.
Monetary and economic considerations; judging of value and prices, money available, and control of cash flow.
Human relations involved: pleasing self and others.[27]

The tasks felt to require high attention, judgment, and planning were the preferred tasks, which were also high in complexity and difficulty.

---

26. D. E. Broadbent, *Decision and Stress* (London: Academic Press, 1971), pp. 10, 15.
27. Rose E. Steidl, "Food Tasks: Complexity, Difficulty and Preference," *Human Ecology Forum* 3 (Summer 1972): 18.

Material Resources. The effect of material resources, particularly household equipment, on the management of household work differs from one's expectations: The time spent on tasks is not necessarily reduced by the use of equipment and the amount of work is also not necessarily reduced.[28] Instead, possession of household equipment tends to reinforce stereotyped task assignments and tends to reduce the amount of help from others.[29] Work may be accomplished with increased ease and standards may be increased because the equipment enables one to do a more thorough job. By having equipment, some individuals or families may undertake tasks that were not formerly done in the home.[30]

THROUGHPUT

The role of home management is to appraise the resources available in a situation, to judge their use in keeping with the goal or event demands, and to develop a plan to be implemented—the throughput of the system.

Planning and implementing household activities involve the concepts discussed previously—standard setting and sequencing actions, controlling and facilitating.

Planning

The clear goal of meeting basic nutritional needs of family members may be accomplished by a wide variety of standards and sequences of action among or within families. Some family members may have traditional breakfast fare, while other members may eat the same sort of food for breakfast as for other meals. Some families prepare unconventional foods that meet the nutritional needs; others may prepare very low-cost foods and have an equal concern for adequate nutrition.

In the past, high standards for household activities, such as house care, have too often been equated with good home management. The concept

28. James N. Morgan, Ismail A. Sirageldin, and Nancy Baerwaldt, *Productive Americans,* Survey Research Center Monograph 43 (Ann Arbor, Mich.: Institute for Social Research, The University of Michigan, 1966), pp. 111–12.
29. Charles Alexander Thrall, "Household Technology and the Division of Labor in Families," Harvard University, Ph.D. dissertation, 1970.
30. Morgan, Sirageldin, and Baerwaldt, p. 112.

1-22

1974, The Register
and Tribune Syndicate

"Why didn't you think of that before I dressed you?"

FIGURE 11.2 Sequencing of activities.

Source: *The Family Circus*, by Bil Keane, reprinted courtesy The Register and Tribune Syndicate.

of lower and upper limits of acceptable variation in standards is a more appropriate view for home management than high or low standards. Flexibility of standards is meaningful in the humanistic trends of society today.

The sequencing of household activities is often shaped by the degree of complexity of the combined internal family and external environments (Figure 11.2).

Among workers in a pharmaceutical company, women who worked a four-day week used the fifth day to catch up on housework.[31] This

---

31. Walter R. Nord and Robert Costigan, "Worker Adjustment to the Four-Day Week: A Longitudinal Study," *Journal of Applied Physchology* 58 (February 1973): 60–66.

catching up probably relates to standard setting as well as sequencing —standards may be changed as more tasks are undertaken or as the homemaker shifts her expectations or desired output.

Sequencing activities may be mentally rehearsed, especially when a situation changes. For example, anticipation of the sequence of activities relating to moving can reduce stress. Changes in a planned sequence will likely occur as feedback information reveals the success of one aspect of the sequence and the problems associated with other aspects.

Implementing

Controlling household activities—that is, checking and adjusting the standards or sequences of planned actions—is accomplished in a variety of ways. Checking against standards is often subjective—the readiness of food or the sheen when waxing a car.

For some homemakers, checking the sequence of household activities may be in relation to a written plan for a day or period of time, while others may plan with a mental sequence of activities. A high specificity of plans can require careful checking to meet the specified standards and sequences. An activity such as redecorating a room can involve very specific plans and frequent checking to insure completion of the activity as planned. For such projects, adjustments are often necessary to accommodate subtle variations from expected effects, as with a somewhat more intense paint color.

As indicated in Chapter 7, the progress or flow of actions can be facilitated positively or negatively by the environmental situation. In one study, the housing type and facilities were related to work being more and less difficult in those tasks that were high in attention, judgment, or planning and in tasks that were low in attention or judgment.[32] The content of the work, the family and community, and the affective and cognitive considerations also affected the work. Since housing and facilities were apparently more important, they are examined in greater detail here as having the potential for facilitating the activities. Figure 11.3 presents a summary of the findings. The role of equipment should be noted because of its reported effect as a positive and negative facilitating factor. This suggests that equipment might just as realistically be a

---

32. Rose E. Steidl, "Factors of Functionality and Difficulty in Homemaking Tasks," *Human Ecology Forum* 3 (Autumn 1972): 10–1.

way to affect the flow of action as it is a time saving device. As such, equipment is viewed as a planned facilitator, used over time to assist the flow of action.

OUTPUT

Output from household activities includes the accomplishment of the task resulting in some degree of satisfaction, resource use, and, at times, fatigue or stress from doing the task.

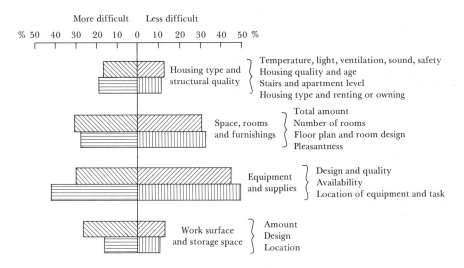

Key: For 622 tasks high in attention, judgment or planning
     ◼ % of 580 responses
     ◼ % of 506 responses

For 414 tasks low in attention or judgment
     ◻ % of 361 responses
     ◻ % of 405 responses

FIGURE 11.3 *Factors about housing and facilities that made work more or less difficult in tasks high in attention, judgment, or planning, and in tasks low in attention or judgment.**

Source: Rose E. Steidl, "Factors of Functionality and Difficulty in Homemaking Tasks," *Human Ecology Forum* 3 (Autumn 1972): 11.

*According to the responses of 208 homemakers in Ithaca, N.Y. vicinity, 1967.

Met Demands

In choosing how to spend their time, people consciously or subconsciously try to maximize their total satisfaction. They may sacrifice satisfaction in one area such as security, achievement, or status to gain in another area and increase the overall sense of well-being. They process information from previous experiences and assess their resources, such as income, age, and knowledge of the available options. The outcome of their efforts toward maximum satisfaction is a set of activities.[33]

Satisfaction from household work varies among individuals, and almost no information is available on the satisfactions men receive from these activities. Work in the 1950's found different satisfactions among women from varying socioeconomic status; higher-status homemakers reported a more favorable attitude toward household work, but with some tendency toward dissatisfaction with the role.[34] In a study of Ohio families, high husband-wife consensus, or marital-role agreement, was related to the wife's satisfaction with her household organization.[35]

In another study of fifty New York state homemakers, one-tenth expressed some dissatisfaction with the way they managed their household work as a whole; separate tasks revealed more dissatisfaction ratings.[36]

For 568 Chicago-area homemakers, reports of satisfaction with the homemaker's role centered on children. Of the responses given by the homemakers, 19 per cent were related to household activities or the home itself, and 13 per cent were concerned with accomplishing activities.[37]

Satisfaction with the way the spouse performs his or her household tasks is lowest when the oldest child is between 6 and 12 years (school-age-children stage) for both husband and wife (Figure 11.4). In the same study, the wife's satisfaction with the way the husband performed his

---

33. F. Stuart Chapin, Jr., "Activity Systems and Urban Structure: A Working Schema," *Journal of American Institute of Planners* 34 (January 1968): 15.

34. Dorothy Greey Van Bortel and Irma H. Gross, "A Comparison of Home Management in Two Socio-Economic Groups," Technical Bulletin 240 (East Lansing, Mich.: Michigan Agricultural Experiment Station, 1954).

35. E. Carolyn Ater and Ruth E. Deacon, "Interaction of Family Relationship Qualities and Managerial Components," *Journal of Marrriage and the Family* 34 (May 1972): 257.

36. Linda Miller Kelsey, "Household Work: Homemakers' Changes and Reasons," Cornell University, M.S. thesis, 1965.

37. Helena Z. Lopata, *Occupation: Housewife* (New York: Oxford University Press, 1971), p. 205.

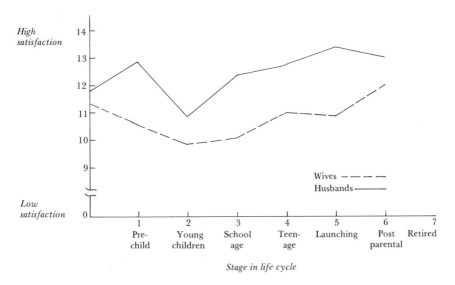

High
satisfaction

Low
satisfaction

Wives — — — —
Husbands ————

Stage in life cycle

FIGURE 11.4 *Satisfaction with the way the spouse performs his or her household tasks, by
family life cycle.*

Source: Wesley R. Burr, "Satisfaction with Various Aspects of Marriage Over the Life
Cycle: A Random Middle Class Sample," *Journal of Marriage and the Family* 32 (February 1970):
34. Copyright (1970) by National Council on Family Relations. Reprinted by permission.

household tasks was highest when the family was at the retired family
life-cycle stage.

Response to specific household activities varies widely. Some persons
like particular household tasks, while other persons find them almost re-
pugnant. Women have reported liking food-related activities over the
years, and mothers of young children have reported liking to care for the
children. No single task dominates the disliked task reports, but cleaning,
ironing, and dishwashing are most often named.[38]

What makes a task liked or disliked is more important for our consideration than the task. It has been proposed that, regardless of the task, similar reasons make a task liked or not liked. Characteristics of tasks were examined in two similar studies with mothers of kindergarten children.

---

38. Francille Maloch, "Characteristics of Most and Least Liked Household Tasks,"
Cornell University, Ph.D. dissertation, 1962, p. 5.

Using the same scale, both groups characterized the most-liked task with the same seven items, although four items characterized the most-liked task for one or the other study.[39]

Reasons for liking task
(both studies)
Could take pride in results.
Found task satisfying.
Results were appreciated
by family.
Could set own pace.
Liked supplies and materials.
Had adequate equipment for
the job.
Liked time spent.

Reasons for liking task
(single study)
Almost always completed
task as planned.
Had much skill for the task.
Found task interesting.
Worked in pleasant location.

Three reasons—pride in results, satisfaction with work, and results appreciated by family—are output factors. The output from a task, satisfaction or lack of it, feeds back to affect succeeding input. Predictably, persons who like a task spend more time on it (input) than do persons who do not like the task.[40] Furthermore, when homemakers rated the reasons why they preferred the most-liked task, they gave "liked time spent" a high rating. The reasons for this attitude toward the least-liked task were in complete agreement in the two similar studies of mothers of preschool children:[41]

Results were short term.
Homemaker disliked time spent.
Task was monotonous.
No creativity required.
Used little mental skill.
Generally no other adult was present.

---

39. Patricia Y. Ronald, Mary E. Singer, and Francille Maloch Firebaugh, "Rating Scale for Household Tasks," *Journal of Home Economics* 63 (March 1971): 178–79.
40. Manning, pp. 7, 10, 13, 16, 18.
41. Ronald, Singer, and Firebaugh, p. 179.

Both of the reasons—"short-term results" and "disliked time spent"—are output reactions from the least-liked task, while the other reasons are mainly inherent in the task itself. Dislike of the time spent was reported for the least-liked task, although, for the same task, homemakers spend less time than those who liked the task. "Perhaps the homemaker who dislikes a task actually accomplishes the task faster—or perhaps the homemaker who likes a task does more of a task, lingers over the task, or does the task more thoroughly."[42]

Resource Use

Emphasis has been placed on resources involved in household activities—especially time, physical capacity, and cognitive resources. Information about the input of time was necessarily based on time-use patterns from research. The findings are not repeated here. Two aspects —fatigue and stress—that may be related to time use, physical capacity, and cognitive resources are discussed as output.

Fatigue and Stress. Fatigue and stress can be a part of the output of the individual's system that feeds back to affect succeeding input. Fatigue is "weariness from bodily or mental exertion";[43] stress is "physical, mental, or emotional strain or tension."[44] The effects of fatigue are decreased attention and motivation, decreased physical and mental performance, and impaired perception and thinking.[45] The decreases may be very important to the family system when demands are high, and fatigue affects performance of activities.

In a laboratory study, the subjects' work loads were increased—a fact that was unknown by the subjects—and they indicated feelings of fatigue during the work period and recovery period. The relation between the ratings and the actual physical work load was high.[46] Homemakers who

---

42. Francille Maloch, "Characteristics of Most and Least Liked Household Tasks," *Journal of Home Economics* 55 (June 1963): 416.

43. Jess Stein, editor-in-chief, *The Random House Dictionary of the English Language* (New York: Random House, 1967), p. 518.

44. Stein, p. 1906.

45. E. Grandjean, "Fatigue: Its Physiological and Psychological Significance," *Ergonomics* 11 (September 1968): 431.

46. J. E. Hueting and H. R. Sarphati, "Measuring Fatigue," *Journal of Applied Psychology* 50 (December 1966): 536.

have relatively high work loads, such as mothers of young children, report fatigue.

Fatigue can occur in many situations other than those in a relatively high work-load period. Situations often associated with fatigue include:

1. Length of work period and postural position
   a. Long period of mental or light physical work in restricted or uncomfortable position
   b. Long working period while standing
   c. Long period of making continuous postural shifts
2. Working under particular task circumstances
   a. Heavy physical tasks, possibly short duration
   b. Disliked tasks
   c. Unaccustomed tasks
   d. Close-attention tasks
3. Working under stressful conditions
   a. Pressures, such as deadlines
   b. Emotional stresses
   c. Insufficient knowledge or information
   d. Information overload[47]

The affective response to tasks can affect fatigue, just as cognitive aspects such as unaccustomed tasks and those requiring close attention can affect fatigue. An unaccustomed task—preserving food, making jelly —can be fatiguing. Fatigue from separate tasks differs from the fatigue felt from the whole job, that is, the feelings of the whole job are permeating.

Circumstances such as deadlines, emotional stresses, insufficient information or knowledge, and information overload contribute to fatigue and stress. Mental overload can cause physiological changes such as increased heart rate and respiration rates, elevated blood pressure, and heart-rate pattern changes.[48]

Families in which both parents work outside the home and single-parent families particularly feel pressures such as deadlines. Close timing

---

47. Steidl and Bratton, p. 8.
48. J. H. Ettema and R. L. Zielhuis, "Physiological Parameters of Mental Load," *Ergonomics* 14 (January 1971): 137.

and coordination of the parents' work schedules and the children's school and activity schedules may be necessary. Planning and implementing household activities around the fixed time requirements can be hectic.

Insufficient information or knowledge can cause uncertainty, stress, and fatigue: parents of a first child caring for a crying baby may feel the stress of not knowing if the crying is a symptom of a serious condition. If the child is not healthy, the uncertainty and stress may prevail in a household.

After medical consultation, suggestions for dealing with chronic fatigue include adequate sleep, suitable daily work-rest routine, avoidance, if at all possible, of excessive stress situations, and a regular schedule of physical exercise or sports.[49]

Economic Value. The economic value of household activities indicates the extent of the homemaking job. An individual who is heavily involved in unpaid productive activity can experience an increased sense of worth if the economic value of unpaid work is generally recognized.

Traditionally, the economic value of unpaid productive work has been excluded from the gross national product (GNP). The service contributions of volunteers in many agencies and groups have not been valued and included in the GNP, nor have contributions of household members, such as household repairs and maintenance, meal preparation, cleaning, chauffeuring, or other services. When the value of goods and services produced outside the market system is excluded, the value of the total economic production is underestimated.

The value of economic contributions in performing household tasks and in physically caring for children can be estimated by real or opportunity cost methods; the value of activities performed can be estimated by real costs. The opportunity method takes into account probable returns from alternative employment while considering the educational level of the individual.

Economists have estimated the value of unpaid productive work at $320 billion annually for a market, or real, valuation of the work and at $398

---

49. R. A. McFarland, "Understanding Fatigue in Modern Life," *Ergonomics* 14 (January 1971): 7.

TABLE 11.8

Average annual dollar value of time contributed by various members in all household work. (All values expressed to nearest $100.)

Number of children	Age in years	Employed-wife households			Nonemployed-wife households		
	Wife	*Wife*	*Husband*		*Wife*	*Husband*	
No children	Under 25	$2,600	$1,100		$3,900	$ 700	
	25–39	2,800	1,100		4,500	900	
	40–54	3,200	600		4,600	1,200	
	55 and over	3,200	900		4,100	1,600	
	Youngest child	*Wife*	*Husband*	*12–17 year-olds*	*Wife*	*Husband*	*12–17 year-olds*
One	12–17	$3,700	$1,400	$ 800	$5,300	$1,600	$ 900
	6–11	4,400	900	–	5,200	1,200	–
	2–5	3,600	1,200	–	5,200	1,400	–
	1	5,000	400	–	5,900	1,400	–
	Under 1	*	*	–	6,600	1,300	–
Two	12–17	$3,600	$1,300	$ 900	$5,600	$1,300	$ 700
	6–11	4,100	1,200	700	5,600	1,300	600
	2–5	4,800	1,400	900	6,400	1,300	600
	1	4,900	2,800	*	6,900	1,300	*
	Under 1	6,200	1,300	*	7,600	1,200	*
Three	12–17	$2,800	$1,200	$ 800	$5,000	$ 800	$ 800
	6–11	4,800	1,200	1,000	5,600	1,300	900
	2–5	5,900	1,700	*	6,200	1,100	900
	1	5,800	2,000	*	6,900	1,300	1,200
	Under 1	5,200	1,700	*	8,000	1,200	*
Four	12–17	$4,600	$1,000	$1,000	$4,700	$ 800	$ 700
	6–11	4,100	700	600	6,100	1,100	800
	2–5	*	*	*	7,000	1,200	600
	1	*	*	*	6,800	1,500	800
	Under 1	*	*	*	8,400	1,700	*
Five–six	12–17	*	*	*	–	–	–
	6–11	*	*	*	$6,600	$1,600	$1,100
	2–5	*	*	*	6,900	1,200	800
	1	*	*	*	5,800	900	*
	Under 1	*	*	*	8,100	1,700	900
Seven–nine	6–11	–	–	–	*	*	*
	2–5	*	*	*	$6,800	$1,800	$ 900
	1	–	–	–	*	*	*
	Under 1	–	–	–	9,400	1,500	*

Kathryn E. Walker and William H. Gauger, "The Dollar Value of Household Work," Information Bulletin 60 (Ithaca, N.Y.: New York State College of Human Ecology, 1973), p. 11.

* Fewer than 4 cases.

– No cases.

billion annually for the opportunity-cost method of valuation.[50] Table 11.8 presents the market valuation of household work.

Unpaid productive work has not been recognized as having economic value until recently because the product is not vendible. Such productive activity, however, is becoming accepted as economic activity even though it remains difficult to evaluate. It is now recognized that services are performed that would require payment if a paid worker performed them. It is also recognized that the value added to products before consumption is part of the total productive process.

If unpaid productive activities are evaluated, they may provide a basis for benefits ordinarily available only to persons gainfully employed outside the home. Legislation has been proposed to allow the work of homemakers to be valued as self-employment income for Social Security coverage, which would provide benefits similar to those available to all other workers under the Social Security system.[51] Persons outside the paid work force have been covered by Social Security only through their spouses. With changing life styles and increasing divorce rates, such proposals recognize the need for alternate methods of providing protection to persons who are otherwise economically vulnerable.

Money estimates may be made to establish the reasonable values of productive contributions that are no longer available to the household because of the death or disability of a family member. Litigation involving premature death and disability is increasing in frequency and in size of settlements. The wife and/or mother's contribution is of especially high value since she typically spends more time in household work than the father or other family members.

An example of the economic contribution of a mother to her family is shown in Table 11.9. The case is of a mother killed in a car-train collision.

---

50. Nancy A. Baerwaldt and James N. Morgan, "Trends in Inter-Family Transfers," in *Surveys of Consumers 1971–72,* eds. Lewis Mandell, George Katona, James N. Morgan, and Jay Schmiedeskamp (Ann Arbor, Mich.: Institute for Social Research, The University of Michigan, 1973), pp. 205–32; Chang Soo Pyun, "The Monetary Value of a Housewife: An Economic Analysis for use in Litigation," *The American Journal of Economics and Sociology* 28 (July 1969): 275; Ismail A. Sirageldin, *Non-Market Components of National Income* (Ann Arbor, Mich.: Institute for Social Research, The University of Michigan, 1969), p. 20.

51. Barbara Jordan and Martha Griffiths, Bills H. R. 12645 and 12646, introduced to the U.S. House of Representatives, 93rd Congress, 2nd Session, February 6, 1974.

TABLE 11.9
Estimated economic contribution lost to the family by death of mother of three children.

Year from death	Children at home — Age of Youngest	Oldest	Unpaid work[a] — Base value	Projected value	Projected net earnings[b]	Projected unpaid and paid (net) value	Estimated personal expenses[d]	Net economic contribution
					Dollars			
	3 children							
1	1	5	8,000	8,000	(3120)	8,000	1,600	6,400
2	1	6	6,900	7,100		7,100	1,600	5,500
3	2	7	6,200	6,600		6,600	1,700	4,900
4	3	8	6,200	6,800		6,800	1,700	5,100
5	4	9	6,200	7,000		7,000	1,800	5,200
6	5	10	6,200	7,200		7,200	1,900	5,300
					Part-time[c]			
7	6	11	4,800	5,750	3,700	9,450	1,900	7,550
8	7	12	4,800	5,900	3,850	9,750	2,000	7,750
9	8	13	4,800	6,100	3,950	10,050	2,000	8,050
10	9	14	4,800	6,250	4,050	10,300	2,100	8,200
11	10	15	4,800	6,450	4,200	10,650	2,200	8,450
12	11	16	4,800	6,650	4,300	10,950	2,200	8,750
					Full-time[c]			
13	12	17	2,800	4,000	8,900	12,900	2,300	10,600
14	13	18	2,800	4,100	9,150	13,250	2,300	10,950
	2 children							
15	14	17	3,600	5,450	9,450	14,900	2,400	12,500
16	15	18	3,600	5,600	9,700	15,300	2,500	12,800
	1 child							
17	16		3,700	5,950	10,000	15,950	2,600	13,350
18	17		3,700	6,100	10,300	16,400	2,600	13,800
19	18		3,200	5,450	10,600	16,050	2,700	13,350
			91,900	116,450	92,150	208,600	40,100	168,500

a Source: Kathryn E. Walker and William H. Gauger, "The Dollar Value of Household Work," Information Bulletin 60 (Ithaca, N.Y.: New York State College of Human Ecology, Cornell University 1973), p. 11.
(The annual increase is based on an annual earnings increment of 3%; all projected values include this increment from year of death.)

b Hourly rate of $3.00 in base year, adjusted for cost of employment at the rate of 40%, and including projected annual earnings increment.
Source: Emma G. Holmes, "Job-Related Expenditures and Management Practices of Gainfully Employed Wives in Ohio," U.S. Dept of Agriculture, Agricultural Research Service, Home Economics Research Report 27 (Washington, D.C.: U.S. Government Printing Office, 1965).

c Part-time = 20 hours; full-time = 40 hours.

d A 3% annual increase in prices was used in the estimate. A personal consumption value may or may not be included in the estimate, but it does recognize that what would have been available to survivors is affected by her consumption.

The three children were less than 1 year, 3 years, and 5 years old. The value of the mother's contribution to the household until the youngest child becomes 18 years of age has been computed with a real-cost approach. The mother was employed as a secretary before marriage, and it is assumed that she would have returned to work part time when the youngest child became 6 years old and full time when the youngest child became 12 years old. Her net economic contribution to the family until the youngest child became 18 was estimated at $134,800.

A case of both parents' dying from a chlorine gas leak resulted in a $235,000 judgment for the loss of the mother's contributions. The children were ages 3, 2, and 1 year at the time of their parents' death.[52]

APPLICATION OF SYSTEMS APPROACH

A systems overview of household activities and employment means that the total picture can be examined—the relation of the activities to other systems and to other demands placed on the family. Listed below are the steps one may take to achieve such an overview, particularly in the case of women's employment outside the home.

Input

Clarify the *goals* for employment and the priorities for maintaining household activities in relation to other goal demands.

Realistically appraise available *resources* or those that can be acquired to help cope with the added pressures from outside employment.

Throughput

Plan realistic standards for tasks; who will do the tasks, including other family members. Plan which goods and services might be purchased rather than done at home. In making plans, consider the compatability of employment with household activities in relation to schedule, days off, sick leave, and so on. In setting standards, consider demands of other family members. In sequencing activities, consider the flexibility they may or may not have.

---

52. John Nussbaum, "3 Orphans Win $1.3 Million in Fatal Chlorine Gas Leak," *The Plain Dealer* (Cleveland), October 24, 1970.

Output

Anticipate the outcomes from household activities in relation to other potential outcomes from employment outside the home as well as the satisfaction of the person who performs the activities and/or is employed. Consider the relation of the output benefits to the input costs —that is, the economic value of the contribution from productive work in the home, which will be altered by outside employment, and the dollar gain from employment outside the home.

One can estimate the potential output from employment outside the home for a specific family by considering what happens, for example, in households with the wife employed outside the home and in those where the wife is not employed. The data in Table 11.8 is based on the time use of different family compositions and is an estimate of the contribution to household activities based on 1971 wage rates. With Table 11.8 it is possible to estimate the differences in values of work contributed to the home when the worker is either employed or not employed outside the home. A person with two children, the youngest child 12 years old, contributes an estimated $5,600 to the household when she is not employed outside the home and $3,600 whenever she is employed (Table 11.8). A child or children 12–17 years old contribute more to household work when the mother is employed. However, the husband's contribution remains about the same ($1,300 annually) whether or not the wife is employed. Whether the reduction in the time spent and the resultant reduction in the estimated value of the contribution is important to the family depends on their values and goals.

A further consideration in the output from the wife's employment outside the home—aside from the estimated value of her contribution to the household—is the net income. The work table (Table 11.10) is for a wife and mother because taxation is based on a male as head of the household and as the main earner. With some modifications for tax purposes, the concept of the table is applicable to a single-parent family, or an individual. The table is based on income tax procedures in 1973. There are continual calls for tax reform to equalize the tax treatment of husbands and wives, married couples, single individuals, and unmarried couples. The table can serve as a checklist for the types of expenses that could be encountered even if dollar estimates are not made. For mothers of young children, the dollar cost of child care may amount to nearly one-half the income earned,[53] but the net cost would likely be less. Employment requires commitment of resources to some expenses which might or might not be chosen by the family—for example, the Social Security tax, a mandatory retirement plan, or a required life insurance plan.

A systems look at the question of employment outside the home includes more than the economic analysis. When employment of the wife and mother appears to be an economic necessity, a broader systems look at the situation might identify other possibilities. The basis for the wife's employment and the stage in the family life cycle affected part of the family system's output in one study: "Both partners are lower in marriage happiness if the wife participates in the labor market out of economic necessity than if she participates by choice . . . . A woman's choice of the labor market over the home market strains the marriage only when there are preschool children in the family."[54]

A professionally employed mother in an urban area recounts another cost of work outside the home:

There is also the matter of fatigue. Whether I actually get less sleep or am more active than other women with children who do not have jobs, or whether the pressure of trying to balance and meet so many responsibilities is the really tiring factor, it would be difficult to say. But it does seem to me frequently that I am more tired than I care to be.[55]

When a family is on welfare or near the low-income line and is eligible for benefits such as medical assistance or living in subsidized housing, the analysis of costs and benefits of working outside the home for a wife and mother or for a woman as head of the household should be made carefully. Society appears to overlook the alterations in household activities required in low-income households when the wife or mother must work outside the home.

---

53. Emma G. Holmes, "Job-Related Expenditures and Management Practices of Gainfully Employed Wives in Ohio," U.S. Dept. of Agriculture, Agricultural Research Service, Home Economics Research Report 27 (Washington, D.C.: U.S. Government Printing Office, 1965), p. 1.
54. Susan R. Orden and Norman M. Bradburn, "Working Wives and Marriage Happiness," *The American Journal of Sociology* 74 (January 1969): 392.
55. Sidney Cornelia Callahan, *The Working Mother* (New York: The Macmillan Company, 1971), p. 117.

TABLE 11.10
Worksheet for estimating net gain or loss from the wife's employment outside the home.

Item	Amount in dollars
Tax deductible expenses	
Transportation on the job, not reimbursed	_____
Specialized work clothing, including maintenance	_____
Dues to unions, professional and business organizations	_____
Tools, licenses, and supplies for job	_____
Professional and business meetings, conferences, conventions	_____
Business entertainment, professional engagements, and so on	_____
Educational expense of maintaining or increasing skills for current job	_____
Child care during employment (for children under 13 years or handicapped)	_____
Professional and business publications	_____
Other specific expenses of producing income	_____
Total tax deductible expense _____	
Total times 100 per cent minus tax percentage rate with wife employed	_____
Expenses not tax deductible	
Extra expense of hired household help including house repair and improvement help	_____
Transportation to work, including parking	_____
Extra expense for general-wear clothing, including maintenance	_____
Extra personal care expense	_____
Employee clubs, gifts, flowers, not required for employment	_____
Work-related parties and special meal expense (entertainment value excluded)	_____
Extra cost of convenience food for home consumption and increased meals away from home, including meals at work	_____
Income tax	
Total income tax with wife employed _____	
Total income tax with wife not employed _____	
Difference—extra tax	_____
Social Security tax	_____
Total expenses not tax deductible	_____
Total expenses related to income production	_____

Item	Amount in dollars
Income	
Gross pay	_____
Employer's contributions	
Retirement plan	_____
Health and accident insurance	_____
Life insurance	_____
Gifts, bonuses, and so on	_____
Value of employee discounts	_____
Other monetary benefits	_____
Gross total income from wife's employment	_____
Net income from wife's employment	
(Difference in gross total income and	
total expenses related to income production)	_____
Economic value of wife's contribution to household work*	
Without wife's employment	_____
With wife's employment	_____
Difference = loss in services	
Net gain from wife's employment	_____
(Difference in net income from wife's	
employment and loss in services)	

*See Table 11.3.

  Source: Adapted from Emma G. Holmes, "Estimating Net Income of Working Wives," *Family Economics Review* ARS 62-5 (March 1962) 4.

MICRO-HABITAT

The micro-habitat, or setting for work and other activities, impinges on both resources and demands in the home managerial system. The micro-habitat is formed partly from output of activities that are internal to the household (noise, odors, space use) and partly from decisions affecting the environment continuously (work-area design).

Space, the factors affecting its use, and the effects of space on performance are discussed first, followed by work-area arrangements and heights, by noise (factors affecting the perception of noise, its effect on work performance, and reduction in intensity), and, finally, by odors. The positive or negative effects of these conditions on current managerial activity describe their facilitating influence.

Space

Factors Affecting Space Use. Living organisms use space and time as a principal organizing system, and everything that is experienced has a spatial context.[56] The spatial context in the home is interrelated with family activities and family qualities.[57] Social class, living patterns, cultural background, views of space use, amount of available space, family life cycle and family size, special needs of family members, equipment design, and work habits all affect the use of space.

Crowded conditions experienced by lower economic families dictate some use of space. Areas must be shared, and privacy may be nonexistent. Living patterns are illustrated in the following report of a Puerto Rican household in the United States:

It is characteristic for all members of the Puerto Rican household to stay together in the living room in the evenings and sometimes all day. Family members often sit together on the sofa watching television and talking during the commercials. There is a steady stream of traffic to the kitchen as each family member raids the refrigerator, but each visit to the kitchen is short. No one stays in the kitchen alone. Additionally, Puerto Ricans tend to use their bedrooms only to sleep in at night. The main living space of the household is the living room.[58]

Northern Europeans and North Americans are similar in their views on space use for personal relationships. Space has been categorized by the use an individual makes of it.

1. *Intimate space* (a clearance of up to 18 inches around an individual) is the zone where physical contact is very likely.
2. *Personal space* (up to an additional 30 inch clearance) is a "protective" zone separating individuals.
3. *Social space* (a clearance of 4–12 feet) is used in conduct of impersonal business with no expectation of touching.

---

56. Edward T. Hall, "Proxemics and Design," *Design & Environment* 2 (Winter 1971): 24.
57. Irwin Altman, Patricia A. Nelson, and Evelyn E. Lett, "The Ecology of Home Environments," U.S. Dept. of Health, Education, and Welfare Final Report, Project No. 0-0502 (Washington, D. C.: U.S. Government Printing Office, 1972), p. 99.
58. Albert E. Scheflen, "Living Space in an Urban Ghetto," *Family Process* 10 (December 1971): 438.

4. *Public space* (12 or more feet clearance) is used for public occasions.[59]

The home provides the setting for activities involving intimate, personal, and, sometimes, social spaces. Space in some homes is so limited that only intimate and personal spaces are available. Findings from one study of an urban ghetto indicate a lack of even personal space. People may prefer an open area around them, but the available space may be limited by the presence of people, furniture or equipment, or by the lack of floor space.[60] Space use varies with space availability (a new Parkinson's law?). Figure 11.5 shows the difference in space use when one edges past a seated person and when one walks past.

Family life cycle and family size affect space use in the household. The presence of children may affect the father's time spent in the house; especially the time of business and professional men seeking privacy to work away from the children.[61] Other occupational groups may not require seclusion for work after employment hours.

Special needs of family members may be an important influence on space use. Housing design often overlooks space requirements of the physically handicapped. Figure 11.6 shows a kitchen work area with limited space for the husband in the wheel chair to assist his wife, who has limited vision, in setting the oven control. Wheelchair use is difficult in frequently used areas such as the bathroom. College campus officials and municipal officials are becoming more alert to the ways in which space can facilitate the activities of persons with special needs.

For persons without aids such as a wheelchair, crutches, or braces, many special needs can be identified. Persons with limited vision may need special space arrangements for their use; pregnant women use space differently; elderly people may confine their space use to the necessities of daily living; obese persons need more space. Body size and build, age, and weight each affect space use.[62]

---

59. Edward T. Hall, *The Hidden Dimension* (Garden City, N. Y.: Doubleday & Company, Inc., 1966), pp. 112–20.
60. Scheflen, p. 443.
61. Ruth H. Smith, Donna Beth Downer, Mildred T. Lynch, and Mary Winter, "Privacy and Interaction Within the Family as Related to Dwelling Space," *Journal of Marriage and the Family* 31 (August 1969): 564.
62. Helen E. McCullough, Kathryn Philson, Ruth H. Smith, Anna L. Wood, and Avis Woolrich, "Space Standards for Household Activities," Bulletin 686 (Urbana, Ill,: Illinois Agricultural Experiment Station, 1962), p. 3.

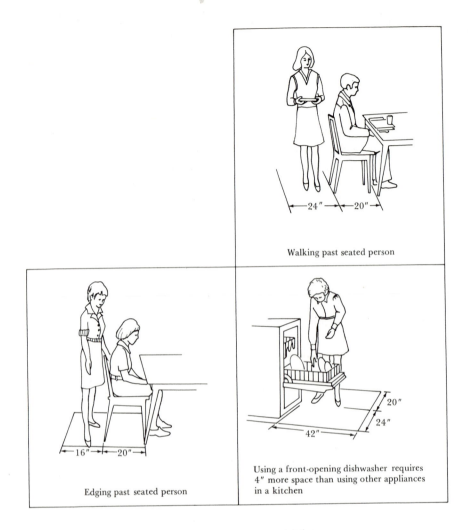

FIGURE 11.5 *Illustrations of clearances for three activities.*

Source: Helen E. McCullough, et al., "Space Standards for Household Activities," Bulletin 686 (Urbana, Ill.: University of Illinois Agricultural Experiment Station, 1962), pp. 9, 11.

Space needs vary with equipment design. The effect can be seen in Figure 11.5 showing a front-opening dishwasher that requires more space than other kitchen appliances. Furniture design may also affect space use.

Work habits can affect space use more than most other factors. Opening a file drawer while standing on the side requires less space than opening the drawer while standing in front. Similarly, space requirements differ when one loads a front-opening dishwasher from the side and when one loads it from the front.

Effects of Space on Performance. Young homemakers who reported on factors that affected their work mentioned space as a factor that made work either more or less difficult, depending on the adequacy. Examples of inadequate space that adversely affected work were: small size of total dwelling space, small size of rooms such as the kitchen and bedrooms, a lack of certain rooms or spaces such as a dining room or eating area, lack of a room for the baby, or lack of outside space.[63]

The homemakers noted positive spatial qualities that made work easier: adequate total dwelling space; a separate, well-planned kitchen; a separate room for the baby; a large room used solely for recreation; and no waste space that required cleaning.[64]

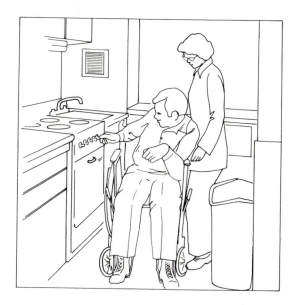

FIGURE 11.6 *Kitchen area with inadequate space for assisting wife with limited vision.*
Source: Marianne Parker and Francille M. Firebaugh, "An Experience in Home Management," *Illinois Teacher* 15 (May-June 1972): 235

63. Rose E. Steidl, "Difficulty Factors in Homemaking Tasks: Implications for Environmental Design" *Human Factors* 14 (October 1972): 476–77.
64. Steidl (October 1972), p. 477.

Work-Area Design

Individuals and families are capable of adapting to work areas as well as to other parts of their environment. A family may readily identify poorly designed spaces while inspecting a house, but these same spaces, if not changed before or soon after the family moves in, are often readily adapted to. Adaptability limits the necessity of well-designed work areas, but it does not reduce the benefits of good design. Evidence is difficult to gather on the effects of space, but individuals who use well-designed areas react with increased satisfaction and pleasure.

Work-Area Arrangement. Many factors affect arrangement of work areas—the existing facilities, the importance or priorities of values, that is esthetic appearance versus highly functional design. Several principles have been developed to arrange work centers to facilitate activities and to minimize the frustrations that result from complex work patterns.

1. Locate the most-used centers first.
2. Place centers to fit the routing of work.
3. Place closely related centers together.[65]

The center concept locates the work surface, storage area, and major appliance or equipment to serve a particular activity.[66] The location or arrangement of work areas is part of the micro-habitat, which is not often easily modified. Many families use housing where the location of utilities determines work-area placement and, thus, limits choices in work-area arrangement.

For kitchens, the principles of work-center arrangement may be applied as follows:

1. Locate the most-used centers first.
   The sink and range (or surface cooking unit) work centers are the most frequently used.
2. Place centers to fit the routing of work.
   The sink is a primary center, and other centers should be placed in relation to it. Questions are often asked about the placement of the dishwasher (dishwashing center) in relation to the sink. The routing of the work to the right or left depends on handedness and work habits. In

---

65. Steidl and Bratton, p. 291.
66. Steidl and Bratton, p. 270.

many cases, the routing of the work is strongly affected by the utility connections and the space available between the sink and the other major equipment.

3. Place closely related centers together.

Sink-range centers and sink-mix centers (if much baking is done) have close relationships, while sink-refrigerator, sink-dish storage, range-mix, range-dish storage, mix-refrigerator, and dish storage-dining centers have somewhat close relationships.[67]

Storage and work-area arrangements deserve close attention when the area is frequently used or when improvements would sufficiently increase the use and enjoyment to justify the improvement costs. Storage locations for equipment and supplies affect body positions and may make awkward reaches necessary in meal preparation.[68] Arrangement of storage areas may be based on several criteria, such as increasing the facilitation of the work, increasing the satisfaction with the work process, protecting children and others incapable of judgment about proper use and care of supplies and equipment, protecting a product from heat or sunlight. Choices in storage design may also be heavily influenced by the visual and esthetic impact.

Whenever the criteria are intended to increase the facilitation of the work, several principles of storage are applicable:

1. Place items so they are easy to see, reach, grasp, and replace.
2. Store items within the worker's limits of reach.[69]

Methods of storing items for easy seeing, reaching, grasping, and replacing include:

a. Storing unlike items one row and one layer deep.
b. Stack only items with compatible dimensions.
c. Leave enough clearance for grasping and replacing items.
d. Organize items in the storage space to minimize searching and facilitate retrieval.[70]

---

67. Steidl and Bratton, pp. 324–27.
68. Florence Ehrenkranz, "Functional Convenience of Kitchens with Different Sink-Dishwasher Locations," *Journal of Home Economics* 57 (November 1965): 711–16; Jessie J. Mize, Frankye E. Bland, Sally Jo Ritchie, and Joseph W. Simons, "Laundry Work Areas for Southern Rural Homes," Bulletin N.S. 42 (Athens, Ga.: Georgia Agricultural Experiment Station, 1957).
69. Steidl and Bratton, pp. 276–77.
70. Steidl and Bratton, pp. 278–79.

Storage can be either independent of or interdependent with work areas. Storing items within the worker's limits of reach is appropriate for storage independent of work areas, but is probably more important in storage that is a part of a work area. In either case, placing frequently used and/or heavy items within normal reach lessens the likelihood of strain due to lifting.[71] For increased exercise, frequently used, light articles may be stored on a lower level and deep knee bends can be used to reach them.

The most advantageous storage for minimum heart rate and energy consumption is between 28 and 52 inches above floor level.[72] Using storage space 4 inches above the floor requires about 16 more heart beats per minute than using storage 52 inches above the floor.[73] The physiological importance of tasks varies for workers, depending on their general state of health, including pregnancy, age, vision, and so on.

Work Heights. Optimum working conditions are desirable for any activity. Work heights are especially important when an activity is done frequently, when it involves heavy lifting, when it is performed for long periods, or when the worker has physical problems.

Unlike Australia and some Scandinavian countries, we in the United States are not oriented toward applying known principles to improve work situations or to individualize work heights in the home or in many institutions such as libraries and schools. Technology is available to make adjustable heights, but the cost exceeds the apparent benefits.

Living styles and work habits affect seated or standing working postures. Meal preparation in the United States typically requires frequent trips between kitchen work centers, with trips between storage, counter, and appliances averaging 111–165 for a meal.[74] Sitting down for work between trips is generally not feasible. The physically handicapped person may need to be seated or be in a wheel chair and, therefore, must modify the trips in meal preparation.

For both sitting and for standing activities, elbow height appears to be the best indicator of preferred work height. If the work surface height is

---

71. Steidl and Bratton, p. 279.
72. Tessie Agan, Stephan Konz, and Lucy Tormey, "Extra Heart Beats as a Measurement of Work Cost," *Home Economics Research Journal* 1: (September 1972), 32.
73. Agan, Konz, and Tormey, p. 32.
74. Steidl and Bratton, p. 272.

too high for the person and the job, the worker's elbow and arm will be in a strained position; if it is too low, the person may adjust his whole body downward, resulting in very poor posture. Recommendations based on elbow height provide for arm positions with freedom of movement.

The average height of American women is 5 ft. 4 in., and the average elbow height is 39.6 inches.[75] The preferred distance below the elbow for standing work is 3 to about 5 inches, depending on the activity. A 36-inch counter height is therefore close to the preferred working surface height for the average woman. For the person who is not of average height, the 36-inch work surface is often 3 inches too high or too low.

The seated working position has additional work-area requirements compared with the standing position. The preferred work-surface height is from one-half inch below to 1 inch above elbow height, and there should be enough room under the work surface for freedom of leg movement. The thickness of the work surface is limited if both optimum work height and adequate leg clearance are provided.[76]

Sitting to perform tasks does not always reduce energy expenditure. For rolling dough, a task that involves pressure exertion, the energy expended is highest when the worker is seated on a chair, next highest when seated on a posture stool, and lowest while standing.[77]

Ironing on a surface 36 inches high while standing requires about 28 per cent more energy than standing quietly, whereas sitting to iron at a 24-inch surface uses about 31 per cent more energy than sitting quietly. Standing to iron at a 28-inch surface requires lowering the body to reach the work surface and uses the most energy.[78]

The critical point in choosing work-surface heights is not energy expenditure, but the total effect on the body in relation to other resources and demands. If work-surface heights are poorly suited to the person who usually does the task, the work might best be done by someone outside the

75. McCullough *et al.*, p. 4.
76. Joan S. Ward and N. S. Kirk, "The Relation Between Some Anthropometric Dimensions and Preferred Working Surface Heights in the Kitchen," *Ergonomics* 13: (November 1970), 786.
77. Martha Richardson and Earl C. McCracken, "Work-Surface Levels and Human Energy Expenditure," *Journal of the American Dietetic Association* 48: (March 1966), 196.
78. Martha Richardson and Earl C. McCracken, "Work-Surface Levels for Laundry Tasks in Relation to Human-Energy Expenditures," *Journal of Home Economics* 58: (October 1966), 666.

home or the work-surface height might be changed. Sometimes a higher stool or a lower chair may be used effectively. The desirability of different work heights for different tasks and for different persons must be balanced with other realities, such as the difficulties in modifying work areas in apartments that are rented, or the effort needed to modify work areas when the family expects to move frequently. Solutions should be sought, however, since the technology is available and the time spent in household activities is not decreasing.

Noise

Noise is unwanted sound. Three characteristics of sound—intensity, frequency, and duration—are important in examining the effects of noise.[79] Sound intensity, or pressure level, is measured in decibels. The decibel is a unit of relative loudness equal to the smallest degree of difference ordinarily detectable by the human ear. The faintest sound detectable has an intensity of 1 dB, the abbreviation for decibel.

Two sounds having similar pressure levels (decibels) can have very different frequency distributions. When measuring sound, frequency can be weighted to correspond with the human ear's response to sound, with decibels at the lower frequencies filtered out.[80] The dBA scale does just that. A noise source with lower frequencies will have a lower dBA level than a dB level with a flat scale. Sound intensities are not cumulative; for example, if a blender is 96 dBA and a dishwasher 74 dBA, the sound level for both operating simultaneously is just above 96 dBA.

Duration of sound is the third characteristic that is particularly important in the home. For industrial surroundings, the desirable limit for steady noise is 90 dBA, with somewhat higher levels allowable if the exposure time is reduced. Sometimes a consistent, intermittent noise is tolerated; unexpected, startling noises are less acceptable. Highly predictable periodic noises are less distracting than irregular noises.[81] In the household environment, noise originates from family members and their pets,

79. Clifford R. Bragdon, *Noise Pollution, The Unquiet Crisis* (Philadelphia: University of Pennsylvania Press, Inc., 1971), p. 51.
80. Bragdon, p. 55; and Robert Alex Baron, *The Tyranny of Noise* (New York: St. Martin's Press, 1970), p. 41.
81. A. John Eschenbrenner, Jr., "Effects of Intermittent Noise on the Performance of a Complex Psychomotor Task," *Human Factors* 13 (February 1971): 62–63.

from household appliances including heating and cooling systems, and from external sources such as neighbors, automobiles, jet airplanes, lawnmowers, and so on.

The decibel level of product-generated household sounds is given in Table 11.11. A blender, wall exhaust fan, doorbell, furnace blower, and several workshop tools exceed the 90 dBA level. Only the furnace blower and perhaps the wall exhaust fan are continuous in operation, and persons are not necessarily near these noise sources for long periods. The workshop tools are probably the noisiest appliances that are used while the individual is very near. Furthermore, they are often used for long periods.

Decibel levels were recorded for 24-hour periods in homes, and the levels ranged from 36–90 decibels.[82] Using the criteria of continuous background sound and relatively high number of peaks in the decibel level during the hour, the noisiest hour during the day for each of twenty homes was recorded, and the equipment in operation was noted. Television sets and washing machines were frequently being operated during these noisiest hours.[83]

Effect of Noise on Performance. Highly mental tasks, such as problem solving or creative thinking, are susceptible to noise disruption, whereas mechanical or manual jobs are not. A noisy environment often impairs one's ability to retrieve previous thoughts.[84] In laboratory studies, complex task performance decreased with increasing noise intensity levels.[85] With simple tasks, it is apparently possible to call on reserve mental and physical capacity and not decrease the output.

A noisy environment may reduce communication effectiveness, which, in turn, may affect performance of an activity. Many home activities involve communication that may vary by family composition and by stage of the life cycle. Communication interference from noisy backgrounds can be an important source of decreased performance of activities. In a recent study, the maximum acceptable background noise level of voice communication was 71 dBA.[86]

---

82. Jessie J. Mize, Fern Tuten, and Joseph W. Simons, "A Study of Sound Levels in Houses," *Journal of Home Economics* 58 (January 1966): 44.
83. Mize, Tuten, and Simons, p. 44.
84. Bragdon, p. 82.
85. Eschenbrenner, p. 62.
86. John C. Webster and M. Lepor, "Noise—You Can Get Used to It," *Journal of the Acoustical Society of America* 45 (March 1969): 751–57.

TABLE 11.11

Product-generated noise levels in home task areas.

Area and product	Sound pressure level			
	30–49 dBA	*50–80 dBA*	*80–90 dBA*	*90+ dBA*
Kitchen				
Refrigerator	x			
Dishwasher		x		
Faucet		x		
Range vent fan			x	
Electric mixer			x	
Knife sharpener			x	
Electric can opener			x	
Blender				x
Wall exhaust fan				x
Bathroom				
Vent fan		x		
Toilet		x		
Electric shaver			x	
Shower			x	
Hair dryer			x	
Laundry area				
Washing machine		x		
Clothes dryer		x		
Sewing machine		x		
Sink drain			x	
Bedroom				
Fan (portable)		x		
Alarm clock		x		
Radio*			x	
Living room				
TV*		x		
Air conditioner		x		
Vacuum cleaner			x	
Hi-fi*			x	
Telephone (6′ 6″ distance)			x	
Doorbell				x
Furnace blower				x
Workshop				
Jig saw		x		
¼″ portable drill		x		
Wood lathe			x	
Sabre saw			x	
8″ radial saw				x
Disc sander				x
Belt sander				x

Byron C. Bloomfield and Donald C. Hay, "The Auditory Environment in the Home,"
Research Report for Koss Corporation, Milwaukee, Wisconsin, 1971.
*At normal listening levels.

Effect of Noise on Individuals and Factors Affecting Noise Perception. Noise, especially that of high intensity and long duration, can cause hearing loss; it can also be annoying, affecting one's emotional or social well-being.[87]

One writer has described the situation within the home as follows: "When one examines the impact of homemade sounds on man, it is his emotional status rather than his hearing acuity that is in the greater danger."[88] The psychological and physiological effects are difficult to measure because of the interrelationships of noise, many health factors, and other environmental influences on task performance.

Ill or convalescent persons are more sensitive to noise than are healthy persons. Noise probably does not cause heart problems, but if a heart condition already exists, noise may aggravate the condition by the physiological responses it elicits. A relaxed, quiet environment is desirable for a convalescing person.[89]

Factors other than health affect one's sensitivity to noise. In Philadelphia neighborhoods, home owners perceived more noise than apartment dwellers. The age, number of years at present address, education, race, sex, and income of respondents did not make significant differences in noise perception.[90]

Age probably affects response to noise in at least one way. As age increases, hearing acuity decreases, and communication interference may occur more readily. In the household, space use may change as persons with somewhat impaired hearing attempt to increase their chances of hearing a person, a TV, or a radio by space separation from other sounds.[91]

Physiological stress apparently resulting from noise may actually be caused by anger or frustration when the noise interferes with auditory signals or distracts from an activity.[92]

Adaptation to noise is important in homes. Laboratory research reveals that adaptation to objectionable noises can be made, but the adaptation it-

---

87. Bragdon, p. 63.
88. Lee E. Farr, "Medical Consequences of Environmental Home Noises," *The Journal of the American Medical Association* 202 (October 16, 1967): 171.
89. Farr, p. 174.
90. Bragdon, pp. 169, 171.
91. Farr, p. 173.
92. Karl D. Kryter, "Non-auditory Effects of Environmental Noise," *American Journal of Public Health* 62 (March 1972): 397.

self reduces one's ability to resolve other environmental stresses.[93] Household noises are usually not threatening, and thus adaptation is appropriate. Reacting to noise that contains a message of danger or threat is desirable—that is, adaptation is undesirable.

Many individuals respond to the source as well as the sound. A motorcycle or snowmobile rider may not find the sounds objectionable, while an onlooker may be annoyed by the noise. A person who is sewing may be oblivious to the sound of the sewing machine, while another person in the room may find it noisy. When children have been "difficult," sounds emanating from them may be noticed although the sounds do not usually register as noise.

Reduction in Sound. Noise can be reduced in the home by the selection of appropriate materials and equipment and by advantageous use of space. Materials for floor coverings and windows can be changed more easily while the wall and ceiling materials may be of a more permanent nature. Research on a variety of carpets found that cotton, wool, and Acrilan absorbed air-borne sound in that order. Hair-jute underlays for carpets are accoustically more effective than foam rubber. Lined cotton, rayon, and rayon-acetate draperies are effective materials while glass fiber draperies have poor sound absorbing qualities.[94]

For some household appliances, makes and models yield varying sound levels in homes. Some food waste disposers are available with improved quietness through added insulation; other disposers may have similar working parts without the insulation. Appliance manufacturers have found that consumers associate power and effectiveness with high sound levels.

The arrangement of the house can help separate quiet and noisy activities for the occupants' greater comfort.[95] If the layout is not optimal and if the noise level becomes irritating at a certain time of day, family members may need to adjust activities. Perhaps the dishwasher can be run when family members are in another room and the washer and dryer can be operated when most household members are away from the house.

---

93. David C. Glass, Jerome E. Singer, and Lucy N. Friedman, "Psychic Cost of Adaptation to an Environmental Stressor," *Journal of Personality and Social Psychology* 12 (July 1969): 209.

94. J. W. Simons, J. J. Mize, and B. C. Haynes, Jr., "Acoustical Properties of Carpets and Draperies," Research Bulletin 38 (Athens, Ga.: Georgia Agricultural Experiment Station, 1968), pp. 47–48.

95. Steidl (October 1972), p. 478.

These suggestions for reduction or alteration in sound after the fact may be quite unappealing to those who believe that noise pollution should be attacked directly. It appears that basic orientation to sound will have to change before marked improvements will be made in household appliances and home furnishings. Many consumers are not willing to pay the additional cost for wall and ceiling insulation and for floor coverings that are effective in reducing noise. As awareness grows that noise within the home is not inevitable and that even noise outside the home may be lessened, perhaps changes will be made at the insistence of the consumer.

Odors and Other Contaminants

Most North Americans prefer minimal olfactory stimulation. Some cooking odors are desirable, but many odors are not savored.[96] North Americans traveling in other countries may be overwhelmed by the variety and extent of odors from humans, animals, and activities. The same three odor sources exist in the household. The presence of odors is not generally harmful to the body unless it creates stress. Home odors vary with the occupants and their personal habits and occupations and with the activities in the home, particularly cooking.

Of concern today is another source of air contamination—propellants from aerosol products. Personal products such as hair sprays, deodorants, anti-perspirants, and shaving lathers, and household products such as oven cleaners, glass cleaners, starches, and furniture finishes each contain propellants that are discharged to the air in the home. With more tightly constructed houses, the air changes are reduced, and contaminants are dissipated more slowly. Measuring the degree of contamination is difficult and isolating the effects on the body is even more difficult.[97]

In summary, the impact of the environment on the household members has been considered primarily from the viewpoint of work-related activities and areas. Space use, work-area design, noise, and other contaminants have been emphasized. The satisfaction and pleasure accompanying good working conditions make it important to provide the best quality micro-habitat possible.[98]

---

96. Hall, 1966, p. 47.
97. Mars Y. Longley, "Contamination in a Semiclosed Environment—The Modern Home," AMRL-TR-69-130, Paper No. 23:325–334 (Wright Patterson Airforce Base, Ohio: Aerospace Medical Research Lab, 1969), p. 333.
98. Steidl (October 1972), p. 482.

SUMMARY

A systems framework can help in examining the management of household activities. Human and material resources are inputs along with goals and events; accidents are events that may or may not result in injury. Typical outputs are used resources such as time spent, physical costs, affective responses, and material resource changes and met demands such as a sense of satisfaction.

Physically handicapped persons or those experiencing stress from work can use input and output information for planning. Probably the most frequent use of the information is in understanding and interpreting the requirements of household work.

Household work activities consume considerable time each day. The number and the age of the children and the wife's employment affect time use. The value of productive activities in the home is estimated at between three and four billion dollars annually. Estimates of the value of unpaid work by individuals are used to verify losses from death and disability and can be used when considering employment outside the home.

Many household work activities are associated with women's traditional roles in the home, but increasingly men and women choose their roles, including the household activities they perform. The systems method of considering the wife's employment outside the home has been illustrated and some potential costs and benefits explored. With more open choices available to men and women, a cost-benefit analysis can be useful in considering employment

The environment's micro-habitat can affect household activities. Space use varies by social class, living patterns, cultural background, amount of available space, family life cycle, family size, special needs of family members, equipment design, and work habits.

Work areas can be designed to facilitate work, to add to visual enjoyment, or both. Principles of arranging work areas for effective work flow include locating the most used centers first, placing centers that are closely related together, and fitting the work route. Well-designed storage can be an important work facilitator. Work heights should accommodate the physical needs of the most frequent user of the area.

Noise, or unwanted sound, can affect both the effectiveness and the enjoyment of activities. Construction materials and methods and household material and equipment can be chosen to minimize noise. Household odors from humans, activities, and animals are part of the micro-habitat and may be pleasant or unpleasant.

METHODS OF MEASUREMENT OR ESTIMATION OF RESOURCES

Time

Depending on the focus of time-use studies, the categories for household work for reporting time may be extensive, few, or limited to only one category. Time use is frequently summarized by major activity, with the recognition that people often engage in more than one activity at a time (overlapping tasks) or they intersperse activities (dovetailing tasks). The method of data collection affects the detail and the managerial insight to be gained.

Researchers use three principal methods to determine time use. In the recall method, the respondent recalls a day's activities and the time spent on each activity. In the diary method, the respondent records time use as the day progresses. In the observation method, an observer photographs or otherwise records work in great detail. Recalling takes less recording time than a diary, but is subject to more error. The diary process may affect activities to some degree, but is less subject to omissions. The observation method is most successful in clarifying the more complex uses of time.

Physical

Physical–Energy. The measure for energy use in the Calorie—a unit that measures the heat output or rate of oxidation of the body. Calories can be determined from the oxygen consumed by the body in a given period.

To measure energy use by oxygen consumption in relatively light activities such as those done in the home, a respirometer can be carried on the back, with a mask or mouthpiece to collect exhaled air for analysis. The older equipment weighs about 8 pounds.[99] Newer instrumentation is lightweight, comfortable, convenient to use, and produces a continuous record of oxygen consumption (Figure 11.7).

Physical–Heart Rate. Heart rate is another indicator of an activity's physical cost. To record the heart rate, electrodes of a transis-

99. Doris E. Elliot and Mary Brown Patton, "Manual Techniques Used in Determining Human Energy Expenditures," Research Circular 121 (Wooster, Ohio: Ohio Agricultural Experiment Station, 1963), pp. 4–5.

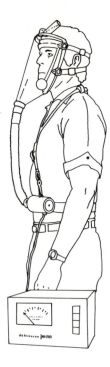

FIGURE 11.7 *Equipment for oxygen consumption (energy) measurement.*

Source: Paul Webb and Samuel J. Troutman, Jr., "An Instrument for Continuous Measurement of Oxygen Consumption," *Journal of Applied Physiology* 28 (June 1970), 868.

torized transmitter may be attached to the chest cavity. The heart beat is transmitted to a remote receiver and recording device. The individual is free to move about without wires, or other restrictions or distractions (Figure 11.8). With some equipment, the heart beat can be transmitted throughout a house, and in the case of astronauts, through outer space.

Relation of Energy and Heart Rate.   Heart rate is closely related to energy expenditure.[100] In one study, the difference in the accumulated heart beat method and the energy expenditure calculated from date col-

---

100. Robert B. Andrews, "The Relationship Between Measures of Heart Rate and Rate of Energy Expenditure," *American Institute of Industrial Engineers Transactions* 1 (March 1969): 9.

lected with the respirometer was 6 per cent.[101] The heart rate apparatus has merit over the respirometer for data collection because it does not interfere with the subject's behavior.

Physical–Body Position. Awkward or excessive reaches and bends are identified by report of the subject or by judgment of trained personnel. There are no standard measures and categories of difficulty for body angles, yet the combinations of angles of bend and body twist represent physical costs of work to consider.

Figure 11.9a is a drawing of an Indian woman in a seated position before beginning a task. Specific points were marked on the individual and on her clothing, as indicated by the darkened marks. Some points were

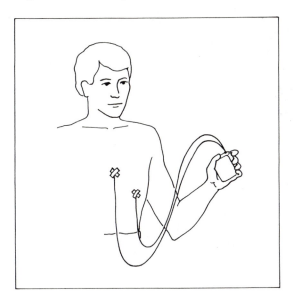

FIGURE 11.8 *Subject fitted to transmitter for telemetering heart rate. The instrument picks up the subject's heart rate and transmits it to a receiver and recorder. This compact and light piece of equipment allows the subject to perform activity unencumbered and at a distance from the recording equipment. The subject wears a garment with a pocket for the transmitter.*

Source: Donald K. Mathews and Edward L. Fox, *The Physiological Basis of Physical Education and Athletics* (Philadelphia: W. B. Saunders Company, 1971), p. 54.

---

101. Robert B. Bradfield, Patricia B. Huntzicker, and George J. Fruehan, "Simultaneous Comparison of Respirometer and Heart-Rate Telemetry Techniques as Measures of Human Energy Expenditure," *The American Journal of Clinical Nutrition* 22 (June 1969): 696–700.

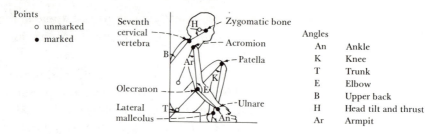

a.   Seated position for Indian woman prior to chapati making, and angles of ankle, knee, trunk, elbow, upper back, head tilt and thrust and armpit.

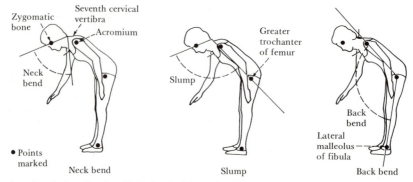

b.   Description of angles of body bend: (1) temple, (2) seventh cervical vertebra, (3) sternal notch, (4) greater trochanter of the femur, (5) acromion process, and (6) lateral malleolus of fibula.

FIGURE 11.9 *Angles of body position, seated and standing.*

Source: a. Adapted from Jagjit Kaur Dhesi and Francille Maloch Firebaugh, "The Effects of Stages of Chapati-Making and Angles of Body Position on Heart Rate," *Ergonomics* 16 (November, 1973): 811-815. b. Sue Wright Trerathan and Francille Maloch, "Angles of Body Bend in Loading Dishwashers," *Journal of Home Economics* 59 (May, 1967): 376.

derived from the photograph, as indicated by the undarkened marks. Figure 11.9b is a sketch of a person loading a dishwasher, with the angles of bend noted.

Body positions, as measured by body angles, are related to energy expenditure and heart rate. Angles involving limb movement are in closer relationship, as might be predicted. The closest relationship between angles and energy for stair climbing was for the angle of knee bend.[102] The angle of knee and ankle bend (which reflect the leg position) had the highest relation to heart rate in a laboratory study.[103]

---

102. Marjorie Branin Keiser and Elaine Weaver, "Body Movements Related to Energy Used," *Journal of Home Economics* 54 (June 1962): 481.
103. Jagjit Kaur Dhesi and Francille Maloch Firebaugh, "The Effects of Stages of Chapati-Making and Body Position on Heart Rate," *Ergonomics* 16 (November 1973): 811–15.

Management by Young Families

12.

Young families, with the challenges of family formation and parenthood, are particularly appropriate to illustrate managerial applications. The shift from dependence on parents or other responsible persons to the assumption of responsibility for one's own welfare and that of a spouse and child has special significance managerially and personally. Gradual changes occur that permit managerial skills and resources to grow along with increased responsibilities. This fact is particularly evident in the timing of parenthood and its accompanying demands, a topic that will receive emphasis throughout this chapter.

The systems orientation highlights the importance of this early stage of life. The continuity and growth of newly formed, open systems such as families depend on the successful interrelation of internal components and on their interaction with external systems. The managerial subsystem includes components critical to the successful functioning of the total system. Contributory factors are reviewed in the following sections.

DEMANDS

The interactions between the personal and the managerial subsystems are particularly great. More goals are formed during the first five years of marriage than at any later period. Goals that derive from the development of family relationships and from the development of management patterns are significantly greater in these early years than are the goals prompted by other areas. Specific family relationship and management goals indicated in a survey of families are:

1. Have (or adopt) and care for children.
2. Limit the number of children.
3. Impart desirable personal values to children.
4. Be able to care for and/or educate relatives outside the nuclear family.
5. Improve family relationships.
6. Improve the home.
7. Increase religious activity.[1]

Other goals that are also important in the first five years and that continue to be relatively more important in succeeding stages are those of financial security and growth, level of living, housing and the living environment, and health.[2] Couples with more education report that more goals evolve. Also, more goals are formed when both the husband and wife are employed at marriage than if only the husband is employed.[3]

Parenthood was once considered a crisis disrupting the system's equilibrium; now, for young couples in general, it is viewed as a transitional, expansive period. One of the obvious, yet critical, needs in this regard is to define or redefine roles with respect to performance of household tasks. Each situation has its own combination of expectations, skills, and resources, however, that leads to variations in responses to the common experience of parenthood. Although the changes are somewhat abrupt, the effects of these changes can be modified by preparation.

Young mothers report various problems. These include feelings of edginess, fatigue, decreased sexual responsiveness, worry about loss of figure and appearance in general, and doubts about their worth as parents. Other problems concern interference from parents and in-laws and decreased contact with persons at work. There are two additional problems that are primarily managerial—interruption of routine habits and changed standards, for example, less tidy housekeeping than desired.[4]

---

1. Cleo Fitzsimmons, Dorothy A. Larery, and Edward J. Metzen, "Major Financial Decisions and Crises in the Family Life Span," North Central Regional Research Publication No. 208 (Lafayette, Ind.: Purdue University Agricultural Experiment Station, 1971), p. 17.
2. Fitzsimmons, Larery, and Metzen, p. 14.
3. Fitzsimmons, Larery, and Metzen, p. 19.
4. Daniel F. Hobbs, Jr., "Parenthood As Crisis: A Third Study," *Journal of Marriage and the Family* 27 (August 1965): 370.

Young fathers report more problems that are managerially related: increased money problems, additional amount of work, interruption of routine habits, and a concern with housekeeping standards. Other personal problems cited are edgy feelings, physical fatigue, wife's decreased sexual responsiveness, and the need to change plans that existed before the child's birth.[5]

The increased money concerns are prevalent, especially for couples married in their teens. High expectations of material goods equivalent to their parents' level of living and the lower incomes of teenage families contribute to their problems.[6] Evidence indicates that the marriages of high-school-age couples involving pregnancies and school dropout face formidable odds. About half the marriages remain intact.[7] In coping with the demands of their particular situations, a predominant pattern in the managerial activity of these young families appears to be a response to event situations rather than to goals.

During these formative years, the presence or absence of goals and the adequacy (or potential adequacy) of resources are important in laying foundations on which building can take place in later stages. The role of resources is discussed in the next section.

RESOURCES

Help from Relatives

Help from parents and other relatives is a resource extension for many young families. Help is given and received in many forms: as outright gifts, as advice, or as assistance in money, goods, or services. An intergenerational study indicates that young couples in the married-child generation frequently receive help with economic and child-care problems, but they also consistently give help as part of a reciprocal relationship (Table 12.1). The parent generation leans considerably more to-

---

5. Hobbs, p. 370.
6. Robert O. Herrmann, "Expectations and Attitudes as a Source of Financial Problems in Teen-Age Marriages," *Journal of Marriage and the Family* 27 (February 1965): 90.
7. Alvin L. Schorr, "The Family Cycle and Income Development," *Social Security Bulletin* 29 (February 1966): 23.

TABLE 12.1

Help received and given in problem areas, by generation.

Problem area	Help	Generation		
		Grandparent	*Parent*	*Married children*
		Per cent		
Economic	Given	26	41	34
	Received	34	17	49
Emotional	Given	23	47	31
gratification	Received	42	37	21
Household	Given	21	47	33
management	Received	52	23	25
Child care	Given	16	50	34
	Received	0	23	78
Illness	Given	32	21	47
	Received	61	21	18

Source: Reuben Hill, *Family Development in Three Generations* (Cambridge, Mass.: Schenkman Publishing Co., Inc., 1970), p. 67.

ward giving than receiving, and the grandparent generation leans toward receiving rather than giving.[8]

Help from relatives provides important benefits at strategic times, but it apparently does not make a significant long-range difference in how families progress financially.[9] An exception is the full-time farm family.[10] The latter is probably affected by the extent to which children interested in following their parents' occupation of farming are assisted in meeting the special demands for capital. But special educational and other advantages provided to family members are directly related to the ability to get

---

8. Reuben Hill, *Family Development in Three Generations* (Cambridge, Mass.: Schenkman Publishing Co., Inc., 1970), p. 16.

9. Ruth E. Deacon and Janet A. Krofta, "Economic Progress of Rural Nonfarm and Part-Time Farm Families," Research Bulletin 976 (Wooster, Ohio: Ohio Agricultural Research and Development Center, 1965), p. 12.

10. Ruth E. Deacon, "The Economic Progress Since Marriage of Ohio Families Farming Full-Time in 1958," Research Bulletin 902 (Wooster, Ohio: Ohio Agricultural Experiment Station, 1962), p. 17.

ahead. The implication is that children who receive less help are able to compensate in other ways and acquire resources comparable to those who receive more tangible aid. It could also be possible that children who receive more assistance tend not to take full economic advantage of it.

In addition to the economic ability to contribute to their newly married children, parents who have a positive attitude toward assistance and parents in a higher social position tend to give more help.[11] On the other hand, the amount of economic support that parents give newly married children is unrelated to the following factors: the social mobility of the married child, parental acceptance of the marriage, the attitude of the married child toward receiving contributions, what parents expect in return for the contributions, whether or not the married child's mother is employed, the closeness within the family, and the distance the child lives from the parents.[12]

When the first child is born, the kind of help wanted from relatives is for routine household work rather than for parental responsibilities. From a sampling of married people of all ages, the wife's marital satisfaction increases with the amount of help received from relatives, and other evidence implies that husbands also respond positively to help. Marital solidarity is strongest, however, when help from kin is received in a wide variety of ways.[13] While help alleviates the strain experienced immediately following the birth of a child, there is also a possibility that it can contribute to the difficulty of adjusting to the first child.[14] Apparently, giving and receiving help with sensitivity to the particular demands at this critical time in the lives of young families has value far beyond tangible assistance.

Income

Young families often begin with relatively low incomes. In 1972, the total family income for families with a head of household under 25

---

11. Alma Beth Clark and Jean Warren, "Economic Contributions Made to Newly Married Couples by Their Parents," Memoir 382 (Ithaca, N. Y.: Cornell University Agricultural Experiment Station, 1963), p. 5.

12. Clark and Warren, pp. 4–5.

13. Robert O. Blood, Jr., *The Family* (New York: Free Press, 1972), p. 194.

14. Daniel F. Hobbs, Jr., "Transition to Parenthood: A Replication and an Extension," *Journal of Marriage and the Family* 30 (August 1968): 417.

years of age averaged $7,716, while that for families with a head of household 25–34 years of age averaged $11,483.[15] An important difference exists in young families, however, and that is the difference in expectations for change in income. Some young families with low educational and skill levels do not have hopes of achieving much more than they presently have, while other families have an optimistic view of their potential. According to one study, expectations of young families were the highest of any age group. Sixty-eight per cent anticipated receiving a higher income in the coming year than they had just earned and only 12 per cent expected a lower income.[16]

Management may differ considerably in families with such varied income expectations. Installment debt might be used by both types of families. If income decreases, such as if the wife does not return to work after having a child, young families could have a problem in meeting debt commitments. When incomes decline, families frequently find it difficult to adjust expenditures, partly because it is difficult to reduce their level of living, but often because their needs continue to increase.

Credit Use

Optimism about the likelihood of increases in earnings and high demands for consumer goods encourage young families to make use of consumer credit. Young families make more use of credit cards than do older families and their use is more likely to involve installment payments rather than the one monthly payment in lieu of a number of cash payments.[17]

In families with the family head under age 25, two-thirds have installment debts.[18] In 1971, the indebtedness of 13 per cent of these families was one-fifth or more of their previous year's income[19]—a level that could have serious implications.

15. U.S. Dept. of Commerce, Bureau of the Census, "Money Income in 1972 of Families and Persons in the United States," Current Population Reports, Series P-60, No. 90 (Washington, D. C.: U.S. Government Printing Office, 1973), p. 7.
16. George Katona, Lewis Mandell, and Jay Schmiedeskamp, *1970 Survey of Consumer Finances* (Ann Arbor, Mich.: The University of Michigan, 1971), p. 18.
17. Lewis Mandell, *Credit Card Use in the United States* (Ann Arbor, Mich.: The University of Michigan, 1972), p. 17.
18. Lewis Mandell, George Katona, James N. Morgan, and Jay Schmiedeskamp, *Surveys of Consumers 1971–72* (Ann Arbor, Mich.: The University of Michigan, 1973), p. 8.
19. Mandell *et al.*, p. 10.

PLANNING AND IMPLEMENTING

Procedures relating to planning and implementing were discussed in Chapters 10 and 11, covering systems applications to financial management and household activities, in which illustrations relating to young families were common examples. These aspects will not be repeated in this section. However, factors that have special impact on the situations of young families in relation to thier planning and implementing will be discussed. These factors include the scope of decisions, the cost of having a child, and the cost of raising a child.

Scope of Decisions

Major decisions that concern the husband's occupation are the most numerous during all intervals of marriage. Housing and mobility decisions rank second. Compared to later periods, however, decisions that relate to financial security and growth and to consumer goods are of greater significance in the first five years of marriage.[20] Clarification of roles for the performance of household tasks is also of major importance. The definition of roles involves interaction between the personal and the managerial systems.

Another basic area of decision making for young families that also involves the personal and managerial systems is planning the number of and spacing of children. The resulting family size and spacing affects the way resources are allocated to meet goals and events most satisfactorily.

Through careful family planning, resources are reconciled with demands (in this case, the goal of having children) and a specific standard for family size and spacing evolves. Factors such as attitudes toward income, adequacy of income, aspirations, wife's labor-force participation, husband's occupation, wife's education, and the family's religion affect both goal demands and resources. Current family income is related to the timing of events such as marriage, the arrival of the first child, and the probability of additional children; but current family income is not related to preferred or expected family size.[21] At all income levels there are families that expect to have a similar number of children.

---

20. Fitzsimmons, Larery, and Metzen, pp. 24–25.
21. Ronald Freedman and Lolagene Coombs, "Economic Considerations in Family Growth Decisions," *Population Studies* 20 (November 1966): 221.

Family-size preferences are affected by attitudes toward future income. In one study, the wives who expected an increase in income anticipated and had more children than wives with different income expectations. Income adequacy also affects family size. Parents expected and had more children when the income was perceived as adequate.[22]

Relative economic status is the relationship between income-earning potential and desired level of living. This relative economic status affects fertility of young adults in the United States. According to Easterlin, a rise in status is accompanied by a rise in fertility.[23]

The high motivation to provide special opportunities for the parents, themselves, or for the children already born has resulted in fewer additional children, with longer intervals between them. For example, high aspirations to provide certain material goods for the children, actual savings and plans for the children's college expenses, participation of the wife in the labor force,[24] and ownership of two cars[25] are all evidences that have accompanied fewer births and wider spacing of children.

The husband's occupation may affect the birth rate; low rates have been associated with professional, clerical, sales, and service workers. Families of farmers, farm laborers, and urban laborers show rather high birth rates over the years.[26] The higher the husband's educational level, the longer couples wait after graduation to have children. Interestingly, the husband's educational level, career mobility, and social origin have not significantly affected family sizes among engineers or scientists.[27]

The wife's educational level has been inversely related to birth rates for white women married between 1940 and 1964 in the United States. As an exception, women with one to three years of high school have had somewhat higher birth rates than less educated women.[28] Religion affects family size and, to some extent, the timing of births.[29]

---

22. Freedman and Coombs, November 1966, p. 221.
23. Richard A. Easterlin, "Relative Economic Status and the American Fertility Swing." in *Family Economic Behavior,* ed. Eleanor Bernert Sheldon (Philadelphia: J. B. Lippincott Co., 1973). p. 215.
24. N. Krishnan Namboodiri, "The Wife's Work Experience and Child Spacing," *The Milbank Memorial Fund Quarterly* 52 (July 1964): 75.
25. Freedman and Coombs, November 1966, p.222.
26. Maria Davidson, "Social and Economic Variations in Childspacing," *Social Biology* 17 (June 1970): 113.
27. Carolyn Cummings Perrucci, "Mobility, Marriage and Child-spacing Among College Graduates," *Journal of Marriage and the Family* 30 (May 1968): 280–81.
28. Davidson, p. 112.
29. Namboodiri, p. 75.

Cost of Having a Child

The economic costs of having a child have risen steadily in the United States as medical costs have risen. Half the total expenses are medical and hospital care (Table 12.2). The estimated costs given in the table include a crib and other nursery items, which may or may not be included since these are often shared within families. If the crib and other nursery items were not purchased, the relative portion of the total for medical and hospital care would be far above 50 per cent.

The total cost of $1,600 in 1971 was considered in 1973 to be within 2–3 per cent of the present cost.[30] Percentages for particular categories will change if medical and hospital costs continue to rise disproportionately to other categories.

In another study in 1971, actual expenditures of a group of families for similar items related to having a child totaled $1,276, on the average. Expenses for the second child were about $200 less—$1,082.[31]

Cost of Raising a Child

The cost of raising a child varies with the family size, standards, and economic level, with the geographical region, and with a rural or an urban location. Whatever contributes to variations in consumer expenditures also causes variations in child-raising costs.

The average cost of raising a child to 18 years has been determined from actual expenditures and has been adjusted for low-cost and moderate economic levels. Costs per child (at 1969 prices), with three children in the family are shown for two regions:[32]

South	Low-cost	$21,710
	Moderate	34,170
North central	Low-cost	23,190
	Moderate	31,770

30. Peter Campbell, "Maternity Costs," (New York: Institute of Life Insurance, 1971); and Sylvia Porter, "What it Costs Now to Have a Baby," *Ladies Home Journal* (January 1970) pp. 32–33.
31. Martha Lanius Adamson, "Birth Expenses for Children Born Between 1968–71 as reported by Fifty Families in Lincoln, Nebraska, 1972," University of Nebraska, M.S. thesis, 1972.
32. Jean L. Pennock, "Child-Rearing Costs at Two Levels of Living, by Family Size," *Family Economics Review* ARS 62–5 (December 1970): 17.

TABLE 12.2
Costs of having a baby in 1971.

Categories	Cost in Dollars	Per cent
Hospital care	553	34.1
4 days @ $97/ day-mother		
@ $20/ day-infant		
Delivery room and circumcision		
set-up		
Medical care	360	22.2
Obstetrical care		
Pediatrician's newborn care		
Circumcision fee		
Infant's layette	75	4.6
Nursery items	339	20.9
Utensils	24	1.5
Bath items	20	1.3
Miscellaneous	63	3.9
Mother's maternity clothing	187	11.5
Total	$1,621	100

Peter Campbell, "Maternity Costs" (New York: Institute of Life Insurance, 1971) (mimeo).

Hospital care—American Hospital Association.
Hospital stay—*Blue Cross Reports*, September 1965.
Medical care—*Medical Economics*, January, 1970 and October 1971.
Layette items—list from U.S. Children's Bureau, *My Baby* magazine;
    —pricing, mid price in Macy's, New York.

No general statement can be made of the effect of rural-urban location on child-raising costs since cost relations in rural and urban areas are inconsistent. For example, transportation costs may be higher for the rural family, while recreation may cost more for the urban family. The effect varies by region, as the following figures for 5-6-person families show:[33]

33. Jean L. Pennock, "Cost of Raising a Child," speech at the 47th Agricultural Outlook Conference, Washington, D. C., February 18, 1970, pp. 18–23.

South	Farm	$21,690
	Rural nonfarm	21,050
	Urban	21,360
North central	Farm	19,460
	Rural nonfarm	19,360
	Urban	22,690
Northeast	Farm	19,770
	Rural nonfarm	23,070
	Urban	19,520
West	Rural nonfarm	25,000
	Urban	23,380

The portion of family income required per child over the 18-year span is about 15–17 per cent.[34] Housing and food comprise 55–60 per cent of the expenditures for raising a child (Table 12.3). Transportation is 13–16 per cent, and education is the smallest, separately listed expense at the low-cost living level. These figures reflect the child-raising costs of the family and do not include society's costs, such as education.

MET DEMANDS

Family Functioning

The level of social adequacy achieved by young families as a group is high, with malfunctioning relatively limited. As indicated in one study, problems are more in the area of finding ways and means to achieve goals and maintain and improve the living environment than in achieving basic satisfactions and goals of a social, emotional, and spiritual nature.[35] These observations were generally confirmed in an intensive

34. Pennock, February 18, 1970, p. 2.
35. Ludwig L. Geismar, *555 Families* (New Brunswick, N. J.: Transaction Books, 1973), p. 51.

TABLE 12.3

Estimated costs at 1969 prices of raising an urban child to age 18 at a low-cost level, by region of the country.

Expenditure	Regions							
	North central		South		Northeast		West	
	Dollars	%	Dollars	%	Dollars	%	Dollars	%
Food	6,030	27	5,600	26	6,180	32	6,300	27
Clothing	2,480	11	2,400	11	2,200	11	2,340	10
Housing	6,840	30	6,340	30	5,880	30	6,920	30
Medical care	1,080	5	1,080	5	900	5	1,280	5
Education	240	1	240	1	120	1	120	1
Transportation	3,640	16	3,320	16	2,460	13	3,780	16
All other	2,380	11	2,380	11	1,780	9	2,640	11
Total	22,690	100*	21,360	100	19,520	100	23,380	100

Jean L. Pennock, "Cost of Raising a Child," speech at the 47th Annual Agricultural Outlook Conference, Washington, D. C., February 18, 1970, pp. 22–23.

* Percentages may not total 100 due to rounding.

study of 555 families with the wife under 30 years old and having had a first child.[36]

The roles of husbands and wives for performing household tasks ordinarily include some balance of sharing and specialization. As the years of marriage increase, the roles become more patterned. Also, the husband's household responsibilities tend to decrease with age.

The husband's decision making apparently varies, however, with the age of the wife. The younger the wife when her first child is born, the more likely she is to be dependent on her husband for responsibility in decision making.[37]

Among young couples with a first child four months old, husbands tended to decide which car to buy and viewed the life insurance choice as theirs. Wives rated life insurance choices as a shared responsibility. The wives' decisions included the family dinner menu, which child-care practices to follow, and how to get the family laundry done. Wives considered

36. Geismar, pp. 19, 51.
37. Robert O. Blood, Jr. and D. M. Wolfe, *Husbands and Wives: The Dynamics of Married Living* (Glencoe, Ill.: Free Press, 1960), p. 43.

decisions about home decoration or furnishings as shared, while husbands reported it to be in the wife's domain. Shared decisions were: which house or apartment to take; how much money the family can afford to spend per week on food; which doctor to call when someone is sick; where to go on vacation; and how to control family finances.[38] The correlation between husband and wife ratings for who makes decisions was lowest for the decisions on house or apartment and child-care practices.[39]

After the first child is born, some variation occurs in patterns of young families about who decides and who performs various tasks. Husbands and wives tend to share the decision making that relates to where to live, where to go on vacation, how to control finances, how much to spend on food, and what doctor to call. They tend to share the job of keeping track of money and bills. But the wife is likely to do the grocery shopping, prepare the food, and call the doctor. She decides about and implements household tasks such as home decorating, meal planning, and child care. The husband decides about and carries through on the selection of a car, life insurance, and the care and repair of the house.[40]

Role patterns are influenced by such factors as education, occupation, skill, age, and interest. The very complexity of these interrelationships makes it difficult to identify the factors that have a major influence. In the individual situation, the roles will be determined by what will work to the best advantage of the individuals involved—that is, if the decisions are made with managerial insight.

Effects of Family Size and Child Spacing on Marital Success

Both the number of and the spacing of children affect marital success, but the couple's control of number and spacing according to their desires is crucial.[41] If the husband and wife have similar goals for family size and spacing, the marriage can be enhanced by reaching the goals. If there are differences between the husband's and wife's desires or between the desires and the actual behavior, the family size and spacing may negatively affect marital success.

---

38. Rebecca Powell Lovingood, "The Effect of Selected Social-Demographic Factors on Household Task Performance of Young Families," The Ohio State University, Ph.D. dissertation, 1973, p. 90.
39. Lovingood, p. 81.
40. Lovingood, pp. 90–91.
41. Harold T. Christensen, "Children in the Family: Relationship of Number and Spacing to Marital Success," *Journal of Marriage and the Family* 30 (May 1968): 288.

During a five-year period of the Detroit studies, 59 of the 1,304 marriages were dissolved. Of the 59, 41 per cent involved premarital pregnancy.[42] The couples with broken marriages had problems such as low economic security and too many children too quickly.[43]

Other research finds that premarital pregnancy is more frequently followed by divorce than is postmarital pregnancy, and that couples having pregnancy shortly after marriage have a higher divorce rate than those with delayed postmarital pregnancy.[44]

USED RESOURCES

Human Resources

Both young mothers and fathers report fatigue as a problem in parenthood. When the output of young parents' resource allocation is fatigue, the system should be examined for factors that contribute to the feelings of tiredness. The physical effort in caring for a child increases as the child increases in weight before walking. Carrying a child upstairs or pushing a child plus packages can require considerable expenditure of energy.[45]

Stress associated with the first child contributes to feelings of fatigue. Not knowing whether a child is really ill or whether his behavior is like that of other babies can be typically stressful. Parenthood stress increases from the second to the fifth month of the first child's life.[46]

Material Resources

Young families are often dissatisfied with their savings and reserve funds.[47] Of young families with the head of the house under 25

42. Lolagene C. Coombs and Zena Zumeta, "Correlates of Marital Dissolution in a Prospective Fertility Study: A Research Note," Appendix F of "Social and Economic Correlates of Family Building Patterns in Detroit," Research Report of Social Security Administration, Grant No. 312(2)-7-248 (March 1970), p. 16.
43. Coombs and Zumeta, p. 11.
44. Christensen, p. 287.
45. June I. Grieve, "Daily Activities of Housewives with Young Children and Estimation of Energy Expenditures," *Ergonomics* 10 (January 1967): 32.
46. Joseph H. Meyerowitz and Harold Feldman, "Transition to Parenthood," *Psychiatric Research Reports* 20 (1966): 79.
47. Katona, Mandell, and Schmiedeskamp, 1971, p. 121.

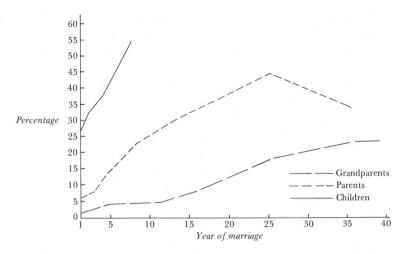

FIGURE 12.1 *Percentage of families having both life insurance and retirement provisions by year of marriage and by generation.*

Source: Reuben Hill, *Family Development in Three Generations* (Cambridge, Mass.: Schenkman Publishing Co., Inc., 1970), p. 132.

years of age in 1971, 20 per cent reported no financial assets and 58 per cent reported less than $1,000.[48]

Figure 12.1 shows that a higher percentage of families in the married children generation have both life insurance and retirement provisions earlier than either the parent or grandparent generation had. For families with the family head younger than 34 years, 78 per cent have life insurance protection.[49]

Effects of Family Size and Spacing on Economic Position

Families that have children shortly after marriage experience economic pressures, accumulate fewer assets, and are more likely to become discouraged with their economic progress than do families with a period of accumulation and economic growth between marriage and the first child.[50] Premarital pregnancy results in the greatest asset dis-

---

48. Mandell, p. 67.
49. Katona, Mandell, and Schmiedeskamp, 1971, p. 117.
50. Ronald Freedman and Lolagene Coombs, "Childspacing and Family Economic Position," *American Sociological Review* 31 (October 1966): 631.

advantage.[51] In one study, couples without premarital pregnancy had 50 per cent more accumulated assets than couples with premarital pregnancy. Further, couples with premarital pregnancy at all educational levels had fewer assets. Income differences are in the same direction, but smaller. Assets for couples with premarital pregnancy for all educational levels averaged $6,620 in 1965 while those for couples without premarital pregnancy averaged $11,400.[52]

In large-scale studies on child spacing in the Detroit area, the rate of premaritally pregnant respondents is reported to be 25 per cent, with the largest percentage from middle-class families.[53] The educational level of couples with premarital pregnancy is generally lower, with the father often dropping out of high school.[54] The economic and educational disadvantage for couples with premarital pregnancy continues through various stages of married life.[55]

Discrepancies between the goals for number of children and the actual number of children among couples with premarital pregnancy in the Detroit study indicate that they were typically less successful with birth-control measures. As a group, they were discouraged with their incomes, despite the gains of a five-year period.[56]

The economic picture is somewhat different for families without premarital pregnancy but with children born a short space apart. The education of these couples is similar to that of couples with longer spaces between children, and the asset and income positions of the two groups are similar. Families with a brief interval between children often have larger families, so that the per capita resource base may be smaller than for those with longer spaces.[57]

Families with longer spaces between children frequently desire and have fewer children and attain a consistency between goals (input) and goal achievement (output). Higher income and asset positions accom-

51. Freedman and Coombs, p. 642.
52. Lolagene C. Coombs, Ronald Freedman, Judith Friedman, and William F. Pratt, "Premarital Pregnancy and Status Before and After Marriage," *American Journal of Sociology* 75 (March 1970): 819.
53. Coombs, Freedman, Friedman, and Pratt, pp. 800, 805.
54. Coombs, Freedman, Friedman, and Pratt, p. 817.
55. Coombs, Freedman, Friedman, and Pratt, p. 800.
56. Lolagene C. Coombs and Ronald Freedman, "Pre-marital Pregnancy, Childspacing, and Later Economic Achievement," *Population Studies* 24 (November 1970): 406.
57. Coombs and Freedman, 1970, p. 406.

pany longer spacing between births, and the per capita resources are greater than for families with shorter spaces between children.

Family size has no consistent relation to income or assets, even after the figures for the length of marriage have been adjusted. Couples with premarital pregnancy with one or two children have the highest income of any size family with premarital pregnancy.[58]

Two case studies appear at the end of the chapter summary. Managerial concepts are identified in the margin.

SUMMARY

Young families form many goals in their early years of marriage; parenthood is an expansive time when the family system changes to meet new goal and event demands. Young fathers and mothers report different problems with parenthood, but the fathers, particularly, report difficulty with financial resources.

Help from relatives is an important resource, but in most cases it is not sufficient to make a difference in the long-run financial picture. Incomes are ordinarily low when the couple is young, and the income decreases with the birth of the first child if the mother chooses not to work outside the home. Credit-use extends the financial resources of young families, and a large portion of couples under 25 have installment debts.

Young families make decisions on a wide variety of topics, some of which affect life chances—occupation, spacing of children.

The cost of having a child is somewhat higher for the first child than for the second child. The cost of raising a child varies by family size, standards, the family economic situation, geographic area, and location.

Decision-making patterns and roles evolve in young families and are affected by education, occupation, skill, age, and interests.

Agreement about family size and child spacing is important in marital success. The family's economic position is affected by family size and child spacing and couples with premarital pregnancy are at the greatest financial disadvantage.

---

58. Coombs and Freedman, 1970, p. 404.

CASE STUDY 1

Pete and Elise Zygor had their first baby, Pam, six months ago. They had married right after high school, and Elise worked for four years prior to Pam's birth to help Pete through school. Pam was born just a few months before his graduation. At that time, Elise quit her job, and their income dropped by more than one-third. Elise feels that a lack of financial resources is one of their biggest problems because Pete is still in training at his job and does not earn very much. He works long hours, and she must take most of the responsibility for the care of the baby.

Goal-directed system
Planning

Resource limitations

Material resources:
money

Having the baby presented real difficulties for them in their small 8'x 35' mobile home. Elise made the middle room into a nursery; after lining the furniture up against the walls and folding up the kitchen chairs, they pull the couch out every night for themselves. With Pam growing older and pulling things over, some items, such as the bird and its cage, have had to go.

Material resource:
space

Reordering personal
priorities and
situational conditions

Pete built shelves in Pam's room to provide storage space and he put an adjustable gate between the living area and the kitchen to keep Pam from being in the way in such a small area and yet she is close enough to see. Elise uses the gate when she prepares meals and washes dishes.

Plans and actions to
facilitate later ones
Dovetailing

Elise felt tired much of the time after Pam was born. She breast-fed Pam and found sleeping and going places quite interrupted by breast-feeding and other aspects of Pam's care. As Pam got a little older, Elise and Pete calculated carefully when to let her sleep through so they could get a full night's sleep.

Planning

Elise's day is oriented to Pam's needs and habits. If Pam does not go to sleep at the usual time, Elise plays with her or rocks her and then does later what she had intended to do.

Adjusting

Two tasks that are done away from home are grocery shopping and laundering. All three usually go grocery shopping. Before they go, Elise writes down a few items and checks the cupboards to see what she needs. She saves newspaper coupons and tries to buy "Specials."

Planning

For the laundry, Elise uses the facility in the mobile-home park either while Pete is home watching Pam or while Pam is napping. Living in the center of the park helps make this possible, since the laundry facility is within sight of their home.

Elise misses her friends at work, but she has almost daily telephone contact with her mother and she also has friends in the park. Most of the residents are young, married college students who also have current resource limitations. She talks to some friends on the phone and takes time for a cup of tea with other friends who stop by. Once in a while, when she feels she has too much to do, she draws the draperies and takes the phone off the hook until she accomplishes what she intended to do.

Personal relations

Facilitating actions

Another situation, with the added complexities of another child and both husband and wife professionally employed, is described here:

CASE STUDY 2

"On a week day we get up at 7:30 and process the children . . . . This semester I've been teaching three mornings . . . . I have had a babysitter who comes every weekday afternoon from 12:00 to 4:00 . . . . One of us is home until noon, and then we're both (at the university) in the afternoon . . . . I go home at 4:00, and between 4:00 and 6:00 it's largely a matter of spending some time with the children and making preparations for dinner. We have a kind of family time just ahead of dinner. We relax over a drink. The little girls join us . . . . After dinner I finish up with the house routine . . . . I usually clear it anywhere between 9:00 and 10:00 . . . . I often don't get out of the kitchen until about 10:00. But anyway, at whatever point I do, I go to my study and I do my desk work . . . . I'm at my desk for about three hours every night, roughly 9:00 to 12:00 . . . . For weekends, during the day Saturday and Sunday I again am with the children, and engage pretty much in household things unless there's something exceptional coming along as there often is—a meeting at the university. And again I do my desk work in the evening."

Resources available to hire help

Standing plan-sequencing

Values

Sequencing

Goals

Sequencing

Management by Low-Income Families

13.

*T*his chapter will focus on some of the special problems low-income families face from a managerial perspective. Attention is centered on how the situations of low-income families can be interpreted managerially. Although an exhaustive analysis of the plight of low-income families is not made, considerable illustrative information is provided to highlight the managerial situations. Background information on low-income families had also been provided in other chapters, such as in Chapter 10 where the problem of defining income adequacy and the extent of poverty were reviewed.

This chapter emphasizes the characteristics and problems of families and individuals with chronically low incomes. Resource inputs such as income, assets, credit, help, and health are discussed first; then, planning and the implementation of plans are considered; and finally, the outputs of resource use and met demands are reviewed from a low-income perspective.

For many people, especially children and the aged, a low-income situation remains for extended periods, while for others, low income may be a temporary situation with realistic expectations of increased income. Young couples and independent individuals may have low incomes while attending school, or a family may experience a low-income period when a member loses his job. Many low-income statistics do not distinguish temporary from long-term low-income status, but in this chapter we stress the implications for managagement of families who experience low income over time.

RESOURCES

Income

Low income for the chronically poor tends to be a multifaceted condition that good management can, at best, only minimize. Many poor people are in the labor force. Five out of six males under age 65 who head poor families worked some time in 1966; most of the nonworkers were disabled.[1] Earnings are often sporadic, seasonal, and low paying, thereby making home management difficult with inadequate and uncertain cash income.

Low-income men and women are most frequently found in low-paying occupations such as unskilled, semiskilled, and low-paying services, particularly domestic service for women.[2] For a welfare recipient, accepting employment is risky because, if layoffs occur, it can mean a lengthy reconsideration of welfare eligibility. Also, welfare recipients often hold only "entry" job status and are unable to get sufficient experience and job seniority to qualify for better jobs.[3]

Although fewer than half the persons below the poverty level received welfare in 1969, 4.4 million of the 7.6 million blacks and other races who were below the poverty level in 1969 received welfare assistance. For whites, 6.7 million of the 16.7 million below the poverty level received welfare.[4]

Welfare assistance, which may be far more stable than wages, does not assure stability in resources. Some recipients face the problems of receiving the welfare check a few days late or of having the money stolen. A writer tells the story of one welfare recipient:

The neighborhood in which this house was located was as depressing and dangerous as the interior of the residence. Though Mrs. Garing was generally afraid to leave her room, one oppressively hot evening she thought to escape the stifling

1. Mollie Orshansky, "The Shape of Poverty in 1966," *Social Security Bulletin* 31 (March 1968): 15.
2. Oshansky, pp. 12–13.
3. Leonard J. Hausman and Hirschel Kasper, "The Work Effort Response of Women to Income Maintenance," in *Income Maintenance,* eds Larry L. Orr, Robinson G. Hollister, and Myron J. Lefcowitz (Chicago: Markham Publishing Company, 1971), p. 96.
4. U.S. Dept. of Labor, Bureau of Labor Statistics, "Black American, A Chart Book," Bulletin 1699 (Washington, D. C.: U.S. Government Printing Office, 1971), pp. 56–57.

confines of her four walls by walking one block to a street vendor's stand. On the way, her purse was snatched, containing all her cash. Ten of the fifteen dollars stolen were owed for rent, overdue because of a delay in mailing the allotment. She attempted to explain to the landlord but he was unsympathetic and verbally abusive.[5]

Migrant workers' resources are especially sporadic.[6] Harvest-time wages may be cut by bad weather, poor crops, or other conditions. One migrant worker said, "I just want a job all year round so money will keep coming in for living expenses."[7]

Assets

Low-income families and individuals often have minimal financial assets to call upon. Almost half the families with less than $3,000 income in 1971 had no assets in checking accounts, savings accounts, certificates of deposit, stocks, bonds, or mutual funds.[8] One-fourth of the low-income families had up to $1,000 in financial assets, a fifth had $1,000–$4,999, and fewer than 10 per cent had more than $5,000 in assets.

For aged, poor couples, the 1968 median of all financial assets other than housing was under $75; for aged couples who were not poor, the median was $2,500 and over. Among older, poor individuals, there were no median assets other than housing.[9]

Housing is an important asset for low-income families, particularly the elderly; it provides a sense of security. Since it is not liquid, housing is a limited resource for emergencies that require immediate dollars. For low-income elderly families, the equity in housing is rather low; 71 per cent of the aged low-income families in 1968 were homeowners with a median

5. Edythe Shewbridge, *Portraits of Poverty* (New York: W. W. Norton and Company, Inc., 1972), p. 93.
6. Glenn R. Hawkes, Minna Taylor, and Beverly E. Bastian, "Patterns of Living in California's Migrant Labor Families," Research Monograph No. 12 (Davis, Calif.: Dept. of Applied Behavioral Sciences, University of California, 1973), p. 19.
7. William A. Rushing, *Class, Culture, and Alienation* (Lexington, Mass.: Lexington Books, D. C. Heath and Company, 1971), p. 113.
8. Lewis Mandell, George Katona, James N. Morgan, and Jay Schmiedeskamp, *Surveys of Consumers 1971–72,* Institute for Social Research (Ann Arbor, Mich.: The University of Michigan, 1973), p. 67.
9. Janet Murray, "Homeownership and Financial Assets: Findings from the 1968 Survey of the Aged," *Social Security Bulletin* 35 (August 1972): 22.

equity of $6,000, and 32 per cent of the elderly low-income individuals were homeowners with a median equity of $7,000.[10]

Credit

"The basic problem of the poor is that they do not have the same ability to repay obligations as do other consumers. Restricted access to the legal credit market by the poor is only one of the many results of an unstable and inadequate income."[11] Low-income families have access to only some of the credit sources available to families with higher incomes. In 1971, 29 per cent of families with an annual income of less than $3,000 had installment debt, mostly less than $500.[12]

Milwaukee residents, who had had their wages garnisheed by retailers or consumer finance companies after leaving welfare and getting a job, were interviewed. When he was asked about continuing business with the creditor who had garnisheed his wages, one husband replied, "I didn't know I could go anywhere else without money." Another replied, "Where else can we make the same payment each week and pick up a new item every time the old bill's about paid up without any change in payments?"[13]

Credit-card use is directly proportional to income; 17 per cent of families with incomes less than $3,000 use credit cards, while 74 per cent of families with incomes of $25,000 and over use credit cards.[14] Low-income, or low socioeconomic-status, families are more likely to use credit cards to repay purchases by monthly installments, while higher income families are more likely to use their cards for convenience, paying the balance at each month's billing.[15]

Using consumer credit can be important to achieve needed flexibility in timing resource inputs to satisfy the family's demands. Buying children's clothes for the beginning of school with consumer credit is an example of middle-class flexibility that low-income families often do not have. Buying

---

10. Murray, p. 11.
11. Report of the National Commission on Consumer Finance, "Consumer Credit in the United States," (Washington, D. C.: U.S. Government Printing Office, 1973), p. 160.
12. Mandell *et al.*, p. 8.
13. Milton J. Huber, "Installment Credit Problems Among Public Welfare Recipients," *Journal of Consumer Affairs* 1 (Summer 1967): 94.
14. Mandell *et al.*, p. 19.
15. H. Lee Mathews and John W. Slocum, Jr., "Social Class and Commercial Bank Credit Card Usage," *Journal of Marketing* 33: (January 1969): 78.

sale items on credit is another strategy used by middle-income families—a strategy not often open to low-income families.

Help

Relatives, friends, churches, and other organizations provide direct and indirect assistance to low-income families. This help is often on an emergency basis, supplementing and bridging gaps that may occur in governmental or formal assistance programs. The gratification of helping others may be the motivating force, but some informal programs are moving toward less patronizing approaches that recognize the dignity of man.

In a California study of low-income families, long-term public assistance families received the most gifts (44 per cent), primarily from organizations and from relatives. Fewer than one-third of the low-income families who never had been on assistance received gifts primarily from relatives.[16] In another study, one-fourth of the poor families received more than moderate help from relatives, while 13 per cent of the nonpoor families received more than moderate help.[17]

Health-Related Resources

Low-income families have a higher incidence of chronic conditions than do other families.[18] Diminished physical and/or mental capacities affect the management of the household either through modified activities or through reduced earnings, if the person is a wage earner. Men with poor health have lower earnings, resulting from the fact that they work fewer total hours and at lower hourly rates than do those in good health.[19]

---

16. Robert C. Stone and Fredric T. Schlamp, *Welfare and Working Fathers* (Lexington, Mass.: Lexington Books, D. C. Heath and Company, 1971), p. 60.
17. Arthur Besner, "Economic Deprivation and Family Patterns," in *Low-Income Life Styles*, ed. Lola M. Irelan, U.S. Dept. of Health, Education, and Welfare, Welfare Administration Publication No. 14 (Washington, D. C.: U.S. Government Printing Office, 1968), p. 17.
18. U. S. Dept. of Health, Education, and Welfare, Public Health Service, *Chronic Conditions and Limitations of Activity and Mobility, United States July 1965–July 1967*, Public Health Service Publication No. 10, Series 10–No. 61 (Washington, D. C.: U.S. Government Printing Office, 1971), p. 7.
19. Joseph M. Davis, "Impact of Health on Earnings and Labor Market Activity," *Monthly Labor Review* 95 (October 1972): 46–49.

Health insurance is important in providing some financial aid in caring for one's health. Persons without health insurance tend to be young —between 17 and 24 years of age. They have low income and low levels of education and are in service or farm-labor occupations. The reason given most often by these persons is that they cannot afford the coverage.[20] Nearly all persons 65 and older are now covered for hospitalization under Medicare (Part A), and over 90 per cent have surgical benefits (Part B).

Medicaid is an alternate program for low-income individuals and families to provide health services under cooperative federal-state agreement. Most eligible persons are either in families with dependent children or are aged, blind, or disabled. Of those using the Medicaid program, 60 per cent are in the Aid to Families with Dependent Children (AFDC) program.[21]

The availability of health-care services determines their use; isolated rural counties in the United States are those seriously lacking in such services.[22] For some urban dwellers, a limited knowledge of how to get around the city, compounded by the maze of health-care facilities and accompanying complicated procedures, makes health-care services also "unavailable."

Community

Knowledge about community resources is a prerequisite to the actual availability of a resource to an individual or family. This knowledge often depends on the person's being literate and exposed to other services or officials. Some groups of low-income individuals join together to take advantage of resources. One person describes her Welfare Rights Organization:

By pooling our knowledge, we helped each other to lose our fear of the bureaucratic multisyllables that even the welfare workers don't always understand. It

20. U.S. Dept. of Health, Education, and Welfare, Public Health Service, *Vital and Health Statistics,* Public Health Service Publication No. 10, Series 10–No. 66, (Washington, D. C.: U.S. Government Printing Office, 1972).

21. James R. Storey, "Public Income Transfer Programs: The Incidence of Multiple Benefits and the Issues Raised by Their Receipt," in *Studies in Public Welfare,* Paper No. 1, Joint Economic Committee (Washington, D. C.: U.S. Government Printing Office, 1972), pp. 32, 39.

22. U.S. Dept. of Agriculture, Economic Research Service for the Committee on Government Operations, *The Economic and Social Condition of Rural America in the 1970's* (Washington, D. C.: U.S. Government Printing Office, 1971), p. 76.

turned out that some children had not been included in grants, money for school bus tickets was being denied, retroactive money was due us, transportation for medical help wasn't paid, the $5 per child hadn't been deducted from outside money before counting it as income, or welfare workers had just added wrong.[23]

The poor prefer intimate interaction experiences in groups that are locally oriented and the reinforcement of existing lifestyles and moral values.[24] "The family and immediate neighborhood are the most meaningful interaction settings for the lower-lower-class person."[25]

Participation in community groups such as the American Legion or Veterans of Foreign Wars (VFW) is very unlikely, even though those groups attract upper-lower-class members, as do church organizations and auxiliaries to the husband's club. In another study of structured recreational programs—bowling, swimming, baton lessons, chess club, bridge, ceramics, and open recreation—definite differences were found by occupational levels. Persons with higher occupational levels participated more in the programs.[26]

Both low- and higher-income families from an urban area in the west used recreational facilities located nearby that were designed for daytime use and did not involve the expense of outfitting for camping.[27] This finding illustrates another important feature of community resources; they must be conveniently located and not involve large additional expenditures by the family if they are to serve families from a range of income levels.

DEMANDS

Goals

Poor people—males and females, blacks and whites, youths and adults —identify their self-esteem with work as strongly as do the nonpoor. They express

---

23. Marie Ratagick, "Two American Welfare Mothers," *Ms.* 1 (June 1973): 75–76.
24. Russell L. Curtis, Jr. and Louis A. Zurcher, Jr., "Voluntary Associations and the Social Integration of the Poor," *Social Problems* 18 (Winter 1971): 341.
25. Curtis and Zurcher, p. 342.
26. Glenn Morris, Richard Pasewark, and John Schultz, "Occupational Level and Participation in Public Recreation in a Rural Community," *Journal of Leisure Research* 4 (Winter 1972): 29.
27. John J. Lindsay and Richard A. Ogle, "Socioeconomic Patterns of Outdoor Recreation Use Near Urban Areas," *Journal of Leisure Research* 4 (Winter 1972): 22.

as much willingness to take job training if unable to earn a living and to work even if they were to have adequate income. They have, moreover, as high life aspirations as do the nonpoor and want the same things, among them a good education and a nice place to live.[28]

Welfare and nonwelfare mothers and fathers consistently rank good health at the top of their goal priorities. The order of ranking varies for the other goals, but the usual order is to have a good education, support a family, be honest, and have good family relations. Having a nice place to live was more important for welfare mothers and fathers than for those not on welfare.[29] Perhaps nonwelfare mothers and fathers had already achieved a nice place to live or did not have difficulty in finding or being accepted in a place to live.

The goal of "a nice place to live" may change to "a place to exist" according to difficulties experienced by low-income persons. A mother now on welfare reports her plight: "No realty company would rent to me with three children and without a full-time job. Since I wasn't on welfare, I couldn't rent anything from the slumlords who usually specialized in welfare recipients. . . . My family was saved from despair at the very last minute: I found a building run by two old women who were drinking away their loneliness and forgot to ask me for references. I got the apartment."[30] With a permanent address, the mother could receive assistance payments.

A report of migrant workers provides another example of changing goals to meet the harsh realities of living. Saving money is difficult in a migrant labor camp, and goals are often changed to "breaking even."[31] "The family from Selma was saving to buy a used car with the money earned picking. . . . They didn't realize they would have to get insurance for the car, which would also cost them quite a bit. In any case, by mid-season, they no longer talked about it, and seemed to have forgotten completely about getting a car."[32]

Middle-class farmers and lower-class farm workers share goals such as economic advantages, good health, and children's success, but have dif-

---

28. Leonard Goodwin, *Do The Poor Want to Work?* (Washington, D. C.: The Brookings Institution, 1972), p. 112:
29. Goodwin, pp. 149–50.
30. Ratagick, pp. 75–76.
31. William H. Friedland and Dorothy Nelkin, *Migrant Agricultural Worker in America's Northeast* (New York: Holt, Rinehart and Winston, 1971), p. 186.
32. Friedland and Nelkin, p. 188.

ferent scales for goals. Workers mentioned such goals as having enough money to meet living expenses, "to make some money to buy a house-trailer to live in," and "to get a $100 check every Saturday night."[33] Farmers mentioned such goals as "to always get a good price for wheat," "to have sufficient income so I can travel six months out of the year," and "to get my land paid off and out of debt to the bank. . . ."[34]

Events

The conditions of families in poverty produce a high incidence of events. Chronically low income, limited schooling and skills, and recurring health problems cannot be easily separated into cause and effect because of their interactions. The frequent need to respond to events often shatters hopes of attaining even minimal goals.

A situation shows how one crisis event is related to other events that affect the family:

The O's went on public assistance in 1961 after Mr. O, a construction worker, had a serious back injury. His surgery and hospital fees were paid by Workmen's Compensation. After the injury, frequent hospitalization and surgery caused Mr. O to lose several jobs. Welfare payments were fairly constant until 1966 when Mr. O became employed again. In 1968, he again required hospitalization and the family needed assistance again. The O's now receive Social Security disability payments, aid from Workmen's Compensation, and food stamps. For these reasons, the Department of Social Services payments were no longer warranted, and their case was closed. Mrs. O feels that their current income is sufficient.[35] The O's were fortunate in having insurance and other services to minimize the extreme financial effects of the injury event, but the uncertainties of recurring health problems have required many adjustments for the O's.

---

33. Rushing, p. 111.
34. Rushing, pp. 110–11.
35. Janet M. Fitchen, "The People of Road Junction: The Participant Observer's Study of a Rural Poverty Area in Northern Appalachia, with Particular Reference to the Problems of Employment of Low Income Women," in *A Study of the Effects on the Family Due to Employment of the Welfare Mother*, vol. III, Report to Manpower Administration, U.S. Dept. of Labor (no date), p. 355.

PLANNING AND IMPLEMENTING

Individual qualities affect planning by low-income families just as with other individuals or families (see Chapter 7). Fatalism, present-time orientation, concreteness, and authoritarianism characterize low-income persons, according to Irelan and Besner.[36] The qualities of fatalism, present-time orientation, and concreteness are particularly appropriate for consideration in relation to planning.

Fatalism—accepting events as inevitable or predestined—limits planning, whenever it occurs. A fatalistic view can mean greater frequency of events because fewer such occurrences are anticipated; a low-income person describes her feelings, "You can't say what's going to happen to you."[37]

In the case of the O family, Mr. and Mrs. O have responded to many events since Mr. O's back injury and now have a limited regular income. They are resigned to the managerial role of responding to circumstances. They are happy with their seven children, ages 1 to 11, having planned originally to have only two or three. They have their ups and downs, but things are usually the same . . . Neither Mr. nor Mrs. O believes that they have much control over what happens to them. "This control is in God's hands and all we can do is to make the best of it. It does not do much good to have ambitions which are not part of His plan." Mrs. O is thus content with her attention to whatever she is doing at the moment.[38]

Closely related to fatalism is a present-time orientation. The suggestion was made in Chapter 7 that individuals are often not present- or future-time oriented. A present-time orientation may be unjustifiably ascribed to a low-income individual or family; the lack of opportunities may give the appearance of present-time orientation.

A writer describes this situation in "the strength and resourcefulness of the people living in the hills and hollows of Appalachia . . . when opportunity strikes, even though it may be modest, these people are ready to

---

36. Lola M. Irelan and Arthur Besner, "Low-Income Outlook on Life," in *Low-Income Life Styles*, ed. Lola M. Irelan, U.S. Dept. of Health, Education, and Welfare, Welfare Administration Publication No. 14 (Washington, D. C.: U.S. Government Printing Office, 1968), p. 7.

37. Fitchen, p. 81.

38. Fitchen, p. 348.

grasp it, provided they have or can acquire the necessary skills. When disaster strikes, they do not go to pieces."[39]

Concreteness is an emphasis on tangible things and acts and makes contingency planning difficult. Forming alternative standards and sequences for indefinite conditions requires the ability to deal in abstract ideas.

Families who do not have experience or ability to process alternative solutions are especially vulnerable to the uncertainties of irregular and fluctuating income or to inadequate income to meet their goal and event demands. Young families with too many pressures may be unable to find adequate solutions soon enough to avoid lost time in establishing basic financial security, formidable debts, or dissolution of the family itself.

An interregional study involving thirteen states found that fatalism, authoritarianism, concreteness, and alienation did not characterize the orientation to job and education of low-income mothers. Present-time orientation was not examined.[40] More research is needed on the impact of individual qualities of low-income families on planning and implementing limited resources to meed demands.

Case studies of individual families reveal evidences of planning and implementing resource use. Mrs. C's story is an example:

Mrs. C, 41, has 12 children. She separated from her first husband after having five children, she had five more and is now married to the father of her last two. . . . She has taken training to get jobs in hospitals and has gained a modicum of status. Her extraordinary drive supplements a great deal of ability. She is capable and reliable and has successfully withstood periods of instability and achieved a degree of economic stability and occupational mobility.[41]

RESOURCE USE AND MET DEMANDS

Met Demands

Maslow's hierarchy of needs for personality development (see Chapter 4), is based on the premise that physiological needs must be

39. U.S. Dept. of Health, Education, and Welfare, Public Health Service, *Mental Health in Appalachia,* Publication No. 1374 (Washington, D. C.: U.S. Government Printing Office, 1965), p. 12.

40. Francille M. Firebaugh, John Woodward, and Ron Daly, "Factors Affecting Value Orientations of Low-Income Mothers," (Preliminary title of draft reporting NC-90 analysis). (Available from Firebaugh.)

41. Fitchen, p. 265.

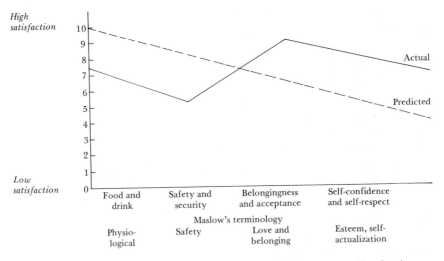

FIGURE 13.1 *Actual and predicted need satisfaction for persons living in a low-income area.*

Source: Adapted from Robert J. Holloway and Richard N. Cardozo, "Consumer Problems and Marketing Patterns in Low-Income Neighborhoods: An Exploratory Study," (Minneapolis, Minn.: University of Minnesota, 1969), p. 14.

satisfied first, then safety needs, love and belonging, esteem, and finally, self-actualization, or fulfillment. Accordingly, persons with low incomes would meet their physiological needs first and higher-order needs would be met in turn. However, one test of Maslow's thesis does not bear this out (Figure 13.1). For a group of low-income homemakers, the need for belonging and acceptance (Maslow's "love and belonging") was satisfied more than the need for safety and security; self-confidence and self-respect were as satisfied as food and drink. Safety may seem beyond the family's control.

Effective managerial responses to event demands are particularly important for low-income families. A probable response by a family to uncontrollable events is to minimize long-range planning and concentrate on making adequate responses to short-term goals and events.

Most people function effectively in some areas, but when difficulties become too great, a nonmanagerial response may occur. Life and circumstances may make overall effective management unlikely, but a concern for the circumstances and for managerial understanding improves the possibilities for successful management.

Resource Use

General Consumer Approach.   Balancing resources with demands means considering the total situation and implies a "rational man." Low-income consumers who fall short of a rational solution in their resource use were described by Richards as follows:

1. Although they spend most of their incomes on basic needs, those who buy durable goods make serious inroads on their incomes.
2. Most do not use more deliberation, consult more sources, or shop more widely, to get the best buys. Instead, many depend on known merchants or relatives for judgments of what to buy.
3. Few have savings of any size; most do not have life insurance, and only half are covered by medical insurance.
4. It is doubtful whether many carry out home production activities to supplement cash purchases.
5. Many probably do not make full use of the programs established to provide services and goods free or at reduced rates.[42]

How defensible are Richards' observations in light of available research findings? Although much information relates to special groups of low-income families or individuals and cannot be generalized for all low-income families, her observations are reviewed below.

The first comment, relating to the effects of the purchase of durable goods, has some basis. For all installment debt, including household durables and automobiles, 13 per cent of the families with less than $3,000 income had 20 per cent of their previous year's income committed to debt payment. The inroad for families with 20 per cent of their income committed to debt payment is serious; however, the extent of low-income families in such a situation is not so large as might be assumed.[43]

The next point, that low-income consumers make minimal deliberation in purchases and that known merchants or relatives provide information for purchases, was not supported in a recent study. Television and newspapers were the most useful sources of information for low-income consumers.[44] Blacks in the St. Louis households rated advice from friends

---

42. Louise G. Richards, "Consumer Practices of the Poor," *Welfare in Review* 3 (November 1965): 10.
43. Mandell *et al.*, p. 10.
44. Carol E. Block, "Prepurchase Search Behavior of Low-Income Households," *Journal of Retailing* 48 (Spring 1972): 9.

as the third most useful source of consumer information, while whites ranked friends as the sixth most useful source.[45] Product information, such as guarantees, prices, brands, new or used condition, was cited as being helpful three times as often as dealer information such as credit terms, service, prices at different stores, reputation of the various dealers. The factor that provided the least help was other people's experience with dealers.[46]

The lack of savings by low-income families is substantiated by statistics collected annually by the Survey Research Center at the University of Michigan. Of families with less than $3,000 income, 42 per cent had no liquid assets in 1970. Those with liquid assets had a median amount of $700.[47] Life insurance, provided by either the employer or the individual, was held by 52 per cent of families with less than $4,999 income.[48] Health insurance coverage is still limited, although Medicaid is providing health services for many.

Richards suggests that home production activities are limited among low-income families. Conditions in many urban apartments and limited housing facilities are not conducive to home production; also, storage for the products, supplies, and equipment for producing goods at home may be inadequate or nonexistent. Using pudding mix and canned spaghetti may, in fact, be cheaper than making a pudding with sugar and eggs and milk or preparing spaghetti from the basic ingredients if roaches or rats or other vermin can infest food supplies in the home.[49]

The fifth point was the failure of low-income families to make full use of programs and services. Although many families do not use available services, the factors that affect the use of services by low-income individuals and families should be recognized. The poor particularly need health services; the bulk of services comes from private physicians, but the poor use emergency rooms and hospital clinics more often than do other groups. They make limited use of preventive services probably because they cannot pay the full cost, cannot be absent from work, cannot arrange

---

45. Block, pp. 9–10.
46. Block, pp. 4–5.
47. George Katona, Lewis Mandell, and Jay Schmiedeskamp, *1970 Survey of Consumer Finances,* Institute for Social Research (Ann Arbor, Mich.: The University of Michigan, 1971), p. 100.
48. Katona, Mandell, and Schmiedeskamp, p. 117.
49. Carolyn Shaw Bell, *The Economics of the Ghetto* (New York: Pegasus, 1970), p. 140.

child care, or cannot get transportation.[50] The poor accept more folk medicine, have greater communication problems with physicians, and have problems in handling organizational details (forms, insurance, medical support payments, and so on). All of these factors contribute to deficiencies in health-service delivery.

A large study on the participation in programs and receipt of benefits found 60 to 75 per cent of all beneficiary households received more than one benefit in each of the areas of the United States that were sampled. One-third received three or more benefits, and 10 to 25 per cent received five or more, depending on area.[51]

Food Purchasing. Low-income families spend a higher portion of their income for food than for other items. Claims have been made that the poor must pay higher prices for food, especially once they are on welfare. Prices do not differ systematically in similar types of stores (chain, independent, or neighborhood) by socioeconomic areas,[52] but differences do occur in the quality of merchandise. No pattern of price changes has been identified if the customers are known to receive welfare checks.[53]

Relatively few chain stores are found in low-income areas. When low-income consumers have transportation, they often shop in chain stores outside their neighborhood;[54] however, many shop in small, conveniently

---

50. Mary W. Herman, "The Poor: Their Medical Needs and the Health Services Available to Them," *The Annals of the American Academy of Political and Social Science* 399 (January 1972): 12.

51. James R. Storey, Alair A. Townsend, and Irene Cox, "How Public Welfare Benefits Are Distributed in Low-Income Areas," in *Studies in Public Welfare* Paper No. 6, Joint Economic Committee (Washington, D. C.: U.S. Government Printing Office, 1973), p. 63.

52. Phyllis Groom, "Prices in Poor Neighborhoods," *Monthly Labor Review* 89 (October 1966): 1085; and B. W. Marion, L. A. Simonds, and Dan E. Moore, "Food Marketing in Low Income Areas: A Review of Past Findings and a Case Analysis in Columbus, Ohio," AE-439 MM/302 (Columbus, Ohio: Cooperative Extension Service, The Ohio State University, 1969), p. vii.

53. Eileen F. Taylor, "Food Prices Before and After Distribution of Welfare Checks . . . Low-Income Areas, Seven Cities, 1969," Marketing Research Report No. 907, U.S. Dept. of Agriculture, Economic Research Service (Washington D. C.: U.S. Government Printing Office, 1970), p. ii; and Marion, Simonds, and Moore, p. vi.

54. Charles S. Goodman, "Do the Poor Pay More?" *Journal of Marketing* 32 (January 1968): 23.

located neighborhood stores where they have established friendships and can get credit.[55]

Low-income consumers, who buy food in small quantities because they lack money or storage or have vermin problems often, although not always, pay higher unit costs. Unit pricing, if it is available and if it is used, helps the consumer make comparisons, but does not alter the reasons for buying smaller amounts.

Buying the large economy size or stocking up when canned goods or staples are on "special" takes more money than buying sporadically in small quantities. The consumer's capital, represented by a well-stocked pantry, is not insignificant and may be more than the poverty-level family can easily amass. Aside from the original investment, the family with a substantial inventory needs storage capacity—to have a bulging cupboard takes not only money and wise buying but also the cupboard space.[56]

Credit Use. One analysis of extensive installment credit use reports that the largest portions of debtors in "some trouble" or "deep trouble," were the unmarried, the poor, and those under 25 or 65 and older. The likelihood of debt trouble was above average for laborers, service workers, and the unemployed and retired.[57] Those with current incomes that varied more than 25 per cent from last year's were more likely to have debt-payment difficulty.[58] Regular, stable incomes facilitate planning (including debt-repayment planning) for low-income families.

A study on family finances showed that 62 per cent of the families with debts and less than $3,000 income made repayments on schedule, while 17 per cent fell behind in their payments and 7 per cent paid in advance. A pattern of whether the other 14 per cent fell behind or paid ahead was not indicated in their responses. At higher income levels, higher percentages of families paid ahead and lower portions fell behind.[59]

---

55. Louis E. Boone and John A. Bonno, "Food Buying Habits of the Urban Poor," *Journal of Retailing* 47 (Fall 1971): 79–84.

56. Bell, p. 140.

57. Mary Ellen Ryan, "An Analysis of Economic and Demographic Characteristics of Consumers Associated with Excessive Installment Debt," The University of Minnesota, M.S. thesis, 1968, pp. 68–69.

58. Ryan, p. 69.

59. George Katona, W. Dunkelberg, G. Henricks, and Jay Schmiedeskamp, *1969 Survey of Consumer Finances,* Institute for Social Research (Ann Arbor, Mich.: The University of Michigan, 1970), p. 33.

SUMMARY

Low-income families and individuals who are chronically limited in resources have been the focus of this chapter. The goals of these families are similar to other income groups, but they differ in extent and are altered by the realities of the situations. The resource limitations are material—income and assets—and human. Limited education and limited occupational skills often complicate the possibilities for increasing material resources.

Planning and implementing the use of resources are probably affected by individual qualities such as fatalism, present-time orientation, and concreteness, although the empirical evidence to support this assumption is limited.

In one low-income neighborhood study, output in the form of met demands was inconsistent with Maslow's hierarchy of needs. Food and drink (physiological needs) and safety and security (safety) were lower than hypothesized by Maslow.

Evidence concerning resource use by low-income individuals and families reveals problems caused by debt, limited home production, and somewhat limited use of services, but certainly not caused by irrational, irresponsive consumer behavior.

Generalizations about low-income families are hard to make; a variety of individuals and families have limited resources, which they use quite differently.

Management by Elderly Individuals and Families

14.

Management *by older individuals and families is important because human and material resources generally decline while goal and event demands do not necessarily decline. This chapter focuses on persons 65 years and older, the primary age for retirement. Retirement seems to be an appropriate time to examine management of family resources because of the changes in the established income and expenditure patterns and the subsequent changes in the lifestyle due to reduced human resources. Because there is a large number of persons 65 years and over, this group is an important one; about ten per cent of the population in the United States in 1970 was in that age category. Projections to the year 2000 show an increase in the proportion of persons aged 75 years or more (Table 14.1).*

DEMANDS

The years of later maturity involve developmental tasks that represent "learning to live with oneself as one changes"; adaptive tasks represent "learning to live in a particular way according to a particular set of values as one changes or as one's culture changes."[1] The developmental tasks for the elderly have been described as regressive in nature:

---

1. Margaret Clark and Barbara Gallatin Anderson, *Culture and Aging* (Springfield, Illinois: Charles C. Thomas Publisher, 1967), p. 394.

TABLE 14.1.
Per cent distribution of the population 65 years and over by age, selected years, 1900 to 2000.

Age	Years			Projected	
	1900	*1950*	*1970*	*1990*	*2000*
			Per cent		
65–69	42.3	40.7	33.9	34.2	29.9
70–74	28.7	27.8	28.0	26.8	26.9
75 and older	29.0	31.5	38.2	39.0	43.2
All 65 and older	100	100	100	100	100

U.S. Dept. of Commerce, Bureau of the Census, "Some Demographic Aspects of Aging in the United States," Series P-23, No. 43 (Washington, D. C.: U.S. Government Printing Office, 1973), p. 7.

Accept and adjust to a debilitating body;
Adjust to a reduction in sexuality;
Readjust to dependence in living paterns;
Accept a different role in the family;
Learn to accept more than one can give when necessary;
Reorient to primary social groups.[2]

Adaptive tasks have been proposed as follows:

Perception of aging and definition of instrumental limitations;
Redefinition of physical and social life space;
Substitution of alternative sources of need-satisfaction;
Reassessment of criteria for evaluation of self;
Reintegration of values and life goals.[3]

---

2. James H. Barrett, *Gerontological Psychology* (Springfield, Illinois: Charles C. Thomas Publisher, 1972), pp. 10–18.
3. Clark and Anderson, pp. 398–414.

Responses of a group of preretired men and women to the question of what they considered to be the main purpose in life reveal both developmental and adaptive tasks. Their answers centered on "the importance of the family" (reorientation to primary social groups), "helpfulness and understanding in interpersonal relationships" (readjustment to dependence-in living pattern, and "coping with life's conditions" (perception of aging and definition of instrumental limitations).[4]

About two-fifths of these preretired persons mentioned material and economic goals to be taken care of prior to full retirement. Mentioned almost as frequently were trvel goals, ranging from sentimental journeys to ancestral lands to camper tours in the United States.[5]

Goals are related to one's situation, and the evolving goals about retirement and concern with saving energy and with the body illustrate this.[6] The circumstances of the elderly vary in their resources, but there is a commonality in recognition of the reality of change.

In a study of almost 900 families in Indiana, Missouri, and Nebraska, retirement-goal formation began to increase at 20–24 years of marriage, peaked at 34–39 years of marriage, and then began to decline.[7] The specific retirement goals were: financial security in retirement; early retirement of husband, wife, or both; retirement in a particular location; and retirement at age 65.[8]

Retirement goals for the families in the study were developed more fully during the late middle years, when couples began diverting attention from other interests and responsibilities to their own security and well-being at a time when some would no longer earn income.[9]

Goals given by the group of couples with 45 plus years of marriage were related to level of living (36%), health (17%), housing and environment (17%), family relations and management (15%), financial security and

---

4. Majda Thurnher, "Goals, Values, and Life Evaluations at the Preretirement Stage," *Journal of Gerontology* 29 (January 1974): 91.

5. Thurnher, p. 87.

6. James E. Birren, "Age and Decision Strategies," in *Decision Making and Age,* eds. A. T. Welford and James E. Birren (New York: S. Karger, 1969), p. 35.

7. Cleo Fitzsimmons, Dorothy A. Larery, and Edward J. Metzen, "Major Financial Decisions and Crises in the Family Life Span," North Central Regional Research Publication No. 208 (Lafayette, Ind.: Purdue University Agricultural Experiment Station, 1971), p. 15.

8. Fitzsimmons, Larery, and Metzen, p. 17.

9. Fitzsimmons, Larery, and Metzen, p. 15.

growth (7%), retirement (5%), income and occupation (2%), and community and involvement (2%).[10]

Relatively little information is available on events—unplanned pertinent occurrences—another form of demands on the individual and family system. A study of injury severity in fire incidents involving apparel found that persons over 65 had a significantly lower percentage of relatively minor burns and a higher percentage of burns covering 50 per cent or more of the body. The author of the study suggests that defensive capabilities are limited with the aged.[11] The elderly are probably less able to respond quickly and effectively to events. When time is not essential, responses to events based on experience can be wise ones.

One event in the life of an individual that can be traumatic is notification of early retirement. In many cases, such an occurrence could have been predicted due to ill health or economic circumstances. Whenever early retirement is not anticipated, receiving such a notice may be an event of major importance.

RESOURCES

Resources that contribute heavily to a person's flexibility in activities and capacity for meeting goals are good health, economic solvency, and social support such as a living spouse, close friend, or relative.[12] The human resources of mental and physical health, family, kin, and friends, and the material resources held by older families are interrelated in their impact on the family management. Sufficient economic resources can purchase services that are difficult to perform when there has been a decline in physical health. Family types, by their resource situations and extent of their problems, are shown in Table 14.2. The author estimated that 25 per cent of the elderly are "totally deprived" or very needy (V), that about half are "typically aged" (II, III, IV), and that another 25 per cent are privileged or "golden sunset families" (I).

---

10. Fitzsimmons, Larery, and Metzen, p. 15.

11. Laura Baker Buchbinder, "Human Activity Patterns and Injury Severity in Fire Accidents Involving Apparel," *Journal of Fire and Flammability/Consumer Products* 1 (March 1974): 4–18.

12. Jaber F. Gubruim, "Toward a Socio-Environmental Theory of Aging," *The Gerontologist* 12 (Autumn 1972, Part 1) 282.

TABLE 14.2

Family resources and problems in older families.

Family type by extent of problems	Material	Human		
	Economic	Physical health	Emotional health	Social—family, kin, friends
I	+	+	+	+
II	+	−	+	+
III	+	−	−	+
IV	−	−	−	+
V	−	−	−	−

Adapted from Gordon F. Streib, "Older Families and Their Troubles: Familial and Social Responses," *The Family Coordinator* (January 1972): 8. Copyright (1972) by National Council on Family Relations. Reprinted by permission.

+ = adequate resources
− = inadequate resources

Among a sample of Old Age Assistance recipients, "those who currently feel disadvantaged in comparison to peers are more likely to perceive a money problem than are respondents who feel that their income is at least equal to that of other old people."[13] Money problems were most often perceived by those in the sample 66–70 years, those living with a spouse, those living in their own home or trailer, those having a special group of friends, and those who had a youthful self-image.[14] "A youthful age-image combined with a desire for consumer items produces the highest problem rates, whereas an older age-image, matched to a lack of consumer interest, is least productive of hardship."[15]

Help from family and friends is often an important resource for elderly individuals and families. One of the regressive developmental tasks noted earlier was learning to accept more than one is capable of giving. Most

13. Thomas Tissue, "Old Age and the Perception of Poverty," *Sociology and Social Research* 56 (April 1972): 336–37.
14. Tissue, p. 338.
15. Tissue, p. 339.

elderly persons are able to give for many years, especially baby-sitting and other services. In a three-generational study, the help received by grandparent families was primarily from parent and married-children families first in the area of illness, and then household management, emotional gratification, and economic assistance.[16]

Earnings are nearly one-third of the total income of the elderly, despite the low labor-force participation rate of older men. Most of the earning of the elderly go to family heads in the 65 through 69 age group. Social Security and other public benefits comprise only about 40 per cent of the income of the elderly but these benefits are often the major or only income source for persons in their seventies and eighties.[17]

The elderly in the United States are predominantly women—11.6 million compared to 8.4 million men.[18] More than one-half the women are widowed or divorced, while almost three-fourths of the men are married. Several factors explain the high proportion of widows: there is a shorter life expectancy for men; wives are generally younger than their husbands; and widowers have a higher remarriage rate than widows, often choosing wives younger than 65.[19]

The resource picture is particularly bleak for elderly women who are alone. "About half of all white, single, aged women and four-fifths of all single, black, aged women are poor."[20] More women today receive social security as retired workers than as dependent wives, according to a sample of recent Social Security recipients.[21] Many families would do better economically if their earnings were considered together for calculating benefits. As the policy currently exists, women receive benefits either as a retired worker or as a dependent, whichever is higher.

---

16. Reuben Hill, *Family Development in Three Generations* (Cambridge, Mass.: Schenkman Publishing Co., Inc., 1970), p. 67.

17. Juanita M. Kreps, *Lifetime Allocation of Work and Income* (Durham,. North Carolina: Duke University Press, 1971), p. 136.

18. U.S. Dept. of Commerce, Bureau of the Census, "U.S. Census of Population: 1970, General Population Characteristics," final report, PC (1)-B1 (Washington, D.C.: U.S. Government Printing Office, 1972), pp. 1–276.

19. U.S. Dept. of Commerce, Bureau of the Census, "Some Demographic Aspects of Aging in the United States," Current Population Reports, Series P-23, No. 43 (Washington, D.C.; U.S. Government Printing Office, 1973), p. 27.

20. Elizabeth M. Heidbreder, "Pensions and the Single Woman," *Industrial Gerontology* (Fall 1972), p. 60.

21. Virginia Reno, "Women Newly Entitled to Retired-Worker Benefits: Survey of New Beneficiaries," *Social Security Bulletin* 36: (April 1973), pp. 3–26.

Widowed black and white women in Chicago have limited contacts with other individuals and organizations. Two-thirds had little or no contact with siblings, two-thirds currently had no children in the home, about three-fifths belonged to no church, and two-thirds belonged to no organization. Many older widows lead lonely lives.[22]

From a study of 486 Ohio residents whose husbands had claimed disability benefits, of those women 60–70 years of age, 58 per cent received no services from their kin. The widowed and divorced received more services than married and single persons, amounting to a higher average number of services.[23]

Resources that are available only through public ownership may be very important to the aged. At a minimum, public transportation is needed by many for grocery shopping and visits to the doctor.[24] In a study of elderly slum dwellers in San Antonio, Texas, very few elderly persons drove cars because they could not afford to maintain them. Public transportation was inadequate, and walking was the only option open to many.[25]

Community services are limited in a number of ways for the elderly. Three reasons are proposed:

1. Too large a social emphasis has been placed both on the roles of the elderly individual to care for himself and on the family to provide services for its members.
2. The economic status of the aged makes them captive consumers of whatever services are available.
3. Our own cultural aversion to old age and to death.[26]

The result of uncoordinated community services is that the needs of individuals are not met; and the social and economic position of the aged person may determine whose needs are met.[27]

---

22. Helena Z. Lopata, "Social Relations of Black and White Widowed Women in a Northern Metropolis," *American Journal of Sociology* 78 (January 1973): 247.
23. Geoffrey Gibson, "Kin Family Network: Overheralded Structure in Past Conceptualizations of Family Functioning," *Journal of Marriage and the Family* 34 (February 1972): 21.
24. Frances M. Carp, "The Mobility of Older Slum-Dwellers," *The Gerontologist* 12 (Spring 1972): 64.
25. Carp, p. 64.
26. Elizabeth W. Markson, Gary S. Levitz, and Maryvonne Gognalons-Caillard, "The Elderly and the Community: Reidentifying Unmet Needs," *Journal of Gerontology* 28 (October 1973): 508.
27. Markson, Levitz, and Gognalons-Caillard, p. 507.

THROUGHPUT

Planning for retirement is difficult because uncertainties are prominent during the time when planning for adequate economic resources must be done. The uncertainties pertaining to one's own situation include time of death of self and spouse, income, retirement needs, especially health care, and date of retirement.[28]

The interaction of the family system with the economic system is dramatically evident with the elderly individual or family, and the results must be taken into account in planning. The effects of inflation on the material resources of the family are particularly serious for individuals who have fixed incomes and assets. Changes are occurring in the Social

TABLE 14.3

Annual budgets for retired couples at three levels of living, urban United States, Autumn 1972.

Budget item	Level of living		
	Lower	*Intermediate*	*Higher*
		Dollars	
Total budget	3,442	4,967	7,689
Total family consumption	3,294	4,661	6,842
Food	989	1,328	1,671
Housing	1,209	1,745	2,730
Transportation	230	448	811
Clothing	172	289	445
Personal care	101	148	217
Medical care	432	434	437
Other consumption	161	269	531
Other items	148	298	584
Personal income taxes	—	8	263

U.S. Department of Agriculture, Agricultural Research Service, Consumer and Food Economics Institute, "BLS Budget Cost Estimates—Autumn 1972," *Family Economics Review* ARS (Winter 1974), 62-5:19.

---

28. James H. Schulz and Guy Carrin, "The Role of Savings and Pension Systems in Maintaining Living Standards in Retirement," *Journal of Human Resources* 7 (Summer 1972): 348.

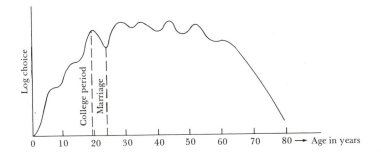

FIGURE 14.1 *Hypothetical curve of social choices, by age.*

Source: Stanford Goldman, "Social Aging, Disorganization, and Loss of Choice," *The Gerontologist* 11 (Summer 1971): 162.

Security system and other retirement systems to gear the payments to the general price level, but many elderly today receive incomes that are woefully inadequate considering the inflation that has existed in the United States in recent years.

Planning for needs in old age is also made difficult by the rising level of living of families and individuals who surround the aged. Anticipation of the effects of this comparison on an individual is not easy.

Retired persons must often plan expenditures more closely than at any time except in the beginning years of marriage. Potential changes in expenditure patterns are: the elimination of employment-related expenditures; a decrease in taxes; a decrease in expenditures for physical activities, with possible increase in recreational expenses; and, of major concern, rising health-care costs.[29]

Budgets for three levels of living have been projected by the Bureau of Labor Statistics (Table 14.3). Since 1972 food costs have continued to rise, and therefore the total family consumption is higher for all levels. Income has risen in actual dollars, but in effective dollars, the income is probably lower.

In long-term planning by the elderly, the need for institutional care is often considered. About 5 per cent of the elderly population in the United

---

29. Gerontological Society, Committee on Research and Development Goals in Social Gerontology, Robert J. Havighurst, Chairman, "Economics of Aging," *The Gerontologist* 9 (Winter 1969): 72.

States live in institutions.[30] Choices are sharply curtailed in many institutional arrangements, and planning is quite different in scope.

Choicemaking generally declines in old age. Social choices are proposed by one writer as fluctuating but generally becoming limited with aging (Figure 14.1). The effect of limited social choices is a narrowing of managerial activity. In recent years, elderly persons have resisted the downturn in social choices, with some choosing to remarry in late years and others, though limited in number, choosing an alternate lifestyle such as communal living.

Planning for retirement seems to be an important prelude to the output of satisfaction. For men who had retired before their company's mandatory retirement age, ill-adjusted retirees were twice as likely to have done little planning as were well-adjusted retirees. Making plans before rather than after retirement is important. For both blue- and white-collar workers with high adjustment to retirement, over 70 per cent had made retirement plans before actual retirement.[31]

Planning for retirement is related to family and individual income. In a large study the group of retired people with the highest incomes had planned and followed their plan to retire at a relatively early time. Two groups with low incomes in retirement were rather old retirees and those who had retired unexpectedly and late.[32]

In a German study of active workers, among the 60–65 age group, extensive plans were related to a positive attitude toward retirement. For retired steelworkers, 70–75 years of age, extensive plans were also related to the positive attitudes toward retirement.[33]

Planning and adjusting to retirement for women should be relatively easy since the man is viewed as the main wage earner and the woman as the secondary, or supplementary, wage earner. The woman in this case is

---

30. U.S. Dept. of Commerce, Bureau of the Census, "Some Demographic Aspects of Aging in the United States," Current Population Reports, Series P-23, No. 43 (Washington, D. C.: U.S. Government Printing Office, 1973), p. 27.

31. Elizabeth M. Heidbreder, "Factors in Retirement Adjustment: White-Collar/Blue-Collar Experience," *Industrial Gerontology* (Winter 1972) p. 77.

32. Richard Barfield and James Morgan, *Early Retirement the Decision and the Experience* (Institute for Social Research, Ann Arbor, Mich.: The University of Michigan, 1969), p. 59.

33. Ursula Lehr and Gernot Dreher, "Determinants of Attitudes Toward Retirement," in *Adjustment to Retirement*, eds. R. J. Havighurst, J. M. A. Munnichs, B. Neugarten, H. Thomae (Assen, The Netherlands: Van Gorum & Comp. N. V., 1970), pp. 129–30.

stereotypically viewed as having necessary employment, but not a career. In other situations, when a woman's employment is viewed as a career, it is proposed that the ease or difficulty of the woman's retirement is similar to a man's.[34]

Widowhood presents special managerial problems. For women who are left with financial resources considerably greater than they have ever managed, money-use planning may be very troublesome. Although general household management may be hard to abandon, many must do so at some point.

The older woman, accustomed to managing her own home, refuses to give it up if she has enough financial and health resources to keep it. Only a widow who is really incapable of self-maintenance lives with married offspring, unless a subculture demands her dependence. The widow often uses a culturally institutionalized explanation, such as "two women can't work in the same kitchen," to justify her unwillingness to live with married children.[35]

In a study of union workers 60 years and older who had planned retirement, changes in the husband's decision-making patterns occurred during the first two years of retirement. Decisions about the husband working and about the care of and repairs to the house that had been made frequently by the husband became almost completely husband dominated.[36] The decisions that were almost equal before retirement, that is, where the husband and wife contributed equally to the decision, became more nearly equal after retirement. The decisions were: what trips to take, when to go to the doctor, what evening activity to engage in, and what to do for relatives. The questions of food expenditures and visits of relatives moved toward being more equal in husband and wife involvement after retirement. What to have for meals became more wife dominated in the two years after the husband's retirement.[37]

For the actual performance of tasks, some changes were noted following retirement. "Husbands tended during the first year of retirement to

---

34. Lehr and Dreher, p. 126.
35. Helena Z. Lopata, "The Social Involvement of American Widows," *American Behavioral Scientist* 14 (September–October 1970): 49.
36. Woodrow W. Hunter, "A Longitudinal Study of Preretirement Education," Department of Health, Education, and Welfare, Welfare Administration, Research Grants Branch Project #151 (Ann Arbor, Michigan: The University of Michigan, 1968), p. 81.
37. Hunter, p. 82.

turn over more of the household tasks to their wives than had been the case before retirement."[38]

In one research project, men and women anticipating retirement reported considering what they wished to do at retirement and making some decisions about anticipated activities and lifestyles. About three-fourths of them were actively making arrangements to implement their plans, while about one-fifth of the men had goals in the discussion stage, and a few had vague goal ideas. In only one-fifth of the cases did planning extend beyond five years into retirement; the focus was mostly on the first year or two of retirement.[39]

Flexibility is an attribute of planning that needs to be high when the elderly person lives in an age-heterogeneous situation.[40] The need for flexibility is less in an age-homogeneous setting, where the variety of situations is reduced and expectations are standardized.[41]

In planning and decision making, use of stored information is necessary. Retrieval of information, generation of ideas, and flexibility in generating alternatives begin to decline around 50 years of age.[42] "It is not known how the individual's taking more time can compensate for lagging facility in finding from within himself the needed information for generating alternatives."[43] Guilford suggests that the elderly should be given simplified presentations of complex problems to allow time for comprehension.

Implementation of plans may be considerably altered by the changes in the physical capacity of the aged. The pace of activities is generally slowed. Checking and adjusting require use of stored information, and the experience of the older person can be helpful whenever a quick response is not necessary.

OUTPUT

Life satisfaction was studied for middle-aged and elderly residents of Virginia, and the major contributions to differences in life satisfaction

38. Hunter, p. 84.
39. Thurnher, p. 87.
40. Gubruim, p. 282.
41. Gubruim, p. 282.
42. J. P. Guilford, "Intellectual Aspects of Decision Making," in *Decision Making and Age*, eds. A. T. Welford and James E. Birren (Basel, Switzerland: S. Karger, 1969), p. 100.
43. Guilford, p. 100.

were socioeconomic status and family income.[44] Somewhat important in differences were health status and participation in activities such as neighboring. For another sample of elderly residents in a housing project, life satisfaction was affected by the constraint or freedom from constraint they felt. Constraint was measured by the ability to perform daily activities and the amount of monthly income.[45] "Among the constrained old people, those who are socially active are more likely to be satisfied and those who are less active are more likely to be dissatisfied."[46]

In rating their personal situation of the past, present, and future, Old Age Assistance recipients realistically rated the past as the best, the present as less good and the future as still lower, while the same respondents rated the national situation as better in the past, lower at present, and exceeding the past five years in the future.[47]

Satisfaction in a situation may be due to factors internal to the individual and family system, or the environment may have a strong influence. Retired residents who lived in an age-integrated community had a higher morale than those in an age-segregated community. The respondents were matched for age, sex, marital status, and religious affiliation. The groups were also matched in participation rates.[48]

Retirement may bring a time when one takes stock of met demands and used resources and the information is fed back to alter goals. Some goals may be recognized as being highly unlikely of ever being met and may be discarded, while others are shifted in priority.

The resource situation of many elderly persons has already been described; the net worth of the elderly families in the United States is made up primarily of the equity in a house. Improvements in private pension systems to supplement the Social Security system in this country along with improved plans for health care may dramatically change the resources used by the elderly. Savings may be less necessary to attain the level of living desired by the aged.[49]

---

44. John N. Edwards and David L. Klemmack, "Correlates of Life Satisfaction: A Re-examination," *Journal of Gerontology* 28 (October 1973): 502.
45. Kenneth J. Smith and Aaron Lipman, "Constraint and Life Satisfaction," *Journal of Gerontology* 27 (January 1972): 78.
46. Smith and Lipman, p. 82.
47. George S. Sternlieb and Bernard P. Indik, *The Ecology of Welfare* (New Brunswick, N. J.: Transaction Books, 1973), p. 159.
48. Houshang Poorkaj, "Social-Psychological Factors and 'Successful Aging,'" *Sociology and Social Research* 56 (April 1972): 299.
49. Schulz and Carrin, p. 363.

ENVIRONMENTS

Housing alternatives open to the elderly include: remaining in one's own home; living in an age-mixing or age-segregation area; or living in a retirement community, in a nursing home, or in extended-care facilities.[50]

Many elderly persons choose the first alternative. Such a choice can mean that an individual or a couple remains in a large house which is appropriate for a big family but not for one or two persons. Staying in the same neighborhood in urban areas that have changed drastically may mean that the risk of crime is great. Older persons often have the disadvantage of having inadequate material and human resources to maintain their homes.[51]

Older people are "likely to be more vulnerable to environmental influences than people in general might."[52] Changing housing is a threatening thing for many older people. In one study of residents of two housing projects, those who moved were significantly poorer in functional health than persons who were not re-housed. The re-housed persons were higher in morale, more satisfied with their housing, more involved in outside activities, and more satisfied with the *status quo* than the comparable persons who lived in the community.[53] More needs to be known about the stresses and challenges associated with environmental changes.

SUMMARY

Goal and event demands change in the lives of the elderly as their situations change. Retirement is often an identifiable point of change. Goals of couples married for 45 years and more focused on level of living,

---

50. James E. Montgomery, "The Housing Patterns of Older Families," *The Family Coordinator* 21 (January 1972): 40–45.
51. John D. Lange, "Alternatives for Action: Housing," The National Forum of State Legislators on Older Americans (Washington, D. C., December 4–6, 1972), pp. 26–27.
52. M. Powell Lawton and Jacob Cohen, "The Generality of Housing Impact on the Well-Being of Older People," *Journal of Gerontology* 29 (March 1974): 201.
53. Lawton and Cohen, p. 200.

health, housing and environment, family relations, and management.

Resources among the elderly are often limited—both human and material—especially among individuals and couples in their seventies and eighties. Problems with money are greater when one has youthful ideas and is interested in consumer goods.

Most elderly give and receive help from other family members. Widowed and divorced women receive more services than any other group of elderly persons. Community resources can be very important to the elderly—public transportation, recreation facilities, and health-care facilities.

Economic planning for old age is made difficult by the living level of those who surround them, by inflation, by generally fixed incomes and assets. Increased social efforts may lessen the problems of individual planning.

Planning by the elderly is marked by reduced choices; patterns of decision making alter with increased equality in some areas, but with greater specialization in other areas. Planning and decision making may be changed by the reduced capacity to generate ideas.

Life satisfaction varies among the elderly just as in any other age group. Socioeconomic status and income contribute to differences in satisfaction; the environment also affects satisfaction, with age-integrated living related, in one study, to higher morale than age-segregated living. Environments may affect the elderly more than other groups; changes in the environment are potentially traumatic.

Universals about aging that have been supported by research follow:

1. In an older population, females outnumber males.

2. The aged always constitute a minority within the total population.

3. Old people tend to shift to more sedentary, advisory, or supervisory roles with less physical exertion and less economic production.

4. In all societies, the mores prescribe some mutual responsibility between old people and their adult children.[54]

---

54. Donald O. Cowgill and Lowell D. Holmes, "Summary and Conclusions: The Theory in Review," in *Aging and Modernization,* eds. Donald O. Cowgill and Lowell D. Holmes (New York: Meredith Corp., 1972), p. 321.

Several variations of the universals seem appropriate to include in our summary:

1. Modern societies have higher proportions of women and especially of widows.

2. Modern societies have higher proportions of people who live to be grandparents and even great grandparents.

3. Retirement is a modern invention; it is found chiefly in modern high-productivity societies.

4. With modernization the responsibility for the provision of economic security for dependent aged tends to be shifted from the family to the state.

The Context and Concepts of Home Management: A Summary

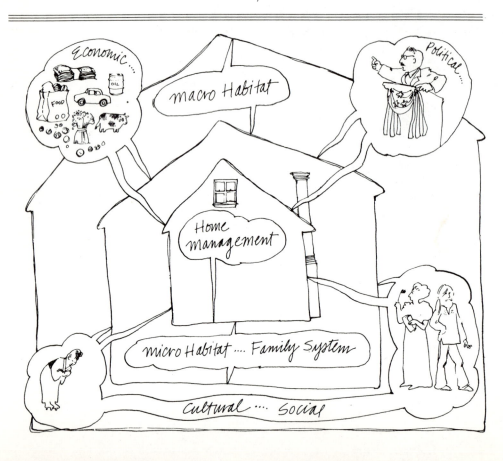

15.

CONTEXT

A managerial problem must be resolved within the context of the situation that gives it meaning. The solution to one managerial problem will probably alter the context of the next managerial problem. Chapters 1 and 2 discuss managerial functions in a context of dynamic interactions of individuals and families with their environment.

The systems format provides a frame of reference for analyzing the goal-directed behavior of families as a managerial response to the current situation. The family system's context changes partly because of changes introduced by previous managerial responses and partly because of changes introduced by other systems. The opportunity to view these interactions in a dynamic context is a special advantage of the systems approach to managerial analysis.

While input, throughput, output, and feedback are processes of any open system, positive feedback with its contribution to the acceptance of change, is important in individual and social management systems. The transitions of life from one stage to another provide a context of continuity and change that is consistent with life's experiences and new demands. Positive feedback provides information for adaptation to changing external situations and recognizes changing satisfactions from experiences that tend to reorient values and redirect goals.

Individuals and families are self-directed systems with continually redefined purposes that affect their potential for effective management. Adaptiveness and growth potential may influence managerial actions in various ways. Marked adaptive and growth differences have been described by the terms "equifinality" and "multifinality." Families may start with quite different demands and resources and eventually arrive at the same end (equifinality); or families in similar beginning situations may reach quite different future situations (multifinality). A systems analysis may emphasize the individuality of specific managerial problems even though the basic systems and their managerial elements retain similar characteristics from system to system and over time.

The environment of any individual and family system has interacting social, biological, and physical relations. No individual system can function effectively by itself—it is ecological in nature. Inputs and outputs relate external systems to individual and family systems; the output of one system becomes input of another system. The physical environment provides the habitat for social systems of either natural or structured space. The external physical environment—the macro-habitat—may be incorporated in the family micro-habitat by economic interchange as with the purchase of furniture and fuel.

Intermediate to the adaptations in the macro-habitat for exchange with the family system is the role of technology, which is the application of knowledge toward useful ends. We are most aware of the ways in which changes in the physical environment are affected by new technological insights, particularly as environmental problems have alerted us to the degradation that may occur if advances are not applied equally to counter and control pollution. In addition to the effects of technology in relation to the physical environment, new techniques or mechanisms applied to political, economic, and social problems are equally illustrative. Changes in traffic patterns, communication, pricing, taxation, or health-care plans are all part of the technological influence on the total environment.

In Figure 2-3, the interrelated impacts of the political and economic systems on each other and on the family system were illustrated. In an interdependent, specialized society no one aspect can function alone. The family system is dependent on the economic system for opportunities to fulfill its economic goals and on the political system for programs, policies, and protection consistent with its rights and needs. In turn, each system is dependent on the family system for appropriate active support in fulfilling its economic and political roles.

The social-cultural system is the broad representation of the many expectations, opportunities for, and actual involvement in social processes. All such relationships have implications for the demands and actual costs and benefits that formal and informal group relations accrue. Involved are such matters as social status, mobility, and role identification, which impinge on individual families differently. Families who "have arrived," those who have no social aspirations, or those who see no effect from or advantage in striving may be indifferent to an available opportunity, but for quite different reasons. The first group may be unresponsive due to high demands and resources they want to protect; the second, due to relative disinterest in the nature of the particular opportunity; and the latter, due to inadequate personal or material resources to take advantage. The nature of the managerial aspect of each situation is different in terms of given demands and resources and the managerial situation to which a new activity would relate. Interpretation in terms of systems terminology, such as relative openness and the responsiveness to negative or positive feedback, are also pertinent.

Systems inputs and outputs have their internal and external relationship effects as subsystem or external system interactions occur. In addition, the situation in which activities of the family system take place changes due to the interaction of external systems with each other within the common social and physical milieu. Within the individual or family system, the personal and managerial subsystems interact to clarify meanings and direct actions toward the personal development and welfare of the individuals and of the total unit.

CONCEPTS

While the context of home management provides insight into the setting for managerial activity, the explication of the nature of any managerial activity that is observed or is anticipated needs to be done with an understanding of the concepts or components, processes, and content integral to managerial interpretation. The purpose of Part Two, Chapters 3 through 9, was to clarify basic conceptualizations underlying all managerial activity of the home regardless of the simplicity or complexity of the question or the scope of alternatives available for solution.

In keeping with the systems format, managerial components need to be identified with the particular aspect of systems that is consistent with both the systems and managerial perspectives. Inputs were identified as the goal and event demands, whether initiated internally or externally to family system, to which the management system responds and which give direction to the nature of the response. Goals were described as following from a value orientation, while events appear unexpectedly but nevertheless require considered action, often superseding responses to goals that are on the agenda before.

The other major input to the management system is resources. These were classified broadly as human and material, according to where the desired capacities or characteristics are located that can be useful in meeting the demands of a situation. In all likelihood, some combination of human and material resources is needed, and making advantageous combinations is part of the managerial problem.

Demands and resources together are, in a sense, the raw materials that give content to management. The meanings associated with values represent their content and subsequent objectives toward which goals are directed. The characteristics or properties of resources that represent their utility or potential satisfaction in utilization are the substantive elements that give content to resource considerations. The potential solutions in the use of means to meet goals are therefore contained in the inputs. The content of a management problem is essentially determined by the nature of the inputs. Meaning and means are thus the essence, the content, as reflected in the goals and resources that provide the objectives and the basis for meeting them in the transformation processes within the boundary of the managerial subsystem.

The transformation, or throughput, function of a managerial system is to plan for and implement the action deemed most likely to achieve the goals with the available means. This process is often referred to as "putting it through the system." What is meant is that the transformation process is the consideration of particular goals and resources that enter into the internal system to be evolved into appropriate plans and actions. Putting a particular question "through the system" means that planning and implementing processes will be applied specifically to the inputs.

Planning and implementing are the identified throughput processes, the managerial subsystems. Through planning, ways of meeting the goals or events are foreseen through two basic components: standard setting, whereby potential outcomes are anticipated in terms of quantitative and qualitative alternatives most nearly matching preferred results with the available resources; and sequencing, by which tasks and their parts are ordered for effective action. Standard setting and sequencing are interrelated in that standards may be affected by the sequence of actions and vice versa. Although alternative standards and alternative sequences may be considered separately, the final plan that most successfully integrates available options will have overall advantages. It is possible, however, to seek the solution that most fully serves a purpose (selecting a twenty-fifth anniversary present) regardless of the time involved or the back-tracking involved in the search. Or, the item most quickly available that will serve a purpose (perhaps put out a fire) may be the need, instead of fully weighing the standards by which the job will be done.

For both standard setting and sequencing, there are aspects that help to identify the nature of their development as plans. Clarity is an aspect that determines how specific or well defined the plan is, compared to a plan's generality. A flexible plan has a defined range within which the acceptable standards may vary or within which the order may vary. A realistic plan is one that will turn out as anticipated. A more complex plan would involve a greater interrelation of persons and scope of standards and/or sequence than one that would be described as more simple. All of these factors have influences on how well a plan can be carried out and/or how well it coincides with the established goals.

For recurring activities, planning is often simplified by determining a plan or procedure that can be called upon whenever a given situation arises. The recurrences may be daily (as with breakfast) or less often (as with mowing the lawn), but such situations would permit standing plans in terms of given standards or a given schedule or pattern of performance. Although many plans are evolved to meet special situations with no intention of reuse, plans or parts of plans once developed are a form of resource since they represent information that may be called upon to simplify related situations that arise.

Plans are a necessary prelude to the action, if achieving goals is on a better than chance basis. The degree to which the action relates to plans is partly dependent on the success of the plan and partly dependent on the degree to which the implementation is effective in insuring that the plans are followed. Through controlling, the standards and sequences that are the output of planning are adhered to or adapted appropriately. Checking and adjusting are the mechanisms through which plans are followed in the action phase.

A plan with well defined guidelines can be readily checked as to whether the order or the anticipated results are being met or can be met within the limits of flexibility that were prescribed by the plans. As actions proceed, it may be apparent that the situation has either changed or is not quite consistent with what was anticipated. In either case, the standards or sequences may need to be changed to relate more closely to the original demand or to the available resources. This is accomplished through feedback to the planning subsystem for appropriate adjustment, a process that ordinarily occurs as the action is progressing. This is why such a change is identified as an adjustment rather than as a new plan—some aspect of the plan remains in the action phase.

The facilitating component of task implementation recognizes individual and environmental conditions that promote (or conversely, inhibit) the flow of actions. A family group that likes most foods is easier to plan meals for than one that has limited likes or allergy problems. A facilitating aspect of a task is one that is ordinarily not central to plans for a given sequence of action but that affects the flow. Setting up a convenient situation for sewing can be a planning activity all its own; but once the situation is there, the planning for a sewing project is more likely to relate to how a particular garment can be cut out, put together, fit, and finished with the desired results. The work situation may have expedited the project, but the awareness of the work situation is often not consciously considered unless it is limiting.

Mechanisms for facilitating actions may be foreseen and built into a plan, such as when special future dates are circled on a calendar to jog the memory to do whatever was planned at an earlier time. Rehearsing a plan can also facilitate the flow of activity at the important time.

Because decisions are a part of every managerial component and of aspects of living beyond the scope of home management, the decision-making process has been identified as a universal one that underlies all social processes, of which management in the home is but one part. Decision processes are involved in every managerial process and function. Decisions are made about values, goals, resources, standards, and sequences, as well as in the action or implementing phase. Even as management could not exist without decision making, it is not the fact of a decision but the nature of the decision that makes it managerial. A planning decision is different from a controlling decision.

Although a planning decision is different from a controlling decision in content, the decision-making process operates in both situations. The decision-making process is basically that of recognizing the nature of the problem, identifying and weighing alternatives, and making the choice in relation to them. While this process is ordinarily identifiable, there are persons who can make decisions intuitively. These are situations where there is a comprehension of the totality of what is involved, if not a fully conscious recognition of all of its elements. These somehow meld into the overall understanding rather simultaneously so that solutions appear to be immediate.

Another concept that is universal with respect to all social process and that is necessary to managerial activities involving interpersonal relations is communication. Communication concerns the processes by which messages are transmitted from a source to a receiver. Messages about management are particular messages, but questions about what facilitates the delivery or reception of messages are communications. Recognition of the factors that promote or complicate either end of the communication process can affect the effectiveness of the managerial role where two or more persons need to receive each other's insights clearly. Barriers to either sending or receiving, such as limited interest, place constraints on the scope of a managerial question that can receive mutual attention; openness tends to contribute to expansiveness in managerial opportunities.

The result of managerial activity is represented by its outputs of met demands and used resources. The goal and event demands were identified as anticipated outcomes which, through the managerial function of planning, became expected outcomes to the extent that available resources allowed. Implementation of plans or expected outcomes lead, in turn, to actual outcomes, the output of management in a systems sense. The role of management is to bring about as close a relationship as possible of the anticipated and actual outcomes. As an open system, the end product, or output, of management is conveyed to its environment.

Met demands indicate that through managerial processes some purpose has been more closely achieved than if no management had occurred. Demands arising from goals are value based and are therefore indicative of meanings which the managerial activity is designed to fulfill or satisfy. To the extent that goals relate to basic values, their achievement may represent a high degree of satisfaction and a special sense of fulfillment. Often such basic achievements are preceded by more limited, shorter-term goals that make the longer-term accomplishment possible. All levels of achievement can carry a sense of fulfillment that is related to meanings having predominant cognitive or affective foundations, although some balance of both the more instrumental or expressive aspects are likely to be present.

Events that elicit responses to meet unanticipated demands are also able to generate a sense of achievement that is dependent on the nature of the event itself. Any such response carries meanings—perhaps of survival or surprise in seeing a special friend unexpectedly—that will yield a particular type of interpretation, depending on the situation.

Used resources, compared to met demands, may be more readily measured. While we may not be fully conscious of resources presumed to be more plentiful, those resources of which we are aware may be categorized as: *exchanging,* where something is given up for something else of compariable value; *transferring,* where something is shared voluntarily or involuntarily; *consuming and protecting,* where attributes are used up for the returns in satisfaction or risk reduction; *producing and saving-investing,* where additions to total resources are anticipated directly or indirectly, investments in human capital being part of the latter.

More than one resource use may occur in the process of meeting a demand. For example, a durable good (a stove) is consumed in part in the preparation or the production of a meal that is done for the enjoyment of consumption or for health maintenance. Uses of resources within the household often go unnoticed because they do not involve interactions with systems external to the household. But many resource reallocations occur as managerial inputs and outputs within the household.

An open system seeks to maintain itself or grow through its exchanges with the environment. This is true of family systems even though this interchange has left families and individual households more vulnerable in a number of ways. By sharing functions such as education or food processing family members have been able to grow intellectually and to enjoy a wide variety of experiences. Even so, eroding of purpose and dissipation of energies are potential hazards.

An open system's environment provides the context, while the given responses of an open system determine the content for the interchanges that take place. The degree of interchange and the direction undertaken within the available potential is affected by the feedback mechanism. For it is through the feedback mechanism that both stability and change are promoted.

Feedback reflects the relation of output to input and represents that part of output that returns as input to affect ongoing or succeeding activities of the system. Responses that support continuity and stability and are not disposed to accept deviations from anticipated outcomes indicate negative feedback influences. Responses supportive of deviations from anticipated results are illustrative of positive feedback. For a social system such as the family, it is through feedback that the unit maintains its continuity in relation to the past and makes appropriate changes in relation to the future.

Feedback may occur between the output and input of a system or subsystem. That is, within the management system, output from the implementing subsystem may become part of the input to the implementing or planning subsystem. Outputs (or information about them) of met demands or used resources may also go to the external environment of the management system within the family system to affect later demand or resource inputs of the system. The output of a met demand may, for example, return directly from the management system to the personal system and affect the value system of family members involved in or affected by the managerial activity. Output from the managerial system may, in addition, return as feedback to the family system after it has entered the environment external to the family. Information regarding interchange with another enviornmental system, perhaps with respect to a satisfactory or unsatisfactory expenditure, may return to reflect effects significant for follow-up activity.

Another source of feedback to the management system results from "nonmanaged" uses of resources that need to be acknowledged because of their effects on available resources for meeting future needs. These actions ordinarily follow from impulses to respond to an opportunity or an event without giving even cursory consideration to the relation of the response to previous plans or to the costs and possible outcomes. Routines and standing plans are not illustrative of nonmanagement because they are presumed to have originated from a managerial process.

APPLICATION

Applications of concepts of home management may take many forms, but two types of applications were illustrated in order to recognize the varied alternatives for viewing managerial problems using a systems format. Two major types of activities—financial and household—were examined first. The other applications focused on special life-cycle or resource situations—low income, young, and elderly. The nature of problems and levels of human and material resources vary greatly among and within the groups and, of course, are highly interrelated.

The complexity of home management is particularly apparent in financial affairs of families. Financial demands are partly influenced by the changing availability of goods and services and by varying aspirations rooted in changing socioeconomic conditions. Changing price levels and patterns of income distribution affect the resource expectations of families in terms of actual income or of ultimate satisfactions to be gained from its use.

Because of varying demands and resources over the life cycle and patterns of income that do not coincide with goals and needs especially at the earlier and later life-cycle stages, planning and implementing activities are the focus of financial management. The role of mechanisms such as record-keeping and budgeting in facilitating the planning and controlling process were considered. The alternatives that credit and savings provide in helping to direct lifetime income most advantageously to serve life goals are important factors in orienting throughput activities to serve longer-term purposes.

Financial management activities contribute to the lifestyle a family desires. Outcomes may be identified in the sense of accomplishment or in the financial position attained.

In comparison to financial management, household activities are more contained in location but more diffuse in ways inputs can be identified and placed into a common frame of reference for effective planning and implementing. No one resource relation can be used to give continuity and meaning to household activities. The element of time probably comes closest, but space availability and use, or implications for changes in the physical environment and in human physical capacity, are all influential inputs that interact as throughput with imprecise interrelations.

A situation can be analyzed in the standard setting and sequencing subsystems of planning from the perspective of the specificity or flexibility that is needed or the feasibility of meeting a goal in the process of implementation. The controlling and facilitating aspects of implementing provide further opportunity to direct or redirect the action in ways considered to be most advantageous. The complexity of management is an aspect affected by both the number of circumstances and persons involved in either planning or implementing.

The output from household activities provides a high portion of what is meaningful to families. The very routine nature of ongoing household activities and its diffuse character often obscure recognition of its importance to the total living pattern until a major change is introduced. This was illustrated by an example of the estimated economic loss to a family of a mother's contribution due to her premature death. Such an estimate of unavailable and unallocated resource inputs and outputs does not do justice to the meaningful, but less tangible, values foregone in unmet goals.

Differences in managerial emphasis introduced over the life cycle were further illustrated by special chapters relating to the young and the elderly. For the young, the special atttention to long-term goal formulation and to the problems of coping with early resource limitations and providing for their long-run adequacy clarifies the dependence of managerial processes on the nature of the inputs. The systems approach makes clear through these applications that the managerial potential is prescribed by the inputs. The outputs, however, are highly variable and dependent on the throughput processes in working with the available inputs.

Planning and implementing are creative aspects of management that have continuing influences on the succeeding goal and resource inputs. For young families, we discussed the interaction of child spacing and the economic position in meeting family goals. While any one managerial response is dependent on the given inputs, which are affected by the environmental situation, the self-directed, adaptive nature of an ongoing system is supportive of the idea that needed change and reorientation can be brought about by the system.

The chapter applying management to low-income situations recognized the possibility that after continual and unsuccessful coping with inadequate resources and uncontrollable events, a disinterest in or inability to respond managerially to situations may occur. This sense of futility may be rooted in circumstances other than low income; but in such instances, efforts to maintain control through longer-range planning may seem impossible when they are dissipated by unforeseen and uncontrollable situations. Reversing an entropic process before the system loses all power of response even at the maintenance level requires resources and strategically placed assistance from the external environment. The help needed may be to remove or control the source of events, to provide opportunities for obtaining needed resources, to encourage development of realistic goals, and to assist in effective planning and implementing processes that can lead to increasing success in achievement. Providing the relevant assistance for the varied problem situations that can occur requires a high degree of insight into the managerial role in strengthening the maintenance and self-actualizing potential of individuals and families.

The purpose of this book has been to contribute to managerial understanding so that the interpretation of components common to situations across the broad spectrum of possibilities and outcomes is possible. The systems approach has provided a useful format for serving this end. The systems view promotes recognition of underlying processes and the context and content of the subject—in this case, the management of individuals and families—can be comprehended as well.

Bibliographical Index

Acker, Joan. "Women and Social Stratification: A Case of Intellectual Sexism," *American Journal of Sociology,* 78 (January 1973), 174–183. **39**

Ackoff, Russell L. "Toward a System of Systems Concepts," *Management Science,* 17 (July 1971), 661–671. **7, 14**

Ackoff, Russell L., and Fred E. Emery. *On Purposeful Systems.* Chicago: Aldine-Atherton, 1972. **129, 130**

Adams, Bert N. "Isolation, Function, and Beyond: American Kinship in the 1960's," *Journal of Marriage and the Family,* 32 (November 1970), 575–597. **40**

Adamson, Martha Lanius. "Birth Expenses for Children Born Between 1968–1971 as reported by Fifty Families in Lincoln, Nebraska, 1972," University of Nebraska, M.S., 1972. **355**

Agan, Tessie, Stephan Konz, and Lucy Tormey. "Extra Heart Beats as a Measurement of Work Cost," *Home Economics Research Journal,* 1 (September 1972), 28–33. **352**

"Alcohol and Home Accidents at the Working Ages," Metropolitan Life Insurance Company, *Statistical Bulletin,* 48 (October 1967, 3–4. **299**

Aldous, Joan. "A Framework for the Analysis of Family Problem Solving," pp. 265–281 in *Family Problem Solving,* eds. Joan Aldous, Thomas Condon, Reuben Hill, Murray Straus, and Irving Tallman. Hinsdale, Ill.: The Dryden Press, Inc., 1971. **108, 109**

Aldous, Joan. "Occupational Characteristics and Males' Role Performance in the Family," *Journal of Marriage and the Family,* 31 (November 1969), 707–712. **88, 90**

Aldous, Joan. "Wives' Employment Status and Lower-Class Men as Husband-Fathers: Support for Moyihan Thesis," *Journal of Marriage and the Family,* 31 (August 1969), 469–476. **80, 81**

Aldous, Joan, and Reuben Hill. "Breaking the Poverty Cycle: Strategic Points for Intervention," *Social Work,* 14 (July 1969), 3–12. **256**

Alexis, Marcus, and Charles Z. Wilson. *Organizational Decision Making.* Englewood Cliffs, N.J.: Prentice-Hall, Inc., 1967 **111, 112, 115**

Allen, Vernon L. See Sarbin, Theodore R.

Altman, Irwin, Patricia A. Nelson, and Evelyn E. Lett. "The Ecology of Home Environments" (U.S. Dept. of Health, Education, and Welfare Final Report, Project No. 0-0502. Washington, D.C.: U.S. Government Printing Office, 1972. **326**

Anderson, Barbara Gallatin. See Clark, Margaret.

Andrews, R. B. "The Additivity of Values of Energy Expenditure of Simultaneously Performed Simple Muscular Tasks," *Ergonomics,* 9 (September 1966), 507–515. **303**

Andrews, Robert B. "The Relationship Between Measures of Heart Rate and Rate of Energy Expenditure," *American Institute of Industrial Engineers Transactions,* 1 (March 1969), 2–10. **342**

Annett, John. *Feedback and Human Behavior.* Baltimore, Md.: Penguin Books, 1969. **235**

Arons, Stephen. "Compulsory Education," *Saturday Review,* 55 (January 15, 1972), 52–57. **140**

Ater, E. Carolyn, and Ruth E. Deacon. "Interaction of Family Relationship Qualities and Managerial Components," *Journal of Marriage and the Family,* 34 (May 1972), 257–263. **187, 188, 225, 312**

Ayers, R. U. See Kneese, Allen V.

Babin, Harriet Salome. "Four Dimensions of Ten Decisions Made by Rural Families," Lousiana State University, M.S., 1971. **123**

Baer, William G. See Wilner, David M.

Baerwaldt, Nancy A., and James N. Morgan. "Trends in Inter-Family Transfers," pp. 205–232 in *Surveys of Consumers 1971–72,* eds. Lewis Mandell, George Katona, James N. Morgan, and Jay Schmiedeskamp. Ann Arbor, Mich.: Institute for Social Research, The University of Michigan, 1973. **319**

Baerwaldt, Nancy. See Morgan, James N.

Barclay, Nancy A. "Decision-Making by Students in the Home Management Residence Course," Pennsylvania State University, M.S., 1963. **110, 116**

Barclay, Nancy Ann. "Organization of Household Activities by Home Managers," The Ohio State University, Ph.D., 1970. **81, 82, 188, 215, 216**

Bardwell, Ann Skinner. "Resource Use of Low-Income Families and its Relationship to Family Patterns of Adjustment to Chronic Maternal Illness," The Ohio State University, Ph.D., 1968. **231**

Bardwell, Ann S. See Deacon, Ruth E.

Barfield, Richard, and James Morgan. *Early Retirement: The Decision and the Experience.* Ann Arbor, Mich.: Institute for Social Research, The University of Michigan, 1969. **394**

Barlow, Robin, Harvey E. Brazer, and James N. Morgan. *Economic Behavior of the Affluent.* Washinton, D.C.: The Brookings Institution, 1966. **286**

Baron, Robert Alex. *The Tyranny of Noise.* New York: St Martin's Press, 1970. **334**

Barrett, James H. *Gerontological Psychology.* Springfield, Ill.: Charles C. Thomas Publisher, 1972. **386**

Bastian, Beverly E. See Hawkes, Glenn R.

Bean, Nancy M. "Decision Class, Linkage, and Sequence in One Central-Satellite Decision Complex: Students' Summer Occupational Choice," Michigan State University, M.S., 1968. **124**

Becker, Gary. "An Economic Analysis of Fertility," pp. 209–240 in National Bureau of Economic Research, *Demographic and Economic Change in Developed Countries.* Princeton, N.J.: Princeton University Press, 1960. **71**

Belding, Harwood S. See Kamon, Eliezer.

Bell, Carolyn Shaw. *The Economics of the Ghetto.* New York: Pegasus, 1970. **380, 382**

Berelson, Bernard, and Gary A. Steiner. *Human Behavior.* New York: Harcourt, Brace & World, Inc., 1964. **38, 40**

Berger, R. M., J. P. Guilford, and P. R. Christensen. "A Factor-analytic Study of Planning Abilities," *Psychological Monographs,* 71 (Whole No. 435), 1957. **177, 179**

Berrien, Kenneth F. *General and Social Systems.* New Brunswick, N.J.: Rutgers University Press, 1968. **14**

Besner, Arthur. "Economic Deprivation and Family Patterns," pp. 15–19 in *Low-Income Life Styles,* ed. Lola M. Irelan (U.S. Dept. of Health, Education, and Welfare, Welfare Administration Publication No. 14). Washington, D.C.: U.S. Government Printing Office, 1968. **371**

Besner, Arthur. See Irelan, Lola M.

Bharadwaj, Lakshmi K. See Wildening, Eugene A.

Bienvenu, Millard J., Sr. "Measurement of Marital Communication," *The Family Coordinator,* 19 (January 1970), 26–31. **131**

Birren, James E. "Age and Decision Strategies," pp. 23–36 in *Decision Making and Age,* eds. A. T. Welford and James E. Birren. New York: S. Karger, 1969. **387**

Blackwell, Roger D. See Kollat, David T.

Blake, Judith. "Income and Reproductive Motivation," *Population Studies,* 21 (November 1967), 185–206. **72, 84**

Bland, Frankye E. See Mize, Jessie J.

Block, Carol E. "Prepurchase Search Behavior of Low-Income House-holds," *Journal of Retailing,* 48 (Spring 1972), 3–15. **379, 380**

Blood, Robert O., Jr. *The Family.* New York: Free Press, 1972. **351**

Blood, Robert O., Jr., and D. M. Wolfe. *Husbands and Wives: The Dynamics of Married Living.* Glencoe, Ill.: The Free Press, 1960. **125, 358**

Blood, Robert O., Jr., and Reuben Hill. "Comparative Analysis of Family Power Structure: Problems of Measurement and Interpretation," pp. 526–535 in *Families in East and West,* eds. Reuben Hill and Rene Konig. The Hague: Mouton & Co., 1970. **125**

Bloom, Benjamin S., and a Committee of College and University Ex-aminers. *A Taxonomy of Educational Objectives: Handbook I: The Cognitive Domain.* New York: David McKay, 1956. **147**

Bloom, Benjamin S. See Krathwohl, David R.

Bloomfield, Byron C., and Donald C. Hay. "The Auditory Environment in the Home," Research Report for Koss Electronics., Inc., Mil-waukee, Wis., 1971. **336**

Bombeck, Erma. "Life Isn't Simple Any More," *Columbus (Ohio) Dispatch,* April 5, 1972. **106**

Bonno, John A. See Boone, Louis E.

Boone, Louis E., and John A. Bonno. "Food Buying Habits of the Urban Poor," *Journal of Retailing,* 47 (Fall 1971), 79–84. **382**

Boulding, Kenneth E. *Economics as a Science.* New York: McGraw-Hill Book Company, 1970. **52**

Boulding, Kenneth E. "The Economics of the Coming Spaceship Earth," pp. 3–20 in *Environmental Quality in a Growing Economy,* ed. H. Jar-rett. Baltimore, Md.: The Johns Hopkins University Press, 1966. **17**

Boulding, Kenneth E. "The Ethics of Rational Decision," *Management Science,* 12 (February 1966), B-161–B-169. **158**

Brackett, Jean. "Urban Family Budgets Updated to Autumn 1972," *Monthly Labor Review,* 96 (August 1973), 70–76. **270, 271**

Bradburn, Norman M. See Orden, Susan R.

Bradfield, Robert B., Patricia B. Huntzicker, and George J. Fruehan. "Simultaneous Comparison of Respirometer and Heart-Rate Tele-metry Techniques as Measures of Human Energy Expenditure," *The American Journal of Clinical Nutrition,* 22 (June 1969), 696–700. **343**

Bragdon, Clifford R. *Noise Pollution, The Unquiet Crisis.* Philadelphia: The University of Pennsylvania Press, Inc., 1971. **334, 335, 337**

Bratton, Esther Crew. See Steidl, Rose E. *Work in the Home.* New York: John Wiley & Sons, Inc. 1968.

Brazer, Harvey E. See Barlow, Robin.

Brix, V. H. *You Are A Computer: Cybernetics in Everyday Life*. New York: Emerson Books, Inc., 1970. **175, 181**

Broadbent, D. E. *Decision and Stress*. London: Academic Press, 1971. **307**

Brown, Kathleen H. "Social Class as an Independent Variable in Family Economics Research," *Journal of Consumer Affairs*, 3 (Winter 1969), 127–136. **93**

Buchbinder, Laura Baker. "Human Activity Patterns and Injury Severity in Fire Accidents Involving Apparel," *Journal of Fire and Flammability/Consumer Products* 1: (March 1974), H-18 **388**

Buckley, Walter. *Sociology and Modern Systems Theory*. Englewood Cliffs, N.J.: Prentice-Hall, Inc., 1967. **9, 10, 11, 14, 233, 235**

Buechner, Helmut K. See Ripley, S. Dillon

Burenstam Linder, Staffan. *The Harried Leisure Class*. New York: Columbia University Press, 1970. **19, 175, 227**

Burk, Marguerite C. "On the Need for Investment in Human Capital for Consumption," *Journal of Consumer Affairs*, 1 (Winter 1967), 123–138. **161**

Burr, Wesley R. "Satisfaction with Various Aspects of Marriage Over the Life Cycle: A Random Middle Class Sample," *Journal of Marriage and the Family*, 32 (February 1970), 29–37. **287, 313**

Bymers, Gwen J., and Mabel A. Rollins. "Classification Systems: Household Expenditures Data and Household Accounts" (Bulletin 1014). Ithaca, N.Y.: Cornell University Agricultural Experiment Station, 1967. **159, 227, 278, 279**

Bymers, Gwen J., and Marjorie Galenson. "Time Horizons in Family Spending—A Study of Household Investment," *Journal of Home Economics*, 60 (November 1968), 709–716. **227, 290**

Callahan, Sidney Cornelia. *The Working Mother*. New York: The Macmillan Company, 1971. **212, 217, 323**

Campbell, Frederick L. "Family Growth and Variation in Family Role Structure," *Journal of Marriage and the Family*, 32 (February 1970), 45–53. **72, 73, 96**

Campbell, Peter. "Maternity Costs." New York: Institute of Life Insurance, 1971, mimeo. **355, 356**

Cardozo, Richard N. See Holloway, Robert J.

Carolson, John. See Nye, Ivan F.

Carp, Frances M. "The Mobility of Older Slum-Dwellers," *The Gerontologist*, 12 (Spring 1972), 57–65. **391**

Carrin, Guy. See Schulz, James H.

Centers, Richard, and Bertram H. Raven. "Conjugal Power Structure: A Re-Examination," *American Sociological Review*, 36 (April 1971),

264–278. **90**

Chapin, F. Stuart, Jr. "Activity Systems and Urban Structure: A Working Schema," *Journal of American Institute of Planners,* 34 (January 1968), 11–18. **312**

Christensen, Harold T. "Children in the Family: Relationship of Number and Spacing to Marital Success," *Journal of Marriage and the Family,* 30 (May 1968), 283–289. **359, 360**

Christensen, P. R. See Berger, R. M.

Churchman, C. West. *The Systems Approach.* New York: Delacorte Press, 1968. **5, 14, 157, 217**

Clark, Alma Beth, and Jean Warren. "Economic Contributions Made to Newly Married Couples by Their Parents" (Memoir 382). Ithaca, N.Y.: Cornell University Agricultural Experiment Station, 1963. **351**

Clark, Margaret, and Barbara Gallatin Anderson. *Culture and Aging.* Springfield, Ill.: Charles C. Thomas Publisher, 1967. **385, 386**

Cleland, David I., and William R. King. *Management: A Systems Approach.* New York: McGraw-Hill Book Company, 1972. **112**

Cohen, Jacob. See Lawton, M. Powell.

Coleman, Richard P. See Rainwater, Lee.

Coles, Robert. "Like It is in the Alley," pp. 126–138, in *Life at the Bottom,* ed. Gregory Armstrong. New York: A Bantam Book, 1971. **78**

Collette, John. See Ludwig, Edward G.

Consumer Product Safety Commission, Bureau of Epidemiology. "Fiscal Year 1973 Tabulation of Data from National Electronic Injury Surveillance System (NEISS), July 1, 1972–June 30, 1973." **298**

Coombs, Lolagene C., and Ronald Freedman. "Pre-marital Pregnancy, Childspacing, and Later Economic Achievement," *Population Studies,* 24 (November 1970), 389–412. **362, 363**

Coombs, Lolagene C., Ronald Freedman, Judith Friedman, and William F. Pratt. "Premarital Pregnancy and Status Before and After Marriage," *American Journal of Sociology,* 75 (March 1970), 800–819. **362**

Coombs, Lolagene C., and Zena Zumeta. "Correlates of Marital Dissolution in a Prospective Fertility Study: A Research Note," Appendix F of "Social and Economic Correlates of Family Building Patterns in Detroit," Research Report of Social Security Administration, Grant No. 312(2)-7-248 (March 1970). **360**

Coombs, Lolagene. See Freedman, Ronald.

Costigan, Robert. See Nord, Walter R.

Cowgill, Donald O., and Lowell D. Holmes. "Summary and Conclusions: The Theory in Review," pp. 305–323 in *Aging and Modernization,* eds. Donald O. Cowgill and Lowell D. Holmes. New York:

Appleton-Century-Crofts, 1972. **399**

Cox, Irene. See Storey, James R.

Crain, Alan J., Marvin Sussman, and William B. Weil. "Effects of a Diabetic Child on Marital Integration and Related Measures of Family Functioning," *Journal of Health and Human Behavior,* 7 (Summer 1966), 122–127. **75**

Crandall, Elizabeth W. "Conceptual Framework I: The Three-Step Managerial Process," pp. 17–34 in *Conceptual Frameworks: Process of Home Management,* Proceedings of a Home Management Conference. Washington, D.C.: American Home Economics Association, 1964. **60**

Crandall, Elizabeth W. See Gross, Irma H.

Croog, Sydney H., Alberta Lipson, and Sol Levine. "Help Patterns in Severe Illness: The Roles of Kin Network, Non-Family Resources, and Institutions," *Journal of Marriage and the Family,* 34 (February 1972), 32–41. **228**

Crosby, Kristan Rinker. "Perceived Levels of Living and Family Welfare," The Ohio State University, M.S., 1970. **244**

Curtis, Russell L., Jr., and Louis A. Zurcher, Jr. "Voluntary Associations and the Social Integration of the Poor," *Social Problems,* 18 (Winter 1971), 339–357. **373**

Cushman, Ella M. *Management in Homes.* New York: The Macmillan Company, 1945. **139**

Dale, Verda M. "An Exploration of the Relationship of Home Managers' Self-Actualization to Participation by Family Members in Home Activities," Michigan State University, Ph.D., 1968. **81**

D'Arge, Ralph C. See Kneese, Allen V.

Davey, Alice J. "Relationship of Family Interaction to Family Environment," Michigan State University, Ph.D., 1971. **132**

Davidson, Maria. "Social and Economic Variations in Childspacing," *Social Biology,* 17 (June 1970), 107–113. **354**

Davis, Joseph M. "Impact of Health on Earnings and Labor Market Activity," *Monthly Labor Review,* 95 (October 1972), 46–49. **371**

Dawson, Judith A. "An Exploratory Study of Long-Range Planning by Families," The Pennsylvania State University, M.S. 1970. **170, 171**

Deacon, Ruth E. "The Economic Progress Since Marriage of Ohio Families Farming Full-Time in 1958" (Research Bulletin 902). Wooster, Ohio: Ohio Agricultural Experiment Station, 1962. **350**

Deacon, Ruth E. "Toward a Philosophy of Home Management," speech, Oregon State University, Corvallis, Oregon, January 24, 1966. **7**

Deacon, Ruth E., and Janet A. Krofta. "Economic Progress of Rural Nonfarm and Part-time Farm Families" (Research Bulletin 976). Wooster, Ohio: Ohio Agricultural Research and Development Center, 1965. **278, 350**

Deacon, Ruth E., Francille Maloch, and Ann S. Bardwell. "Relationship of Maternal Health to Family Solidarity Among Low-Income Families in 28 Appalachian Counties" (The Ohio State University Research Foundation Project 2072). Columbus, Ohio: The Ohio State University School of Home Economics, 1967. **76**

Deacon, Ruth E. See Ater, E. Carolyn

Deacon, Ruth E. See Maloch, Francille. "Components . . ."

Deacon, Ruth E. See Maloch, Francille. ". . . Framework . . ."

Deacon, Ruth E. See Meeks, Carol B.

Dechert, Charles R. "The Development of Cybernetics," *The American Behavioral Scientist,* 8 (June 1965), 15–20. **5, 7**

de Jesus, Carolina Maria. *Child of the Dark.* New York: E. P. Dutton & Co., Inc., 1962. **176**

Dhesi, Jagjit Kaur, and Francille Maloch Firebaugh. "The Effects of Stages of Chapati-Making and Angles of Body Position on Heart Rate," *Ergonomics,* 16 (November 1973), 811–815. **344, 345**

Dickerscheid, Jean Dearth. "Development of a Method of Measuring the Effects of a Preschool Child on the Mother's Heart Rate," The Ohio State University, Ph.D., 1967. **305**

Diesing, Paul. *Reason in Society.* Urbana, Ill.: University of Illinois Press, 1962. **120, 122, 161, 163**

Dorsey, Jean Muir. See Nickell, Paulena.

Downer, Donna Beth, Ruth H. Smith, and Mildred T. Lynch. "Values and Housing—A New Dimension," *Journal of Home Economics,* 60 (March 1968), 173–176. **99**

Downer, Donna Beth. See Smith, Ruth H.

Dreher, Gernet. See Lehr, Ursula.

Driver, Michael J. See Schroder, Harold M.

Duff, Raymond S., and August B. Hollingshead. *Sickness and Society.* New York: Harper & Row, Publishers, 1968. **74, 75**

Dunkelberg, W. See Katona, George.

Dunsing, Marilyn. See Schnittgrund, Karen.

Dunsing, Marilyn M. See Hafstrom, Jeanne L.

Duvall, Evelyn M. *Family Development.* Philadelphia: J. B. Lippincott Company, 1971. **67**

Easterlin, Richard A. "Relative Economic Status and the American Fertility Swing," in *Family Economic Behavior,* ed. Eleanor Bernert Sheldon (Philadelphia: J. B. Lippincott Co., 1973), p. 215. **354**

Easton, David. *A Framework for Political Analysis*. Englewood Cliffs, N.J.: Prentice-Hall, Inc., 1965. **24**

Edwards, John N., and David L. Klemmack. "Correlates of Life Satisfaction: A Re-examination," *Journal of Gerontology*, 28 (October 1973), 497–502. **397**

Ehrenkranz, Florence. "Functional Convenience of Kitchens with Different Sink-Dishwasher Locations," *Journal of Home Economics*, 57 (November 1965), 711–716. **331**

Eilon, Samuel. "What Is a Decision?" *Management Science*, 16 (December 1969), B172-B-189. **112**

Eisenman, Russell, and Diane J. Foxman. "Creativity: Reported Family Patterns and Scoring Methodology," *Psychological Reports*, 26 (April 1970), 615–621. **177**

Elliot, Doris E., and Mary Brown Patton. "Manual Techniques Used in Determining Human Energy Expenditures" (Research Circular 121). Wooster, Ohio: Ohio Agricultural Experiment Station, 1963. **341**

Elliot, Doris E., Mary Brown Patton, and Mary Edna Singer. "Energy Expenditures of Women Performing Household Tasks" (Bulletin 939). Wooster, Ohio: Ohio Agricultural Experiment Station, 1963. **304**

Emery, Fred E. See Ackoff, Russell L.

Engel, James F. See Kollat, David T.

Erdoes, Richard. "My Travels with Medicine Man John Lame Deer," *Smithsonian*, 4 (May 1973), 30–38. **141**

Eschenbrenner, A. John, Jr. "Effects of Intermittent Noise on the Performance of a Complex Psychomotor Task," *Human Factors*, 13 (February 1971), 59–63. **334, 335**

Ettema, J. H., and R. L. Zielhuis. "Physiological Parameters of Mental Load," *Ergonomics*, 14 (January 1971), 137–144. **316**

Evans, Richard H., and Norman R. Smith. "A Selected Paradigm of Family Behavior," *Journal of Marriage and the Family*, 31 (August 1969), 512–517. **93**

Fagen, R. E. See Hall, A. D.

Farr, Lee E. "Medical Consequences of Environmental Home Noises," *The Journal of the American Medical Association*, 202 (October 16, 1967), 171–174. **337**

Feldman, Harold. See Meyerowitz, Joseph H.

Ferber, Robert, and Lucy Chao Lee. "Husband-Wife Influence in Family Purchasing Behavior," *The Journal of Consumer Research*, 1 (June 1974), 43–50. **126**

Firebaugh, Francille M., John Woodward, and Ron Daly. "Factors Affecting Value Orientations of Low-Income Mothers." (Submitted for publication, 1974). **377**

Firebaugh, Francille M. See Dhesi, Jagjit Kaur.

Firebaugh, Francille M. See Parker, Marianne.

Firebaugh, Francille M. See Ronald, Patricia Y.

Fitchen, Janet M. "The People of Road Junction: The Participant Observer's Study of a Rural Poverty Area in Northern Appalachia, with Particular Reference to the Problems of Employment of Low Income Women," pp. 1–121 in *A Study of the Effects on the Family Due to Employment of the Welfare Mother,* Vol. III, Report to Manpower Administration, U.S. Dept. of Labor (n.d.). **211, 375, 376, 377**

Fitzsimmons, Cleo, Dorothy A. Larery, and Edward J. Metzen. "Major Financial Decisions and Crises in the Family Life Span" (North Central Regional Research Publication No. 208). Lafayette, Ind.: Purdue University Agricultural Experiment Station, 1971. **66, 67, 126, 153, 254, 348, 353, 387, 388**

Fletcher, Joseph. *Moral Responsibility.* Philadelphia: The Westminster Press, 1967. **140**

Fowler, Evelyn Sue. "Factors Related to the Economic Well-being of the Family," Purdue University, Ph. D., 1972. **243**

Fox, Edward L. See Mathews, Donald K.

Foxman, Deane J. See Eisenman, Russell

Freedman, Ronald, and Lolagene Coombs. "Childspacing and Family Economic Position," *American Sociological Review,* 31 (October 1966), 631–648. **73, 361, 362**

Freedman, Ronald, and Lolagene Coombs. "Economic Considerations in Family Growth Decisions," *Population Studies,* 20 (November 1966), 197–222. **353, 354**

Freedman, Ronald. See Coombs, Lolagene C. (March 1970)

Freedman, Ronald. See Coombs, Lolagene C. (Nov. 1970)

Friedland, William H., and Dorothy Nelkin. *Migrant Agricultural Workers in America's Northeast.* New York: Holt, Rinehart and Winston, 1971. **374**

Friedman, Judith. See Coombs, Lolagene C.

Friedman, Lucy N. See Glass, David C.

Fruehan, George J. See Bradfield, Robert B.

Fuchs, Victor R. "Toward a Theory of Poverty," pp. 69–91 in *The Concept of Poverty* (Chamber of Commerce of the United States Task Force on Economic Growth and Opportunity). Washington, D.C.: Chamber of Commerce of the United States, 1965. **251**

Galanter, E. See Miller, George A.

Galbraith, John Kenneth. *The Affluent Society.* Boston: Houghton Mifflin Co., 1958. **30**

Galenson, Marjorie. See Bymers, Gwen J.

Garfinkel, Irwin "The New Jersey Income Maintenance Experiment," *Journal of Consumer Affairs,* 6 (Summer 1972), 1–11 **29**

Garland, T. Neal. See Poloma, Margaret M.

Garrett, Gerald. See Nye, Ivan F.

Gauger, William H. See Walker, Kathryn E.

Geismar, Ludwig L. *555 Families.* New Brunswick, N.J.: Transaction Books, 1973. **357, 358**

Gibson, Geoffrey. "Kin Family Network: Overheralded Structure in Past Conceptualizations of Family Functioning," *Journal of Marriage and the Family,* (February 1972), 13–23. **391**

Glass, David C., Jerome E. Singer, and Lucy N. Friedman. "Psychic Cost of Adaptation to an Environmental Stressor," *Journal of Personality and Social Psychology,* 12 (July 1969), 200–210. **338**

Gognalona-Caillard, Maryvonne. See Markson, Elizabeth W.

Goldman, Stanford. "Social Aging, Disorganization, and Loss of Choice," *The Gerontologist,* 11 (Summer 1971), 158–162. **393**

Goodman, Charles S. "Do the Poor Pay More?" *Journal of Marketing,* 32 (January 1968), 18–24. **381**

Goodman, Mary Ellen. *The Individual and Culture.* Homewood, Ill.: The Dorsey Press, Inc., 1967. **37**

Goodwin, Leonard. *Do the Poor Want to Work?"* Washington, D.C.: The Brookings Institution, 1972. **374**

Gotshalk, D.W. *Patterns of Good and Evil.* Urbana, Ill.: University of Illinois Press, 1963. **145**

Gough, Harrison, and Alfred B. Heilbrun. *The Adjective Check List Manual.* Palo Alto, Cal.: Consulting Psychologists Press, 1965. **81**

Grandjean, E. "Fatigue: Its Physiological and Psychological Significance," *Ergonomics,* 11 (September 1968), 427–436. **315**

Green, Gloria P. "Relative Importance of CPI Items," *Monthly Labor Review,* 88 (November 1965), 1346–1349. **37**

Grieve, June I. "Daily Activities of Housewives with Young Children and Estimation of Energy Expenditures," *Ergonomics,* 10 (January 1967), 25–33. **360**

Grieve, June I. "Heart Rate and Daily Activities of Housewives with Young Children," *Ergonomics,* 15 (March 1972), 139–146. **305**

Griffiths, Martha. See Jordan, Barbara.

Groom, Phyllis. "Prices in Poor Neighborhoods," *Monthly Labor Review,* 89

(October 1966), 1085–1090. **381**

Gross, Irma H., and Elizabeth W. Crandall. *Management for Modern Families.* New York: Appleton-Century-Crofts, 1963. **235**

Gross, Irma H., Elizabeth W. Crandall, and Marjorie M. Knoll. *Management for Modern Families.* New York: Appleton-Century-Crofts, 1973. **235**

Gross, Irma H. See Van Bortel, Dorothy Greey.

Gubrium, Jaber F. "Toward a Socio-Environmental Theory of Aging," *The Gerontologist,* 12 (Autumn 1972, Part 1), 281–284. **388, 396**

Guilford, J. P. "Intellectual Aspects of Decision Making," pp. 82–102 in *Decision Making and Age,* eds. A. T. Welford and James E. Birren. Basel, Switzerland: S. Karger, 1969. **396**

Guilford, J. P., R. M. Berger, and P. R. Christensen. "A Factor-analytic Study of Planning" (Reports from the Psychological Laboratory, No. 12). Los Angeles: University of Southern California, 1955. **177**

Guilford, J. P. See Berger, R. M.

Guilford, Joan S. "Prediction of Accidents in a Standardized Home Environment," *Journal of Applied Psychology,* 57 (June 1973), 306–313. **297, 299**

Hafstrom, Jeanne L., and Marilyn M. Dunsing. "Satisfaction and Education: A New Approach to Understanding Consumption Patterns," *Home Economics Research Journal,* 1 (September 1972), 4–12. **289**

Hafstrom, Jeanne. See Schnittgrund, Karen.

Hahn, Gerald J. "Evaluation of a Decision Based on Subjective Probability Estimates," *IEEE Transactions on Engineering Management,* EM-18 (February 1971), 12–16. **113**

Hahn, Julia Mae Schriver. "Families' Control of the Allocation of Financial Resources for the College Education of Their Children," The Pennsylvania State University, M.S., 1968. **204**

Hall, A. D., and R. E. Fagen. "Definition of Systems, *General Systems,* 1 (1956), 18–28. **14**

Hall, Douglas T. "A Model of Coping with Role Conflict: The Role Behavior of College Educated Women;" *Administrative Science Quarterly,* 17 (December 1972), 471–486. **41**

Hall, Edward T. "Proxemics and Design," *Design & Environment,* 2 (Winter 1971), 24–25, 58. **326**

Hall, Edward T. *The Hidden Dimension.* Garden City, N.Y.: Doubleday & Company, Inc., 1966. **131, 327, 339**

Halliday, Jean R. "Relationships Among Certain Characteristics of a Decision Event: Decision Procedure, Decision Context, and Decision-Maker," Michigan State University, Ph.D., 1964. **111**

Handel, Gerald. See Rainwater, Lee.

Hansen, Donald A., and Reuben Hill. "Families Under Stress," pp. 782–819 in *Handbook of Marriage and the Family,* ed. Harold T. Christensen. Chicago: Rand McNally & Company, 1964. **157**

Hausman, Leonard J., and Hirschel Kasper. "The Work Effort Response of Women to Income Maintenance," pp. 89–104 in *Income Maintenance,* eds. Larry L. Orr, Robinson G. Hollister, and Myron J. Lefcowitz. Chicago: Markham Publishing Co., 1971. **368**

Havas, Nick, and Hugh M. Smith. "Customers' Shopping Patterns in Retail Food Stores" (U.S. Dept. of Agriculture, Economic Research Service, Marketing Economics Division ERS-99). Washington, D.C.: U.S. Government Printing Office, 1962. **207**

Havelock, Ronald G. *Planning for Innovation.* Ann Arbor, Mich.: Institute for Social Research, The University of Michigan, 1969. **127, 128, 129, 130, 135, 136**

Havelock, Ronald G. *Planning for Innovation through Dissemination and Utilization of Knowledge.* Ann Arbor, Mich.: Institute for Social Research, The University of Michigan, 1971. **10**

Hawkes, Glenn R., Minna Taylor, and Beverly E. Bastian. "Patterns of Living in California's Migrant Labor Families" (Research Monograph No. 12). Davis, Calif.: Dept. of Applied Behavioral Sciences, University of California, 1973. **369**

Hay, Donald C. See Bloomfield, Byron C.

Hayghe, Howard. "Labor Force Activity of Married Women," *Monthly Labor Review,* 96 (April 1973), 31–36. **34, 35**

Haynes, B. C., Jr. See Simons, J. W.

Hedgepeth, William, and Dennis Stock. *The Alternative: Communal Life in New America.* New York: The Macmillan Company, 1970. **149, 189**

Heidbreder, Elizabeth M. "Factors in Retirement Adjustment: White-Collar/Blue-Collar Experience," *Industrial Gerontology* (Winter 1972), pp. 69–79. **394**

Heidbreder, Elizabeth M. "Pensions and the Single Woman," *Industrial Gerontology* (Fall 1972), pp. 52–62. **390**

Heilbrum, Alfred B. See Gough, Harrison.

Helfrich, Margaret L. *The Social Role of the Executive's Wife* (Monograph No. 123). Columbus, Ohio: Bureau of Business Research, The Ohio State University, 1965. **89**

Helfrich, Margaret L., and Barbara J. Tootle. "Economic Profile of the American Business Executive," *Bulletin of Business Research,* 46 (November 1971), 4–7. **89**

Henderson, James Mitchell, and Richard E. Quandt. *Micro-economic Theory.* New York: McGraw-Hill Book Company, 1971. **42**

Henricks, G. See Katona, George.

Herman, Mary W. "The Poor: Their Medical Needs and the Health Services Available to Them," *The Annals of the American Academy of Political and Social Science,* 399 (January 1972), 12–21. **381**

Herrmann, Robert O. "Expectations and Attitudes as a Source of Financial Problems in Teen-age Marriages," *Journal of Marriage and the Family,* 27 (February 1965), 89–91. **349**

Hill, Reuben. "Decision Making and the Family Life Cycle," pp. 113–141 in *Social Structure and the Family: Generational Relations,* eds. Ethel Shanas and Gordon F. Streib. Englewood Cliffs, N.J.: Prentice-Hall, Inc., 1963. **66**

Hill, Reuben. *Family Development in Three Generations.* Cambridge, Mass.: Schenkman Publishing Co., Inc., 1970 **131, 170, 171, 173, 174, 212, 213, 217, 233, 254, 255, 282, 283, 284, 350, 361, 390**

Hill, Reuben. "Judgment and Consumership in the Management of Family Resources," *Sociology and Social Research,* 47 (July 1963), 446–460. **86**

Hill, Reuben. "Modern Systems Theory and the Family: A Confrontation," *Social Science Information,* 10 (October 1971), 7–26. **7**

Hill, Reuben. See Aldous, Joan.

Hill, Reuben. See Blood, Robert O., Jr.

Hill, Reuben. See Hansen, Donald A.

Hill, Reuben. See Silverman, William.

Hobbs, Daniel F., Jr. Parenthood As Crisis: A Third Study," *Journal of Marriage and the Family,* 27 (August 1965), 367–372. **68, 348, 349**

Hobbs, Daniel F., Jr. "Transition to Parenthood: A Replication and an Extension," *Journal of Marriage and the Family,* 30 (August 1968), 413–417. **351**

Hollingshead, August B. "A Two-Factor Index of Social Position." New Haven, Conn.: Hollingshead, 1957. **92**

Hollingshead, August B. See Duff, Raymond S.

Holloway, Robert J., and Richard N. Cardozo. "Consumer Problems and Marketing Patterns in Low-Income Neighborhoods: An Exploratory Study." Minneapolis, Minn.: University of Minnesota, 1969. **378**

Holmes, Emma G. "Estimating Net Income of Working Wives," *Family Economics Review,* ARS 62–5 (March 1962), 3–5. **325**

Holmes, Emma G. "Job-Related Expenditures and Management Practices of Gainfully Employed Wives in Ohio" (U.S. Dept. of Agriculture, Agricultural Research Service, Home Economics Research Report 27). Washington, D.C.: U.S. Government Printing Office, 1965. **320, 323**

Holmes, Lowell D. See Cowgill, Donald O.

Holmstrom, Lynda Lytle. *The Two-Career Family*. Cambridge, Mass.: Schenkman Publishing Company, 1972. **184**

Hook, Nancy C., and Beatrice Paolucci. "The Family as an Ecosystem," *Journal of Home Economics*, 62 (May 1970), 315–318. **20**

Houriet, Robert. *Getting Back Together*. New York: Coward, McCann & Geoghegan, Inc., 1971. **128, 131**

House, James S. See Laumann, Edward O.

Howe, Leland W. "Group Dynamics and Value Clarification," *Penneys Forum*, (Spring/Summer 1972). **20**

Huber, Milton J. "Installment Credit Problems Among Public Welfare Recipients," *Journal of Consumer Affairs*, 1 (Summer 1967), 89–97. **370**

Hueting, J. E., and H. R. Sarphati. "Measuring Fatigue," *Journal of Applied Psychology*, 50 (December 1966), 535–538. **315**

Hungerford, Nancy I. "An Approach to the Study of Managerial Control," Cornell University, M.S., 1970. **214, 218**

Hunt, G. M. See Rusk, Howard.

Hunter, Woodrow W. "A Longitudinal Study of Preretirement Education" (Department of Health, Education, and Welfare, Welfare Administration, Research Grants Branch Project #151). Ann Arbor, Mich.: The University of Michigan, 1968. **395, 396**

Huntzicker, Patricia. See Bradfield, Robert B.

Huth, Tom. "30,000 a Year 'Permits' Dissatisfaction," *The Washington Post* (May 13, 1973). **147**

Hyman, Herbert H., and Charles R. Wright. "Trends in Voluntary Association Memberships of American Adults: Replication Based on Secondary Analysis of National Sample Surveys," *American Sociological Review*, 36 (April 1971), 191–206. **94**

Indik, Bernard P. See Sternlieb, George S.

Irelan, Lola M., and Arthur Besner. "Low-Income Outlook on Life," pp. 1–12 in *Low-Income Life Styles*, ed. Lola M. Irelan (U.S. Dept. of Health, Education, and Welfare, Welfare Administration Publication No. 14). Washington, D.C.: U.S. Government Printing Office, 1968. **151, 376**

Jaeger, Carol. See Pennock, Jean L.

Jeffers, Camille. *Living Poor*. Ann Arbor, Mich.: Ann Arbor Publishers, 1967. **98**

Johnson, Richard A., Fremont E. Kast, and James E. Rosenzweig. *The Theory and Management of Systems*. New York: McGraw-Hill Book Company, Inc., 1963. **184**

Jordan, Barbara, and Martha Griffiths. Bills H. R. 12645 and 12646, introduced to the U.S. House of Representatives, 93rd Congress, 2nd Session, February 6, 1974. **319**

Judson, J. S. See Rusk, Howard.

Kahn, R. L. See Katz, D.

Kamon, Eliezer, and Harwood S. Belding. "The Physiological Cost of Carrying Loads in Temperate and Hot Environments," *Human Factors,* 13 (April 1971), 153–161. **306**

Kasper, Herschel. See Hausman, Leonard J.

Kassarjian, Harold H. "Personality and Consumer Behavior: A Review," *Journal of Marketing Research,* 8 (November 1971), 409–418. **83**

Kast, Fremont E., and James E. Rosenzweig. "General Systems Theory: Applications for Organization and Management," *Academy of Management Journal,* 15 (December 1972), 447–468. **9, 14**

Kast, Fremont E., and James E. Rosenzweig. *Organization and Management, A Systems Approach.* New York: McGraw-Hill Book Company, 1970. **119, 168, 173**

Kast, Fremont E. See Johnson, Richard A.

Katona, George. *The Mass Consumption Society.* New York: McGraw-Hill Book Company, Inc., 1964. **170, 243**

Katona, George, W. Dunkelberg, G. Henricks, and Jay Schmiedeskamp. *1969 Survey of Consumer Finances.* Ann Arbor, Mich.: Institute for Social Research, The University of Michigan, 1970. **382**

Katona, George, Lewis Mandell, and Jay Schmiedeskamp. *1970 Survey of Consumer Finances.* Ann Arbor, Mich.: Institute for Social Research, The University of Michigan, 1971. **230, 263, 352, 360, 361, 380**

Katona, George, and Eva Mueller. "A Study of Purchase Decisions," pp. 30–36 in *Consumer Behavior,* Vol. 1, ed. Lincoln H. Clark, New York: New York University Press, 1955. **175**

Katona, George, Burkhard Strumpel, and Ernest Zahn. *Aspirations and Affluence.* New York: McGraw-Hill Book Company, Inc., 1971. **244**

Katona, George. See Mandell, Lewis.

Katz, D., and R. L. Kahn. *The Social Psychology of Organizations.* New York: John Wiley & Sons, Inc., 1966. **231, 232**

Kaye, Stanley. "Ego Identity, Time Perspective, Time Conceptualization, and Planning," New York University, Ph.D., 1968. **177**

Keiser, Marjorie Branin, and Elaine Knowles Weaver. "Body Movements Related to Energy Used," *Journal of Home Economics,* 54 (June 1962), 479–482. **345**

Kelsey, Linda Miller. "Household Work: Homemakers' Changes and Reasons," Cornell University, M.S., 1965. **312**

Kerckhoff, Alan C. "Status-Related Value Patterns Among Married Couples," *Journal of Marriage and the Family,* 34 (February 1972), 105–110. **155**

King, William R. See Cleland, David I.

Kirk, N. S. See Ward, Joan S.

Kiser, Clyde V. "Changing Patterns of Fertility in the United States," *Social Biology,* 17 (December 1970), 302–315. **214**

Klemmack, David L. See Edwards, John N.

Knapp, Mark L. See McCroskey, James C.

Kneese, Allen V., R. U. Ayers, and Ralph C. D'Arge. *Economics and the Environment.* Baltimore, Md.: The Johns Hopkins University Press, Inc., 1970. **22**

Knoll, Marjorie M. See Gross, Irma H.

Kohn, Melvin L. *Class and Conformity, A Study in Values.* Homewood, Ill.: The Dorsey Press, 1969. **79, 93**

Kolasa, Blair J. *Introduction to Behavioral Science for Business.* New York: John Wiley & Sons, Inc., 1969. **80**

Kollat, David T., James F. Engel, and Roger D. Blackwell. "Current Problems in Consumer Behavior Research," *Journal of Marketing Research,* 7 (August 1970), 327–332. **83**

Kollat, David T., and Ronald P. Willett. "Customer Impulse Purchasing Behavior," *Journal of Marketing Research,* 4 (February 1967), 21–31. **206, 207, 209**

Komarovsky, Mirra. *Blue-Collar Marriage.* New York: Random House, Inc., 1962. **131**

Konz, Stephan. See Agan, Tessie.

Koontz, Harold, and Cyril O'Donnell. *Principles of Management: An Analysis of Managerial Functions.* New York: McGraw-Hill Book Company, 1972. **115**

Krathwohl, David R., Benjamin S. Bloom, and Bertram B. Masia. *A Taxonomy of Educational Objectives: Handbook II: The Affective Domain.* New York: David McKay, 1964. **146**

Kreps, Juanita M. *Lifetime Allocation of Work and Income.* Durham, N.C.: Duke University Press, 1971. **390**

Krofta, Janet A. See Deacon, Ruth E.

Kristeller, E. See Rusk, Howard.

Kryter, Karl D. "Non-auditory Effects of Environmental Noise," *American Journal of Public Health,* 62 (March 1972), 389–398. **337**

Kyrk, Hazel. *The Family in the American Economy.* Chicago: University of Chicago Press, 1953. **35, 258**

Lancaster, Reta R. "Case Studies of the Decision-Making of Ten Non-College Educated Homemakers," University of Kansas, M.S., 1966. **112**

Lange, John D. "Alternatives for Action: Housing," The National Forum of State Legislators on Older Americans, Washington, D.C., December 4–6, 1972. **398**

Larey, Dorothy A. See Fitzsimmons, Cleo.

Larson, Carol E. See McCroskey, James C.

Lasswell, Thomas E. *Class and Stratum*. Boston: Houghton Mifflin Co., 1965. **39, 43, 92**

Laumann, Edward O., and James S. House. "Living Room Styles and Social Attributes: The Patterning of Material Artifacts in a Modern Urban Community," *Sociology and Social Research,* 54 (April 1970), 321–342. **99**

Lawton, M. Powell, and Jacob Cohen. "The Generality of Housing Impact on the Well-Being of Older People," *Journal of Gerontology,* 29 (March 1974). 194–204. **398**

Lee, Hanson W. See Weisbrod, Burton A.

Lee, Lucy Chao. See Ferber, Robert.

Lefcourt, Herbert M. "Belief in Person Control: Research and Implications," *Journal of Individual Psychology,* 22 (November 1966), 185–195. **215**

Lehr, Ursula, and Gernet Dreher. "Determinants of Attitudes Toward Retirement," pp. 116–137 in *Adjustment to Retirement,* eds. R. J. Havighurst, J. M. A. Munnichs, B. Newgarten, H. Thorne. Assen, The Netherlands: Van Gorcum & Comp. N.V., 1970. **394, 395**

Lepor, M. See Webster, John C.

Lett, Evelyn E. See Altman, Irwin.

Levine, Sol. See Crogg, Sydney H.

Levinger, George. "Task and Social Behavior in Marriage," *Sociometry,* 27 (December 1964), 433–488. **296**

Levitz, Gary S. See Markson, Elizabeth W.

Lindsay, John J., and Richard A. Ogle. "Socioeconomic Patterns of Outdoor Recreation Use Near Urban Areas," *Journal of Leisure Research,* 4 (Winter 1972), 19–24. **30, 373**

Lipman, Aaron. See Smith, Kenneth J.

Lipson, Alberta. See Croog, Sydney H.

Longley, Mars Y. "Contamination in the Semiclosed Environment—The Modern Home" (AMRL–TR–69–130, Paper No. 23: 325–334). Wright Patterson Airforce Base, Ohio: Aerospace Medical Research Lab, 1969. **339**

Lopata, Helena Z. *Occupation: Housewife*. New York: Oxford University Press, 1971. **66, 67, 68, 89, 121, 203, 211, 312**

Lopata, Helena Z. "The Life Cycle of the Social Role of Housewife," *Sociology and Social Research,* (October 1966), 5–22. **68**

Lopata, Helena Z. "The Social Involvement of American Widows," *American Behavioral Scientist,* 14 (September-October 1970), 41–58. **395**

Lopata, Helena Z. "Social Relations of Black and White Widowed Women in a Northern Metropolis," *American Journal of Sociology,* 78 (January 1973), 241–248. **391**

LoSciuto, Leonard A. See Wells, William D.

Lovingood, Rebecca Powell. "The Effect of Selected Social-Demographic Factors on Household Task Performance of Young Families," The Ohio State University, Ph.D., 1973. **359**

Luce, Gay Gaer. "Biological Rhythms in Psychiatry and Medicine" (U.S. Dept. of Health, Education, and Welfare, Public Health Service Publication 2088), Washington, D.C.: U.S. Government Printing Office, 1970. **189**

Ludwig, Edward G., and John Collette. "Disability, Dependency and Conjugal Roles," *Journal of Marriage and the Family,* 31 (November 1969), 736–739. **76**

Lynch, Mildred T. See Downer, Donna Beth.

Lynch, Mildred T. See Smith, Ruth H.

Magee, John F. "Decision Trees for Decision Making," *Harvard Business Review,* 42 (July–August 1964), 126–138. **113, 114**

Magrabi, Frances M. "An Empirical Test for Decision Rule," *Journal of Consumer Affairs,* 3 (Summer 1969), 41–51. **112**

Magrabi, Frances M., and W. H. Marshall. "Family Developmental Tasks: A Research Model," *Journal of Marriage and the Family,* 27 (November 1965), 454–458. **69**

Maloch, Francille. "Characteristics of Most and Least Liked Household Tasks," Cornell University, Ph.D., 1962. **313, 315**

Maloch, Francille, and Ruth E. Deacon. "Components of Home Management in Relation to Selected Variables" (Research Bulletin 1042). Wooster, Ohio: Ohio Agricultural Research and Development Center, 1970. **49, 76, 95, 183, 185, 186, 188, 193, 196, 205, 207, 209, 211, 215**

Maloch, Francille, and Ruth E. Deacon. "Proposed Framework for Home Management," *Journal of Home Economics,* 58 (January 1966), 31–35. **49, 106**

Maloch, Francille, and C. R. Weaver. "Orientation of Expenditures to Day of Pay," *Journal of Consumer Affairs,* 5 (Summer 1971), 137–144. **282**

Maloch, Francille. See Deacon, Ruth E.

Maloch, Francille. See Trevathan, Sue Wright.

Mandell, Lewis. *Credit Card Use in the United States.* Ann Arbor, Mich.: The

University of Michigan, 1972. **352, 361**

Mandell, Lewis, George Katona, James N. Morgan, and Jay Schmiedes-kamp. *Surveys of Consumers 1971–72*. Ann Arbor, Mich.: Institute for Social Research, The University of Michigan, 1973. **262, 263, 352, 369, 370, 379**

Mandell, Lewis. See Katona, George.

Manning, Sarah L. "Time Use in Household Tasks by Indiana Families" (Research Bulletin No. 837). Lafayette, Ind.: Purdue University Agricultural Experiment Station, 1968. **76, 96, 97, 300, 302, 314**

Manning, Sarah L., and Ethel L. Vatter. "Financial Management Practices of Families with Steady or Fluctuating Incomes" (Bulletin 997). Ithaca, N.Y.: Cornell University Agricultural Experiment Station, 1964. **282**

Manning, Sarah L. See Williams, Flora L.

Marion, B. W., L. A. Simonds, and Dan E. Moore. "Food Marketing in Low Income Areas: A Review of Past Findings and a Case Analysis in Columbus, Ohio" (AE–439 MM–302). Columbus, Ohio: Cooperative Extension Service, The Ohio State University, 1969. **381**

Markson, Elizabeth W., Gary S. Levitz, and Maryvonne Gognalona-Caillard. "The Elderly and the Community: Reidentifying Unmet Needs," *Journal of Gerontology*, 28 (October 1973), 503–509. **391**

Marshall, W. H. See Magrabi, Frances M.

Masia, Bertram B. See Krathwohl, David R.

Maslow, Abraham H. *Motivation and Personality*, 2nd ed. New York: Harper & Row, Publishers, 1970. **80**

Mathews, Donald K., and Edward L. Fox. *The Physiological Basis of Physical Education and Athletics*. Philadelphia: W. B. Saunders Company, 1971. **304, 343**

Mathews, H. Lee. "Causes of Personal Bankruptcies, Columbus, Ohio" (Monograph No. 133). Columbus, Ohio: The Ohio State University Bureau of Business Research, 1968. **290**

Mathews, H. Lee, and John W. Slocum, Jr. "Social Class and Commercial Bank Credit Card Usage," *Journal of Marketing*, 33 (January 1969), 71–78. **370**

Mathews, H. Lee. See Slocum, John W., Jr.

Mathiesen, Thomas. "The Unanticipated Event and Astonishment," *Inquiry*, 3 (Spring 1960), 1–17. **154**

McCracken, Earl C. See Richardson, Martha.

McCroskey, James C., Carol E. Larson, and Mark L. Knapp. *An Introduction to Interpersonal Communication*. Englewood Cliffs, N.J.: Prentice-Hall, Inc., 1971. **127**

McCullough, Helen E., Kathryn Philson, Ruth H. Smith, Anna L. Wood, and Avis Woolrich. "Space Standards for Household Activities" (Bulletin 686). Urbana, Ill.: University of Illinois Agricultural Experiment Station, 1962. **327, 328, 333**

McFarland, R. A. "Understanding Fatigue in Modern Life," *Ergonomics,* 14 (January 1971), 1–10. **317**

Meeks, Carol B., and Ruth E. Deacon. "Values and Planning in the Selection of a Family Living Environment," *Journal of Home Economics,* 64 (January 1972), 11–16. **141**

Mesthene, E. G. *Technological Change.* Cambridge, Mass.: Harvard University Press, 1970. **19, 42**

Metzen, Edward J. See Fitzsimmons, Cleo.

Meyerowitz, Joseph H., and Harold Feldman. "Transition to Parenthood," *Psychiatric Research Reports,* 20 (1966), 78–84. **360**

Miller, David W., and Martin K. Starr. *The Structure of Human Decisions.* Englewood Cliffs, N.J.: Prentice-Hall, Inc., 1967. **151**

Miller, George A., E. Galanter, and K. H. Pribram. *Plans and Structure of Behavior.* New York: Henry Holt and Co., 1960. **208**

Miller, Herman P. *Rich Man, Poor Man.* New York: Thomas Y. Crowell Company, Inc., 1971. **251, 252, 253**

Miller, James R., III. *Professional Decision-Making, A Procedure for Evaluating Complex Alternatives.* New York: Praeger Publishers, 1970. **111**

Miller, S. M., and Pamela A. Roby. *The Future of Inequality.* New York: Basic Books, Inc., 1970. **29**

Mize, Jessie J., Frankye E. Bland, Sally Jo Ritchie, and Joseph W. Simons. "Laundry Work Areas for Southern Rural Homes" (Bulletin N.S. 42). Athens, Ga.: Georgia Agricultural Experiment Station, 1957. **331**

Mize, Jessie J., Fern Tuten, and Joseph W. Simons. "A Study of Sound Levels in Houses," *Journal of Home Economics,* 58 (January 1966), 41–45. **335**

Mize, J. J. See Simons, J. W.

Montgomery, James E. "The Housing Patterns of Older Families," *The Family Coordinator,* 21 (January 1972), 40–45. **398**

Montgomery, James E. "Impact of Housing Patterns of Marital Interaction," *The Family Coordinator,* 19 (July, 1970), 267–275. **97**

Moore, Dan E. See Marion, B. W.

Moore, Wilbert E. *Man, Time, and Society.* New York: John Wiley & Sons, Inc., 1963. **213**

Morgan, James N. "Housing and Ability to Pay," *Econometrica,* 33 (April 1965), 289–306. **85**

Morgan, James N. "Some Pilot Studies of Communication and Consensus in the Family," *Public Opinion Quarterly,* 32 (Spring 1968), 113–121. **170**

Morgan, James N. See Baerwaldt, Nancy A.

Morgan, James N. See Barfield, Richard.

Morgan, James N. See Barlow, Robin.

Morgan, James N. See Mandell, Lewis.

Morgan, James N., Ismail A. Sirageldin, and Nancy Baerwaldt. *Productive Americans.* Ann Arbor, Mich.: Institute for Social Research, The University of Michigan, 1966. **84, 87, 97, 300, 308**

Morris, Glenn, Richard Pasewark, and John Schultz. "Occupational Level and Participation in Public Recreation in a Rural Community," *Journal of Leisure Research,* 4 (Winter 1972), 25–32. **30, 373**

Morris, William T. "Intuition and Relevance," *Management Science,* 14 (December 1967), B-157–B-165. **106**

Mott, Paul E., *et al. Shift Work.* Ann Arbor, Mich.: The University of Michigan Press, 1965. **90**

Mount, John F. See Myers, James H.

Mueller, Eva. See Katona, George.

Mumaw, Catherine R. "Organizational Patterns of Homemakers Related to Selected Predispositional and Situational Characteristics," The Pennsylvania State University, Ph.D., 1967. **82, 190, 195, 216**

Mumaw, Catherine R., and Addreen Nichols. "Organizational Styles of Homemakers: A Factor Analytic Approach," *Home Economics Research Journal,* 1 (September 1972), 34–43. **215**

Mumaw, Catherine R. See Nichols, Addreen.

Mumey, Glen A. *Personal Economic Planning.* New York: Holt, Rinehart and Winston, Inc., 1972. **272**

Murphy, Kathryn R. "Contrasts in Spending by Urban Families," *Monthly Labor Review,* 87 (November 1964), 1249–1253. **228**

Murray, Henry A., *et al. Explorations in Personality.* New York: Oxford University Press, 1938.M **80**

Murray, Janet. "Homeownership and Financial Assets: Findings from the 1968 Survey of the Aged," *Social Security Bulletin,* 35 (August 1972), 3–23. **369, 370**

Musgrave, Richard A. "Cost-Benefit Analysis and the Theory of Public Finance," *Journal of Economic Literature,* 7 (September 1969), 797–806. **29**

Myers, Anna Mae. "Class and Interrelatedness of Decisions Ensuing from the Decision of Wives to Seek Employment," Virginia Polytechnic Institute, M.S., 1967. **124**

Myers, James H., and John F. Mount. "More on Social Class vs. Income as Correlates of Buying Behavior," *Journal of Marketing,* 37 (April 1973), 71–73. **94**

Namboodiri, N. Krishnan. "The Wife's Work Experience and Child Spacing," *The Milbank Memorial Fund Quarterly,* 52 (July 1964), 65–77. **214, 354**

Napier, Ted L. "Rural-Urban Differences: Myth or Reality?" (Research Bulletin No. 1063). Wooster, Ohio: Ohio Agricultural Research and Development Center, 1973. **95**

Nelkin, Dorothy. See Friedland, William H.

Nelson, Patricia A. See Altman, Irwin.

Newman, William H., Charles E. Summer, and E. Kirby Warren. *The Process of Management.* Englewood Cliffs, N.J.: Prentice-Hall, 1967. **150**

Nichols, Addreen. "Person-centered and Task-centered Styles of Organization," Michigan State University, Ph.D., 1964. **188, 195**

Nichols, Addreen, Catherine R. Mumaw, Maryann Paynter, Martha A. Plonk, and Dorothy Z. Price. "Family Management," *Journal of Marriage and the Family,* 33 (February 1971), 112–118. **124, 195, 196**

Nickell, Paulena, and Jean Muir Dorsey. *Management in Family Living.* New York: John Wiley & Sons, Inc., 1967. **29, 234**

Nord, Walter R., and Robert Costigan. "Worker Adjustment to the Four-Day Week: A Longitudinal Study," *Journal of Applied Psychology,* 58 (February 1973), 60–66. **309**

Norris, Ruby Turner. *The Theory of Consumer's Demand.* New Haven, Conn.: Yale University Press, 1952. **282**

Nussbaum, John. "3 Orphans Win $1.3 Million in Fatal Chlorine Gas Leak," *The Plain Dealer* (Cleveland, Ohio), October 24, 1970. **321**

Nye, Ivan F., John Carolson, and Gerald Garrett. "Family Size, Interaction, Affect and Stress," *Journal of Marriage and the Family,* 32 (May 1970), 216–226. **73**

O'Brien, Carol B., and Dorothy Z. Price. "An Investigation of the Traditional Concept of Management," *Quarterly Bulletin* of the Michigan Agricultural Experiment Station, 44 (May 1962), 714–725. **213, 215**

O'Donnell, Cyril. See Koontz, Harold.

Ogle, Richard O. See Lindsay, John Jay.

Ohnmacht, Fred W. "Personality and Cognitive Referents of Creativity: A Second Look," *Psychological Reports,* 26 (February 1970), 336–338. **110**

Orden, Susan R., and Norman M. Bradburn. "Working Wives and Marriage Happiness," *The American Journal of Sociology,* 74 (January 1969), 392–407. **323**

Orshansky, Mollie. "Counting the Poor: Another Look at the Poverty

Profile," *Social Security Bulletin,* 28 (January 1965), 3–29. **250**

Orshansky, Mollie. "The Shape of Poverty in 1966," *Social Security Bulletin,* 31 (March 1968), 332. **368**

Oyer, E. Jane, and Beatrice Paolucci. "Homemakers' Hearing Losses and Family Integration," *Journal of Home Economics,* 62 (April 1970), 257–262. **76**

Pahl, Bernd. See Vroom, Victor

Paolucci, Beatrice. "Managerial Decision Patterns," *Penney's Fashions and Fabrics* (Fall/Winter 1963). **172**

Paolucci, Beatrice. See Hook, Nancy C.

Paolucci, Beatrice. See Oyer, E. Jane.

Papanek, Hanna. "The Two-Person Career," *American Journal of Sociology,* 78 (anuary 1973), 90–110. **88**

Parker, Marianne, and Francille M. Firebaugh. "An Experience in Home Management," *Illinois Teacher,* 15 (May-June 1972), 233–238. **329**

Parsons, Talcott. *The System of Modern Societies.* Englewood Cliffs, N.JM: Prentice-Hall, Inc., 1971. **39, 40, 41, 43**

Pasewark, Richard. See Morris, Glenn.

Patton, Mary Brown. See Elliot, Doris E.

Paynter, Maryann. See Nichols, Addreen.

Pennock, Jean L. "Child-Rearing Costs at Two Levels of Living, by Family Size," *Family Economics Review,* ARS 62–5 (December 1970), 16–17. **355**

Pennock, Jean L. "Cost of Raising a Child," speech at the 47th Annual Agricultural Outlook Conference, Washington, D.C., February 18, 1970. **356, 357, 358**

Pennock, Jean L., and Carol M. Jaeger. "Household Service Life of Durable Goods," *Journal of Home Economics,* 56 (January 1964), 22–26. **22, 23**

Perrucci, Carolyn Cummings. "Mobility, Marriage and Child-spacing Among College Graduates," *Journal of Marriage and the Family,* 30 (May 1968), 273–282. **354**

Philson, Kathryn. See McCullough, Helen E.

Plonk, Martha A. "Exploring Interrelationships in a Central-Satellite Decision Complex," *Journal of Home Economics,* 60 (December 1968), 789–792. **123, 124, 172**

Plonk, Martha A. See Nichols, Addreen.

Pollay, Richard W. "The Structure of Executive Decisions and Decision Times," *Administrative Science Quarterly,* 15 (December 1970), 459–471. **110**

Poloma, Margaret M., and T. Neal Garland. "The Married Professional

Woman: A Study in Tolerance of Domestication," *Journal of Marriage and the Family,* 33 (August 1971), 531–540. **89**

Poorkaj, Houshang. "Social-Psychological Factors and 'Successful Aging,' " *Sociology and Social Research,* 56 (April 1972), 289–300. **397**

Porter, Sylvia. "What it Costs Now to Have a Baby," *Ladies Home Journal,* 87 (January 1970), 32–33. **355**

Pratt, Lois. "Conjugal Organization and Health," *Journal of Marriage and the Family,* 34 (February 1972), 85–95. **126**

Pratt, William F. See Coombs, Lolagene C.

Preisz, Lois Hessacker. "An Investigation of Credit Usage Among Young Married Couples in Western Oregon," Oregon State University, M.S., 1971. **283**

Pribram, K. H. See Miller, George A.

Price, Dorothy Z. "Social Decision-Making," pp. 14–21 in *The Family: Focus on Management* (Proceedings of a National Conference). Washington, D.C.: The American Home Economics Association, 1969. **120**

Price, Dorothy Z. See Nichols, Addreen.

Price, Dorothy Z. See O'Brien, Carol.

Projector, Dorothy S. *Survey of Changes in Family Finances.* Washington, D.C.: Board of Governors of Federal Reserve System, 1968. **229**

Pyun, Chang Soo. "The Monetary Value of a Housewife: An Economic Analysis for use in Litigation," *The American Journal of Economics and Sociology,* 28 (July 1969), 271–284. **319**

Quandt, Richard E. See Henderson, James Mitchell.

Rados, David L. "Selection and Evaluation of Alternatives in Repetitive Decision Making," *Administrative Science Quarterly,* 17 (June 1972), 196–206. **119**

Rainwater, Lee. *Behind Ghetto Walls.* Chicago: Aldine Publishing Co., 1970. **100**

Rainwater, Lee. "Fear and House-As-Haven in the Lower Class," *Journal of the American Institute of Planners,* 32 (January 1966), 23–30. **102**

Rainwater, Lee, Richard P. Coleman, and Gerald Handel. *Workingman's Wife.* New York: Oceana Publications, Inc., 1959. **94, 194**

Rapoport, Rhonda, and Robert N. Rapoport. "The Dual Career Family," *Human Relations,* 22 (February 1969), 3–30. **89**

Rapoport, Robert N. See Rapoport, Rhonda.

Ratagick, Marie. "Two American Welfare Mothers," *Ms.,* 1 (June 1973), 74–77, 112. **373, 374**

Raven, Bertram H. See Centers, Richard.

Regan, Mary C. "Family Patterns and Social Class" (Research Monograph

#5). Davis, Cal.: University of California, 1967. **131, 132**

Reno, Virginia. "Women Newly Entitled to Retired-Worker Benefits: Survey of New Beneficiaries," *Social Security Bulletin,* 36 (April 1973), 3–26. **390**

Rescher, Nicholas. "What Is Value Change? A Framework for Research," pp. 68–109 in *Values and the Future,* eds. Kurt Baier and Nicholas Rescher. New York: The Free Press, 1969. **142**

Rice, Ann Smith. "An Economic Life Cycle of Childless Families," Florida State University, Ph.D., 1965. **69**

Rice, Robert R. "The Effects of Project Head Start and Differential Housing Environments Upon Child Development," *The Family Coordinator,* 18 (January 1969), 32–38. **97**

Richards, Louise G. "Consumer Practices of the Poor," *Welfare in Review,* 3 (November 1965), 1–13. **379**

Richardson, Martha, and Earl C. McCracken. "Energy Expenditures of Women Performing Selected Activities" (U.S. Dept. of Agriculture, Agricultural Research Service, Home Economics Research Report 11). Washington, D.C.: U.S. Government Printing Office, 1960. **303**

Richardson, Martha, and Earl C. McCracken. "Energy Expenditures of Women Performing Selected Activities While Sitting and Standing," *Journal of the American Medical Women's Association,* 16 (November 1961), 861–865. **304**

Richardson, Martha, and Earl C. McCracken. "Work-Surface Levels and Human Energy Expenditure," *Journal of the American Dietetic Association,* 48 (March 1966), 192–198. **333**

Richardson, Martha, and Earl C. McCracken. "Work-Surface Levels for Laundry Tasks in Relation to Human-Energy Expenditures," *Journal of Home Economics,* 58 (October 1966), 662–668. **333**

Richardson, Reta Hamilton. "Stimuli in Homemaking Activities Associated with Heart Rate Changes in Women from Two Socioeconomic Levels," The Ohio State University, Ph.D., 1969. **305**

Riesman, David, and Howard Roseborough. "Careers and Consumer Behavior," in *Consumer Behavior,* ed. Lincoln H. Clark. Vol. II. New York: New York University Press, 1955. **36**

Ripley, S. Dillon, and Helmut K. Buechner. "Ecosystem Science as a Point of Synthesis," *Daedalus,* 96 (Fall 1967), 1192–1199. **17**

Ritchie, Sally Jo. See Mize, Jessie J.

Roby, Pamela A. See Miller S. M.

Rodgers, Roy H. *Improvements in the Construction and Analysis of Family Life Cycle Categories.* Kalamazoo, Mich.: Western Michigan University, 1962. **66**

Rogers, Everett M., with F. Floyd Shoemaker. *Communication of Innova-*

tions. New York: The Free Press, 1971. **127, 128**

Rollins, Mabel A. See Bymers, Gwen J.

Romino, Imogene. "Financial Management Practices of 52 Couples with Teenage Wives in Baltimore County, Maryland," The Pennsylvania State University, M.S., 1970. **283**

Ronald, Patricia Y., Mary E. Singer, and Francille Maloch Firebaugh. "Rating Scale for Household Tasks," *Journal of Home Economics,* 63 (March 1971), 177–179. **314**

Roseborough, Howard. "Some Sociological Dimensions of Consumer Spending, *Canadian Journal of Economics and Political Economy,* 26 (August 1960), 454–464. **36**

Roseborough, Howard. See Riesman, David.

Rosenzweig, James E. See Johnson, Richard A.

Rosenzweig, James E. See Kast, Fremont E.

Ross, John A. "Social Class and Medical Care," *Journal of Health and Human Behavior,* 3 (Spring 1962), 35–40. **155**

Rossi, Alice S. "Barriers to the Career Choice of Engineering, Medicine, or Science among American Women," pp. 51–127 in *Women and the Scientific Professions,* eds. J. A. Mattfeld and C. G. Van Aken. Cambridge, Mass.: M.I.T. Press, 1965. **91**

Rotter, Julian B. "Generalized Expectancies for Internal Versus External Control of Reinforcement," *Psychological Monographs,* 80 (Whole No. 609), 1966. **176**

Rushing, William A. *Class, Culture, and Alienation.* Lexington, Mass.: Lexington Books, D. C. Heath and Company, 1971. **369, 375**

Rusk, Howard, E. Kristeller, J. S. Judson, G. M. Hunt, and M. Zimmerman. "A Manual for Training the Disabled Homemaker" (Rehabilitation Monograph 8, 2nd ed.). New York: New York University Institute of Physical Medicine and Rehabilitation, 1971. **304**

Ryan, Mary Ellen. "An Analysis of Economic and Demographic Characteristics of Consumers Associated with Excessive Installment Debt," University of Minnesota, M.S., 1968. **290, 382**

Safilios-Rothschild, Constantina. "Family Sociology or Wives' Family Sociology? A Cross-Cultural Examination of Decision-Making," *Journal of Marriage and the Family,* 31 (May 1969), 209–301. **125**

Safilios-Rothschild, Constantina. *The Sociology and Social Psychology of Disability and Rehabilitation.* New York: Random House, 1970. **75**

Sarbin, Theodore R., and Vernon L. Allen. "Role Theory," pp. 488–558 in *The Handbook of Social Psychology,* Vol. I., ed. Gardner Lindzey and Elliott Aronson. Reading, Mass.: Addison-Wesley Publishing Co., Inc., 1968. **40, 41, 43**

Sarphati, H. R. See Hueting, J. E.

Scheflen, Albert E. "Living Space in an Urban Ghetto," *Family Process,* 10 (December 1971), 429–450. **326, 327**

Scheibe, Karl E. *Beliefs and Values.* New York: Holt, Rinehart and Winston, Inc., 1970. **158**

Schlamp, Fredric T. See Stone, Robert C.

Schmiedeskamp, Jay. See Katona, George.

Schmiedeskamp, Jay. See Mandell, Lewis.

Schnittgrund, Karen, Marilyn Dunsing, and Jeanne Hafstrom. "Children and Money . . . Attitudes and Behavior of 52 Grandparent and Parent Families," *Illinois Research,* 15 (Spring 1973), 12–13. **279, 281**

Schomaker, Peggy K., and Alice C. Thorpe. "Financial Decision-Making As Reported by Farm Families in Michigan," *Quarterly Bulletin,* 46 (November 1963), 335–352. **110**

Schorr, Alvin L. "The Family Cycle and Income Development," *Social Security Bulletin,* 29 (February 1966), 14–25, 47. **283, 349**

Schottland, Charles I. "Government Economic Programs and Family Life," *Journal of Marriage and the Family,* 29 (February 1967), 7–123. **27**

Schroder, Harold M., Michael J. Driver, and Siegfried Streufert. *Human Information Processing.* New York: Holt, Rinehart and Winston, Inc., 1967. **178, 179**

Schultz, John. See Morris, Glenn.

Schulz, James H., and Guy Carrin. "The Role of Savings and Pension Systems in Maintaining Living Standards in Retirement," *Journal of Human Resources,* 7 (Summer 1972), 343–365. **392, 397**

Schweitzer, Stuart O. "Occupation Choice, High School Graduation, and Investment in Human Capital," *Journal of Human Resources,* 6 (Summer 1971), 321–332. **83**

Searls, Laura G. "Leisure Role Emphasis of College Graduate Homemakers," *Journal of Marriage and the Family,* 28 (February 1966), 77–82. **71**

Shewbridge, Edythe. *Portraits of Poverty.* New York: W. W. Norton & Company, Inc., 1972. **369**

Shibutani, Tamotsu. "A Cybernetic Approach to Motivation," pp. 330–336 in *Modern Systems Research for the Behavioral Scientist,* ed. Walter Buckley. Chicago: Aldine Publishing Company, 1968. **181**

Shoemaker, F. Floyd. See Rogers, Everett M.

Sirageldin, Ismail A. See Morgan, James N.

Silverman, William, and Reuben Hill. "Task Allocation in Marriage in the United States and Belgium," *Journal of Marriage and the Family,* 29 (May 1967), 353–359. **67, 68**

Solow, Robert M. "The Economist's Approach to Pollution and Its Control," *Science,* 173 (August 6, 1971), 498–503. **19**

Sonnenfeld, J. "Variable Values in Space and Landscape: An Inquiry into the Nature of Environmental Necessity," *Journal of Social Issues,* 22 (October 1966), 71–82. **98**

Stager, Paul. "Conceptual Level as a Composition Variable in Small-Group Decision Making," *Journal of Personality and Social Psychology,* 5 (February 1967), 152–161. **116**

Starr, Martin K. *Management: A Modern Approach.* New York: Harcourt Brace Jovanovich, Inc., 1971. **167**

Starr, Martin K. See Miller, David W.

Steele, Marguerite. "The Effect of a Selected Group of Variables on the Meal Type," Plan B Report for the M.S., The Ohio State University, 1970. **90**

Steidl, Rose E. "Difficulty Factors in Homemaking Tasks: Implications for Environmental Design," *Human Factors,* 14 (October 1972), 471–482. **210, 211, 217, 218, 219, 220, 329, 338, 339**

Steidl, Rose E. "Factors of Functionality and Difficulty in Homemaking Tasks," *Human Ecology Forum,* 3 (Autumn 1972), 10–11. **310, 311**

Steidl, Rose E. "Food Tasks: Complexity, Difficulty and Preference," *Human Ecology Forum,* 3 (Summer 1972), 17–19. **307**

Steidl, Rose E., and Esther Crew Bratton. *Work in the Home.* New York: John Wiley & Sons, Inc., 1968. **20, 86, 188, 189, 192, 219, 302, 303, 304, 316, 330, 331, 332**

Stein, Bruno. *On Relief.* New York: Basic Books, Inc., Publishers, 1971. **250, 252**

Steiner, Gary A. See Berelson, Bernard.

Sternlieb, George S., and Bernard P. Indik. *The Ecology of Welfare.* New Brunswick, N.J.: Transaction Books, 1973. **397**

Stock, Dennis. See Hedgepeth, William.

Stone, Robert C., and Fredric T. Schlamp. *Welfare and Working Fathers.* Lexington, Mass.: Lexington Books, D. C. Heath and Company, 1971. **371**

Storey, James R. "Public Income Transfer Programs: The Incidence of Multiple Benefits and the Issues Raised by Their Receipt," in *Studies in Public Welfare* (Paper No. 1, Joint Economic Committee). Washington, D.C.: U.S. Government Printing Office, 1972. **372**

Storey, James R., Alair A. Townsend, and Irene Cox. "How Public Welfare Benefits are Distributed in Low-Income Areas," in *Studies in Public Welfare* (Paper No. 6, Joint Economic Committee), Washington, D.C.: U.S. Government Printing Office, 1973. **252, 381**

Straus, Murray A. "Communication, Creativity, and Problem-solving Ability of Middle- and Working-Class Families in Three Societies," *The American Journal of Sociology*, 73 (January 1968), 417–430. **133**

Straus, Murray A. "Social Class and Farm-City Differences in Interaction with Kin in Relation to Societal Modernization," *Rural Sociology*, 34 (December 1969), 476–495. **174, 175**

Streib, Gordon F. "Older Families and Their Troubles: Familial and Social Responses," *The Family Coordinator*, 21 (January 1972), 5–20. **389**

Streufert, Siegfried. See Schroder, Harold M.

Strumpel, Burkhard. "Economic Life Styles, Values and Subjective Welfare—An Empirical Approach," in *Family Economic Behavior: Problems and Prospects*, ed. Eleanor Bernert Sheldon. Philadelphia: J. B. Lippincott Company, 1973, pp. 69–125. **242, 243**

Strumpel, Burkhard. See Katona, George.

Summer, Charles E. See Newman, William H.

Sussman, Marvin. See Crain, Alan J.

Tallman, Irving. "The Family As a Small Problem Solving Group," *Journal of Marriage and the Family*, 32 (February 1970), 94–104. **133**

Taylor, Eileen F. "Food Prices Before and After Distribution of Welfare Checks . . . Low-Income Areas, Seven Cities, 1969" (Marketing Research Report No. 907, U.S. Dept. of Agriculture, Economic Research Service). Washington, D.C.: U.S. Government Printing Office, 1970. **381**

Taylor, Minna. See Hawkes, Glenn R.

Thorpe, Alice C. See Schomaker, Peggy K.

Thrall, Charles Alexander. "Household Technology and the Division of Labor in Families," Harvard University, Ph.D., 1970. **308**

Thurnher, Majda. "Goals, Values, and Life Evaluations at the Preretirement Stage," *Journal of Gerontology*, 29 (January 1974), 85–96. **387, 396**

Thurow, Lester C. "The Optimum Lifetime Distribution of Consumption Expenditures," *The American Economic Review*, 59 (June 1969), 324–330. **356**

Tissue, Thomas. "Old Age and the Perception of Poverty," *Sociology and Social Research*, 56 (April 1972), 331–344. **389**

Toffler, Alvin. *Future Shock*. New York: Random House, Inc., 1970. **41, 92, 106, 141**

Tootle, Barbara J. See Helfrich, Margaret L.

Tormey, Lucy. See Agan, Tessie.

Townsend, Alair A. See Storey, James R.

Trevathan, Sue Wright, and Francille Maloch. "Angles of Body Bend in Loading Dishwashers," *Journal of Home Economics,* 59 (May 1967), 375–377. **344**

Tribble, Mildred F. "Relationships Among Five Dimensions of Twenty-five Home and Family Decisions," Louisiana State University, M.S., 1970. **123**

Troutman, Samuel J., Jr. See Webb, Paul.

Turner, Ralph H. *Family Interaction.* New York: John Wiley & Sons, Inc., 1970. **133, 134**

Tuten, Fern. See Mize, Jessie J. (1966)

Tyler, Gus. "Generation Gap or Gap Within a Generation?" *Dissent,* 18 (April 1971), 145–154. **128**

Van Bortel, Dorothy Greey, and Irma H. Gross. "A Comparison of Home Management in Two Socio-Economic Groups" (Technical Bulletin 240). East Lansing, Mich.: Michigan Agricultural Experiment Station, 1954. **312**

Vatter, Ethel L. See Manning, Sarah L.

Vincent, Clark E. "Family Spongia: The Adaptive Function," *Journal of Marriage and the Family,* 28 (February 1966), 29–36. **9**

Vroom, Victor, and Bernd Pahl. "The Relationship Between Age and Risk-Taking Among Managers," *Experimental Publication System* Issue 9, Ms. No. 339-12 (December 1970). **118**

Waldman, Elizabeth. "Marital and Family Characteristics of the U.S. Labor Force," *Monthly Labor Review,* 93 (May 1970), 18–27. **84**

Walker, Florence S. "A Proposal for Classifying Self-Imposed House-keeping Standards," *Journal of Home Economics,* 60 (June 1968), 456–460. **180**

Walker, Kathryn E. ARS Summary Report of "Time Used for Household Work," Department of Consumer Economics and Public Policy, New York State College of Human Ecology, Cornell University, June 15, 1971, mimeo. **302**

Walker, Kathryn E. "Homemaking Still Takes Time," *Journal of Home Economics,* 61 (October 1969), 621–624. **69, 70, 300, 301**

Walker, Kathryn E. "Household Work Time: Its Implication for Family Decisions," *Journal of Home Economics,* 65 (October 1973), 7–11. **300**

Walker, Kathryn E. "How Much Help for Working Mothers?" *Human Ecology Forum,* 1 (Autumn 1970), 13–15. **72**

Walker, Kathryn E. "Time-Use Patterns for Household Work Related to

Homemakers' Employment," USDA Agricultural Research Service, 1970 National Agricultural Outlook Conference, Washington, D.C., February 18, 1970. **73, 90, 92**

Walker, Kathryn E., and William H. Gauger "The Dollar Value of Household Work" (Information Bulletin 60). Ithaca, N.Y.: New York State College of Human Ecology, Cornell University, 1973. **318, 320**

Ward, Joan S., and N. S. Kirk. "The Relation Between Some Anthropometric Dimensions and Preferred Working Surface Heights in the Kitchen," *Ergonomics,* 13 (November 1970), 783–797. **333**

Warren, E. Kirby. See Newman, William H.

Warren, Jean. Figure adapted from class notes. Ithaca, N.Y.: New York State College of Home Economics, Cornell University. **285**

Warren, Jean. See Clark, Alma Beth.

Weaver, C. R. See Maloch, Francille.

Weaver, Elaine Knowles. See Keiser, Marjorie Branin.

Webb, Paul, and Samuel J. Troutman, Jr. "An Instrument for Continuous Measurement of Oxygen Consumption," *Journal of Applied Physiology,* 28 (June 1970), 867–871. **342**

Webster, John C., and M. Lepor. "Noise—You Can Get Used to It," *Journal of the Acoustical Society of America,* 45 (March 1969), 751–757. **335**

Wechsler, Henry, *et al.* "Alcohol Level and Home Accidental Injuries," U.S. Public Health Service Grant #UI 00022–02, Research Progress Report, October, 1967 (unpublished). **297, 298, 299**

Weckstein, Richard S. "Welfare Criteria and Changing Tastes," *American Economic Review,* 52 (March 1962), 133–153. **35, 242**

Weil, William B. See Crain, Alan J.

Weisbrod, Burton A., and Hansen W. Lee. "An Income-New Worth Approach to Measuring Economic Welfare," *American Economic Review,* 58 (December 1968), 1315–1329. **252**

Wells, William D., and Leonard A. LoSciuto. "Direct Observation of Purchasing Behavior," *Journal of Marketing Research,* 3 (August 1966), 227–233. **205, 206**

Wetters, Doris. "Creative Aspects of Homemanager's Resourcefulness," The Pennsylvania State University, Ph.D., 1967. **86**

Wheeler, Sister Madeleine. "Communication Behavior and Task Collaboration in Families of Low Socio-economic Levels," The Pennsylvania State University, Ph.E., 1971. **131**

Whitehead, Clay Thomas. *Uses and Limitations of Systems Analysis.* Santa Monica, Calif.: Rand Corp., 1967. **169, 171**

Whyte, William H., Jr. "Budgetism: Opiate of the Middle Class," *Fortune,* 53 (May 1956), 133–137. **277**

Wildening, Eugene A., and Lakshmi K. Bharadwaj. "Aspirations, Work Roles and Decision-Making Patterns" (Research Bulletin 266). Madison, Wis.: University of Wisconsin, 1966. **96**

Willett, Ronald P. See Kollat, David T.

Williams, Flora L., and Sarah L. Manning. "Net Worth Change of Selected Families," *Home Economics Research Journal,* 1 (December 1972), 104–113. **288**

Wilner, Daniel M., and William G. Baer. "Sociocultural Factors in Residential Space," (mimeo. prepared for Environmental Control Administration of the U.S. Dept. of Health, Education, and Welfare and the American Public Health Association, 1970. **98**

Wilner, Daniel M., and William G. Baer. "Sociocultural Factors in Residential Space" (abstract of position paper), *Proceedings of the First Invitational Conference on Health Research in Housing and Its Environment,* Arlie House, Warrenton, Virginia, March 17-19, 1970. **99**

Wilson, Charles Z. See Alexis, Marcus.

Winter, Mary. See Smith, Ruth H.

Wohlwill, Joachim F. "The Physical Environment: A Problem for a Psychology of Stimulation," *Journal of Social Issues,* 22 (October 1966), 29–38. **98**

Wolfe, D. M. See Blood, Robert O., Jr.

Wood, Anna L. See McCullough, Helen E.

Wood, Sharon F. "Day-to-Day Decision-Making of College Educated Homemakers," The Pennsylvania State University, M.S., 1966. **110, 116**

Woolrich, Avis. See McCullough, Helen E.

Wright, Charles R. See Hyman, Hebert H.

Zahn, Ernest, See Katona, George.

Zielhuis, R. L. See Ettema, J. H.

Zimmerman, M. See Rusk, Howard.

Zumeta, Zena. See Coombs, Lolagene C.

Zurcher, Louis A., Jr. See Curtis, Russell L., Jr.

Zwaagstra, Atje Pat. "Factors Related to Family Financial Problems and Perceived Adequacy of Income," Purdue University, M.S., 1971. **243**

Subject Index

Unemployment, risk of, 259
Unemployment insurance, 27
Unplanned shopping, 206
Used resources, 8, 21, 56, 62, 225–230, 235, 360–363, 409, 410, 411
Utility, 161

Values, 140–148, 155, 164
  changes in, and societal factors, 142
  characteristics of, 143–146, 164
  cognitive domain in, 145, 147–148, 164
  content of, 146–148, 164
  differences in, and location, 95
  dollar, fixed and variable, 159
  economic, of household activities, 317–321
  and family life cycle, 99
  feedback and, 235
  goals and, 144, 145, 149, 164, 409
  influence of social status on, 92–93
  nature of, 140–143, 164
  objective, 145–146, 164
  qualitative-quantitative, 182
  subjective, 145–146, 164
  trade-off, 116–117

Waste disposal problems, 22–23
Wealth, 252–253, 286

Welfare programs, 27–29, 368–369, 374
Welfare Rights Organization, 372–373
Widows, widowers, 390, 391, 395
Women
  career, 395
  employed outside home, 33, 34, 68, 84, 89, 90, 322–323, 324–325, 395
  families headed by, 79
  planning and adjusting to retirement by, 394–395
  predominance of, among elderly, 390
Work
  habits of, and space use, 328–329
  payment to children for, 281
  and self-esteem, 373–374
Work-area design, 330–334

Young families, 347–365, 413
  case studies of, 364–365
  decision making in, 93, 94
  goals of, 347–348, 413
  income of, 351–352
  met demands of, 357–360
  planning and implementing by, 353–357
  problems of, 348–349, 360
  resources of, 349–352
  use of credit by, 261
  used resources of, 360–363